PATHWAYS

of RECONCILIATION

Perceptions on Truth and Reconciliation
ISSN 2371-347X

PATHWAYS
of RECONCILIATION

*Indigenous and Settler Approaches to
Implementing the TRC's Calls to Action*

Edited by Aimée Craft and Paulette Regan

UNIVERSITY OF MANITOBA PRESS

Pathways of Reconciliation: Indigenous and Settler Approaches to
Implementing the TRC's Calls to Action
© The Authors 2020

24   23   22   21   20   1   2 3   4   5

University of Manitoba Press
Winnipeg, Manitoba, Canada
Treaty 1 Territory
uofmpress.ca

Cataloguing data available from Library and Archives Canada
Perceptions on Truth and Reconciliation, ISSN 2371-347X ; 2
ISBN 978-0-88755-854-2 (PAPER)
ISBN 978-0-88755-856-6 (PDF)
ISBN 978-0-88755-855-9 (EPUB)
ISBN 978-0-88755-880-1 (BOUND)

Cover image: *The Beach* by Georgina Laing (Cootes), Uchucklesaht First
Nation, n.d., tempera on paper, courtesy of Georgina Laing.
From the collection of the Residential and Indian Day School Art
Research Program at University of Victoria.
Cover design by Kirk Warren
Interior design by Jess Koroscil

Printed in Canada

The University of Manitoba Press acknowledges the financial support for
its publication program provided by the Government of Canada through
the Canada Book Fund, the Canada Council for the Arts, the Manitoba
Department of Sport, Culture, and Heritage, the Manitoba Arts Council,
and the Manitoba Book Publishing Tax Credit.

Funded by the Government of Canada | Canadä

With deepest respect to residential school survivors whose courageous and tireless actions speak truth to power and whose vision and wisdom guides us on pathways of reconciliation.

CONTENTS

INTRODUCTION

A I M É E   C R A F T   A N D   P A U L E T T E   R E G A N [1]

There are often many roads that lead to the same destination. This can make the journey interesting, challenging, unique, and worthwhile. Sometimes, in fact, the journey becomes more significant than the arrival at any particular place and the distance travelled, and lessons learned along the way are the purpose of the voyage. The title of this volume—*Pathways of Reconciliation*—reflects our profound belief that reconciliation is not only an ultimate goal but a decolonizing process of journeying in ways that embody everyday acts of resistance, resurgence, and solidarity, coupled with renewed commitments to justice, dialogue, and relationship building.[2] Reconciliation is, after all, according to the *Final Report* of the Truth and Reconciliation Commission of Canada (TRC), "an ongoing process of establishing and maintaining respectful relationships."[3]

However, these relationships among Indigenous peoples, settler Canadians, and the Canadian state cannot exist in a vacuum. If reconciliation is to be more than rhetoric or purely symbolic, there must be concrete actions that achieve real societal change,[4] particularly in a context that arises out of a recognized cultural genocide.[5] Structural, systemic, and institutional racism and discrimination must be eliminated. Reparations must be made on several fronts, ranging from apologies and monetary compensation to establishing decolonial processes to return lands and dismantle structures of oppression and power that have led to the cultural genocide that has been perpetrated against Indigenous peoples in Canada for over a century and a half. This also includes the rejection of colonial legal assumptions, such as the Doctrine of Discovery and *terra nullius*, that have systematically dispossessed, marginalized, and impoverished Indigenous peoples within their own territories, and a disruption of the legal systems that perpetuate those entrenched legal and political assumptions.[6]

The Truth and Reconciliation Commission found that conflicting views between Crown perspectives and Indigenous understandings of reconciliation persist:[7] "What is clear to this Commission is that Aboriginal peoples and the Crown have very different and conflicting views on what reconciliation is and how it is best achieved. The Government of Canada appears to believe that reconciliation entails Aboriginal peoples' accepting the reality and validity of Crown sovereignty and parliamentary supremacy in order to allow the government to get on with business. Aboriginal people, on the other hand, see reconciliation as an opportunity to affirm their own sovereignty and return to the 'partnership' ambitions they held after Confederation."[8]

Getting on with business and building a relationship are very different objectives and have vastly differing outcomes. This explains the current political context in which we find Indigenous governments and the Canadian government at odds on the terms of the nation-to-nation relationship. The ethos of relationship from an Indigenous perspective embodies the agreement to work together that was articulated by Indigenous nations in treaty making, while the government's perspective, supported by the legal jurisprudence of the Canadian courts, supports a vision of reconciling the prior occupation of Canada by Indigenous peoples with assumed Crown sovereignty.[9]

The TRC calls for the United Nations Declaration on the Rights of Indigenous Peoples to be the framework for reconciliation in twenty-first-century Canada: "Aboriginal peoples' right to self-determination must be integrated into Canada's constitutional and legal framework and into its civic institutions in a manner consistent with the principles, norms, and standards of [UNDRIP]."[10] In 2016 the federal government committed to the full implementation of UNDRIP and in 2017 supported a private member's bill that aims to ensure that this goal is achieved. The bill, an Act to ensure that the laws of Canada are in harmony with the United Nations Declaration on the Rights of Indigenous Peoples, was passed in the House of Commons on 30 May 2018, but died on the floor of the Senate in June 2019.[11] Implementing UNDRIP requires significant change to existing structures and governing institutions of power. Sheryl Lightfoot, in the Conclusion of this book, provides a thoughtful analysis of the change that must happen in order to even come close to the implementation of UNDRIP in a Canadian context.

If the TRC's vision of reconciliation is fully implemented, Indigenous cultural knowledge, governance systems, and laws will be regenerated, and Indigenous nations will be restored to their rightful place as self-determining equal partners in Confederation. The TRC cautioned that it will take several generations and much difficult work to repair the harms inflicted on Indigenous peoples through the residential school system and other institutional policies and practices of colonialism. New knowledge of and respect for diverse Indigenous cultures, histories, and ways of life must be generated through collaborative dialogue and education.

It is particularly important that non-Indigenous people, with critical thought and sustained kindness, engage in decolonial acts and processes of reconciliation in ways that do not place the burden of change or relationship building more heavily on Indigenous peoples.[12] Non-Indigenous people must be responsible and accountable for undertaking their own decolonization.[13]

Since the TRC's calls to action were released in June 2015, people in governments; churches; non-profit, professional, and community organizations; corporations; schools and universities; associations; and clubs have asked: "How can I participate in reconciliation?" They have asked this question of themselves and others. The answer is not always straightforward or simple and requires knowledge, action, respectful engagement, and sustained commitment. This is in part because there is a range of opinions on the usefulness of reconciliation as a mechanism for authentic societal change. The theory and concept of reconciliation have been widely debated by Indigenous and non-Indigenous scholars, activists, artists, and community members. Critics reject a liberal model of reconciliation that enables the Canadian settler state to make modest adjustments to "recognize" and "accommodate" Indigenous peoples in existing political, legal, and institutional structures and systems in ways that ultimately perpetuate colonialism. They argue instead for a deeply decolonizing resurgence of culturally diverse Indigenous political philosophies, governance systems, and laws that support self-determination and land-based ways of life. This is the necessary foundation for renegotiating a decolonial relationship between Canada and Indigenous peoples—one in which non-Indigenous people can also work for justice, equity, and responsible land stewardship in solidarity with Indigenous people.[14]

Prior to the release of the TRC *Final Report*, some critics cautioned that the commission's mandate was too narrow and its recommendations would do little to change the colonial status quo. Yet, as we note above, the TRC calls for the United Nations Declaration to be the framework for reconciliation in Canada, and, as Paulette Regan points out elsewhere, the commission's vision of reconciliation "is contingent on the land-based resurgence of Indigenous cultures, languages, knowledge systems, oral histories, laws, and governance structures. . . . The commission's work lays the foundation for a decoloniz-ing paradigm shift in how reconciliation is conceptualized, negotiated, and practiced in formal and informal settings."[15]

The essays in this volume engage with a variety of approaches to recon-ciliation (within a variety of reconciliation frameworks, either explicit or implicit) and illustrate the complexities of reconciliation. They provide valuable insights into the lessons learned as Indigenous and non-Indigenous people take action on reconciliation in practical terms. The volume canvasses various pathways of reconciliation from Indigenous and non-Indigenous perspectives, reflecting a diversity of approaches to the reconciliation mandate that was given to all Canadians by the TRC. The following chapters discuss grassroots initiatives, education (both informal and institutional), and varied attempts to engage with and implement some of the TRC's Calls to Action. Together, the authors, including academics, practitioners, students, and ordi-nary citizens, demonstrate the importance of trying and learning from new and creative approaches to thinking about and practising reconciliation. The authors describe the general and specific challenges and opportunities of reconciliation as they reflect on what they have learned from their attempts (both successful and less successful) in the process.

The volume is organized thematically to explore various pathways of recon-ciliation: reframing, learning and healing, researching, and living. However, all of these pathways are integrated and mutually dependent. Together, the chapters illustrate how theoretical approaches to reconciliation combined with practical initiatives can shift attitudes and stimulate actions that can lead to real societal change. They will challenge you as a reader to think about what reconciliation actually is, what it can achieve, and what obligations flow from a deep commitment to reconciliation. Authors explain how they have been a part of learning, healing, educating, researching, and living in ways that aim at reconciliation.

Some of these chapters were initially presented as part of the conference "Pathways to Reconciliation," co-sponsored by the University of Manitoba, the National Centre for Truth and Reconciliation, and the University of Winnipeg in June 2016.[16] However, these conference papers represented only a few of the hundreds of important reconciliation initiatives that are underway across the country in response to the T RC's call to reconciliation. To broaden the scope of the volume to better reflect the range and diversity of reconciliation projects across all levels and sectors of society in post-T RC Canada, we subsequently issued a call for papers. The following chapters outline a series of varied perspectives, initiatives, and practices relating to reconciliation, reflecting individual and collective pathways.

Sometimes over the course of a journey, we must walk alone. At other times we share the pathway with fellow travellers. Such is the case with Canada's journey of reconciliation.

Sometimes we do the work of reconciliation or preparation for reconciliation on our own. And sometimes we come together to share parts of the journey forward. Along the way we may let go of long-held beliefs and attitudes and old colonial stories and systems that keep us stuck on a road of unequal power relations, colonial violence, and ongoing injustice. This is the pathway of reframing. On occasion we must stop to consider where we have been, where we need to go, and how best to get there; we must rethink our concepts and plans accordingly. We will dialogue to learn new ways of being that help to heal old wounds and inspire us to new actions. This is the pathway of learning and healing. At times we may need to gather new information about ways to make our journey more meaningful and share our findings more broadly with others. This is the pathway of research. We may also learn from the experience of journeying itself, being open to the gifts we are given as we stumble along, unsure of our footing but willing to risk continuing on anyway, with humility and courage. This is the pathway of living.

These various pathways are not linear: they overlap and intertwine, making new connections of head, heart, and spirit. Sometimes we must lead the way. At other times we must circle back to unlearn old ways or to encourage others to join us. The journey of reconciliation is imperfect and difficult. We will often be tempted to abandon our efforts in the face of overwhelming barriers. While we acknowledge reconciliation's flaws, particularly the potential for replicating rather than transforming settler colonialism in Canada, we encourage readers to reflect on the teachings revealed in the chapters of this volume. We believe that the authors' insights demonstrate the rich potential that reconciliation holds for all of us if we are willing to stay the course.

Reframing

In the first part of the book, different theoretical and contextual approaches to reconciliation are explored, engaging with the TRC's approach, Indigenous aspirations for reconciliation, and with international transitional justice contexts that have given rise to varied mechanisms and measurements of reconciliation.

In his chapter David MacDonald looks at a survey that probed settler perceptions of reconciliation and revealed support for the proposition that reconciliation is about equality and that there is a general lack of willingness to acknowledge settler privilege as part of a colonial interdependent relationship with Indigenous peoples. He argues that we must move beyond liberal multicultural and civil rights frameworks (built on liberal concepts of equality operating within the institutional and ideological boundaries of the settler state) in order to participate in transformative or "unsettling" reconciliation that accounts for Indigenous self-determination and sovereignty.

Speaking to four decades of truth and reconciliation commissions rooted in transitional justice in societies recovering from mass violence, Régine Uwibereyeho King and Benjamin Maiangwa focus on the 1994 Rwandan genocide. They illustrate a model of participatory justice and community healing, called *gacaca*, which struggled with its retributive and restorative application. They identify lessons that may serve Canadians as they seek to implement the TRC's Calls to Action, through a justice system that emanates from communities' traditional values and history.

Based on an extensive evaluation of reconciliation-monitoring literature on the national discourse of reconciliation, Cody O'Neil offers considerations for the National Council for Reconciliation as they undertake the task of examining indicators of reconciliation. While explicitly engaging with the challenges and inherent assumptions of research and measurement, accepting that measurement may be a tool equally of colonization and decolonization, he suggests indicators that aim to capture the framework of reconciliation put forward by the TRC (including the rights contained in UNDRIP) that could both challenge and contribute to the ongoing process of reconciliation in Canada.

In comparing the Canadian TRC to the Maine Wabenaki-State Child Welfare Truth and Reconciliation Commission, Rachel George considers calls from Indigenous peoples to have their truth heard in a formal process and to work towards healing and change. However, she questions the ultimate ability of such processes to move beyond a victimization model toward a true expression of self-determination as a potential or desired outcome.

Learning and Healing

Restorying, educating, dialoguing, and reforming systems are at the heart of the agenda for change that appears throughout the chapters of Part 2. These authors explore, from their own individual perspectives and fields of study, the potential for reconciliation and some of the very important challenges that present themselves along the journey.

Indigenous scholar Erica Jurgens reflects on her personal experience as an intergenerational survivor to argue for the resurrection of Indigenous historiography through original literacies and the (re)writing of distorted colonial settler historiography. She argues that education institutions bear responsibility for transforming historical consciousness, particularly relating to Indigenous nationhood and settler colonialism, in order to (re)right dominant narratives and to repair historical amnesia.

Building on the concept of "peace in the woods," a term used in forest governance, Melanie Zurba and John Sinclair examine attempts to develop culturally relevant models of transitional governance, guided by collaborative principles. Using a "post-conflict pedagogy" in the case of forestry relations in northwestern Ontario, they explore the potential for reconciliation through structural shifts in forest governance.

Researching

While reconciliation is focused on action, there are research initiatives that support the careful consideration of the theories and practices that underlie various approaches to reconciliation. Putting forward their case studies as methods of engaging and learning, each of the authors in Part 3 provides a critical reflection on their contextualized approaches to reconciliation.

In the spirit of Calls to Action 93 and 94, Cathy Rocke and Régine Uwibereyeho King designed a pilot project aimed at the "urgent need to advance the understanding of reconciliation" and the "urgent need for more dialogue between Aboriginal peoples and new Canadians." They present the findings of a pilot project that, through interviews, explored newcomers' current understanding of reconciliation and perceptions of the kind of reconciliation that could work in the Canadian context.

Tracey Carr and Brian Chartier have conducted interviews with support workers and Elders to better understand the needs of residential school survivors and their families for healing, as well as to examine the role of mental health professionals in the healing process. They concluded that the needs of the survivors were generally framed in connection to culture, support programs, and forgiveness, and that health care support should be framed around an understanding of culture and personal history and continuity in care, as well as proper diagnoses.

Living

As mentioned above, meaningful societal change is required in order to journey toward reconciliation. The authors in Part 4 provide some concrete examples, from their unique perspectives on their approach to reconciliation, aimed at improving relationships between Indigenous and non-Indigenous Canadians.

Centred on apologies, Peter Bush's chapter reviews church apologies and considers how apology repetition (from the perspective of "speakers" and "hearers") shapes the relationship between churches and Indigenous peoples "so they might walk together."

As a veteran child welfare worker, Mary Anne Clarke asks difficult questions of the system (particularly in Manitoba) and draws parallels to the colonial assimilation and cultural genocide agenda of the Indian Residential School agenda. She suggests that to achieve reconciliation, child welfare must be decolonized and transformed into proactive, community-specific systems based on Indigenous self-determination.

Andrea Walsh describes the repatriation of a collection of seventy-five children's paintings created at the Alberni Indian Residential School (1959 to 1964) to survivors and their families. This important commemorative project links art, commemoration, and repatriation to the hard work of healing and reconciliation, shared through the paintings and stories of survivors.

In March 2016 the Research Unit at the National Centre for Truth and Reconciliation (NCTR) hosted an interdisciplinary roundtable, "Reconciliation and/or Resurgence: Emerging Research Pathways." Thirty-one invited scholars from across Canada participated in a two-and-a-half-day dialogue guided by Elders and facilitated by NCTR research staff. The purpose of the roundtable was to inform the NCTR's research strategy by bringing together a small but growing group of Indigenous and settler scholars across multiple disciplines who are beginning to explore the complex relationship between oppositional discourses of reconciliation and Indigenous resurgence. Key themes emerged, and, the following year, the NCTR partnered with the University of Victoria to hold a symposium for Indigenous scholars (from Indigenous studies, politics, and law) to engage on the theme of resurgence in an era of reconciliation.[17] A further publication is being prepared following that symposium. And we expect there will be many more of these important conversations, ongoing, for many years to come.

The reconciliation dialogue is only just beginning and it is likely to never end. Pathways will be carved, mistakes will be made, and we will probably step on each other's toes along the way. Yet we must not squander the rich opportunities before us, ones that will enable us to learn and change as we journey towards a renewed relationship. We hope that this volume will serve as a source of inspiration and become an essential tool for others who are developing and implementing their own decolonizing transformative approaches to reconciliation.

Notes

1   Aimée Craft was the founding director of research at the National Centre for Truth and
    Reconciliation (NCTR). Paulette Regan was the former senior advisor on research and reconcili-
    ation at the NCTR, and the senior researcher and lead writer on the *Reconciliation* volume of the
    TRC *Final Report.*

2   During its mandate, the TRC elaborated ten principles of reconciliation it viewed as essential for
    Canada to "flourish in the twenty-first century." These principles informed the TRC's work and
    shaped the TRC's Calls to Action:

    1. The *United Nations Declaration on the Rights of Indigenous Peoples* is the framework for
        reconciliation at all levels and across all sectors of Canadian society.

    2. First Nations, Inuit, and Métis peoples, as the original peoples of this country and as self-de-
        termining peoples, have Treaty, constitutional, and human rights that must be recognized and
        respected.

    3. Reconciliation is a process of healing of relationships that requires public truth sharing,
        apology, and commemoration that acknowledge and redress past harms.

    4. Reconciliation requires constructive action on addressing the ongoing legacies of colo-
        nialism that have had destructive impacts on Aboriginal peoples' education, cultures and
        languages, health, child welfare, the administration of justice, and economic opportunities
        and prosperity.

    5. Reconciliation must create a more equitable and inclusive society by closing the gaps in
        social, health, and economic outcomes that exist between Aboriginal and non-Aboriginal
        Canadians.

    6. All Canadians, as Treaty peoples, share responsibility for establishing and maintaining mutu-
        ally respectful relationships.

    7. The perspectives and understandings of Aboriginal Elders and Traditional Knowledge
        Keepers of the ethics, concepts, and practices of reconciliation are vital to long-term
        reconciliation.

    8. Supporting Aboriginal peoples' cultural revitalization and integrating Indigenous knowledge
        systems, oral histories, laws, protocols, and connections to the land into the reconciliation
        process are essential.

    9. Reconciliation requires political will, joint leadership, trust building, accountability, and
        transparency, as well as a substantial investment of resources.

    10. Reconciliation requires sustained public education and dialogue, including youth engage-
        ment, about the history and legacy of residential schools, Treaties, and Aboriginal rights, as
        well as the historical and contemporary contributions of Aboriginal peoples to Canadian
        society. (Truth and Reconciliation Commission of Canada, *What We Have Learned,* 3–4).

3   TRC, *Final Report,* vol. 6, 11, *Reconciliation.*

4   TRC, *What We Have Learned,* 11–12.

5   A key TRC finding is that the residential school system was a central element in Canada's broader
    Aboriginal policy of assimilation, "which can be best described as 'cultural genocide.'" *TRC Final
    Report,* vol. 1, 3.

6   As part of the ninety-four Calls to Action, the TRC specifically called for the repudiation of the
     Doctrine of Discovery and *terra nullius*. However, as many have argued, this requires a dismantling of
     the institutions that have been structured by, and continue to benefit from, these legal assumptions.

7   The Truth and Reconciliation Commission was part of the Indian Residential Schools Settlement
     Agreement (IRSSA). For a comprehensive overview of the circumstances leading up to the IRSSA,
     see: TRC, *Final Report*, vol. 1, *The History, Part 2*, 551–79. For the TRC mandate, see *Honouring
     the Truth*, app. 1; and *Calls to Action*, 319–37.

8   TRC, *What We Have Learned*, 25.

9   See, for example, this thoughtful piece on the assumption of Crown sovereignty: Ryan Beaton,
     "De Facto and de Jure Crown Sovereignty: Reconciliation and Legitimation at the Supreme
     Court of Canada," *Constitutional Forum* 25 (2018): 27. A. Craft, "Neither Infringement nor
     Justification—the SCC's Mistaken Approach to Reconciliation," in *Renewing Relationships:
     Indigenous Peoples and Canada*, ed. B. Gunn and K. Drake (Saskatoon: University of
     Saskatchewan Native Law Centre, 2019), 59–82.

10   TRC, *What We Have Learned*, 28.

11   For status of Bill C-262, see: https://www.parl.ca/LegisInfo/BillDetails.aspx?Language=E&-
     billId=8160636&View=0. For the text of the bill, see: http://www.parl.ca/DocumentViewer/
     en/42-1/bill/C-262/third-reading.

12   The application of reconciliation as articulated by the courts perpetuates an unequal balanc-
     ing of interests that marginalizes Indigenous aspirations, in favour of broader societal interests.
     As Aimée Craft writes, "The court promotes an unequal division of the 'reconciliation burden,'
     disproportionately privileging the Canadian public over Indigenous people within their own lands
     and territories." Aimée Craft, "Neither Infringement nor Justification – The SCC's Mistaken
     Approach to Reconciliation," in *Renewing Relationships: Indigenous Peoples and Canada*, ed. B.
     Gunn and K. Drake (University of Saskatchewan Native Law Centre, 2019), 75.

13   Regan, *Unsettling the Settler Within*.

14   See, for example, Coulthard, *Red Skin*; Asch, Borrows, and Tully, *Resurgence and Reconciliation*;
     Simpson, *As We Have Always Done*; Henderson and Wakeham, *Reconciling Canada*; Hill and
     McCall, *The Land We Are*; Manuel and Derrickson, *Reconciliation Manifesto*; Simpson, *Dancing
     on Our Turtle's Back*; Alfred, *Wasáse*.

15   Regan, "Reconciliation and Resurgence," 209–27.

16   This edited volume is part of a series—Perceptions on Truth and Reconciliation—in collab-
     oration between the University of Manitoba Press and the National Centre for Truth and
     Reconciliation. The first volume in this series was *A Knock on the Door: The Essential History
     of Residential Schools from the Truth and Reconciliation Commission of Canada* It is an edited
     summary of the TRC *Final Report* Executive Summary, with a contextualizing foreword by Phil
     Fontaine, a key leader in the fight to bring to light the cultural genocide of residential schools, and
     an afterword by Aimée Craft, past director of research at the NCTR, to explain what remains to
     be uncovered about the dark history of the residential school experience, the ongoing legacy of the
     schools, and research on and for reconciliation. There is so much we have yet to understand about
     the legacy of residential schools and our pathways of reconciliation.

17   In September 2018 the University of Victoria Faculty of Law welcomed the first cohort of
     students who will study the Canadian common law and Indigenous legal orders transystemically.
     For more information on the JD/JID program, see https://www.uvic.ca/law/about/indigenous/
     jid/index.php.

Part One

REFRAMING

CHAPTER 1

PAVED WITH COMFORTABLE INTENTIONS

Moving beyond Liberal Multiculturalism and Civil Rights Frames on the Road to Transformative Reconciliation

DAVID B. MACDONALD[1]

A few months before Donald J. Trump was elected president of the United States in 2016, Barack Obama held up a gilded mirror to celebrate Canada. Addressing Parliament in a spirit of bilateral friendship, the now former U.S. president had this to say:

> It's our enduring commitment to a set of values—a spirit, alluded to by Justin, that says no matter who we are, where we come from, what our last names are, what faith we practice, here we can make of our lives what we will. It was the grit of pioneers and prospectors who pushed West across a forbidding frontier. The dreams of generations— immigrants, refugees—that we've welcomed to these shores. The hope of run-away slaves who went north on an underground railroad. "Deep in our history of struggle," said Dr. Martin Luther King, Jr., "Canada was the north star.... The freedom road links us together."[2]

To this he added: "More than any other system of government, democracy allows our most precious rights to find their fullest expression, enabling us, through the hard, painstaking work of citizenship, to continually make our countries better. To solve new challenges. To right past wrongs. And, Prime Minister, what a powerful message of reconciliation it was—here and around the world—when your government pledged a new relationship with Canada's First Nations."[3]

Broken down into its key components, Obama's speech embodied many of the triumphalist beliefs of settler Canadians in their approach to how best to seek reconciliation with Indigenous peoples. He told us, first, that Canada is fundamentally a settler society, formed by settler determination and hard work against a wilderness beset with obstacles. Settlers are the founders and hosts, welcoming newcomers to a land of prosperity and tolerance.

Second, Canada is an acknowledged leader in civil rights and race relations, a beacon of hope for many, including those African Americans who sought refuge here. Third, the fact that Canada is a democracy, which can be imputed as the best form of government, means it has the institutional ability to solve any problem, including past wrongs against Indigenous peoples. Distorting Audre Lorde, Obama told his appreciative audience that there is nothing wrong with the master's house that the master's tools cannot fix. In retrospect, Canada now seems even better when compared with the malignant nationalism that has triumphed after Obama's departure.

This chapter is divided into four sections. The first engages with framing theory and outlines the differences between what I see as liberal and transformative reconciliation, and their related terms: soft and hard Indigenous rights. I argue that the Truth and Reconciliation Commission's (TRC) views of reconciliation weave soft and hard, liberal and transformative forms of reconciliation together.

However, as the second section of this chapter posits, through a critical reading of the 2016 Environics survey on settler perceptions of Indigenous peoples, most settler respondents understand reconciliation primarily in terms of liberal equality; at least this is how they responded to the survey's understanding of reconciliation. Both the U.S. civil rights movement and Canadian multiculturalism help frame how reconciliation might be conceptualized—as providing economic and other forms of equality to Indigenous peoples within the beliefs, institutional structures, and ideological boundaries of the settler state. This has also been noted in Australia, where equality, instead of land and Indigenous autonomy, is advanced. There is a growing literature that critiques the equation of economic equality on settler terms with reconciliation.[4]

The third and fourth sections detail some of the problems of state-controlled narratives of multicultural and civil rights—in particular their wilful forgetting of the long lineages of communities of colour in what is now Canada and their feigned ignorance of anti-Black racism. By advancing a liberal frame that does not threaten the dominance of Stephen Harper's traditional "old stock" settler, these policies confine expressions of difference and collective rights to areas that do not threaten settler society. The same frames have been used to suppress Indigenous peoples and their *sui generis* rights to self-determination, and may continue to do so in the future.

Settler Comfort and the Liberal Frame

Defining "settler" is not straightforward. While a mental image of smiling Euro-Canadians may leap to mind, there is sometimes a question mark about racialized people (in my case, mixed-race Indians from Trinidad by way of Regina), since we function within a white-dominated system that privileges white settler comfort and marks out European identities as normal and unproblematic, while representing others as "ethnic" or "multicultural."[5] Further, given the European origins of the settler colonial system in Canada, racialized peoples are commonly seen in settler colonial studies as, in the words of Lorenzo Veracini, "*appellants* facing a political order that is already constituted," rather than as settlers who are "*founders* of political orders and carry their sovereignty with them."[6]

However, given that many racialized people, like me, see their primary identity as "Canadian," a self-identity as "settler" may be valid. One might define "settler" in its broadest sense as everyone who is not Indigenous, while also making distinctions where appropriate between European settlers and settlers of racialized origin, based on the inherent racial hierarchies on which the settler state was constructed and still depends. "Settler," in my view, is preferable to the more supposedly neutral terms used by the Environics survey (discussed later), such as "Canadians," "the public," and the "mainstream." Terms such as these obfuscate the coloniality of settler-Indigenous relationships and whitewash settler dominance at the expense of Indigenous peoples.[7]

While racialized people are often more attuned to Canada's racist ways, in general most settlers have traditionally ascribed to what Sherene Razack terms a "fantasy" view of national history, insofar as we tend to disavow notions of conquest, invasion, and genocide, promoting instead myths of peaceful settlement.[8] Constance Backhouse has similarly identified Canada's tendency to define itself as "not a racist country, or at least is much less so than

our southern neighbour, the United States." Her work laments the continued existence of a "'mythology of racelessness' and 'stupefying innocence.'"[9]
At the same time it is clear, as Augie Fleras observes, that "discrimination
and racism are not simply relics from the past, but are so deeply ingrained
and structurally embedded that any chance of disappearing in the foresee-
able future is nil to none."[10]

Certainly we have long maintained what Paulette Regan calls a "myth of
innocence" over how and why Indigenous knowledge, cultures, languages,
laws, and governance traditions have been virtually erased from mainstream
history and society.[11] We are now slowly changing our view of history and,
with it, our primarily negative perceptions of Indigenous peoples. But there
is considerable avoidance and ignorance still. For example, as Erica Jurgens
argues in Chapter 5, this "great forgetting" has erased evidence of early nation-
to-nation relationships between Indigenous people and settlers, which would
disrupt the settler narrative of the English and French as the true founding
nations of Canada.

Newcomers to Canada (recent immigrants and refugees) often confront
racism as well. Racism has historically marginalized racialized people inside
Canada, while also helping to erect unequal barriers to immigration. Work
by settler colonial theorists such as Lorenzo Veracini outlines a triangular
model of how settler states operate, with three groups occupying the same
geographic space but with very different endowments of political power and
resources. At the top of the triangle are European settlers, with Indigenous
peoples and later migrants (often people of colour) at the bottom. As he puts
it, "Settlers are *founders* of political orders and carry their sovereignty with
them (on the contrary, migrants can be seen as *appellants* facing a political
order that is already constituted)."[12]

The focus for non-European peoples, whether their families have been
in Canada for centuries or since last week, is to assimilate into the European
settler mainstream and to do so quickly and quietly. A national poll of almost
4,000 Canadians, released in late 2016 by CBC and Angus Reid, revealed
that 68 percent of respondents felt that "minorities should be doing more
to fit in with mainstream society instead of keeping their own customs and
languages." Angus Reid's executive director observed of the findings: "there
are real limits on what Canadians . . . are prepared to put up with in terms
of accommodation and the sense of the mosaic versus the melting pot."[13]
The wording is instructive: difference is something to be "accommodated,"

to be put up with, but only in a shallow sense and only, it seems, within limits. Further, the term "mainstream" is undefined, but for most readers there would be little doubt that mainstream equals settler values and ways of doing things.

In this chapter I assess how settlers have tried to make "reconciliation" comfortable by framing it as something familiar and non-threatening, in much the same way they have sought to use multiculturalism as a means of promoting assimilation. A frame is a way of organizing and interpreting reality through an ensemble of preconceived ideas. Framing theory suggests that when actors are seeking to implement new policies or ideas, they will package these, as Loren Cass notes, "in a way that resonates with existing norms and with the interests of the target audience."[14]

Canadian settlers, like the members of most societies, operate according to what we might call an "unconscious ideology," a common-sense understanding made up of unquestioned assumptions that underpin how we view the world. The conception that Canada is tolerant, kind, apologetic, and more civilized than the United States is rarely subject to sustained problematization. Indeed, people are uncomfortable when their established views of reality are articulated and criticized, and that discomfort can show itself as defensive behaviour, denial, and anger.[15]

Obama paid deference to what we might call a liberal frame: the belief in a society and governance system based on individual rights and equality, guaranteed by Western settler institutions and derived from European social contract theory and European forms of law and philosophy. This frame has been at the core of Canada's settler governance traditions, as Anishinaabe theorist Dale Turner observes, and has strongly influenced multicultural policies and its relationship with Indigenous peoples.[16]

I argue here that most settlers are comfortable with Western liberal principles of equality. The most popular ideas of reconciliation are framed as closing gaps, making Indigenous peoples equal with settlers, working to create a shared vision of a harmonious future. While Environics president Michael Adams claims that "the door to reconciliation is truly open," it would be more prudent to suggest that the door is at best half open.[17] This is because we are not recognizing the unsettling and discomforting effects of what I call "transformative reconciliation," which is actually what this process should be about.

Liberal reconciliation frames are designed to settle the settler within, without, in fact, requiring the settler to acknowledge themselves as a settler or to reflect on a relational and inherited coloniality with Indigenous peoples. This type of reconciliation ensures a high level of what Robin DiAngelo calls "racial comfort," at least for white settlers, who can feel the frisson of reconciling without acknowledging their own privilege and continued colonization of Indigenous lands through their participation in the settler state.[18]

It is tempting for political leaders to frame reconciliation in this way to avoid what DiAngelo calls "race-based stress," which can lead to "white fragility," a defensive reaction where white people feel threatened, even by thoroughly liberal-based demands for an end to discrimination. As DiAngelo observes: "Whites often confuse comfort with safety." For those who do not understand their own privilege and fear losing what they have in some respects, this becomes unsettling.[19]

However, to actually achieve any substantive effects, reconciliation may *need* to be unsettling. It will result in new political arrangements, where Indigenous peoples self-determine their own futures either inside or outside Canada, or some combination of both.

As I will outline, liberal notions of equality are insufficient for bringing about meaningful and transformative reconciliation, although they are useful in the short term and can address some of the urgent and obvious problems in Indigenous communities that result from ongoing colonization. In what I call "liberal reconciliation," the focus is similar to the existing frame around civil rights and multiculturalism; it is about respect, a level playing field, and equal access to the opportunities afforded by the Western settler state.

This form of reconciliation can be positive if it helps build Indigenous capacity for self-determination but also contains inherently assimilatory ideals: *to be comfortable like us, they should become like us.*

Transformative reconciliation, by contrast, is about fundamentally problematizing the settler state as a colonial creation, a vector of cultural genocide, and one that continues inexorably to suppress Indigenous collective aspirations for self-determination and sovereignty. In this type of reconciliation, we will see the rollback of settler state control over Indigenous individuals and communities, commensurate with the restoration of Indigenous lands, cultures, laws, languages, and governance traditions. Transformative reconciliation will centre Indigenous rights to self-determination, highlighted in articles 3 and 31 of the United Nations Declaration on the Rights of Indigenous Peoples (UNDRIP). We might understand Indigenous self-determination as "the right to political autonomy, the freedom to determine political status and to freely pursue economic, social and cultural development."[20] This should be seen, Damien Short argues, as "central to a 'just' response to colonial dispossession and the resultant political and social subordination of indigenous peoples."[21] Further, the idea of creating a shared future together may not be what all Indigenous peoples want, and "is challenged by the existence of indigenous nations that have never shared a comprehensive vision with the colonisers nor wish to."[22]

We need to understand as settlers that Indigenous views of reconciliation may be incommensurable with the status quo of the settler state.

Sheryl Lightfoot's work on soft and hard Indigenous rights in the international context can help illustrate what settler Canadians have tended to support, versus what they have not. While the dividing line between soft and hard is somewhat blurred, the terms are useful for my argument.

Soft rights are collective rights to language, culture, spiritual beliefs and practices, educational systems, and other forms of identity. These are perceived as extensions of current human rights norms and practices, and while they may impose some obligations, these obligations can be met largely within the existing structures of the settler state. Even with a transfer of some level of symbolic recognition, and funds, the state retains its power. Lightfoot puts it: "While recognition and protection of soft rights involves some change to thinking about the inclusion of collective rights in the international human rights consensus and the complementarity of collective rights to individual rights, the changes required by states and the UN system to secure these rights are not as fundamental as the changes brought forward by hard rights and thus the majority of states accepted soft rights much more readily."[23]

Lightfoot's soft rights, similar to what I call liberal reconciliation, are not incidental to the reconciliation process and should be seen as an important aspect of it. To rework Adams's comment, this is still part of opening the reconciliation door, and seeking soft rights and economic equality is crucial to the well-being of Indigenous peoples as individuals and communities.

Chief Robert Joseph, when addressing the Liberal Party convention in 2016, outlined the scope of Indigenous inequality, noting how poverty affects half of First Nations children. He identified a suicide rate five to seven times higher than for non-Indigenous peoples, with a life expectancy considerably lower, while reminding his audience that some 130,000 First Nations people need new houses. True reconciliation, he argued, cannot take place unless these matters are dealt with in a satisfactory manner.[24]

Lightfoot's framework might identify these as soft rights because the legitimacy and capacity of the settler state providing them is not in jeopardy.
Indeed, the settler state may *increase* its legitimacy if it is publicly seen to be
responding effectively to these gross injustices.

Mick Dodson noted this problem two decades ago, observing that settler
policies towards Indigenous peoples "constructed on the basis of perceived
need and comparative disadvantage" gave a false impression of the history
and reality of the relationship. He cautioned against basing delivery of rights
on a foundation of compassion. Rather: "As long as indigenous peoples are
dependent on the perception of need and the compassion of the other, we
remain in a position of dependence. Whether the response is benevolent
or withholding, our position as powerless recipients is subtly reinforced."[25]

Hard rights, by contrast, exemplified by "self-determination and land
rights for Indigenous nations, with or without statehood" are less commen-
surable with the current structures of the settler state, and remove settlers'
ability to exercise their compassion in either providing or denying it. Instead,
the focus is on the exercise of Indigenous rights. Potentially, "state territorial sovereignty" is under question when issues of hard rights are raised.[26]

Audra Simpson has cogently addressed some of the distinctions between
liberal and transformative views in her work on Mohawk sovereignty.
Indigenous peoples, she argues, need to be correctly understood as "nation-
als with sovereign authority over their lives and over their membership and
living within their own space, which has been 'held for them' in the form
of reservations."[27]

A focus on culture and soft rights is self-serving for the state, occluding
Indigenous sovereignty and hiding the fact that this sovereignty still exists.[28]
Indigenous political traditions, Simpson argues, are "not the 'culture' that
multiculturalism sought to protect and preserve."[29] Instead, Simpson's view
promotes Indigenous national self-determination efforts as changing our
understanding of territory and political power, "as a sovereignty within multiple sovereignties."[30]

The TRC in their *Reconciliation* volume advocated forms of both soft
and hard rights, although, as I outline later, they pull back from recommendations that could imperil Canada's claims to Westphalian, or state,
absolute sovereignty.

Certainly, most TRC recommendations go well beyond the sort of liberal
rights that we might see embodied in civil rights or multicultural ideals.[31] At

one level, the TRC asserts, equality and inclusivity inform the process, with a focus on "closing the gaps in social, health, and economic outcomes that exist between Aboriginal and non-Aboriginal Canadians."[32] Reconciliation includes "constructive action on addressing the ongoing legacies of colonial- ism that have had destructive impacts on Aboriginal peoples' education, cultures and languages, health, child welfare, administration of justice, and economic opportunities and prosperity."[33] While this focus on gap closing might be seen on the surface to reproduce the problems Dodson identified in the Australian context, the TRC has largely framed soft rights arguments through a hard rights frame. This is so, given that the denial of these soft rights has been used to weaken Indigenous self-determination efforts in the past and present. Further, achieving these equality rights may build capac- ity for Indigenous peoples to collectively self-determine their own futures.

The *Reconciliation* volume also endorsed more overt forms of hard rights, with an emphasis on Indigenous law, land, sovereignty, and self-determina- tion.[34] This is to include revitalizing Indigenous legal traditions, and "cultural revitalization and integrating Indigenous knowledge systems, oral histories, laws, protocols, and connections to the land into the reconciliation process are essential."[35] UNDRIP is presented as "the framework for reconciliation at all levels and across all sectors of Canadian society," and Indigenous peoples are fully acknowledged as "the original peoples of this country and as self-de- termining peoples, [with] Treaty, constitutional, and human rights that must be recognized and respected."[36] Central to this is decolonization, "from the debilitating impacts and ongoing legacy of denial by States of Indigenous peoples' inherent sovereignty, laws, and title to the lands, territories, and resources."[37] Treaties will prove central here, as "a sacred obligation that commits both parties to maintaining respectful relationships and sharing lands and resources equitably."[38]

Recommending a new royal proclamation will, for the TRC, confirm on the settler side the rights and obligations of the treaty relationships. This would include "an official disavowal of the Doctrine of Discovery," full implementation of UNDRIP, and full reconciliation of "Aboriginal and Crown constitutional and legal orders to ensure that Aboriginal peoples are full partners in Confederation, including the recognition and integration of Indigenous laws and legal traditions in negotiation and implementation processes involving Treaties, land claims, and other constructive agree- ments."[39] Indigenous laws and protocols will confirm the resurgence of

Indigenous communities as self-determining. They will also rectify the power imbalance, creating a more partnership-oriented ethos.

This partnership, however, will be determined by Indigenous peoples and on their own terms. As the TRC outlines: "Without Indigenous law and protocol establishing the common ground on which the parties meet—reconciliation will always be incomplete. At the same time, we recognize that Indigenous forms of reconciliation will not be available to the Canadian state until First Nations, Inuit, and Métis peoples decide to offer them, leaving significant power in the hands of Indigenous peoples."[40]

This counters the prevailing view that settlers are empowered to demarcate the parameters of reconciliation. The TRC argues that any moving on will depend on Indigenous decisions. While a liberal reconciliation model would allow the settler state to respond to Indigenous inequality through the apportionment of soft rights within the existing framework of the state, a transformative model would return decision-making power to Indigenous peoples. They would decide whether progress was being made on reconciliation.

However, the TRC did not devote much of its word count to problematizing how best self-determination could be defined, and neither did it engage with any potential ramifications of any process that could have a negative impact on existing Canadian Westphalian sovereignty. For example, their vision of reconciliation is one "that fully embraces Aboriginal peoples' right to self-determination within, and in partnership with, a viable Canadian sovereignty."[41]

As such, the TRC's version of Indigenous self-determination appears to fall short of achieving Simpson's "sovereignty within multiple sovereignties."[42] Reconciliation might not result in a more complex model of sovereignty, where Indigenous nations use their own passports and sign treaties and other agreements with other countries. For example, Sid Hill, the Tadodaho (traditional leader) of the Onondaga of the Six Nations Confederacy, has used a Haudenosaunee passport to travel outside of Canada and recently articulated: "We are a sovereign nation recognized by the United States under the 1794 Treaty of Canandaigua signed by George Washington."[43]

Similarly, the Chiefs of Ontario understand the treaties as "living, international agreements, which remain valid today and continue to affirm our sovereign relationships." Speaking for the fourteen Indigenous nations whose traditional territory is within the province of Ontario, the Chiefs are clear:

"We are and always have been original Nations that have never relinquished our title, rights, language, culture, and governance by way of Treaty to the British Crown or the successor state of Canada."[44]

The TRC's mandate has arguably restricted its ability to promote a robust sense of hard rights. Article 4(c) of its mandate suggests that the TRC was to "build upon the work of past and existing processes, archival records, resources and documentation, including the work and records of the Royal Commission on Aboriginal Peoples [RCAP] of 1996."[45] Since RCAP had already made extensive recommendations, the TRC was not obliged to reiterate them, although it could have done so. Suggesting specific changes to the nature of sovereignty could have strayed well beyond its commonly accepted parameters as expressed in its mandate. Further, while recommending that UNDRIP frame the reconciliation process was bold, Article 46(1) ensures that UNDRIP neither authorizes nor encourages "any action which would dismember or impair, totally or in part, the territorial integrity or political unity of sovereign and independent States."[46] UNDRIP, while path breaking in many respects, has had to dilute its hard rights provisions in order to gain agreement by signatory states. As I will outline in the third and fourth sections, civil rights equality and multiculturalism frameworks have been privileged in settler understandings of reconciliation. Both ensure a sense of forward movement and progress along the road to reconciliation but are also designed to make that process comfortable for settler Canadians by confining it to relatively safe areas that will not upset status quo institutions, values, and identities of the settler state.

"Safe" does not mean "easy," but it does mean that problems can be solved primarily by changing attitudes and policies and adding funding to deal with long-term government neglect.

The Environics Survey

In June 2016 the Ottawa-based public policy firm Environics released a survey based on telephone discussions with 2,001 non-Indigenous respondents during a three-week period in early 2016.[47] The survey sought to gauge settler knowledge and impressions of Indigenous peoples and issues, in particular the Indian Residential Schools (IRS) and the work and recommendations of the TRC. The survey featured three, primary, different types of questions, some asking for a basic choice between two or three responses,

such as Question 5: "Over the past few years, has your impression of Aboriginal Peoples gotten better, gotten worse, or stayed the same?" A second
type asked respondents to choose from a range of finite options, such as
Question 3: "Do you think each of the following is very important, somewhat important, not very important, or not at all important in defining
Canada . . . Aboriginal history and culture . . . Bilingualism . . . Multiculturalism . . . Land and geography . . . The health care system." A third type
was open-ended questions, such as Question 2: "What do you think makes
Canada unique?"[48] Respondents were triaged into streams after answering
certain questions a certain way. For example, if they answered that they had
generally positive impressions of Indigenous peoples, they would be asked
why in an open-ended way, for example, Question 6A: "Why do you say
your impression has gotten better?"[49]

The results buttress my arguments in this chapter: a large proportion of
settler respondents view reconciliation through a liberal frame, mediated
through civil rights and multicultural tropes. They were not offered the
option to choose a transformative model of reconciliation, so it is not clear
from the survey whether they would have approved or rejected this view of
reconciliation. Overall, the survey revealed the following four salient points:

- Lack of knowledge about the IRS system, the work of the
  TRC, and its recommendations.

- Support for the proposition that reconciliation is primarily
  about equality.

- Mixed perceptions of Indigenous distinctiveness; weak
  acceptance of Indigenous unique status coupled with support
  for settling land claims.

- Lack of willingness to see settler privilege as part of a colonial
  and interdependent relationship with Indigenous peoples.

First, respondents demonstrated a low level of knowledge about Indigenous
peoples, histories, and contemporary issues. While 66 percent of respondents
claimed some knowledge of the IRS system, when broken down by thematic
area (organized by unprompted responses), the results were not encouraging. If we factor in what percentage of the total sample of respondents claim
to know anything, we get far lower statistics, indicated by round brackets.

When asked, 42 percent of the "knowledgeable" 66 percent (28 percent of the total sample) could "recall something" about "abuse and molestation of students," 29 percent (19 percent) about "general mistreatment . . . and discrimination," 31 percent (21 percent) about the impact of being separated, 18 percent (12 percent) on cultural impact of language and culture loss, and a mere 4 percent (2.6 percent) could "recall something" on cultural genocide.[50]

While Environics praises this level of knowledge, let us be clear about their findings: 72 percent of total respondents claim to know nothing about Survivor abuse, and 88 percent know nothing about language and culture loss. Given this, it is perhaps not surprising that self-reported impressions of Indigenous peoples over the past few years have not changed for 61 percent of respondents,[51] or that 79 percent of respondents want to learn more about Indigenous cultures, which seems fully consistent with a liberal paradigm.[52]

Environics featured a question related to cultural genocide, but it was rather convoluted, measuring people's disagreement with the statement "Canada's residential schools policy was not an intentional effort to destroy Aboriginal culture and connection to the land." The 42 percent who agree with this statement are interpreted as "reject[ing] the idea of cultural genocide," although that term does not feature in the question itself. Given that only 2.6 percent of respondents connected the term "cultural genocide" with the IRS system, it is not clear how respondents could give an informed opinion.[53]

Second, when asked what "reconciliation" meant to them (a question where respondents provide their own unprompted definitions), respondents answered that it was primarily about social and economic equality. Perceptions of reconciliation bear similarities with how multiculturalism was framed from the 1980s and after, as what Fleras dubs "equity multiculturalism" of the 1980s and 1990s, with its focus on a "level playing field," as well as the "civic multiculturalism" from the mid-1990s and after, with a focus on "living together."[54]

Indeed, "equality remains a dominant theme," Environics argued, which they broke down into support for "mutual respect and living together in harmony," with respondents viewing reconciliation as "fair policies" and a "level playing field" (at 18 percent). Similarly, reconciliation could be seen as Indigenous peoples and the federal government cooperating and "working together" (11 percent), with both sides listening, communicating, and in dialogue (7 percent).[55] Expanding the centrality of equality and harmony,

Environics revealed: "Some think of reconciliation as getting along better (14%), finding common ground and coming together (14%), both sides listening to each other (12%). . . . Fewer Canadians also spoke about actions to repair the damage caused by Indian residential schools: compensation (5%), help or counsel to care for the affected (4%), improving support from government (1%) and recognizing Aboriginal rights (1%)."[56]

Economic and social inequality are recognized as serious problems, with 59 percent identifying a "large gap in the standard of living."[57] The gap is crucial for most respondents, with 72 percent agreeing that "reconciliation will be impossible as long as Aboriginal peoples remain socio-economically disadvantaged."[58] Key priorities comprised ending discrimination, increasing funding for on-reserve housing and schools and for safe drinking water, reviving Indigenous languages, and a mandatory curriculum about Indigenous culture and history.[59]

Environics observes that anti-Indigenous racism is a particularly acute problem. While other groups (such as Canadian Muslims) are also targeted, for Indigenous peoples, "it appears to be more deeply rooted and resistant to change."[60] When discussing challenges, respondents prioritized "struggles Aboriginal peoples face in being accepted into the Canadian social fabric." This included "stigma" for being Indigenous, which resulted in "inequality and discrimination" and "isolation and related social issues," alongside "threats to Aboriginal culture and traditions or to their self-identity."[61] Note that Environics failed to problematize the "social fabric" as being created by settlers, and, within a liberal model, the question seems to privilege the removal of barriers to Indigenous integration within the settler state.

In terms of how widespread anti-Indigenous attitudes are: "Two-thirds strongly (24%) or somewhat (41%) agree with the statement 'Most Canadians are prejudiced against Aboriginal peoples, whether or not they are conscious of it.'"[62]

The third point revealed by the survey was that respondents had problems seeing Indigenous peoples as possessing a unique legal and historical status predating Canada and also guaranteed by the Constitution; they similarly encountered problems seeing Indigenous peoples as a unique definitional element in understanding Canadian identity. For example, when asked in general terms about what makes Canada unique, 43 percent of respondents proffered "multiculturalism and diversity," with "land and geography" a distant second (17 percent), followed by "freedom and democratic system" at 14 percent, and the "'nice,' 'friendly,' 'humble' nature of the populace" at 11 percent. Indigenous peoples came in at 2 percent.[63]

Added to their poor contributions to Canadian uniqueness, the distinct, constitutionally recognized rights of Indigenous peoples failed to mark them out as unique. Respondents were split on this issue. Fifty-two percent of respondents did agree that Indigenous peoples "have unique rights as the first inhabitants of the continent," while, by contrast, a significant minority at 41 percent countered that "they are just like other cultural or ethnic groups in Canada's multicultural society." Worryingly although predictably, the prairie provinces, which contain a large proportion of Indigenous peoples, had the lowest support for uniqueness recognition.[64]

The survey did not ask questions about Indigenous governance traditions, Indigenous law, colonialism, settler identities, race, white privilege, UNDRIP, self-determination, sovereignty, or nation-to-nation relationships. Most of these terms were scrupulously avoided; treaty rights were barely explored. Most questions were confined to areas that would fall into the liberal reconciliation and soft rights category.

However, when asked about hard rights issues, respondents were generally positive, which suggests some hope for the future, if the Trudeau government is able to reframe the status of Indigenous peoples and how reconciliation could look. For example, some 66 percent "endorse providing Aboriginal communities full control over the natural resources on their traditional territories," while 60 percent were in favour of "settling all outstanding land claims with First Nations, Métis and Inuit people regardless of what this might cost."[65] This may seem a bit dissonant with this less positive view, endorsed by 45 percent, that "Aboriginal communities do not need control over their land and resources to be successful."[66] However, this means that for respondents, settling land claims was not a precondition to however they defined Indigenous "success." Interestingly: "The importance given to challenges associated with land claims/treaty rights has dropped significantly since 2008 (when 18% identified it as the most important issue); this decline is most noticeable in Ontario and among high income earners."[67]

Indigenous representation within the existing settler political system was roundly popular for respondents. Seventy-six percent were in favour of there being "an Aboriginal representative at every meeting of the country's First Ministers," while 73 percent favoured "requiring at least one Aboriginal Minister in the federal cabinet." A smaller majority of 63 percent were in favour of creating "a new parliamentary committee composed of Aboriginal MPS from all parties to review all laws from an Aboriginal perspective." Support for "the creation of an Aboriginal political party" was far lower at 49 percent.[68] Notably, none of these suggestions went much further than what Quebec already has, and, indeed, guaranteed Indigenous seats (as in New Zealand for Māori), supreme court membership, and other such issues are not broached by the survey.

The fourth point is a general lack of willingness amongst respondents to accept responsibility for the continuing negative effects of settler colonialism on Indigenous peoples. When Environics asked about the three biggest obstacles to social and economic equality, equal proportions of respondents (26 percent) blamed the policies of the governments and "Aboriginal peoples themselves." Only 18 percent cited the "attitudes of the Canadian public" as the primary cause.[69] Following this attitude, a large proportion of respondents felt that Indigenous peoples "have a sense of entitlement in terms of receiving special consideration and financial benefits from governments that are not available to other Canadians." Support for this contention was 66 percent overall, with particularly strong majorities in the prairie provinces and amongst older respondents.[70]

A large proportion of respondents also felt that Indigenous peoples were being given privileged access to various social services, despite obvious and well-publicized evidence to the contrary. To whit: "Canadians are most likely to believe that Aboriginal peoples are treated as well as or better than others when it comes to the health care system (62%) and the workplace (63%), in comparison to the education system (49%) and the criminal justice system (48%)."[71]

The troubling nature of the findings continues with regards to how settlers view their own privilege and positionality. While many respondents acknowledged the problems of structural racism and prejudice, only 33 percent agreed with the statement "Mainstream Canadian society today benefits from ongoing discrimination against Aboriginal peoples," versus 71 percent who disagreed.[72]

Interestingly, while Environics stratified respondents by age, region, and gender, they provided little information about socio-economic status. Class and perceptions of Indigenous peoples were poorly correlated; the word "class" was not used in the report at all.[73] When socio-economic status was briefly alluded to, poorer, younger people seemed to be more in favour of

Indigenous hard rights than richer people. Those "with lower household incomes" tend to more readily recognize the unique rights of Indigenous peoples. One of the most pro-Indigenous groups, the "Young Idealists," has "lower than average household incomes." By contrast, those most resistant to hard rights tended to be the "Dismissive Naysayers," with "higher than average incomes," and "Informed Critics," who are the "most affluent of the five groups."[74]

The overall thrust of the survey is that Canadians recognize that discrimination and social and economic inequality are serious problems. They are prepared to concede certain soft rights to Indigenous peoples, and are supportive of concluding land claims and allowing Indigenous "control" over traditional lands. The survey, however, did not address many aspects of transformative reconciliation, which makes it difficult to say whether respondents would or would not favour moving forward with harder forms of rights.

This is a common problem with surveys. For example, Angus Reid in its 2015 and 2018 surveys also does not cover transformative reconciliation, instead focusing on the more liberal aspects. The 2018 survey, "Truths of Reconciliation," labelled Indigenous peoples and "Indigenous Canadians," and 53 percent agreed with the following statements: "Overall, Indigenous Canadians would be better off . . . integrating more into broader Canadian society, even if that means losing more of their own culture and traditions"; "In modern Canada, Indigenous people should have no special status that other Canadians don't have"; and "Canada spends too much time apologizing for residential schools—it's time to move on." In these cases the questions assume Indigenous rights stem from prior occupancy rather than any *sui generis* rights per se, and there is no mention of treaties or the Constitution. The questions also assume that settlers should have the power to determine whether further integration is an acceptable idea, as well as when and how Canada should "move on."[75] Reconciliation Canada's 2017 report, based on a survey they commissioned, similarly suggests that respondents were in favour of liberal forms of reconciliation.[76]

Because issues of sovereignty, self-determination, and law were not raised in the Environics survey, it is difficult to gauge settler support for hard rights that might actually change the way Canadians and Indigenous sovereignties are perceived and operate. Support for Indigenous control also seems to contradict a feeling of Indigenous entitlement and the widespread ignorance of the IRS system and the work of the TRC.

The Liberal Multicultural Frame

Thomas Axworthy has observed that Justin Trudeau's development of a "true partnership with Canada's indigenous peoples" could be "as defining for Trudeau as French-English reconciliation was for his father."[77] Were this to be the case, the balance would need to be shifted, since, as I will argue here, both biculturalism and multiculturalism developed at the expense of Indigenous peoples, and this exploitative relationship continues still.

Christine Inglis has described our system as a "programmatic-political" form of multiculturalism, given that the state has developed "specific types of programs and policy initiatives designed to respond to and manage ethnic diversity." This is an expansion beyond the mere acknowledgement of ethnic diversity, known as "demographic-descriptive" multiculturalism.[78]

The state has long viewed multiculturalism as attractive because of its ability to maintain the dominance of white settlers, who continue to set default Canadian values, creating the boundaries for what is to be tolerated or discouraged. Himani Bannerji observed some time ago that multiculturalism "establishes anglo-Canadian culture as the ethnic core culture while 'tolerating' and hierarchically arranging others around it as 'multiculture.'"[79] That multiculturalism is about integration into the settler state is taken for granted by many settlers.

In a 2015 Environics survey, respondents were both very pro-immigration (57 percent) and pro-multiculturalism. However, this had less to do with a celebration of difference than the view that immigration was good for the economy while also being effective in its capacity to submerge competing cultures into dominant white settler society. To the proposition "Ethnic groups should try as much as possible to blend into Canadian society and not form a separate community," 75 percent of respondents concurred, a level unchanged from previous iterations of the survey between 2004 and 2010.[80] This should come as no surprise, since from a policy perspective Citizenship and Immigration Canada defines a central goal of multiculturalism as promoting "the long-term integration of ethnic and religious communities, including the adoption of Canadian values."[81] These, needless to say, are not defined but assumed.

Settler state governments have long played the game of conflating Indigenous hard territorial and political rights with softer linguistic and cultural rights for ethnic communities. Under Pierre Trudeau, liberalism informed *both* the assimilatory 1969 White Paper and the 1971

Multiculturalism Act. White Paper liberalism, after all, sought to turn Indigenous peoples into Indigenous individual citizens, who would relinquish their "special status" as a "race apart in Canada" to become instead "Canadians of full status," as Trudeau announced in August 1969.[82] He found it inconceivable "that in a given society one section of the society [should] have a treaty with the other section of the society," given that everyone "must be all equal under the laws."[83]

Ironically, Trudeau's liberalism overtly favoured French Canadian nationalism—they were the only ones deserving of any special collective status in his national vision. In other words, there was to be more recognition and reward for the subsidiary colonizing power in Canada, while Indigenous peoples were to be unilaterally stripped of their legal rights.

Canadian multiculturalism since that time has involved the thin recognition of some community cultural traits, as part of the escalator towards the integration of non-Europeans into the settler state and its values. Yes, some level of cultural expression is tolerated, but only until, as Fleras notes, such cultural differences "get in the way of full citizenship and equal participation." In practice, in order for such diversity to be respected, it is best "stripped of history or context, and consistent with Canada's self-proclaimed prerogative for defining the outer limits of acceptable differences."[84] The framing of multiculturalism as a tolerance and even celebration of diverse otherness, often non-European identities, has paradoxically helped the erasure of the non-European communities who also helped found the country. As Bannerji notes, the way multiculturalism is framed presents people of colour as curiosities, either new to the country or as somehow other to whatever mainstream Canada is supposed to be, even, as is often the case, when their families have been here for generations. Conversely, Bannerji observes, hegemonic whiteness in the ways settler identities are understood allows "all white people, no matter when they immigrate to Canada or as carriers of which European ethnicity, [to] become invisible and hold a dual membership in Canada, while others remain immigrants generations later."[85]

For example, much of Black history in what is now Canada has been erased, sometimes through attempted or actual physical destruction, like the slave cemetery in St. Armand, Quebec, and Africville in Nova Scotia.[86] Early Black presence as slaves and those fleeing slavery goes back to the foundation of the American colonies,[87] and even though Black loyalists predate the formation of the country, Rinaldo Walcott observes: "The most recent migrations have taken precedence in the popular imagination and there-fore authorities tend to locate blackness as new to the nation."[88] In what he calls a "double move," the Official Languages Act positions English and French Canadians outside the multicultural framework, identifying them and their cultures as foundational, essentially whitewashing the nation by acknowledging non-white peoples only as "the contaminants within, but in proscribed ways."[89]

Canada's thin multiculturalism frame also informs the thin recognition of Indigenous cultures, languages, laws, governance systems, and spiritual prac-tices. There is a tendency to frame Indigenous rights as somehow analogous to cultural claims by ethnic communities, and, as Environics demonstrates, respondents have a tendency to conflate reconciliation with equality. Pierre Trudeau's injunction, "No citizen or group of citizens is other than Canadian, and all should be treated fairly,"[90] translates into temporary government measures to ensure fairness—to ensure that those who are below the expec-tations set by the settler state can rise to it. Policies designed to foster equality are by definition temporary, because once equality is reached, the policies can end, and if the policies do not achieve equality, they need to end on the basis that they are not achieving their desired effect.

As Fleras notes, liberal multiculturalism will "ensure that individuals are treated as equals when their differences prove disadvantaging—as long as the concessions are needs based and temporary."[91] Applying the same logic of temporary assistance to Indigenous peoples, Will Kymlicka has argued for distinct rights for Indigenous peoples on the basis of their vulnerabil-ity. As such, "the rights accorded to Aboriginal groups are justified only 'if there actually is a disadvantage with respect to cultural membership, and if the rights actually serve to rectify the disadvantage.'"[92] Further, Kymlicka constrains Aboriginal rights through his own sense of "justice": "One could imagine a point where the amount of land reserved for indigenous peoples would not be necessary to provide reasonably external protections, but rather would simply provide unequal opportunities to them. Justice would then require that the holdings of indigenous peoples be subject to the same redis-tributive taxation as the wealth of other advantaged groups, so as to assist the less well off in society."[93]

Kymlicka and others like him will therefore decide when Indigenous peoples are approaching the barrier of justice and when they have crossed the line. Like an infusion pump monitoring an IV drip, they will deliver a sufficient quantity of government-mandated sugar water to promote equality, then presumably taper it off and discontinue the flow entirely when equality is reached.

This is problematic for any notion of reconciliation because it puts the ball squarely in the court of the settler state. They can decide when Indigenous peoples have had enough of a helping hand to attain equality within the institutional and ideational framework of the settler state, and how much is enough.

Equality and the Civil Rights Framework

Walking with tens of thousands of other people in the pouring rain was for many people one of the highlights of the 2013 Vancouver National Event. Organized by Reconciliation Canada, the march was opened by a moving tribute to IRS Survivors by Martin Luther King Jr.'s daughter Bernice King, who addressed the sodden crowd on the fiftieth anniversary of her father's "I have a dream" speech. She had a message for the crowd: "the way forward . . . is going to be through choosing non-violence." A choir sang civil rights–era spirituals. King urged the crowd to avoid hate, to seek positive transformation. She spoke with passion, but much of her speech, while rousing, said very little about the distinct situation of Indigenous peoples in a settler state.[94]

Echoing the liberal discourse of multiculturalism, Bernice King spoke volubly about a liberal form of equality, and hence a liberal understanding of reconciliation. Civil rights is, after all, largely about privileges or rights that are legally enforceable. According to the Cornell Law School, examples would include "freedom of speech, press, and assembly; the right to vote; freedom from involuntary servitude; and the right to equality in public places." Under this rubric, violations of civil rights occur when the rights of "an individual are denied or interfered with because of their membership in a particular group or class."[95]

Back in 1963 Martin Luther King put it that "we've come to our nation's capital to cash a check." That cheque was the Declaration of Independence, and King sought equality, or, as he described it, the fulfilment of the "promise that all men, yes, black men as well as white men, would be guaranteed the 'unalienable Rights' of 'Life, Liberty and the pursuit of Happiness.'" King's speech was resoundingly successful in part because of its continued faith in the American ideal, which King contrasted with the reality of American practice: "we refuse to believe that the bank of justice is bankrupt. We refuse to believe that there are insufficient funds in the great vaults of opportunity of this nation." He then continued with probably the most salient passage: "I have a dream that my four little children will one day live in a nation where they will not be judged by the color of their skin but by the content of their character."[96]

King pitched his speech not only to African Americans but also to white liberals, and so he both tragedized and legitimated the American political experiment simultaneously. The philosophy behind the American social contract, King argued, was legitimate, but the execution of its terms was discriminatory. King pushed for a larger share of the existing pie but held back from reinterpreting the concept of a pie, the mode of its production, or the composition of its filling.

This is starkly different from theorists like Charles Mills, who in *The Racial Contract* argues that there never was any promissory note for Black people. The contractarian basis of the American republic was inequality—white parasitism was foundational to the republic, for without slave labour, the social system could not have functioned effectively.[97]

Bernice King's speech, while seeming to talk past the Indigenous–settler context, may have made white Americans uncomfortable, exposing their fragility, given that civil rights equality is a long way from being achieved, and white Americans display discomfort when the pendulum seems to swing in a direction favourable to African Americans. Take, for example, the widespread negative reaction to so-called reverse discrimination. In a June 2016 survey, the Brookings Institution revealed that the majority of white Americans believe that "discrimination against whites . . . is as big a problem as discrimination against blacks and other minorities." This problematic view was embraced by wholly 66 percent of white members of the working class.[98] The study demonstrates a major dissonance between white and Black people over the extent of anti-Black racism. For example, 88 percent of African Americans "say the country needs to continue making changes for blacks to have equal rights with whites," a figure that is only 53 percent for whites.[99]

The civil rights equality frame is a problem in Canada at two levels. First, as already outlined, it provides only a limited soft rights liberal view of reconciliation, well short of affirming the hard rights of Indigenous peoples.

Second, the frame locates civil rights issues as an *American* problem that has no analogue in Canada.

Promoting civil rights seems relatively unproblematic if it is framed as correcting what white Americans have done to Black Americans. While white settlers deny a history of Black people in what is now Canada, so too is there a marked tendency to ignore and deny the reality of anti-Black racism. Desmond Cole notes that Toronto's naïveté about the city's widespread racism towards Black people is "because we want to tell ourselves that it's not happening here, and we especially want to tell ourselves that we are not the United States of America."[100] Yet, racism has always been present. It is, as Backhouse describes, "a deeply embedded, archly defining characteristic of Canadian history."[101]

Indeed, Anthony Morgan describes "today's black Canadian experience" as constituted by "extreme marginalization and disadvantage; restricted access to housing; racial profiling in policing, security, education and child welfare; criminalization; over-representation in the criminal justice system; high levels of unemployment; and disproportionate and extreme poverty."[102] Doug Saunders too has noted widespread discrimination against Black Canadians, in terms of "employment, in housing and especially in the policing and justice systems." Black Lives Matter's spread and success in major Canadian cities is thus a domestic phenomenon, the result of the lived experiences of racism and violence by Black people.[103] The settler state record of civil rights is hardly ideal. For example, Black inmates in federal prisons increased by 69 percent from 2005 to 2015, while the percentage of Black children and youth in Toronto's child welfare system is now 41 percent, even though they comprise only 8 percent of Toronto's youth population. Coupled with the epidemic of police carding, defined "as random police checks that disproportionately target black people," and the shooting by police of Jermaine Carby and Andrew Loku, it is clear that something is seriously wrong.[104]

Black Lives Matter has been working in solidarity with Idle No More, and in April 2016 they occupied the Indigenous Affairs offices in downtown Toronto. Idle No More youth organizer Erica Lee asserted that both groups were united by the recognition that Toronto and other cities were constructed on stolen Indigenous land. Both groups, she argued, came together in "understanding why indigenous youth are being pushed to kill ourselves in a colonial context, and to recognize that police violence is impacting black lives, indigenous lives and racialized lives in this country." The two groups, in occupying

Indigenous and Northern Affairs Canada (INAC) offices, join together. As Lee puts it: "we're taking back this land and we're taking back our lives."[105]

Overall, we are faced with four settler perceptions that may hinder the reconciliation process. The first is the perception that reconciliation is or should be about equality or a "level playing field," and should not be about "uniqueness," or rewarding an unfair sense of "entitlement," especially when white settlers feel they have little responsibility for the current crises of Indigenous peoples. Tied to this is a second point: the belief that the way settler Canada has dealt with "diversity" through its multicultural-ism policies constitutes a laudable framework for understanding what types of (temporally and financially limited) duties the settler state has vis-à-vis Indigenous peoples. This ignores the white settler–dominated approach to integration and "Canadian values," the erasure of non-Europeans as found-ing communities, and the general climate that sees non-Europeans as visibly other. Black, Asian, Indian, and other communities helped found Canada alongside Dutch, Greeks, Spanish, and Italians. Their contributions should be better recognized.

The third issue concerns the belief that the U.S. civil rights movement is a model for reconciliation. Again, equality becomes important, and settlers dream of ways that the "promissory note" can at last be cashed. Like King assured his audience, they want to feel that the state is not bankrupt, that the underlying liberal principles of Canada remain legitimate and praisewor-thy. This is at one level to confuse soft and hard rights, liberal reconciliation within the framework of the settler state with Indigenous self-determina-tion, and, as I stressed earlier, it also ignores the longevity and continuation of anti-Black racism in this country.

Finally, there is simply no evidence that a significant proportion of settler Canadians view their state as a settler state or themselves as settlers, or even as white people. Only a tiny proportion of respondents felt any personal or collective responsibility for cultural genocide, let alone UN-defined genocide. Faith in the beneficence of a liberal universal ideology remains unaltered by the increase in knowledge about the IRS system and the work of the TRC.

Mainstream media has proven deficient in reframing the situation. Rather than overtly challenging Euro-Canadians to see themselves as priv-ileged settlers and take responsibility for the current status of Indigenous peoples, the media has tended to focus attention on Indigenous peoples as the problem, while eliding the larger settler colonial context behind the historical trauma that many Indigenous peoples face as a result of ongoing colonization.

In their work on media bias and the TRC, Rosemary Nagy and Emily Gillespie note that the media has in most cases focused on the promotion of reductive frames, on individual Survivor experiences of physical and sexual abuse, trauma, and healing. The system is blamed primarily on "mistakes," suggesting that had it operated properly, most of the abuses would not have occurred. Reductively framing stories about Indigenous peoples suggests that the IRS system was an historical artifact, a product of mentalities and policies confined to an earlier, long since passed, period of Canadian history, with no current manifestations.[106] Genocide and cultural genocide are not discussed, and the crimes of the system have generally been blamed on individuals: stern-faced nuns, predatory priests, greedy bureaucrats, and callous police officers.

As DiAngelo's work outlines, white audiences are generally more accepting of a reductive treatment, in that "whites are usually more receptive to validating white racism if that racism is constructed as residing in individual white people other than themselves."[107] An expansive view, by contrast, stresses the interconnections and continued legacies of all relationships between Indigenous peoples and settlers. This includes territorial dispossession; the imposition of colonial educational, justice, governance, and other systems; Indian residential schools; the Sixties Scoop; Indigenous imprisonment; other forms of structural racism; and, more generally within Canadian settler society, Nagy and Gillespie say, "deeply ingrained colonial attitudes and patterns of behaviour."[108]

By contrast, when media is freed from settler control, Indigenous peoples have agency to reinterpret the frames through which current events are understood. Brad Clark's comparative analysis of Aboriginal Peoples Television Network (APTN) versus mainstream settler channels highlights how settlers have chosen a "'problem people' frame," seeing negative issues arising as the fault of Indigenous peoples. By contrast, APTN respects Indigenous peoples, and uses instead a "'social conditions as context' frame" to engage with the fuller picture behind news events, including colonization and cultural genocide.[109]

Conclusions

What can we conclude from all of this? The Environics survey represented a mix of responses, but leaned most heavily in the direction of a liberal reconciliation agenda, marked primarily by efforts to reduce discrimination and inequality. This focus can be seen as positive and productive if settlers understand that these soft rights goals are part of a process of supporting Indigenous capacity building to better enable Indigenous self-determination. Hard rights are about restoring the nation-to-nation, government-to-government dynamic that was originally present.

Those of us who are settler Canadians need to engage in more critical reflection about ourselves as settlers, and learn far more about Indigenous peoples, languages, and cultures but also governance traditions, law, and treaties. It must become clear at some point (soon) in the reconciliation process that the state may be required to roll back its sovereignty to facilitate the Indigenous resurgence to take hold, for Indigenous *sui generis* rights to self-determination to go forward.

Critical Race Studies may help us to partially conceptualize where we are currently located as settlers in the reconciliation process. Derald Wing Sue has outlined a series of five phases on the road to a racially healthy society. This might function as the basis for evaluating some, and only some, phases of an Indigenous–settler reconciliation process in Canada.[110]

Most white Americans operate within what Wing Sue calls the "Conformity Phase," marked by strong ethnocentrism, a lack of awareness of whiteness in racial terms, and limited contact with and understanding of other ethnic groups. This leads to the prevalence of stereotyping, "and a strong belief in the universality of values and norms governing behavior." This phase is marked by forms of "denial and compartmentalization."[111]

A large proportion of respondents to the Environics surveys appears to fall into this category, with a smaller proportion falling into the next category, that of "Dissonance." As Wing Sue explains, this stage occurs when "the White person is forced to deal with the inconsistencies that have been compartmentalized or encounters information or experiences at odds with denial." This is the first stage in white people actually acknowledging their own cultural values and racial identity as not being common sense and universal but grounded in a particular set of hierarchical assumptions.[112]

For the more self-aware, the "Resistance and Immersion Phase" follows, epitomized by white people seeing "racism everywhere." At this stage, whiteness is acknowledged. This is a phase of serious critical reflection, remorse, anger at white society, guilt over one's own now-acknowledged privilege, and a sense that society as the person knows it is based on lies and obfuscation. What follows are "Introspection" and "Integrative Awareness" phases.[113]

Surveys and other gauges of settler public opinion suggest that most Canadian settlers (including settlers of racialized origin) are located at these initial two phases, and while they are acquiescent to the need for the government to work towards reducing inequality, and even settling land claims, they are not self-reflective in terms of their own responsibilities and positionalities. Regarding newcomers, the CBC/Angus Reid poll demonstrates that assimilation into the settler mainstream continues to be uncritically defined as the end goal of immigration policy.

Wing Sue is clear that many people will never progress higher than the first one or two phases. Indeed, white American society has not progressed far beyond the conformity phase, as the Brookings survey illustrates. Additionally, applying five phases from an American civil rights context to an Indigenous–settler reconciliation context may transplant very different standards for measuring progress towards reconciliation. As I have noted elsewhere, critical race theory based on a framework of civil rights has little to say about colonialism; this makes it incomplete.[114]

As such, we need to move well beyond Wing Sue's phases in the sense that seeking to eradicate oppression and create a non-racist identity are insufficient final goals for reconciliation—they are potentially only the ground floor. At least two or three more phases are thus needed to gauge progress on reconciliation according to what the TRC has recommended. This would imply not only recognizing white settler privilege and seeking to end it in favour of equality but to change the actual system, not just of its *racially oppressive* structures, which prevent equality of conditions and opportunity, but of its *colonizing* structures as well, which impose settler colonial institutions, systems, languages, and values over those of Indigenous nations. This would include a hard rights focus, with an emphasis on Indigenous law, land, sovereignty, and self-determination.[115] However, as discussed earlier, the TRC mandate has precluded recommendations that could complicate or render uncomfortable the exercise of Canadian sovereignty, hence the focus on, as Peter McClaren notes, "Aboriginal peoples' right to self-determination within, and in partnership with, a viable Canadian sovereignty."[116]

On a positive note, the Trudeau government is providing some measure of hope that the country can progress further along the road to transformative reconciliation than it did under Harper. Despite the government's obvious neoliberal and resource-extractive agenda, and the continuation of many policies from the Harper era, the government's pledge to harmonize Canadian law with UNDRIP holds promise. Trudeau's "unfinished business of confederation," taken to its logical conclusion, could mean partial deconfederation in terms of the rolling back of the Westphalian absolute sovereignty enjoyed by the Canadian state. By this, I mean the full settler recognition of the bounced cheques symbolized by Crown breaches of the treaties, both the written and extensive oral agreements between Crown representatives and Indigenous representatives.

However, the contours of Indigenous self-determination and the exercise of hard rights will be different for each Indigenous nation. There will be no one universal solution, and this is precisely the point. It does not fall to settler academics or government officials to define what should be done and how. The better path is to encourage the relationship to develop, and to better understand what Indigenous peoples require in their nation-to-nation relationships. So far, the reconciliation process for the proportion of Canadians who know anything about it has involved miniscule sacrifices. This may change, and Canada has the potential to demonstrate new forms of complex sovereignty, sovereignties within sovereignties, and Indigenous nations with control over their own laws, peoples, and lands.

Notes

1   My thanks to Paulette Regan, Malissa Bryan, Aimée Craft, Audra Simpson, Sheryl Lightfoot, Kiera Ladner, Cody O'Neil, Pat Case, Malinda Smith, and Curtis Nash. The research and writing of this chapter is made possible by SSHRC Insight Grant 430201.

2   "President Barack Obama's Speech."

3   Ibid.

4   On Australia, see: Short, *Reconciliation and Colonial Power*, 5–6. Australia's "Reconciliation Barometer" is a prime example of liberal reconciliation, as it is focused on measuring outcomes such as "Equality and Equity," "Unity," and "Historical Acceptance." See: Reconciliation Australia, "2018 Australian Reconciliation Barometer," https://www.reconciliation.org.au/wp-content/uploads/2019/02/final_full_arb-full-report-2018.pdf. In the Canadian context, see Manuel and Derrickson, *Reconciliation Manifesto*. Manuel and Derrickson advocate the return of Indigenous lands as a central aspect of reconciliation.

5   See, for example, Thobani, *Exalted Subjects*; Lawrence and Dua, "Decolonizing Antiracism."

6   Veracini, *Settler Colonialism*, 3.

7   Environics, *Canadian Public Opinion*, 3.

8   Razack, "Introduction," 2.

9   Backhouse, *Colour-Coded*, 14.

10 Fleras, *Politics of Multiculturalism*, 61.

11 Regan, *Unsettling the Settler Within*, 106.

12 Veracini, *Settler Colonialism*, 3.

13 Proctor, "CBC-Angus Reid Institute."

14 Cass, "Norm Entrapment and Preference Change," 41.

15 Weber, *International Relations Theory*, 4–5.

16 Turner, *This Is Not a Peace Pipe*, 13.

17 Adams, "Door to Reconciliation."

18 DiAngelo, "White Fragility," 60.

19 Ibid., 54, 60–61.

20 Short, *Reconciliation and Colonial Power*, 20.

21 Ibid.

22 Ibid., 21–22.

23 Lightfoot, *Global Indigenous Politics*, 29–30.

24 Kusch, "Liberal Convention Opens."

25 Dodson, "Towards the Exercise," 68.

26 Lightfoot, *Global Indigenous Politics*, 29–30.

27 Simpson, *Mohawk Interruptus*, 16.

28 Ibid., 20.

29 Ibid., 159.

30 Ibid., 187.

31 TRC, *Final Report*, vol. 6, *Reconciliation, passim.*

32 Ibid., 16.

33 Ibid., 16.

34 Ibid., 4.

35 Ibid., 11–12, 16.

36 Ibid., 16.

37 Ibid., 32.

38 Ibid., 34–35.

39 Ibid., 37–38.

40 Ibid., 78–79.

41 Ibid., 21.

42 Simpson, *Mohawk Interruptus*, 187.

43 Hill, "My Six Nation Haudenosaunee," 30.

44 Chiefs of Ontario, "Understanding First Nation Sovereignty."

45 TRC, "Our Mandate."

46 UN General Assembly, *United Nations Declaration*, 18.

47 Environics, *Canadian Public Opinion on Aboriginal Peoples*, 2.

48 Ibid., 3–4, 33, 84–85.

49 Ibid., 36.

50 Ibid., 29–30.

51 Ibid., 12.

52 Ibid., 17.

53 Ibid., 31.

54 Fleras, *Politics of Multiculturalism*, 69.

55 Environics, *Canadian Public Opinion on Aboriginal Peoples*, 34.

56 Ibid., 33.

57 Ibid., 22.

58 Ibid., 39.

59 Ibid., 6, 36.

60 Ibid., 1.

61 Ibid., 19.

62 Ibid., 26.

63 Ibid., 9.

64 Ibid., 14.

65 Ibid., 36.

66 Ibid., 38.

67 Ibid., 19.

68 Ibid., 43.

69 Ibid., 21–22.

70 Ibid., 23.

71 Ibid., 27.

72 Ibid., 28.

73 Ibid., 2.

74 Ibid., 14, 47, 50.

75 Angus Reid, "Canadians on Indigenous Issues: Focus on Reserves Final Survey Questionnaire –
     Post Pre-Test Feedback (19 March 2018)," http://angusreid.org/wp-content/uploads/2018/06/
     Canadians-on-Indigenous-Issues-Final.-March-20.pdf; Angus Reid, "Truths of Reconciliation:
     Canadians Are Deeply Divided on How Best to Address Indigenous Issues," 7 June 2018,
     http://angusreid.org/indigenous-canada/. For an older survey with similar types of ques-
     tions and terminology see: Angus Reid, "Truth and Reconciliation: Canadians See Value
     in Process, Skeptical about Government Action," 9 July 2015, http://angusreid.org/
     aboriginal-truth-and-reconciliation/.

76 Reconciliation Canada, "CANADIAN RECONCILIATION LANDSCAPE."

77 Axworthy, "In the North."

78 Inglis, "Multiculturalism."

79 Bannerji, *Dark Side of the Nation*, 78.

80 Environics, *Canadian Public Opinion About Immigration*, 7.

81 Citizenship and Immigration Canada, "Annual Report on the Operation of the Canadian
     Multiculturalism Act—2013–2014," Citizenship and Immigration Canada, http://www.cic.gc.ca/
     english/resources/publications/multi-report2014/3.asp (accessed 15 July 2016).

82 Trudeau, "Justice in Our Time," 631.

83 Ibid., 632.

84 Fleras, *Politics of Multiculturalism*, 82–83.

85 Bannerji, *Dark Side of the Nation*, 112.

86 Walcott, *Black Like Who?*, 136.

87 Ibid., 137.

88 Ibid., 150.

89 Ibid., 137.

90 Trudeau, "Justice in Our Time," 632.

91 Fleras, *Politics of Multiculturalism*, 82.

92 Quoted in Turner, *This Is Not a Peace Pipe*, 64.

93 Quoted in ibid., 65–66. .

94 "Bernice King's Speech at the Walk for Reconciliation," Reconciliation Canada, 27 September 2013, http://reconciliationcanada.ca/staging/bernice-kings-speech-at-the-walk-for-reconciliation/ (accessed 15 July 2016).

95 Cornell Law School, "Civil Rights."

96 King, "I Have a Dream."

97 Mills, *Racial Contract.*

98 Jones et al., *How Immigration and Concerns,* 2.

99 Pew Research Center, "On Views of Race and Inequality, Blacks and Whites are Worlds Apart," Pew Research Center, 27 June 2016, http://www.pewsocialtrends.org/2016/06/27/on-views-of-race-and-inequality-blacks-and-whites-are-worlds-apart/ (accessed 15 July 2016).

100 "Occupied Canada."

101 Backhouse, *Colour-Coded,* 17.

102 Morgan, "Suffocating Experience."

103 Saunders, "Why Black Canadians."

104 Kassam, "Canada Is Hailed."

105 "Occupied Canada."

106 Nagy and Gillespie, "Representing Reconciliation," 11–13.

107 DiAngelo, "White Fragility," 61.

108 Nagy and Gillespie, "Representing Reconciliation," 11–12.

109 Clark, "Framing Canada's Aboriginal Peoples," 43, 49–51.

110 Wing Sue, *Multicultural Social Work Practice,* 111–12.

111 Ibid., 122.

112 Ibid., 123–24.

113 Ibid., 124–26.

114 McClaren, "White Terror"; Nylund, "Critical Multiculturalism."

115 McClaren, "White Terror," 4.

116 Ibid., 21.

CHAPTER 2

PERCEPTIONS ON TRUTH AND RECONCILIATION

Lessons from Gacaca in Post-Genocide Rwanda

RÉGINE UWIBEREYEHO KING AND
BENJAMIN MAIANGWA

Over the last four decades, truth and reconciliation commissions (TRCs) have been used as a means to redress past wrongs and to heal and reconcile people in post-conflict societies. For the most part, the TRC model is a form of transitional justice recommended for use in societies recovering from mass violence in the Global South. Accordingly, at least forty TRCs have been implemented there.[1]

The TRC model was originally not perceived as a model applicable for wealthy countries of the Global North with well-established democracies and judicial systems.[2] However, in recent years, countries such as Australia and Canada have experimented with the TRC model to deal with their colonial realities. This model holds a certain appeal for government bodies and multilateral organizations precisely because legal prosecutions are judged to be too costly, time-consuming, and difficult for national judicial systems and emerging democracies.[3] Moreover, a judicial system on its own is insufficient for acknowledging the broad scope of historical abuses committed against a particular social group (i.e., Indigenous peoples) as well as for redressing wrongs, healing intergenerational traumas, and rebuilding better and, in the words of Oliver Richmond, "sustainable forms of reconciliation."[4]

The literature review presented in this chapter relates to a model of TRC that managed to bring together the people of Rwanda for legal justice and community healing after the 1994 genocide against the Tutsi. We recognize that the conception and implementation of national TRCs vary due to the nature of the wrongs done, the historical circumstances, and the socio-political contexts in which they operate. The intention of this chapter is not to compare TRCs; rather, we believe that lessons learned from past TRCs can be useful for new implementations that share the basic goals of revealing historical atrocities, establishing accountability, and seeking social healing.

An understanding of context is crucial to the conceptualization and implementation of a TRC. In this chapter we focus on the lessons that can be learned from the TRC model that was implemented in post-genocide Rwanda, known as *gacaca*. "Gacaca" literally means "grass" or "lawn," and is a system of participatory, community justice. After the 1994 genocide against the Tutsis in Rwanda, the government of Rwanda took this traditional communal dispute mechanism and reshaped it into a national program designed to respond to the national wounds of the genocide. The formal institution of gacaca can be perceived as a homegrown TRC because of its roots in the traditional model known to all Rwandan people.

The analysis of interdisciplinary literature on gacaca reveals mixed and controversial evaluations. Like other TRCs gacaca struggled with the management of retributive and restorative justice. Accordingly, notions and processes of community healing and reconciliation must find expression between these two poles within which all TRCs operate. This explains some of the diversity of perspectives held by different actors, as some put a stronger emphasis on, or operate within the world of, retributive justice, while others value the restorative pathway.

As authors, we hope that lessons learned from the formal gacaca process in Rwanda will be useful for Canadians as they seek ways to implement their TRC's Calls to Action. Taking into account all the interdisciplinary perspectives and our own experience, both in Rwanda and in Canada, we submit that some of the most important lessons are: (1) the need to take local community context and experiences of peace building into account, especially Indigenous values and needs; (2) the need to be flexible in implementing the TRC's Calls to Action—through vigilant monitoring—given that there are divergent perspectives on how people interpret the atrocities committed in their communities; and (3) the need to move beyond Western liberal legalistic justice processes to combine retributive and restorative justice as practised by communities at the grassroots.

By recognizing Indigenous values, needs, and cultural resources in peace building and social transformation processes in contexts like Canada and Rwanda where some variants of transitional justice were implemented, formerly oppressed people can find their voice, claim and retain their agency, heal past hurts, and rebuild societal relationships. Being flexible in implementing the TRC's Calls to Action could be particularly helpful while implementing Call to Action 29, which calls for the Canadian government to work collaboratively with "plaintiffs not included in the Indian Residential Schools Settlement Agreement to have disputed legal issues determined expeditiously on an agreed set of facts."[5] The combination of retributive and restorative justice in a TRC context suggests that the foundations of reconciliation (truth, mercy, peace, justice, healing, respect, etc.), which may seem contradictory, are in fact interdependent.

Most importantly, we submit that Canadians should emulate Rwanda's experiment with a justice system that emanates from the people's traditional values and history in revealing the truths of their pasts and in working for a shared and better future. In Rwanda gacaca brought together opposing communities and led to local ownership of the transitional process. In Canada it has the potential to accomplish even more.

Background of Rwanda's TRC

The 1994 genocide against the Tutsi in Rwanda resulted in the brutal killing of between 800,000 and 1 million Tutsis, along with some moderate Hutus.[6] The Tutsi genocide was state-sponsored and lasted only 100 days. The killers were former friends, colleagues, neighbours, and, in some cases, relatives, all of whom operated under the gaze of underfunded and ill-equipped United Nations peacekeepers.[7] The country was in chaos when the genocide ended in July 1994. Many Rwandans identified themselves as "the walking dead." They were destitute and wounded physically and psychologically, houses had been destroyed, and family properties and possessions had been looted. Banks, schools, churches, and government institutions were severely damaged and non-functional.

Estimates of the number of raped Tutsi women range between 250,000 and 500,000. Sexual violence was clearly a genocide tactic.[8] Many were purposely infected with HIV/AIDS so that they would experience a slow, painful death. Survivors were often the sole living members of their families.

The genocide produced contrasting population flows in and out of Rwanda. Approximately 1 million descendants of former Tutsi refugees, who had fled the country during the Rwandan independence movement in the late 1950s and early 1960s, now returned to their homeland after more than three decades in refugee camps in neighbouring countries. At the same time, at the close of the genocide, about 2 million Rwandans fled the country. The majority of these were Hutus, including genocidaires, who feared retaliation from the army that had ended the genocide. There are no exact figures on how many Hutus were killed en route to or within refugee camps in neighbouring countries. Similarly, there are no reliable statistics on the number of Hutu women and girls who were raped in the camps by former genocidaires. Régine Uwibereyeho King, this chapter's first author, helped with the repatriation of people from the Eastern Democratic Republic of Congo, where she witnessed an alarming number of teenage girls who carried their own young children.

In 1996 many of the camps were destroyed and a significant number of refugees were forced to return to Rwanda. By the end of 1996, Rwandan prisons were already filled with genocide suspects beyond their holding capacity. It is estimated that prisons that had been constructed for 10,000 prisoners now held up to 150,000 men and women.[9] They could not stand to absorb even more genocidaire suspects returning from the camps.

Over the next years both Rwandans and non-Rwandans had many questions and few answers about how survivors, perpetrators, their families, and returnees were to live together in the same communities. Dr. Simon Gasibirege, a Rwandan psychologist, summarized the puzzle of post-genocide Rwanda with these words: "How is it possible to live together in peace and security when neighbors have killed the parents or siblings from the household next door? How can social harmony be rebuilt when one group blames another for war, exile and lost years in refugee camps or prisons? How can we conceptualize and implement reconciliation, peace building, and sustainable development projects in a society that is imploded, disoriented, and reduced to chaos?"[10] Rendering justice to the perpetrators on behalf of the victims was a major challenge facing the remnants of the Rwandan justice system and the international community.

As early as November 1994, the United Nations Security Council created the International Criminal Tribunal for Rwanda (ICTR), which was to operate from Arusha, Tanzania. However, the ICTR was established to deal only with high-level genocide suspects—those who were classified as Category 1 cases, which included people who had planned and organized killings as well as perpetrators of sexual crimes, including rape. Technically, these crimes were under the jurisdiction of the Rwandan national courts, which could impose sentences ranging from twenty-five to thirty years of imprisonment (for those who confessed) to capital punishment (for those convicted without confession).[11] However, the Rwanda national courts were no longer functional. Few judges were left in the country and they were not equipped to deal with the severity and volume of genocide crimes. It was not until 1996 that legal personnel and basic equipment were put in place and the national courts could begin to prosecute genocide suspects.[12]

By 1999 it became obvious that the national courts and the ICTR would be unable to address the overwhelming number of genocide cases. It is estimated that more than 761,000 people were complicit in the 1994 genocide; this provides an indication of the breadth of genocide participation.[13] Thousands of inmates languished in prisons, and from the survivors' perspective, there had been no justice or compensation for the death of loved ones and the loss of property.

By the year 2000 it was painfully evident that the ICTR and the national courts were slow and ineffective in the task of rendering the kind of justice many Rwandans desired.[14] This growing frustration motivated the Rwandan government to draw on an Indigenous, or "homegrown," system of justice known as gacaca. In the next section we explain the meanings of gacaca and its functioning.

State-Sanctioned Gacaca

Before the genocide, gacaca existed as a traditional community mechanism for resolving disputes. These included inheritance, civil liability, theft, and family relationships.[15] The traditional gacaca had the power to sanction the violation of shared community rules in order to reconcile the parties in conflict. The process required defendants to confess their crimes, express remorse, and seek the forgiveness of injured parties. At the end of the process, both the offended and offenders shared a drink with other community members to symbolize reconciliation.[16] After the genocide the government of Rwanda transformed traditional gacaca into a state-sanctioned system that had the power to try certain categories of genocide crimes within communities.[17]

The national gacaca program was launched officially in June 2002 in two pilot phases, and was further developed in 2004 before it was inaugurated nationwide in 2005.[18] The rationale for gacaca's establishment in post-genocide Rwanda stemmed from the government's effort to expedite the genocide cases that had proven cumbersome for domestic and international courts and to provide an alternative setting for local solutions to genocide issues.[19] The main objectives of the state-sanctioned gacaca were to establish the truth of the genocide, to speed up prosecution processes, to eradicate impunity, to reconcile aggrieved communities, and to render justice to victims and perpetrators.[20] It is essential to recognize that the formal gacaca, from the outset, had a dual mandate to render both retributive and restorative justice to perpetrators and victims.[21]

As a state-sanctioned system, gacaca established a separate court for each cell and sector of Rwanda, along with a General Assembly, a Bench, and a Coordinating Committee. The entire intervention was steered by approximately 250,000 officials,[22] while its formal implementation was done in phases involving the active participation of all community members.

During the preliminary stages of gacaca, Rwandans were first asked to draw up a list of who was living in their area during the genocide and then identify those who were dead. After the list of victims was composed, people were required to create a list of community members involved in the genocide. The judges classified the perpetrators into criminal categories using information drawn from different phases of information gathering. Government monitors supervised this work at each stage.[23]

It is important to note that the judges, also known as *inyangamugayo* or "people with integrity," were not lawyers. Rather, they had been officially elected. The criteria of their election included being over eighteen years of age and being perceived as a person with social integrity in the community. The state-sanctioned gacaca did not qualify to hold trials for genocide suspects of Category 1 crimes, which involved the masterminds of the genocide. Nevertheless, it had the power to hold jurisdiction over Categories 2, 3 and 4 as defined by the Organic Law.[24] Category 2 crimes included notorious murderers such as those who tortured others or mutilated their bodies, suspects who killed or intended to kill, and their accomplices in such acts.[25] Category 3 included those who conducted "serious attacks without the intent to cause the death of the victims," and Category 4 comprised crimes against property.[26]

Community judges had the power to impose punishment on those found guilty, including imprisonment, community service, or compensation for stolen property. The degree of punishment depended on the nature of the crimes committed, the willing nature of confessions, and the perpetrator's age in 1994.[27] Unlike other legal systems the state-sanctioned gacaca courts encouraged suspects to confess their crimes either before being formally accused or during the actual gacaca trials; they encouraged victims to work toward forgiveness and reconciliation within the community; and community members' participation was mandatory.[28] The state-sanctioned gacaca courts completed the majority of cases brought before it and officially ended in June 2012.[29]

This state-sanctioned gacaca received both praise and criticism from its launch until its conclusion, both within and across disciplines such as anthropology, law, ethics studies, criminal justice, communication studies, international development studies, and peace and conflict studies. Rather than conducting an interdisciplinary comparative analysis, we chose to do a critical examination of the strengths and weaknesses of the formal gacaca, drawing from these disciplines, to evaluate its merit and extract lessons that may inform newer TRCs, including Canada's, as Canadians search for ways to implement the ninety-four Calls to Action.

The critical analysis of interdisciplinary literature on gacaca is supplemented by the personal experiences of the first author. She was born and raised in Rwanda, survived the genocide, and became a Canadian citizen a decade ago. She is intrigued by the TRC models of both her countries.

Gacaca Literature Review

Anthropological Literature

Scholars from anthropology take an ethnographic orientation by immersing themselves in people's day-to-day lives, observing and interpreting their patterns of interaction and perspectives in situated contexts.[30] To date, anthropologists have variously acclaimed or condemned the state-sanctioned gacaca as a tool of transitional justice.

For instance, before the establishment of the program, Elizabeth Neuffer conducted a study in Rwanda that analyzed people's dreams and fears about the prospective courts.[31] The study showed that many Rwandans were optimistic that the courts would provide a sense of closure and an inclusive avenue in which both witnesses and perpetrators could meet and move together toward social harmony. Similarly, Lyn Graybill[32] and Stephanie Wolters[33] propose that Rwandans were hopeful about the credibility of the process during the initial stages. Their participation was motivated by a confidence that the formal gacaca would reveal the truth of the genocide. They also believed that the process would encourage apology and forgiveness, and promote reconciliation. Notwithstanding, Graybill notes in another study that despite the initial overwhelming support for gacaca, enthusiasm for the process lessened after alleged killings in 2003 "of some witnesses who had planned to testify."[34]

Anne Kubai suggests that the state-sanctioned gacaca procedures were democratic because they were based on transparent rules that were communicated to the participants.[35] Janine Clark's paper praises the gacaca process for giving voice to perpetrators and victims, and for providing a setting for the healing of traumatic wounds.[36] She argues that the inclusion of local people made the process conducive to grassroots reconciliation.[37]

In a ten-year field study, Phil Clark confirmed that many Rwandans were receptive of the formal gacaca program because of their prior experience with the traditional model.[38] They claimed that their participation in the formal gacaca procedures unburdened them of the trauma they had been living with. As an example, many survivors reported experiencing relief when they located and buried their deceased relatives.[39]

Anuradha Chakraverty's field research is far more critical of the gacaca process.[40] Chakraverty condemns what she refers to as gacaca's one-sidedness, arguing that its courts humiliated and prosecuted only Hutus, while ignoring the atrocities committed by the Rwandan Patriotic Front (RPF).[41] This perceived lopsidedness of the formal gacaca has also been highlighted as one of its major drawbacks by Barbara Oomen and Janine Clark.[42]

Other studies raised different critiques. For example, Timothy Longman employed an ethnographic analysis of interviews and focus group discussions conducted in three local communities to claim that far from resolving conflicts and promoting restorative justice, as its advocates claim, the formal gacaca only heightened ethnic divisions and insecurity, and consolidated the power base of an authoritarian regime.[43] Longman criticizes the Rwandan government's policy for portraying Tutsis as the only victims of the genocide and branding Hutus as the perpetrators.[44] Thus, he concludes that if the state had not dictated that Tutsis were the only victims in formal gacaca trials, and if all sides had been given equal rights and attention at the courts, the process might have engendered true reconciliation in Rwanda.[45]

Similarly, Alexandre Dauge-Roth raises questions about the contribution of the state-sanctioned gacaca to trauma healing.[46] On a positive note, Dauge-Roth draws on the testimony of a woman who lost over 270 family members to the genocide to illustrate that the formal gacaca provided the context for some people to collectively face their past.[47] However, the author acknowledges the woman's—and other survivors'—frustration with their inability to define and negotiate "the rules and the conditions under which they face the perpetrators,"[48] which might have allowed the government to use the formal gacaca jurisdiction and the policy of national unity and reconciliation to impose "a constraining context of dialogue" that influenced who could say what and when.[49] In this research the portrayed woman condemned the fact that survivors were forced to make many concessions, including forgiving perpetrators against their will.[50]

As this body of literature indicates, Rwandans were initially hopeful and had high expectations that gacaca would facilitate truth telling and restore community relationships. However, the eventual levels of satisfaction differed based on individual experiences and the influence of the government's involvement during the state-sanctioned gacaca.

Normative, Legal, and Ethical Literature

Legal scholars provided a mixture of positive and negative critiques of the state-sanctioned gacaca from its early stages. Some of them took polarized positions either for or against its implementation, while others offered more nuanced critiques. For instance, at the beginning of the formal gacaca, William Schabas offered a positive view of the process, describing it as a decentralized system of justice spearheaded by non-state and non-Western professionals, which could serve as an example for other post-conflict societies where large-scale prosecution of perpetrators of crimes is deemed impossible.[51] While the formal gacaca was perceived as a homegrown model,[52] it was also emblematic of other TRCs. In another review of studies on gacaca, Judith Herrmann concluded that the formal gacaca process successfully incorporated the five dimensions of TRCs: accountability, establishing the truth, reparations for wrongdoing, reconciliation, and reformation of institutions.[53]

Maya Sosnov was critical of the formal gacaca's performance, maintaining that the process was problematic because it was state-sanctioned and -controlled, and that it was challenging to get both sides (perpetrators and victims) to believe and participate in it.[54] On the objective of speeding up the genocide trials, Sosnov argues that the state-sanctioned gacaca courts were unable to operate more expeditiously than the national and the international criminal courts on Rwanda, or even to eradicate the culture of impunity.[55] Sosnov criticizes the formal gacaca for not considering charges of violence against members of the RPF after the genocide.[56] It is worth noting that on the general charge of impunity, Anne-Marie de Brouwer and Etienne Ruvebana argue that the formal gacaca actually did eradicate the culture of impunity by prosecuting those responsible for genocide.[57]

Coel Kirkby argues that branding many Hutus as killers raised questions about the legitimacy of the state-sanctioned gacaca model because it "create[d] corresponding categories of moral guilt and innocence."[58] However, unlike other scholars who condemn gacaca as a state-controlled process, Kirkby finds that the grassroots nature of the formal gacaca shields it from manipulation by the state. He also argues that international monitoring groups like Penal Reform International have not observed any significant state interference in the formal gacaca process.[59] At the same time, Kirkby questions the legitimacy of the formal gacaca because of its use of judges who lacked formal legal training to adjudicate on genocidal crimes.[60] This author fears that the lack of competency might have led to false convictions, particularly in the absence of state-funded defence counsels.[61] In addition, Kirkby acknowledges that the absence of a compensation program by the government greatly undermined the reconciliation and rehabilitation processes of survivors.[62] Nevertheless, the author positively evaluates the restorative philosophy that underpinned the formal gacaca, particularly with regards to commuting convicted genocidaires from imprisonment to community service.[63]

Scholars who use a strict legal framework of analysis have been more critical. From a normative standpoint, Dadimos Haile argues that the formal gacaca violated the fundamental principles of fair trial standards, thus breaching the Rwandan Constitution, the African Charter on Human and Peoples' Rights (ACHPR), and other relevant international human rights systems.[64] Haile deplores the lack of training for state-sanctioned gacaca judges, thereby raising serious questions about their legal competence and direction of the process.[65] He also highlights the oft-cited criticism of the formal gacaca as being a state-controlled process that discriminated against Hutus[66] and denies the positive evaluation made in some studies that the state-sanctioned gacaca achieved its stated objectives of speedy trials, public participation, and the discovery of the truth.[67] For this reason, the formal gacaca has been perceived in many quarters as a vengeful rather than a reconciliatory process.[68]

Other scholars echo similar sentiments by arguing that the formal gacaca did not adhere to fair trial and due process in regard to legal and human rights.[69] It is also alleged that the lack of protection for witnesses resulted in attempts to obliterate evidence, violent attacks (including murder), and the destruction of homes.[70]

Regarding the objective of discovering the truth of the past, Haile argues that the state-sanctioned gacaca did not have the capacity to confirm the veracity of defendants' testimonies.[71] Bert Ingelaere concurs that "the general perception of the absence of truth by the Rwandan population seems to be one of the most problematic aspects of the court system."[72] On the whole, Haile claims that the concrete contribution of the formal gacaca to transitional justice in Rwanda lies in the fact that the courts merely fulfilled the government's moral imperative to punish genocidaires.[73]

Regarding the goal of strengthening Rwandan communities' capacity to resolve their own problems, Sosnov argues that the formal gacaca was not a reflection of the customary model because it relied on state coercion.[74] In addition, Sosnov denies that the state-sanctioned gacaca promoted reconciliation and unity, because it was not able to produce a completely truthful version of the genocide. She concludes that the process served only to create ethnic divisions without providing compensation and material benefits to survivors.[75]

Most respondents provided a contrasting evaluation in the study by de Brouwer and Ruvebana.[76] They indicated that the formal gacaca promoted reconciliation and provided the context for dialogue between Hutus and Tutsis. Some respondents acknowledged that their personal security was threatened by the process and that they were concerned by the lack of compensation.[77] Nevertheless, de Brouwer and Ruvebana's study found that many Rwandans believed that the formal gacaca produced speedy trials of genocidaires and provided a place for survivors to tell their truth, to their benefit.[78]

The state-sanctioned gacaca has also been criticized for being far too ambitious, particularly regarding its goal of providing retributive and restorative justice simultaneously.[79] It seems legitimate to hold that the formal gacaca's objectives were idealistic and exceeded the capabilities of the local courts. Nevertheless, Phil Clark insists that the formal gacaca remains an ingenious hybrid model of transitional justice, which fulfilled its objectives of "retributive, deterrent, and restorative justice, with the ultimate aim as restorative."[80] He further claims that by synthesizing the relevant dimensions of justice, the formal gacaca was able to punish genocide perpetrators in ways that facilitated important non-legal results, including the reconciliation of divided communities.[81] Clark makes the important assertion that the dominant legal literature on the formal gacaca failed to recognize its achievements and impact.

While many critiques of the state-sanctioned gacaca focused on its legal and reconciliatory processes, a few scholars have broadened its scope to examine the role of the international community in its conceptualization, implementation, and publicity. The next section examines the influence of international donors in the formal gacaca process.

International Development Studies
In this section, we review the literature that explores the external influences on the national gacaca program, particularly those tied to funding and publicity. From an international development perspective, Barbara Oomen challenges the perception that the state-sanctioned gacaca was purely a state-driven initiative.[82] She submits that the idea of using customary systems of dispute resolution to administer transitional justice in Rwanda was first broached by representatives of the donor community.[83] Ingelaere has also reported that powerful countries from the Global North invested generously in Rwanda's post-genocide judicial activities, particularly in the case of the formal gacaca courts.[84] In fact, Roger MacGinty argues that, for a time, "the gacaca system was the darling of the international community: a poster child for local-level restorative justice projects."[85] The 2011 Human Rights Watch report on gacaca argues that the process would not have been established without the generosity of international donors.[86]

Major international donors and NGOs contributed to the state-sanctioned gacaca initiative such that by 2002, they had financed the recruitment and training of over 250,000 judges and purchased equipment and facilities for the 11,000 jurisdictions of the courts.[87] The donors included leading Western countries and regional organizations such as the Netherlands, Belgium, Austria, Switzerland, the United States, and the European Union (EU).[88] Most of these countries and government bodies supported the formal gacaca process for about ten years.[89] The funding levels are estimated at $3 million from the US, €7 million from the EU, and £700,000 from the UK department for International Development.[90]

There were additional non-financial contributions from international research institutes, who wrote and disseminated research and policy papers about the process to the wider international community. One such initiative was Penal Reform International (PRI). In its report on gacaca, PRI claims that it supported the development of its inception, and that over the years it gave independent advice, training, and support to the Rwandan government, the international community, and academics.[91] Peter Uvin and Charles Mironko similarly argue that the contribution of international donors resulted in the sharing of information on the formal gacaca proceedings to the world outside of Rwanda.[92]

It should not be assumed that all international donors were enthusiastic about the idea of establishing the state-sanctioned gacaca. There was an initial inertia due to concerns about gacaca's judicial standards. However, according to Ingelaere, the international donor community eventually developed interest in the process due to the awareness that the TRC model "was the less bad of two possible options for tackling the past—on the one hand classical (retributive) justice, which would not be able to manage and resolve the past wrongs, and, on the other hand, imperfect, unknown and revolutionary justice."[93]

Oomen argues that external influence in gacaca led to a strict organization of the process and resulted in the loss of some of the traditional components of gacaca, in that crimes such as "genocide, rape and sexual violence were far from the subjects that were discussed [using gacaca] in the old days, such as land conflicts and family matters."[94] Roger MacGinty makes this point clear: "Fundamentally, the adoption of the [formal] gacaca courts by the central government and their funding and promotion by external [liberal] peace-support agents challenged the very organic qualities that made the gacaca system so attractive in the first place."[95] As a result, the process lost some local support.

While some legitimate concerns were raised about gacaca's dependence on international donors, it was clear that a post-accord recovering society like Rwanda needed the strong support of the international community to launch and sustain gacaca.

Peace and Conflict Studies Literature

Peace and conflict studies take an interdisciplinary approach, drawing on the findings of different disciplines while furthering discussions on factors that promote or hinder peace building and reconciliation. A significant theme in the literature deals with the ways issues of gender and rape were handled in the formal gacaca proceedings, with a related topic being residual trauma and its impact on people affected by violence.

On a positive side the state-sanctioned gacaca was applauded for trusting women and prioritizing their active participation.[96] Studies noted that the formal gacaca provided space for women's participation and for their voices to be heard, even if the results may not have brought them justice.[97] Alana Tiemessen asserts that gacaca recognized women's leadership and role in the reconciliation process and rehumanized them by expanding their identity beyond simply that of victim.[98]

Unfortunately, Tiemessen's optimism is countered by studies that found that the formal gacaca trials lacked a gender perspective useful for transitional justice.[99] In analyzing the experience of Rwandan sexual crime survivors, Sarah Wells found that the public nature of the formal gacaca actually exposed victims to shame and jeopardized their chances of receiving support from their community.[100] In a similar vein Brittany Olwine alludes to the fact that the formal gacaca allowed for sexually abused women to be publicly shamed, even though the underlying goal of the courts was to respect cultural practices and use community-centred ideas to administer justice and promote reconciliation.[101] Olwine argues that Rwanda's deeply entrenched patriarchal system and intolerance toward rape victims made women victims susceptible to community rejection. Accordingly, they were discouraged from testifying against their perpetrators during the formal gacaca.[102] Therefore, despite the participatory nature of the formal gacaca, Peter Uvin and Charles Mironko, Sarah Wells, and Nicole Ephgrave all contend that its courts did very little to address gendered genocide-related crimes, which left the patriarchal norms of shaming rape victims unchallenged.[103] It can be argued that gacaca did not qualify or was not expected to hold trials for Category 1 crimes. However, such cases slipped into the gacaca hearings because the national courts and ICTR were very slow in bringing perpetrators of sexual crimes to trial.

A further critique from a gendered perspective is that the gacaca courts considered only the experience of a particular group of Tutsi women, even though violence was also directed at moderate Hutu women.[104] As a result,

Ephgrave claims, official discourse recognized only Tutsi women as legitimate victims of the genocide.[105] This perceived selectivity of victims in the state-sanctioned gacaca courts led Wells to conclude that the process yielded incomplete truth about the Rwandan genocide.[106] Crucially, Wells berates the formal gacaca for not providing health care and economic opportunities for women survivors, which she claims were far more relevant to the women than participating in a process in which they had little faith.[107]

Other scholars write about the traumatic experience that women and other witnesses endured in the formal gacaca courts. In an attempt to predict the potential benefits and shortcomings of the courts, Ervin Staub's seminar with community leaders in Rwanda indicated that the formal gacaca's trials could potentially retraumatize survivors and even instigate renewed anger and hostility among Rwandans if they were not psychologically prepared.[108]

Other studies confirmed these concerns. A phenomenological study by Ulrika Funkeson, Emilie Schröder, Jacques Nzabonimpa, and Rolf Holmqvist demonstrated that women who participated in the formal gacaca proceedings found the process to be both depressing and traumatic.[109] Some of the participants described feeling psychologically stressed and ill after offering their testimonies.[110] Others expressed heartbreak at the lack of credibility in the perpetrators' testimonies and their rejection of the victims' personal testimonies.[111] Nevertheless, many respondents stated that they experienced relief after testifying at the formal gacaca trials, while others acknowledged that witnessing in this process led to forgiveness, reunification, and reconciliation between perpetrators and victims.[112] The study by de Brouwer and Ruvebana confirms both the cathartic and retraumatizing impacts of the formal gacaca.[113]

Some studies focus on the state-sanctioned gacaca's role in peace building and reconciliation in general. Longman's study assessed its potential to bring about peace and reconciliation in post-genocide Rwanda.[114] Echoing the arguments made in the preceding sections, Timothy Longman argues that the formal gacaca's partial success in holding trials for thousands of individuals responsible for genocide crimes and allowing communities to develop accounts of the past was compromised by the reinforcement of ethnic divisions, because only Hutu genocidaires were prosecuted while alleged RPF crimes were excluded. Thus, there was an impression of "victors' justice."[115]

Stephanie Wolters, Cori Wielenga, and Geoff Harris similarly query the one-sidedness of gacaca, arguing that the courts were more retributive than restorative because they dealt only with Hutu crimes, thereby diminishing the full participation of Hutus in the process.[116] Moreover, the fact that only Tutsis could identify themselves as survivors within the formal gacaca jurisdiction is, according to Susan Thomson, an aberration of the national unity and reconciliation that the state aimed to achieve through these courts.[117] As a result of this perceived one-sidedness of gacaca justice, Longman questions whether the formal gacaca ultimately promoted peace and reconciliation in post-genocide Rwanda.[118]

Other logistical and practical issues were alleged to have compromised the state-sanctioned gacaca's capacity to promote peace and reconciliation. These included the unstable and fluctuating participation of citizens and even judges. Farmers and salaried workers claimed they could not afford to leave their farms and work unattended to be present at the court hearings.[119] Furthermore, Uvin and Mironko argue that the formal gacaca courts represented "a dramatic rethinking of the functions of justice in a post-conflict society, stressing community participation over legal procedure and adding a degree of restorative justice."[120] But they also indicate that the formal gacaca was susceptible to manipulation by the people it was meant to serve due to its near total dependence on witnesses' willingness to testify.[121]

How are we to understand these diverse claims and findings? Was gacaca a needed mechanism of justice and reconciliation in post-genocide Rwanda? Are there lessons to learn for other post-accord societies? In the next section, we respond to these questions by critically examining the different issues raised in the reviewed literature regarding gacaca's efficacy as a transitional justice mechanism.

Literature Discussion

We have shown that there are profound disagreements and controversies within evaluations of the formal gacaca. Timothy Donais cites questions raised about the "extent to which the country's ethnic conflict has been resolved rather than merely suppressed."[122] Measured against the idealized liberal legal framework,[123] some researchers advance that the state-sanctioned gacaca (1) violated the principles of fair trial standards; (2) lacked the legal capacity to confirm the veracity of testimonies;[124] and (3) offered no protection to survivors and perpetrators who were attacked for testifying at gacaca courts. As we have shown, literature from this line of thought consistently alleges that the formal gacaca was an undemocratic, state-controlled process, a one-sided victor's justice that humiliated and prosecuted Hutus, exonerated Tutsis from crimes committed by the RPF, and overlooked gender considerations.[125]

On the other hand, scholars who evaluate the formal gacaca more positively argue that the process was well received among many Rwandans who felt their participation would unburden them of atrocities they had committed or suffered.[126] This perception was largely based on their experience with the customary gacaca.[127] A number of scholars argue that the formal gacaca process gave local people, including women, shared space to participate in and negotiate the micro-politics of healing and reconciliation through oral testimony. For example, Jacques Fierens asserts that the formal gacaca made it possible to administer justice in post-genocide Rwanda, even if unsatisfactorily.[128] Anne Kubai concurs that gacaca was "the most viable and perhaps the only way to bring the entire community to trial by the community and for the community."[129]

It is striking that these divergent conclusions can be expressed by scholars of the same professional background and can be found even in comments on the same research projects. We argue that these mixed reviews are due to the varying personal backgrounds and expectations scholars brought with them as they examined the formal gacaca. They may also have been influenced by previous biases and perceptions; Donais writes that these polarized evaluations may be influenced by the tensions that generally exist between the goals of international criminal law and transitional justice as embodied in the liberal peace model.[130] Additionally, divergent perspectives may be related to the fact that the formal gacaca, and for that matter other TRCs, are often caught in the tension between retributive and restorative justice.

These controversies also have their counterparts in the experiences of those who were exposed to the genocide. The following example can help readers to understand the mixed evaluations and perceived outcomes of the formal gacaca.

As stated in the background of this chapter, Régine Uwibereyeho King was born and raised in Rwanda. During the genocide she and her family members were targeted for killing. She survived, along with a few family members, including her brother, who suffered machete wounds at the hands of the men who attacked him.

Shortly before the attack he had tried to conceal himself behind a neighbour's house. The neighbour shouted when she saw him, thereby summoning the gang of killers. They beat him with clubs, cut his tendons with machetes, and inflicted wounds on his head and chest. They stripped him of his clothing and left him for dead.

In the immediate aftermath of the genocide, the neighbour experienced deep remorse for her wrongdoing and apologized to the mother of the victim, who still lived in the community. Years later, in a gacaca court, the victim offered his testimony. And while he was still speaking, the same woman neighbour came forward, kneeled, and begged publicly for his forgiveness. Conversely, the leader of the killing group who had personally inflicted the victim's wounds denied the accusations against him. When Régine later asked her brother about his disposition at the trial, he replied: "I went to the gacaca hearing with mercy in my two hands. One wanted it and asked for it. I gave it to her. One did not want it, did not ask for it, and I took it back." At the hearing other community witnesses reported that the accused had committed further genocide crimes in the village. He denied participation in all of them. Based on his denial and dishonesty, he was sentenced to nineteen years' imprisonment.

These two individuals (the woman neighbour and the accused man) faced the testimony of the same person. The victim told his story and was willing to offer forgiveness based on a confession of wrongdoing that almost cost him his life. The two individuals responded differently: one was remorseful; the other, unapologetic. It is, therefore, presumable that their subsequent understanding and evaluations of gacaca would be remarkably different.

This local case study helps shed light on the mixed perspectives on gacaca as a form of TRC. In the next section, we attempt to draw out the lessons that can be learned, particularly the ones that should be considered when implementing the Calls to Action recommended by the Canadian TRC.

Lessons to Learn from Gacaca

Kristin Doughty provides a useful approach for evaluating complex processes such as the state-sanctioned gacaca,[131] a methodology that, we submit, has been missing in most assessments of the formal gacaca. Doughty suggests that researchers must take into consideration the context in which the state-sanctioned gacaca was conceived and operated. Scholars are urged to shift their focus from a strict legal evaluation of the community courts to consider the potential benefits of the model in Rwandan communities. Accordingly, Doughty urges scholars to locate gacaca's proceedings, such as oral testimonies, in a context in which people rely on mutual interdependence in a densely populated country, where they still share the same means of transportation, work at similar businesses, and worship at the same churches.[132] The TRCs operating in the countries of the Global North, such as Canada, may not share this mode of communal lifestyle. Nevertheless, each society has a set of values and expectations of what a healthy community might look like. In the Canadian context these characteristics may need some adjustments to incorporate Indigenous values, needs, and communitarian lifestyle.

Based on her experience as a Rwandan researcher, the first author would add that the complex nature of the formal gacaca goes beyond the crimes committed, to include consideration of the conditions in which they occurred and how the perpetrators, victims, and bystanders understood and interpreted the crimes committed in their communities. Looking at the previous case example, both the neighbour and the victim understood the offence committed in a similar manner and forgiveness was experienced. The attacker, however, clearly had a divergent perspective and experience in the courts.

Many of the scholarly publications reviewed in this paper reflect the diverse and sometimes controversial evaluations of the formal gacaca. Yet, most studies acknowledged that an inclusive and community-based TRC approach, such as the formal gacaca, was crucial in post-genocide Rwanda. In the very society that experienced violence, inclusion may take different forms to fit the context of those involved in the TRC. According to the first author's informal observation of the 2016 "Pathways to Reconciliation" conference, held in Winnipeg, Manitoba, participants (both Indigenous and non-Indigenous) seemed to express various wants and needs, which suggests different expectations and levels of satisfaction with the implementation of the Calls to Action. These Calls to Action are quite specific and aim at rewriting historical and contemporary settler colonial injustice bedevilling Indigenous people in areas of child care, language and culture, health care, justice, and human rights. In particular, the Calls to Action underscore the need for, as Matt James calls it, "an exceedingly reluctant Canadian federal government"[133] to accept its role in perpetrating acts of cultural genocide through residential schools and to implement the goals of the United Nations Declaration on the Rights of Indigenous Peoples as prerequisites for the emancipation of Indigenous populations.[134] Some scholars have started to write on the strengths and limitations of the TRC's mandate and the strategic decisions the commission made to frame its implementation in an international context.[135] We suggest systematic monitoring and evaluations of the new initiatives that are forming in Canada following the TRC recommendations; other authors in this volume have offered insight into what that might look like.[136] Such evaluations will be useful in identifying and strengthening the positives from the Canadian TRC.

Other critiques drew attention to the speed of the formal gacaca and questioned its ultimate efficacy. The response to such concerns is perhaps best addressed by the 2012 comprehensive statistics of the National Service of gacaca courts. They estimate that it cost the ICTR $1.5 billion USD to complete seventy-five trials over a period of eighteen years. In contrast, the formal gacaca trials cost approximately $52 million USD and handled an estimated two million genocide cases over the course of ten years. Broken down, one suspect cost the formal gacaca fifty dollars USD, while one suspect required the ICTR to invest $20 million USD.[137] If Rwandans had relied on the ICTR model to render justice at the community level, most people would have been long dead before being able to testify or brought to trial.

Many have argued that, freed from state oversight, the formal gacaca might have sidestepped some of its alleged shortcomings, such as exacerbating existing ethnic divisions, being one-sided, and coercing people to testify. More than any other criticism, it was the allegation of excessive state control that our literature review identified as the most serious issue compromising the fulfillment of the formal gacaca objectives, whether that state control is attributed to the leadership style of the current president,[138] or to the influence of the international donors.[139] Again, we urge that the context be adequately considered. While some testimonies undoubtedly created distress and contentions, Rwandans were already deeply divided, especially along ethnic lines. The formal gacaca played a crucial role in creating a space for people of different ethnic backgrounds to come together and deal with their differences.

The intense criticisms of the formal gacaca from the perspective of criminal law for failing to follow due process and pursuing contradictory goals of retribution and restoration seem disproportionate and one-sided. We submit that the researchers failed to account for the multi-dimensional perspectives of peace building and transitional justice that the state-sanctioned gacaca embodied. The critiques are mostly based on a Western liberal concept of justice,[140] which measures the failure of the formal gacaca against legal principles found in penal court systems of developed economies.[141] However, Phil Clark argues that this Western legal perspective fails to account for the hybrid nature of the formal gacaca process,[142] which relates to John Paul Lederach's notion of "the paradox of reconciliation."[143] Lederach asserts that reconciliation is built on a paradox, "which links seemingly contradictory but in fact interdependent ideas and forces."[144]

Charity Wibabara, a Rwandan scholar, conducted a thorough analysis of the existing literature on the customary and formal gacaca and compared the contribution of the formal gacaca to that of the ICTR and the national courts.[145] She has helped to put into perspective the expectations, critiques, and outcomes of each of these justice systems. In the following paragraphs, we will summarize her findings along with those of other scholars who have paid attention to the social context of post-genocide Rwanda.

Wibabara agrees with the criticisms that the formal gacaca lacked legal representation for the accused and witnesses. There were no public prosecutors or trained attorneys. However, she submits that this was not a matter of simple oversight. The procedural rights of due process, including the right to legal representation, were sacrificed to gain a more participatory process in which the accused, the victims, and judges were on equal footing. She notes that other rights, such as being presumed innocent until proven guilty, were observed in order to individualize crimes and not condemn an entire ethnic group.[146] Chiseche Mibenge adds that the formal gacaca process was more accessible to many Rwandans as opposed to the more distant and detached ICTR and the domestic courts.[147] Mibenge reckons that while the formal gacaca lacked formal judicial procedures, it established "individual criminal responsibility without undue delay, and was well capable of carrying out expedient trials and determining questions of guilt or innocence."[148]

Divergences from the Western legal system were not a matter of oversight in the Rwandan or in the Canadian TRC. The alleged shortcomings of the formal gacaca included charges of failing to address the root causes of the genocide[149] and focusing only on selective testimonies of Tutsis.[150] The victims of Indian Residential Schools and the Elders adopted a victim-centred approach. By focusing on the articulation of the struggles in the residential schools as a way for the survivors to claim their voice and respect, and demanding that Canada listens, learns, and takes responsibility for the damage caused, the victim-centred approach also presented its own strengths and limitations, particularly overlooking the structural issues and their implications in a country where, as James states, "the perpetrators and the beneficiaries of the injustices continue to be socially dominant."[151]

In the case of TRC Rwanda, like Doughty,[152] Towner acknowledges that the community setting in which the formal gacaca took place or the bottom-up truth telling in Canada[153] demanded focus. The state-sanctioned gacaca was established precisely to deal with genocide crimes committed over 100 days in 1994.[154] This does not mean that other crimes were not valued as serious. The fact that court proceedings were conducted in the immediate communities in the presence of survivors, perpetrators, and their family members allowed for a comprehensive assessment of the testimonies, thus reinstating a sense of justice, closure, and finality.[155] Similarly, it was beyond the scope of community hearings to impose comprehensive financial and social reparations on those who deliberately took the lives of neighbours during the genocide. Wibabara gives the example of perpetrators being given lenient forms of punishment, such as community service in lieu of jail time, for those who confessed their crimes and asked for forgiveness. Reparations for loss of loved ones and for permanent disabilities (physical and psychological) were beyond the limitations of the formal gacaca process.[156]

Arguably, the formal gacaca courts attempted to reveal the truth about the genocide, promote community-based justice, and provide a local context for reconciliation to take place. When these goals are taken into consideration, the charge that the project was too ambitious must be challenged. We return to Lederach's position that reconciliation is a paradox that involves expressions of the pain, provides a place for truth and mercy to be combined, and gives time and place for justice and peace to meet.[157] In more specific terms, Lederach contends that reconciliation deals with the following three paradoxes: (1) reconciliation brings about an encounter between the expression of past hurts and the search for a better future; (2) reconciliation provides a meeting place for truth and justice, where past injustices are exposed and friendships are renewed; and (3) reconciliation gives time and place for justice and peace, creating the possibility to redress past wrongdoing and envision a shared future.[158]

Although these ideas and forces seem contradictory, Lederach argues that they are in fact interdependent.[159] Local TRC processes, like the formal gacaca, tend to give voice to aggrieved populations and serve as a place where justice and mercy meet, thus paving the way for reconciliation. Conceived in this way, we argue that Rwanda's attempt at combining retributive and restorative justice through the formal gacaca offered a robust pathway for reconciliation for affected communities. Similarly, Indigenous people in Canada face their own paradox as they attempt to weave together hard and soft rights; reconciliation between individuals and reconciliation between nations; and learning how to extend mercy without losing truth or sacrificing justice on the altar of reconciliation. Community involvement and the kind of justice that seeks truth, peace, mercy, and healing are constitutive elements of reconciliation that can benefit other societies adopting the TRC model.

Having made this positive evaluation, we would warn that the romanticization of the formal gacaca approach as the "best possible pathway" to reconciliation should be scrutinized. As the Canadian TRC's *Reconciliation* volume aptly notes, Indigenous law, like any other legal system, is not frozen in the past and neither is it monolithic. It affirms that Indigenous law is dynamic, adapting over time to address the changing circumstances of Indigenous people.[160]

Literature on the formal gacaca has clearly shown the complicated nature of community-based hearings in post-genocide Rwanda despite broad popular support for re-establishing social harmony. This underlines the importance of considering the context of each TRC, its focus and outcomes, both mid-term and long term. New TRCs should pay attention to contextual issues that need to be addressed and the different pathways that can help rebuild a sense of harmony, healing, and justice. In Canada, for example, residential schools were the focus of its TRC. Canadians will need to continue to examine the TRC recommendations and link them to the current and future experiences of Indigenous people in their relationships with the government of Canada and other citizens to determine better ways of moving forward.

One way of strengthening the relationship among Indigenous people, non-Indigenous people, and the Canadian government is for the government to begin to integrate and formally recognize the concepts and principles of oral history and legal traditions of Indigenous law, which were integral to the TRC process itself and have a critical role to play post-TRC. As long as Indigenous people are denied the space and mandate to use their socio-legal resources to actualize their aspirations and needs as a people, and, as the *Reconciliation* volume notes, as long as they are not "recognized as possessing the responsibility, authority, and capability to address their disagreements by making laws within their communities"[161] to transform their socio-political situation, it would be delusional to expect that truth and reconciliation can be attained within Indigenous communities.

In Rwanda, we recognize that the formal gacaca was not perfect, but that it made an important contribution to restoring community relationships. Gacaca was established within a context of severe socio-economic dislocation and institutional breakdown, and, as Markus Zimmer says, demonstrated the resilience, "tenacity and the imagination that spawned the experiment."[162]

Conclusion

The legal system on its own cannot initiate reconciliation. Confessions, forgiveness, and reconciliation need to happen at the community level. The formal gacaca, like any other TRC, was limited in what it could conceivably accomplish. The passage of time will be required for the next generation to assess the outcome of building a sustainable culture of reconciliation and trust. As de Brouwer and Ruvebana have found, gacaca is only one of the processes of reconciliation in Rwanda, which provided many citizens opportunities with far-reaching impacts for the relationship of future Rwandans.[163]

The traditional and state-sanctioned gacaca emphasized community participation. As Nicholas Jones and Rob Nestor's article indicates, one of the strengths of the formal gacaca has been that it allowed local people to take responsibility for making decisions as opposed to relying on liberal technocrats or international specialists who are disconnected from the forces of local conflicts and peace-building realities.[164] Community participation creates the possibility of reconciliation between families of survivors and perpetrators.

We also emphasize that the process of bringing people together does not need to be expensive in comparison with the formal judicial system. However, there is a need to continue providing tangible support in terms of economic opportunities, health care, and housing to countless Rwandans who are still reeling from the effects of the genocide.[165] Without these tangible psychological, social, and material supports, especially in light of the fact that the formal gacaca did not include any compensation, it may be unrealistic to expect forums like gacaca to deal with the intangible transgenerational trauma of the 1994 genocide.

We conclude that gacaca provided a framework within which Hutu and Tutsi could come together and address genocide-related issues. In post-gacaca

Rwanda, civil society organizations and grassroots actors have shown a desire to apply this conceptual framework to other community initiatives in which they address social issues, such as poverty, domestic violence, and trauma healing, and further cross-community conversations on reconciliation. We submit that through bringing community members together, the formal gacaca planted seeds for a shared future, and might yet do so again.

Notes

1   Nagy, "Truth and Reconciliation Commission," 200.

2   Ibid.

3   Venter, "Eliminating Fear," 585–87.

4   Richmond, "Peace During and After," 517.

5   Truth and Reconciliation Commission of Canada (hereafter TRC), *Calls to Action*, 3. To learn how the government of Canada is responding to the Truth and Reconciliation Commission's Calls to Action 25 to 42, see Canada, Justice, 2018, https://www.aadnc-aandc.gc.ca/eng/1524502695174/1524502748151 (accessed 27 February 2019). See also CBC, "Beyond 94, Truth and Reconciliation in Canada."

6   Towner, "Documenting Genocide," 300; Haile, "Rwanda's Experiments," 10.

7   Corey and Joireman, "Retributive Justice," 73; Waldorf, *Transitional Justice*, 6; King, "Healing Psychosocial Trauma," 134.

8   De Brouwer and Chu, "Men Who Killed Me," 11.

9   Burnet, *Women in Africa*, 136.

10 Gasibirege, *Lien entre Guérison*, 7.

11 Le Mon, "Rwanda's Troubled Gacaca Courts," 17; Ingelaere, *Gacaca Courts in Rwanda*, 13.

12 Wibabara, *Gacaca Courts*, 109.

13 Le Mon, "Rwanda's Troubled Gacaca Courts," 16.

14 Barria and Roper, "How Effective," 362; Le Mon, "Rwanda's Troubled Gacaca Courts," 16; Brehm, Uggen, and Gasanabo, "Genocide, Justice," 335.

15 Schabas, "Genocide Trials and Gacaca Courts," 891; Check, "Ethnicity and Arms Proliferation," 4–5.

16 Wibabara, *Gacaca Courts*, 165.

17 In this paper, we utilize "customary" or "traditional gacaca" to refer to the traditional mechanism that existed in Rwanda before the genocide, and "formal" or "state-sanctioned gacaca" to refer to the renewed form of the customary system that was transformed into a TRC for Rwanda. We use the terms "formal," "state-sanctioned," and "national" synonymously.

18 Longman, "Trying Times for Rwanda," 50; Thomson, "Darker Side of Transitional Justice," 380.

19 Thomson and Nagy, "Law, Power and Justice," 16; De Brouwer and Ruvebana, "Legacy of the Gacaca Courts," 963.

20 Kirkby, "Rwanda's Gacaca Courts," 100; Kubai, "Between Justice and Reconciliation," 56; Le Mon, "Rwanda's Troubled Gacaca Courts," 16.

21 Corey and Joireman, "Retributive Justice," 73; King, "Healing Psychosocial Trauma," 134; Neuffer, "Kigali Dispatch," 18; Oomen, "Donor-Driven Justice," 902.

22 Schabas, "Genocide Trials and Gacaca Courts," 893.

23 Oomen, "Donor-Driven Justice," 904.

24 Mibenge, "Enforcing International Humanitarian Law," 415; Carter, "Justice and Reconciliation," 50; Lahiri, "Rwanda's Gacaca Courts," 323.

25 Brehm, Uggen, and Gasanabo, "Genocide, Justice," 336.

26 Schabas, "Genocide Trials and Gacaca Courts," 893.

27 Carter, "Justice and Reconciliation," 50; Tiemessen, "After Arusha," 61; Wibabara, *Gacaca Courts versus the International,* 1–263.

28 Carter, "Justice and Reconciliation," 51.

29 Pozen, Neugebauer, and Ntaganira, "Assessing the Rwanda Experiment," 36; Brehm, Uggen, and Gasanabo, "Genocide, Justice," 337.

30 Lambert, Glacken, and McCarron, "Employing an Ethnographic Approach," 20–21.

31 Neuffer, "It Takes a Village," 19.

32 Graybill, "Pardon, Punishment, and Amnesia," 1123.

33 Wolters, "Gacaca Courts," 67.

34 Graybill, "Pardon, Punishment, and Amnesia," 1123.

35 Kubai, "Between Justice and Reconciliation," 55.

36 Clark, "Learning from the Past."

37 Ibid., 16.

38 Clark, "Bringing the Peasants," 198.

39 De Brouwer and Ruvebana, "Legacy of the Gacaca Courts," 946; Clark, "Bringing the Peasants," 202; Longman, "Assessment of Rwanda's Gacaca Courts," 308.

40 Chakravarty, "'Partially Trusting' Field Relationships."

41 The Rwandan Patriotic Front (RPF) was a former guerilla army led by the current Rwandan president Paul Kagame, which stopped the 1994 genocide. But their alleged involvement in retaliatory attacks and killings of about 10,000 to 100,000 Hutus (Barria and Roper, "How Effective," 353) and the fact that the members of this movement were not tried during the gacaca process have raised many questions about the goal of reconciliation pursued by the Kagame administration (Le Mon, "Rwanda's Troubled Gacaca Courts," 18); see: Chakravarty, "'Partially Trusting' Field Relationships," 264.

42 Oomen, "Donor-Driven Justice," 105; Clark, "Learning from the Past," 17.

43 Longman, "Trying Times for Rwanda," 49.

44 Ibid., 51–22.

45 Ibid., 52.

46 Dauge-Roth, "Testimonial Encounter."

47 Ibid., 173.

48 Ibid.

49 Ibid.

50 Ibid., 175–76.

51 Schabas, "Genocide Trials and Gacaca Courts," 895.

52 Brehm, Uggen, and Gasanabo, "Genocide, Justice," 247.

53 Judith Herrmann, "A Critical Analysis of the Transitional Justice Measures Incorporated by Rwandan Gacaca and Their Effectiveness," *James Cook University Law Review* 19 (2012): 92.

54 Sosnov, "Adjudication of Genocide," 138–39.

55 Ibid., 140.

56 Ibid., 142.

57 De Brouwer and Ruvebana, "Legacy of the Gacaca Courts," 950.

58 Kirkby, "Rwanda's Gacaca Courts," 116.

59 Ibid., 111.

60 Ibid., 106.

61 Ibid., 109–11.

62 Ibid., 112–13.

63 Ibid., 107.

64 Haile, "Rwanda's Experiments in People's Courts," 21.

65 Ibid., 23.

66 Ibid., 28.

67 Ibid., 37.

68 Corey and Joireman, "Retributive Justice," 86; Wolters, "Gacaca Courts," 68.

69 Mibenge, "Enforcing International Humanitarian Law," 422; Apuuli, "Procedural Due Process," 18.

70 Kubai, "Between Justice and Reconciliation," 59; Le Mon, "Rwanda's Troubled Gacaca Courts," 17.

71 Haile, "Rwanda's Experiments in People's Courts," 41.

72 Ingelaere, "Does the Truth Pass," 513.

73 Haile, "Rwanda's Experiments in People's Courts," 48.

74 Sosnov, "Adjudication of Genocide," 145–46.

75 Ibid., 142–45.

76 De Brouwer and Ruvebana, "Legacy of the Gacaca Courts," 952.

77 Ibid., 953–72.

78 Ibid., 947–48.

79 Fierens, "Gacaca Courts," 915.

80 Clark, "Hybridity, Holism, and Traditional Justice," 829.

81 Ibid., 830.

82 Oomen, "Donor-Driven Justice," 902.

83 Ibid.

84 Ingelaere, "Gacaca Courts in Rwanda," 47.

85 MacGinty, *Gilding the Lily*, 357.

86 Human Rights Watch, *Justice Compromised*, 127.

87 Oomen, "Donor-Driven Justice and Its Discontents," *Development and Change*, 902–3; Brehm, Uggen, and Gasanabo, "Genocide, Justice," 335.

88 Human Rights Watch, *Justice Compromised*, 127.

89 Ibid.

90 MacGinty, *Gilding the Lily*, 357.

91 Penal Reform International, *Eight Years On*, 17.

92 Uvin and Mironko, "Western and Local Approaches," 228.

93 Ingelaere, "Gacaca Courts in Rwanda," 47.

94 Oomen, "Donor-Driven Justice," 903.

95 MacGinty, *Gilding the Lily*, 358.

96 Tiemessen, "After Arusha," 57–76.

97 Kombo, "Their Words, Actions, and Meaning," 321.

98 Tiemessen, "After Arusha," 63.

99 Wells, "Gender, Sexual Violence and Prospects"; Ephgrave, "Women's Testimony and Collective Memory."

100 Wells, "Gender, Sexual Violence and Prospects," 183.

101 Olwine, "One Step Forward," 653.

102 Ibid., 654.

103 Uvin and Mironko, "Western and Local Approaches," 227; Wells, "Gender, Sexual Violence and Prospects," 192; Ephgrave, "Women's Testimony and Collective Memory," 184.

104 Ephgrave, "Women's Testimony and Collective Memory," 186.

105 Ibid.

106 Wells, "Gender, Sexual Violence and Prospects," 183.

107 Ibid., 194.

108 Staub, "Justice, Healing, and Reconciliation," 27.

109 Funkeson et al., "Witnesses to Genocide," 375–76.

110 Ibid., 377.

111 Ibid., 378.

112 Ibid., 380–81.

113 De Brouwer and Ruvebana, "Legacy of the Gacaca Courts," 958.

114 Longman, "Assessment of Rwanda's Gacaca Courts," 304–12.

115 Ibid., 304.

116 Wolters, "Gacaca Courts," 68; Wielenga and Harris, "Building Peace and Security," 17.

117 Thomson, "Darker Side," 378.

118 Longman, "Assessment of Rwanda's Gacaca Courts," 304.

119 Ibid.; Kirkby, "Rwanda's Gacaca Courts," 109.

120 Uvin and Mironko, "Western and Local Approaches," 226–27.

121 Ibid., 227.

122 Cited in Donais, *Peacebuilding and Local Ownership*, 6.

123 Brehm, Uggen, and Gasanabo, "Genocide, Justice," 338.

124 Haile, "Rwanda's Experiments in People's Courts," 41.

125 Chakravarty, "'Partially Trusting' Field Relationships," 264.

126 De Brouwer and Ruvebana, "Legacy of the Gacaca Courts," 946; Clark, "Bringing the Peasants," 202; Longman, "Assessment of Rwanda's Gacaca Courts," 308.

127 Clark, "Bringing the Peasants," 198.

128 Fierens, "Gacaca Courts," 919.

129 Kubai, "Between Justice and Reconciliation," 59.

130 Ibid., 384–85.

131 Doughty, "Law and the Architecture," 420.

132 Ibid., 425.

133 James, "On Carnival and Context," 488.

134 For more details on the Calls to Action, see TRC, *Calls to Action*.

135 See James, "On Carnival and Context."

136 See O'Neil in this volume.

137 Wibabara, *Gacaca Courts versus the International*, 224–26.

138 Cited in Donais, *Peacebuilding and Local Ownership*, 6.

139 Oomen, "Donor-Driven Justice," 904; Schotsmans, "But We Also Support Monitoring," 392.

140 Zimmer, "Rwanda's Gacaca Courts," 2.

141 De Brouwer, and Ruvebana, "Legacy of the Gacaca Courts in Rwanda," 972.

142 Clark, "Hybridity, Holism, and Traditional Justice," 807.

143 Lederach, *Building Peace*.

144 Ibid., 30.

145 Wibabara, *Gacaca Courts versus the International*, 216–61.

146 Ibid.

147 Mibenge, "Enforcing International Humanitarian Law," 422.

148 Ibid.

149 Haile, *Rwanda's Experiments in People's Courts*, 1–52.

150 Towner, "Documenting Genocide," 298.

151 On the strengths and limitations of the Canadian TRC's strategic decisions that the Commission made regarding the implementation of the victim-centred approach, see James, "A Carnival of Truth?," 2.

152 Doughty, "Law and the Architecture," 419–37.

153 Towner, "Documenting Genocide," 296.

154 Ibid.

155 Ibid.

156 Wibabara, *Gacaca Courts versus the International*, 207–9.

157 Lederach, *Building Peace*, 30–31.

158 Lederach, *Building Peace*. See also: Maiangwa and Byrne, "Peacebuilding and Reconciliation."

159 Lederach, *Building Peace*, 30.

160 TRC, *Final Report,* vol. 6, *Reconciliation,* 52.

161 Ibid., 51.

162 Zimmer, "Rwanda's Gacaca Courts," 2.

163 De Brouwer and Ruvebana, "Legacy of the Gacaca Courts in Rwanda," 962.

164 Jones and Nestor, "Sentencing Circles."

165 De Brouwer and Ruvebana, "Legacy of the Gacaca Courts in Rwanda," 976.

CHAPTER 3

MONITORING THAT RECONCILES

Reflecting on the TRC's Call for a National Council for Reconciliation

CODY O'NEIL

Among the ninety-four Calls to Action outlined in the Truth and Reconciliation Commission's (TRC) Executive Summary report is the call for a National Council for Reconciliation. According to the commission, this council would "monitor, evaluate, and report annually to Parliament and the people of Canada on the Government of Canada's post-apology progress on reconciliation to ensure that government accountability for reconciling the relationship between Aboriginal peoples and the Crown is maintained in the coming years."[1]

Among the indicators to be reported on are the number of Indigenous children in care, education funding, various health indicators (such as infant mortality, life expectancy, suicide), and the overrepresentation of Indigenous peoples in the justice and correctional systems. While its list is not intended to be comprehensive, it does identify one possible starting point for evaluating Canada's post-TRC reconciliation process. In the spirit of this Call to Action, I hope to identify some possible pitfalls and promises of such a project and to pose an introductory set of questions concerning how a National Council for Reconciliation might decide on other indicators and conceive of its efforts to evaluate reconciliation going forward.

I begin by offering a brief reflection on measurement more generally in order to address concerns that naturally come up when one is contemplating the task of measurement in the context of colonialism. I then consider the national context of South Africa, where the national discourse of reconciliation has undergone significant changes as it evaluates reconciliation in the post-apartheid and post-TRC era. After identifying the lessons to be learned from South Africa's reconciliation monitoring project, I consider the Canadian TRC's framing of reconciliation. Finally, I offer some concluding thoughts on a selection of indicators that might capture the expansive framework of reconciliation presented by the TRC. I hope that these reflections prove valuable to the National Council for Reconciliation as it begins its work of monitoring reconciliation in Canada.

Measurement and Its Discontents

It is hard to ignore the long history of mobilizing measurement for the purpose of conquest. As Sherene H. Razack reminds us in the introduction to *Race, Space, and the Law: Unmapping a White Settler Society*: "The subject who maps his space and thereby knows and controls it, is also the imperial man claiming the territories of others for his own. . . . Maps sought to measure, standardize, and bind space, keeping the environment on the outside. Mapping the 'New World' enabled Samuel de Champlain, for instance, to feel himself master of the lands he would eventually claim for the king of France."[2]

In short, measurement is not without its colonial contradictions and genocidal consequences. This should be clear from the historical and current record of colonialism. Steadfast in their commitment to domination, colonizers have long sought to measure in order to master. After all, keeping tabs on the forces that threaten colonial rule is required to maintain this rule. For this reason it should be no surprise that the enterprise of measurement and its self-appointed masters continue to rear their colonial heads in the present.

It was only in 2013 that Ian Mosby's research revealed an unprecedented series of nutritional experiments carried out on Indigenous peoples by the Canadian government in cooperation with leading Canadian nutrition experts. Between 1942 and 1952, Mosby writes, there were "controlled experiments conducted, apparently without the subjects' informed consent or knowledge, on malnourished Aboriginal populations in Northern Manitoba and, later, in six Indian residential schools."[3]

As Mosby makes clear, the experiments regarded Indigenous peoples as "experimental materials" and residential schools and Indigenous communities as "laboratories" for the purpose of pursuing "different political and professional interests."[4] This ought to remind us why it is a common refrain that Indigenous peoples have been "researched to death."[5] Whether it is surveying Indigenous lands in order to steal them, studying Indigenous knowledges in order to sell them, or counting Indigenous children in order to assimilate them, the ways in which measurement has accelerated Indigenous plunder and advanced settler prosperity are far from a historical aside. Often done in the name of "research," the practice of measuring the colonized is saturated in a cherished colonial catalogue of biological, cultural, and geographic classifications. Given this reality, it is not unreasonable to hold that measurement has served a crucial role in sustaining colonization.

That measurement has and continues to privilege the political and professional interests of the colonizers must be taken seriously by any agent in the business of measurement, including the National Council for Reconciliation. While the history of measurement is not reducible to the history of colonialism, its practice is certainly coloured by past and present colonial projects, regardless of which disciplinary banner it is conducted under. This should produce what is an obvious cause for hesitation in confronting the old adage that "to measure is to know."

To naturalize the meaning of measurement as inherently colonial, however, would be to surrender to the historical forces of colonialism—forces that have nothing natural about them. Indeed, suggesting that measurement is somehow synonymous with conquest erases the historical use of measurement both before the colonial era and as a means of resistance that Indigenous peoples continue to employ in the struggle for decolonization. In a world where "findings" are continually misrepresented or simply fabricated to protect colonial privilege, it is imperative to contest the colonial ends to which measurement is so often directed. Against this reality it is both effective and often necessary to wield measurement as a weapon against those who continue to abuse it.

The TRC's call for a National Council for Reconciliation, which includes a host of indicators that would systematically expose the ongoing colonial character of the Canadian state in sectors critical to maintaining its rule, such as child welfare or the criminal justice system, is one example of how measurement might serve the resistance of Indigenous peoples and their allies.

However, it is not sufficient to merely challenge colonial modes of measurement from the standpoint of those being measured. We must also challenge the assumption that the practice of measurement is colonial property to begin with.[6] Dismantling the master's house with the master's tools may or may not be necessary. What *is* necessary is to recognize when a tool (in this case, measurement) does not belong to the master alone. Put another way, we must guard against the dismissal and denial of measurement as practised by Indigenous peoples and nations.

If the concern is not then with measurement per se, this leaves the question of what to measure and how to measure it. What can we learn from reflecting on our intentions behind measuring and the metrics that these intentions produce? What kinds of new or previously ignored metrics might be identified through such reflection? If measurement is to be recognized not only as a tool of colonialism but as a potential tool of decolonization, these questions are critically important. In South Africa a decade-long effort to monitor reconciliation offers some potential answers.

The Case of South Africa: Radical Reconciliation

In its report "Reconciliation as Framework for Preventing Conflict and Sustaining Peace," the United Nations Development Programme writes: "In order to measure reconciliation this requires the acceptance of the concept and its objectives at different levels of society, and an attempt to continue forging a shared understanding of what it means."[7] This statement poses the immediate problem of how to monitor reconciliation in the face of competing definitions of the term. What definition do we use for the purpose of monitoring, and what type of societal transformation underpins this definition?

One attempt to answer these questions can be seen in the South African Reconciliation Barometer (SARB), a national public opinion poll released annually by the Institute for Justice and Reconciliation (IJR) since 2003 to monitor progress in the post-apartheid reconciliation process. This poll was released every year in the form of a "Reconciliation Barometer" survey. After ten years, in 2013, the survey underwent a substantive conceptual shift in response to changing public perception (partly revealed by the poll itself) that national discourse on reconciliation had become increasingly disconnected from the material reality of ongoing economic inequality. In the introduction to its 2013 survey, the IJR writes:

> Political analysts of reconciliation discourse have more recently demonstrated that the focus tends to be on the therapeutic aspects of the concept, rather than the material. . . . This pattern has been seen in South Africa where there is a leaning towards the psychological and interpersonal aspects of reconciliation. As a result the language of reconciliation has been criticised for being at best fluffy and meaningless and at worst ideological. Almost 20 years after the transition, the Reconciliation Barometer survey finds that for ordinary citizens issues of economic inequality and material injustice are the biggest blocks to reconciliation faced today.[8]

In an effort to emphasize this ongoing contradiction of material injustice, the IJR chose to adopt a new conceptual framework, titled "Confronting Exclusion: Time for Radical Reconciliation." Explaining its decision to adopt the concept of radical reconciliation, the IJR stated: "This term [radical] grounds reconciliation in a new direction which places the connection between economic justice and reconciliation at the centre of radical reconciliation."[9]

The IJR thus maintains what has become something of a catchphrase among critics of state-sanctioned models of reconciliation around the world: there can be no reconciliation without restitution.[10] At bottom, these critiques claim that reconciliation cannot be reduced to an apology for an isolated historical injustice—and certainly not celebrated as a means of transcending this injustice—without actually confronting the material basis for injustice that continues to produce inequality in the present.

As T.O. Molefe has made clear in the South African context, this means recognizing apartheid for what it was in material terms: "a state-sponsored criminal enterprise that directed national resources disproportionately among the population and used national resources to deny huge swathes of the population opportunities for development, economic activity and education."[11] Molefe's call, which partly inspired the conceptual shift in the IJR's Reconciliation Barometer, is to rethink reconciliation. They argue that economic inequality must be foregrounded as the primary contradiction demanding resolution in any political process that claims to be restoring the former friendliness of a relationship turned antagonistic (assuming it was ever friendly to begin with).

Radical reconciliation is thus a call to move beyond a politics of recognition—in the form of apology, multicultural lip service, or otherwise—to a politics of restitution.[12] Failure to do so, Molefe suggests, is to succumb to the "totalizing effects" of the "reconciliation ideology" that has become so characteristic of post-apartheid South Africa.

The IJR's concerted response to the increasing romanticization of the reconciliation process, one revealed more recently in the SARB's 2013 findings, is most evident in its use of a Living Standards Measure (LSM) in its public poll. Developed by the South African Audience Research Foundation, the LSM is designed to provide a measure of material exclusion experienced by South African citizens. In addition to other variables, such as education and telecommunications, the LSM considers "the degree of urbanisation, dwelling type, levels of consumption, access to services, social activities, ownership of assets and employment of household helpers."[13] At its core the LSM allows for all survey responses to be broken down according to the socio-economic status of the respondent.

One revealing finding is that white South Africans in the uppermost LSM category report that there are no South Africans who are socio-economically worse off than they are, suggesting that they are comparing themselves only with other white South Africans. As the report points out: "This finding is important for the concept of radical reconciliation as it posits that economic justice is central to reconciliation and requires shared concern for the plight of the economically excluded across race and class groups."[14]

This conclusion coincides with other findings that reveal how few white South Africans (28.5 percent) actually agree with the statement that "reconciliation is impossible if those disadvantaged by apartheid are still poor by race."[15] Taken together, these findings suggest that economic restitution is not particularly high on the reconciliation radar for white South Africans, whose dominant understanding of reconciliation falls short of moving beyond the need to "forgive those who hurt others."[16]

For this reason, the 2013 SARB concludes: "It is only by creating a collective awareness around the inequalities which continue to exist that we can shape a shared identity based on the principles of justice and transformation."[17] How such a collective awareness can be created beyond reading the report (the academic language of which is not particularly accessible) is not described in any detail to the reader.

The IJR's decision to emphasize economic inequality demonstrates a reflective response to a concern that certain discussions fail to recognize: material restitution for historical and ongoing injustice is a fundamental requirement, if not a precondition, for reconciliation. What the IJR reconceptualizes as "radical reconciliation" is therefore nothing less than a call to resolve the contradiction of economic inequality that continues to define the socio-economic landscape of South Africa, a landscape that continues to produce public perceptions of reconciliation that are symptomatic of one's own socio-economic status. For these reasons the IJR has developed a decidedly economic indicator to measure the reconciliation process: only when socio-economic gaps among South Africans start to close can one say with confidence that reconciliation is under way.

Material vs. Immaterial Inequality

The SARB's emphasis on economic inequality notwithstanding, the IJR's concept of radical reconciliation should not be read as a dismissal of those indicators often perceived as less material metrics of reconciliation. Everyday experiences of social interaction across racialized groups, for example, remain central to the IJR's framing of reconciliation. This is evidenced by its use of such indicators as interracial contact, interracial preconceptions, and interracial tolerance, as well as acknowledgement of apartheid's injustice, forgiveness, and a commitment to more dialogue—all of which could be categorized as qualitative in character.

To avoid reproducing the often unnecessary tension between material and immaterial indicators of reconciliation, along with the assumption that one is measurable while the other is not, the IJR report instead interrogates the nature of the relationship between the two. Instead of interpreting qualitative indicators (such as public perception of reconciliation) in addition to quantitative indicators (such as annual household income), the report produces an analysis of the former *according to* the latter (and vice versa).

As the finding regarding white South Africans' failure to perceive their own economic privilege suggests, qualitative perceptions of injustice and quantitative measures of economic inequality are not mutually exclusive: it is only by understanding white South Africans' socio-economic status as a condition for their collective (mis)perception of their own privilege that we can ultimately learn something about the state of reconciliation in contemporary South Africa. As the report makes clear: "Inclusive development and economic transformation is not only imperative for material justice, but also for reconciliation across the country's historical, cultural and racial divides. However, it is important that we do not swing from one extreme to the other, emphasising the economic and political at the expense of the psychological and philosophical. Instead we need to re-think reconciliation in ways which emphasise the relationship between the psychological and material, interpersonal and structural."[18]

In other words the point is not to dissect the difference between public perception and the material reality of economic inequality, or to interpret public perception as a proxy for material change.[19] The point is to understand how public perception is symptomatic of socio-economic status, and that this perception can in turn play a determining role in reproducing a given socio-economic system.[20]

On precisely this point the SARB asserts that it would be unthinking to separate the "material inequality of class relations" quantitatively expressed by the Living Standards Measure from the "symbolic inequality of cultural dominance" qualitatively expressed as "white privilege" and "denial."[21] In other words, public perceptions cannot be understood in isolation from the material conditions of economic inequality, just as economic inequality cannot be understood in isolation from public perceptions necessary to sustain this inequality. Any process of reconciliation that seeks to resolve these interdependent inequalities must take this reality seriously. By extension any project that seeks to monitor such a process must select indicators—and offer an interpretation of these indicators—that accurately reflect this reality.

Reflecting on the concept of radical reconciliation one year after its adoption, the IJR writes: "The aim is not to lose the transcendent call of reconciliation to transform suffering, disconnection and violence into understanding, connection and healing at a national level, but it asks us to confront the searing contradictions which remain with us. It aims to ground the transcendent in the everyday, so that reconciliation becomes a daily practice."[22]

For this reason the IJR argues for a model of reconciliation that cannot be reduced to an either/or logic that would have us debate the reliability of material versus immaterial indicators and then debate some more about which is measurable and which is not. Instead, the IJR proposes a model of reconciliation that requires transforming society from the perspective of everyday economic realities, regardless of whether these realities are registered quantitatively or qualitatively.

There are critical lessons to be learned from this conceptual shift in the South African Reconciliation Barometer over its ten years of publication. First and foremost is its critical response to what reconciliation is *not*. As noted above, the report's conceptual framework of "radical reconciliation" responds to the convenient, idealistic, and indeed colonial illusion that reconciliation can be achieved without restitution. The new hypotheses and indicators of reconciliation outlined in the IJR's report have been selected to remain accountable to this demand.

While the report does not offer a single definition of reconciliation nor a detailed blueprint for the specific societal transformation being sought, it does address the dilemma of competing definitions of reconciliation through its emphasis on economic justice as a fundamental requirement. Any definition or roadmap for reconciliation that fails to recognize this requirement will, according to the framework of the report, prevent genuine reconciliation.

How we choose to define "reconciliation" has serious implications for the kinds of indicators we use to monitor whether or not we are achieving it. Answering this question demands clarity regarding what reconciliation is not, which requires questioning fundamental material realities like ongoing economic inequality and setting aside those indicators that would suggest these realities can be ignored. It is a matter of questioning on whose terms reconciliation is being defined and contesting the often colonial assumptions underlying indicators thought to be reliable metrics of reconciliation. That the South African Reconciliation Barometer Report has attempted to both reflect on and respond to the changing public discourse of reconciliation and its critics in South Africa makes it a valuable resource for thinking about how a National Council for Reconciliation in Canada might go about monitoring reconciliation over time.

That being said, I am not suggesting that the IJR's framing of reconciliation and its monitoring tools should be applied wholesale to other national contexts, since we must pay careful attention to the particular historical circumstances and social formations that pertain there. For instance, the selection of "commitment to national unity" as an indicator of reconciliation would cause serious suspicion in the settler colonial context of Canada, where such language is charged with overtones of assimilation and genocide.

After all, it was "national unity" being called for in the aggressively assimilatory White Paper of 1969, whereby political inclusion under the banner of
national unity implied the dispossession of Indigenous nationhood and the
integration of Indigenous peoples within the Canadian political economy.[23]
This brand of reconciliation is certainly not compatible with Indigenous
self-determination.

Furthermore, the IJR speaks of "developing policy and provoking new
analysis and theory on reconciliation in *post-conflict* societies."[24] In South
Africa, there was a formal break with legislative apartheid followed by a
transition (at least nominally) to a democratic dispensation. It is question-
able whether a transitional justice framework of this sort and its language of
"post-conflict" retains the same critical purchase in the settler colonial context
of Canada, where colonialism is an ongoing process marked by the continued
dispossession of Indigenous lands and the suppression of Indigenous sovereignty. In this context, the language of "post-colonial" or "post-conflict" is
surely a contradiction in terms.[25]

Despite these differences, the IJR's call to root our understanding of
reconciliation in a requirement of economic justice is still extremely relevant in the Canadian context.[26] In turning to the Truth and Reconciliation
Commission of Canada's own rethinking of reconciliation, we can ask: What
kinds of indicators might emerge from a framing of reconciliation that is
founded on the principle of Indigenous self-determination and grounded
in Indigenous legal orders and knowledges?

The Case of the Canadian State: Rhetorical Reconciliation

In order to understand the Canadian TRC's reframing of "reconciliation"
in its *Final Report*, it is necessary to provide some historical background to
the term, which predates the TRC. While the term is employed by the Royal
Commission on Aboriginal Peoples (RCAP) of 1996, notably in the context of Indigenous peoples' right to "fashion their own destiny and control
their own governments, lands and resources" as self-determining nations,
the term is more of a secondary reference than a foundational concept of
RCAP.[27] With Prime Minister Stephen Harper's statement of apology to
former students of Indian Residential Schools in 2008, however, the term
entered a new era of public significance.

Although the apology concludes with reference to the TRC and thus to the work that was yet to come, the term soon became associated with the apology and the conservative agenda of the prime minister who issued it. That is, residential schools could now be framed as a "sad legacy" conveniently relegated to the colonial past, all the while ignoring the ongoing inequalities of the colonial present. This understanding of reconciliation as a rhetorical device designed to forgive the Canadian state and its loyal settler subjects of its own wrongdoing in order to move on with its colonial business as usual would motivate much future criticism of the apology and of the "reconciliation" rhetoric that this apology came to signify in certain political circles.[28]

In parallel to the case of South Africa, this critical discourse is concerned with the contradiction of reconciliation without restitution. In Canada, after all, the language of "renewing the relationship" between Indigenous peoples and non-Indigenous Canadians (or between Indigenous nations and Canada) has long been a state-sponsored scandal manufactured as a means of protecting and reproducing colonial privileges.[29] As Glen Coulthard makes clear, the relationship between Indigenous peoples and Canada remains colonial to the core, prefigured by the capitalist drive of a settler colonial state and its attendant legal infrastructure, which finds its material base in the ongoing dispossession of Indigenous lands, lives, and labour for the purpose of capital accumulation.[30]

According to such critiques, any rhetoric of reconciliation that does not take this material reality seriously is inescapably idealist, representing an imaginary relationship between Indigenous peoples and the Canadian state. That the Harper government would systematically fail to follow through on the few promises it made to Indigenous peoples, such as the promise to build tens of thousands of homes on reserves, is but one indication of the post-apology failure to address the economic injustice so characteristic of the Canadian colonial present.

In light of this historical background to the term "reconciliation" prior to the TRC, we are forced to question its current conversational vogue, especially when uttered by representatives of the Canadian state as the pathway to a "new" relationship going forward. Critics of the term would have us ask whether "reconciliation" has become a buzzword spoken in abstraction from the ongoing reality of dispossession, or used as a rhetorical replacement for the resurgence of Indigenous lifeways that run counter to and embody alternatives to Canada's settler colonial structures.[31] It is not enough, as Rachel

George writes in this volume, to merely rethink our national narratives or to decolonize the settler mind. We might instead ask whether the aspirations we assign to the term—along with how we evaluate these aspirations—address the reality of injustice that persists in the present.

The practice of reconciliation, like that of measurement, is not reducible to its ruling class definition. Neither is it predefined or impervious to more radical readings that could point toward a truly emancipatory relationship. By determining what reconciliation is not, we can clear the way for what it could be. To consider such a clearing, I turn to the Truth and Reconciliation Commission of Canada's framing of *reconciliation as relationship*.

The Case of the Canadian TRC: Relational Reconciliation

With the release of its *Final Report* in December 2015, the Truth and Reconciliation Commission of Canada responded to the discursive dominance of rhetorical reconciliation by refusing to relegate the history of residential schools to an isolated chapter of the past. That the schools were but one element of a much larger and longer project of genocide is thrown into bold relief in the opening paragraph of the Commission's Executive Summary: "For over a century, the central goals of Canada's Aboriginal policy were to eliminate Aboriginal governments; ignore Aboriginal rights; terminate the Treaties; and, through a process of assimilation, cause Aboriginal peoples to cease to exist as distinct legal, social, cultural, religious, and racial entities in Canada. The establishment and operation of residential schools were a central element of this policy, which can best be described as 'cultural genocide.'"[32]

The Commissioners were also very clear about the fact that while the schools may have closed, the relationship between Canada and Indigenous peoples remains a colonial one. Foregrounding the ongoing inequalities of Canada's colonial present, the TRC's framing of reconciliation has significant parallels to South Africa's model of radical reconciliation. That there can be no reconciliation without restitution is expressed in the TRC's Legacy Calls to Action, which directly address ongoing inequality in such areas as child welfare, health, education, and language and culture. This assertion is made more explicit in its fourth and fifth principles of reconciliation, which recognize the need to "address the ongoing legacies of colonialism" and to close the "gaps in social, health, and economic outcomes that exist between Aboriginal and non-Aboriginal Canadians," respectively.[33]

This is not to suggest that the TRC's framing of reconciliation is without its contradictions concerning economic justice. The requirement of land restitution, for instance, is for the most part absent from the *Final Report*. However, it is worth highlighting that the TRC recognized that this question (among others concerning economic justice) was given hearing in the Royal Commission on Aboriginal Peoples, which declared that "there must be a fundamental reallocation of lands and resources" for Indigenous nations to be fully self-determining.[34]

The question of economic restitution is also coloured by the report's lack of clarity on the question of reconciling Indigenous and Crown sovereignties. Call to Action 45 certainly lends itself to a radical reading of what repudiating the Doctrine of Discovery and *terra nullius* might mean for the future of Canadian sovereignty and its colonial claims to the land.[35] Yet, it remains ambiguous as to what sort of colonial constraints the TRC's "new vision for Canada" might place on a truly unconditional affirmation of Indigenous self-determination. This vision, after all, is "one that fully embraces Aboriginal peoples' right to self-determination *within, and in partnership with*, a viable Canadian sovereignty," where the qualifier "viable" remains undefined.[36]

From the standpoint of Canada's capitalist mode of production, Crown sovereignty serves to protect and reproduce the relation between capital and the state. In this scenario the Canadian state demands the ongoing dispossession of Indigenous lands for the purpose of capital accumulation. It has been argued that this reality is fundamentally irreconcilable with Indigenous sovereignty and the persistence of non-capitalist economies in Canada, which pose a significant threat to the structuring logic of capital accumulation.[37] If Canadian sovereignty, as the constitutional guardian of the Canadian political economy, is indeed parasitic upon Indigenous sovereignty, then the possibility of genuine reconciliation would demand nothing less than the disintegration of the Canadian capitalist economy. That this contradiction of reconciling sovereignties, which is perhpas a contradiction of reconciling economies, remains unresolved by the Supreme Court of Canada's definition of "reconciliation" is revealing in this regard.

I emphasize this point because the question of ongoing economic inequality and its attendant discourse of "closing the gaps" remains mired in an undeniable economic contradiction: those on one side of the gap (though to drastically different degrees) depend upon the existence of this gap for their own socio-economic well-being. In other words, the discourse of bringing Indigenous peoples "up to speed" with non-Indigenous Canadians, which can sometimes mean according to decidedly non-Indigenous indicators of well-being, conceals the existence of a parasitic settler economy whose very wealth and "prosperity" are premised upon the ongoing dispossession of Indigenous lands.[38] The same could be said of Canada's deceivingly high ranking on the United Nations Human Development Index,[39] which stands in stark contrast to the vastly lower ranking of First Nations.

This is certainly not to suggest that the gaps cannot or should not be closed. As Phil Fontaine highlights in the TRC's Executive Summary report, Canada has a responsibility to "bridge the past to a future in which the gap in the quality of life and well-being between Aboriginal and non-Aboriginal people vanishes, where First Nations poverty is eradicated, where our children have the same opportunities and life chances as other children, and the promises of our treaties are fulfilled."[40] Rather, we must recognize what this responsibility very likely demands: that the contradiction of inequality internal to the Canadian capitalist economy be resolved. Theorizing, practising, and monitoring a process of reconciliation that is capable of transcending this contradiction are therefore essential.

The TRC's reframing of reconciliation also goes beyond a strictly restitution-based model of reconciliation in its decision to centre Indigenous legal orders as essential to the reconciliation process. The report states: "Establishing respectful relationships also requires the revitalization of Indigenous law and legal traditions. It is important that all Canadians understand how traditional First Nations, Inuit, and Métis approaches to resolving conflict, repairing harm, and restoring relationships can inform the reconciliation process."[41]

Underpinned by its adoption of the United Nations Declaration on the Rights of Indigenous Peoples (UNDRIP) as the foundational framework for reconciliation, the TRC presents a relationship-based model of reconciliation grounded in Indigenous knowledge systems, where "the perspectives and understandings of Aboriginal Elders and Traditional Knowledge Keepers of the ethics, concepts, and practices of reconciliation are vital to long-term reconciliation."[42] At the TRC's Traditional Knowledge Keepers forum, Elders and Knowledge Keepers made a critical point. They told the commission that while there was no word for reconciliation in their languages, they knew many concepts, teachings, laws, ceremonies, protocols, and practices that have been used by their respective nations for millennia to resolve conflicts, repair harms, and restore good relations among diverse peoples and with the Earth. From this holistic and long-term perspective, the TRC affirms that a just and genuine reconciliation must be rooted in the resurgence of Indigenous nations and ways of life.[43]

Furthermore, the commission asserts that the cultural revitalization and integration of "Indigenous knowledge systems, oral histories, laws, protocols, and connections to the land into the reconciliation process are essential."[44] It is worth emphasizing that Indigenous connections to the land constitute a definitive feature of the TRC's decidedly *relational* framework for reconciliation. This framework, titled "Reconciliation as Relationship," derives from the TRC's assertion that reconciliation cannot be reduced to any single relationship, whether between Indigenous peoples and non-Indigenous Canadians, between Indigenous nations and the Canadian state, between oneself and one's family, or between the human and the non-human world. On this latter point, the commission states: "Reconciliation between Aboriginal and non-Aboriginal Canadians, from an Aboriginal perspective, also requires reconciliation with the natural world."[45]

It is on the basis of this relational framework that the TRC goes beyond singular concern with the question of economic justice to an even more demanding and ultimately decolonizing framework that challenges Eurocentric models of conflict resolution and instead centres Indigenous legal orders, knowledge systems, and relationships to the natural world as inseparable from the reconciliation process. The TRC's call to decolonize Indigenous–Crown relations and establish genuine nation-to-nation relationships is thus a call to transform not only the economic and political but also the social, legal, and cultural relationships between Indigenous peoples and settlers on the basis of mutual respect and peaceful coexistence on and with the land. According to this vision of relational reconciliation, demanding one form of transformation without the other would be to deny the reality of their interdependence.

Conclusion: Monitoring Relational Reconciliation

The need to monitor progress is reflected in the TRC's call for a National Council for Reconciliation, as described in the introduction to this essay.

Having addressed certain concerns with the practice of measurement more generally, and having identified some of the pitfalls and promises of monitoring reconciliation through an analysis of the South African Reconciliation Barometer, I wish to pose some concluding thoughts concerning how a National Council for Reconciliation might conceive of its efforts to monitor reconciliation. These thoughts are not delivered as a comprehensive blueprint for reconciliation-monitoring efforts. Rather, I hope they may prove helpful in guiding a selection of indicators that more fully capture the expansive framework of relational reconciliation presented by the TRC, indicators that could be monitored over time to reveal whether or not this framework is being fulfilled.

In comparing the IJR's framework for radical reconciliation and the TRC's framework for relational reconciliation, what are the implications for monitoring reconciliation over time? We can conclude that the call to address ongoing economic injustice is a central point of convergence. Both the IJR and the TRC take the position that without fundamental restitution, reconciliation will remain a rhetorical exercise in the service of colonialism. In the case of the South African Reconciliation Barometer, the indicators of reconciliation are in keeping with this position, reflecting the relationship between economic justice and reconciliation. In the case of the TRC, the Legacy Calls to Action constitute an initial inventory of indicators for reconciliation in such areas as child welfare, education, health, language and culture, and justice. These calls make it clear that the relationship between Indigenous peoples and Canada cannot be bettered without addressing the ongoing impacts of colonial institutions at all levels and across all sectors of Canadian society.[46]

The TRC's ten Principles of Reconciliation put forth in its *Final Report* provide a powerful guide for selecting indicators of reconciliation that are accountable to the TRC's framework. For example, in what way are the "perspectives and understandings of Aboriginal Elders and Traditional Knowledge Keepers of the ethics, concepts, and practices of reconciliation" being considered in the selection of indicators? What indicators or other indicia of reconciliation might be identified within particular Indigenous legal orders?[47]

Not all indicators need to be devised anew. The United Nations Declaration on the Rights of Indigenous Peoples, for instance, outlines an extensive list of articles that can serve as indicators in their own right, or from which indicators can be derived. Similarly, with the TRC's Calls to Action and the National Inquiry into Missing and Murdered Indigenous Women and Girls' Calls for Justice, action taken in response should be monitored accordingly. One such project for the TRC's Calls to Action is already under way and available online.[48]

In the words of the TRC, reconciliation is not an end goal, but rather "an ongoing process of establishing and maintaining respectful relationships."[49] Based on this framework, relational reconciliation is not a tepid call for everyone to just "get along" but a transformative call to reimagine and remake relationships. As such, indicators of reconciliation should not be limited to those items that can be "checked off" a list at the expense of those indicators that require different modes of evaluation. This is especially true if the list is overdetermined by what are assumed to be "standard" determinants of well-being, success, progress, etc.[50]

It is also essential to identify and frame indicators in a way that does not reproduce the colonial narrative of the "Indian problem." One example would be the difference between monitoring health outcomes as opposed to monitoring government failure to address these health outcomes. There is a serious risk (and a long history) of framing socio-economic indicators in such a way that Indigenous peoples are presented as broken, as opposed to the brokenness of the Canadian state or its settler population.[51]

Moreover, there is no shortage of indicators that reveal a great deal about whether or not fundamental features of the relationship between Indigenous nations and Canada are being resolved. Canada's ongoing genocide against Indigenous women, girls, and 2SLGBTQQIA people, its ongoing failure to resolve outstanding land claims and honour Treaties with Indigenous nations, and its ongoing resistance to justice for Indigenous children are but a few examples.

As Leanne Simpson points out: "At the end of Trudeau's term, we should have more land than we do now. The environment should be in better shape."[52] The status of land claims, the actual outcomes of settlement agreements, the exercise of Indigenous jurisdiction, and the fulfillment of Treaty obligations could provide indicators regarding the so-called land question. Environmental assessment on the terms and according to the laws and legal processes of Indigenous nations could provide indicators regarding the shape of the environment. This would be in keeping with the TRC's assertion that reconciliation requires reconciliation with the natural world.

What may appear to some as less obvious indicators of reconciliation—in such areas as the arts, community organizing, solidarity within social movements, community "re-storying" efforts,[53] and public memory—should also be given hearing as indicators in their own right.

Whether it is developed in the form of a report or otherwise, a reconciliation monitoring project must serve not only as an evaluative tool to gauge whether or not progress is being made over time but as a stimulant to national conversation on the topic of reconciliation itself. What does public perception polling tell us about the forms of reconciliation that people perceive themselves as committed to? And what do these various degrees of commitment to various forms of reconciliation reveal about the dominance of certain reconciliation frameworks over others, and the need to contest these frameworks?[54]

Ultimately, a project of this sort should provide an informative and valuable resource (including the often overlooked factors of readability and accessibility) that will contribute to the ongoing and future efforts of Indigenous nations, communities, organizations, and movements committed to decolonization. Its indicators should not be considered in isolation from one another but rather in relationship with one another. It is essential to present these relationships in a way that is not merely descriptive—reporting on the status of a specific indicator and letting it speak for itself—but in a way that encourages collective and effective action to change the reality being indicated. In this sense we might demand that the project is not merely one of reconciliation monitoring but also monitoring that reconciles.

Notes

1 On the National Council for Reconciliation, see: TRC, *Calls to Action*, 53–56; TRC, *Final Report*, vol. 6, *Reconciliation*, 232–33.

2 Razack, "Introduction," 12.

3 Mosby, "Administering Colonial Science," 145. As Mosby makes clear in conclusion: "In the end, these studies did little to alter the structural conditions that led to malnutrition and hunger in the first place and, as a result, did more to bolster the career ambitions of the researchers than to improve the health of those identified as being malnourished," 148.

4 Ibid.

5 The discipline of anthropology has what is perhaps one of the more publicly acknowledged histories of such research. For a more recent account of the historical and contemporary relationship between anthropology and Indigenous peoples, see: Starn, "HERE COME THE ANTHROS." For a critical response to Starn's piece, see: Simpson, "Settlement's Secret."

6 To suggest that any one people (in this case, the colonizers) possesses a monopoly on measurement would be to erase those modes of measurement developed by Indigenous peoples according to their own legal and knowledge systems before colonial contact, modes that continue to be practised today in the face of ongoing dispossession. See, among others: Cajete, *Native Science*; D'Arcy, "No Empty Ocean"; Mann, *New Revelations*; and Pascoe, *Dark Emu* on this topic.

7 United Nations Development Programme, "Reconciliation as Framework," 27.

8 Wale, *Confronting Exclusion*, 8.

9 Ibid., 9.

10 In the Canadian context, these critiques include Alfred, "Restitution Is the Real Pathway"; Belcourt, "Opinion"; Coulthard, *Red Skin*; Regan, *Unsettling the Settler Within*; Simpson, *Dancing on Our Turtle's Back*; Simpson, *Mohawk Interruptus*; Watts and King, "TRC Report a Good Start"; among others.

11 Molefe, "T.O. Molefe."

12 On the politics of recognition and multiculturalism in settler colonial contexts, see: Povinelli, *Cunning of Recognition*; Bannerji, *Dark Side of the Nation*; Hale, "Neoliberal Multiculturalism"; Muehlmann, "How Do Real Indians"; and Coulthard, *Red Skin*.

13 Wale, *Confronting Exclusion*, 14.

14 Ibid., 41.

15 Ibid., 33.

16 Ibid., 38.

17 Ibid., 35.

18 Ibid., 8.

19 See Hirsch, MacKenzie, and Sesay, "Measuring the Impacts," 398.

20 That ideological perception is not without its material consequences substantiates this claim. In the case of interracial perception, for instance, the consequences are undeniably material in character. Being shot to death at the hands of a police force or property owner whose actions are fuelled

by institutionally installed perceptions of racialized criminality is but one example of the mutually reinforcing relationship between public perceptions and the material inequality that these perceptions serve to sustain.

21 Wale, *Reflecting on Reconciliation*, 29.

22 Ibid., 10.

23 On the settler state's drive for political economic purity, see: Wolfe, *Traces of History*; Coulthard, *Red Skin*.

24 Wale, *Reflecting on Reconciliation*, 46 (my emphasis).

25 This point has long been made by Indigenous scholars and more recently by theorists of settler colonialism. As Linda Tuhiwai Smith writes: "This is best articulated by Aborigine activist Bobbi Sykes, who asked at an academic conference on post-colonialism, 'What? Post-colonialism? Have they left?'" (*Decolonizing Methodologies*, 24). The Rwanda Reconciliation Barometer also draws on the language and theory of post-conflict in its understanding of reconciliation, noting the following major feature of reconciliation: "whether seen as a process or an end, it occurs after the official conclusion to a conflict, and thus generally aims to resolve 'invisible' conflict" ("Rwanda Reconciliation Barometer," 17).

26 One such earlier critique came from the Royal Commission on Aboriginal Peoples in 1996, from which the TRC draws heavily in its own findings.

27 See, for instance: vol. 5: *Renewal: A Twenty Year Commitment*. The document *Highlights from the Report of the Royal Commission on Aboriginal Peoples* also contains passing references to "reconciliation," notably with reference to the proposal of a new Treaty process as a means to "lead the way to reconciliation between Aboriginal and non-Aboriginal people," available at https://www.aadnc-aandc.gc.ca/eng/1100100014597/1100100014637.

28 As already noted, such critiques include Alfred, "Restitution Is the Real Pathway"; Belcourt, "Opinion"; Coulthard, *Red Skin*; Regan, *Unsettling the Settler Within*; Simpson, *Dancing on Our Turtle's Back;* Simpson, *Mohawk Interruptus;* Watts and King, "TRC Report a Good Start"; among others.

29 Alfred, *Wasáse*; Regan, *Unsettling the Settler Within*.

30 Coulthard, *Red Skin*.

31 On the use of reconciliation and decolonization as a metaphor, see: Tuck and Yang, "Decolonization." On the more recent literature of Indigenous resurgence, see: Simpson, *As We Have Always Done; Dancing on Our Turtle's Back;* Corntassel, "Re-envisioning Resurgence"; Hunt, "Ontologies of Indigeneity"; Simpson, *Mohawk Interruptus*; and Coulthard, *Red Skin*.

32 TRC, *Honouring the Truth*, 1.

33 TRC, *Final Report*, vol. 6, *Reconciliation*, 16.

34 Ibid., 21–23. Regarding land restitution, it is also worth noting that the TRC's adoption of UNDRIP as its principal framework for reconciliation is not without its implications regarding the assertion of Indigenous title. See, for instance: Calls to Action 51 and 52.

35 TRC, *Final Report*, vol. 6, *Reconciliation*, 230.

36 Ibid., 21.

37 See: Coulthard, *Red Skin*. On the logic of primitive accumulation more generally, see: Nichols, "Disaggregating Primitive Accumulation." On the Canadian capital–state relation, see: McCormack and Workman, *Servant State*. See also George in this volume.

38 One need only consider such emblematic examples as the resource extraction or real estate devel-
    opment industry, the criminal justice system, or the child welfare system to begin discerning the
    centrality of Indigenous dispossession to the accumulation of settler capital. In Manitoba, for
    instance, one could argue that the hydro economy depends on continued access to Indigenous
    lands and waters for further resource development. That the vast majority (71 percent) of
    Canadians disagrees with the statement that they benefit from ongoing discrimination against
    Indigenous peoples would suggest that the economic parasitism of the Canadian settler economy
    remains largely unacknowledged (see MacDonald in this volume). For a more detailed account
    of how settlers of various classes benefit from the ongoing dispossession of Indigenous lands, see:
    Battell-Lowman and Barker, *Settler: Identity and Colonialism.*

39 See Jurgens in this volume.

40 TRC, *Honouring the Truth*, 217.

41 TRC, *Final Report*, vol. 6, *Reconciliation,* 11.

42 Ibid., 16.

43 Ibid., 11–13. See also Regan, "Reconciliation and Resurgence."

44 Ibid., 16.

45 Ibid., 13.

46 This call for the fundamental transformation of settler colonial institutions is reflected in Clarke's
    analysis of CFS in this volume, in which she calls for the eventual elimination of CFS as a settler
    colonial institution, while maintaining that a necessary first step is to at least provide equal
    funding to children in care regardless of whether they are on- or off-reserve.

47 On the use of Indigenous legal principles for evaluating community justice initiatives, see
    Napoleon and Friedland, "Gathering the Threads."

48 CBC, "Beyond 94."

49 TRC, *Final Report*, vol. 6, *Reconciliation,* 11.

50 Overdetermining the state of reconciliation according only to public perception and conventional
    socio-economic indicators fails to recognize that these modes of measurement are an incomplete
    indication of the state of reconciliation. This risk of overdetermination must be recognized and
    responded to. The recent work of Margo Greenwood et al. (*Determinants of Indigenous Peoples'
    Health*) is one example of a response to this risk in the context of health, by stressing the impor-
    tance of moving beyond conventional social determinants of health (income, education, etc.)
    to considering Indigenous perspectives and experiences on health and health care in Indigenous
    communities across Canada.

51 Eve Tuck's distinction ("Suspending Damage") between "damage-centred" and "desire-centred"
    research could provide a powerful model for the selection of indicators in this regard. As Mary
    Anne Clarke highlights in this volume, the impact of federally and provincially imposed indicators
    of housing standards on Indigenous children who are then forced into "care" as a result ought to
    remind us of how so-called good intentions are often synonymous with colonial intentions.

52 Simpson, "Smudgier Dispossession."

53 Corntassel, Chaw-win-is, and T'lakwadzi, "Indigenous Storytelling," 139.

54 On precisely this point, see MacDonald and Zurba and Sinclair in this volume.

CHAPTER 4

A MOVE TO DISTRACT

Mobilizing Truth and Reconciliation in Settler Colonial States

RACHEL (YACAAʔAŁ) GEORGE[1]

Forced to confront legacies of trauma emerging from the twentieth century, often referred to as "the century of genocide,"[2] political discourse shifted globally to centre notions of morality and to explore morality's linkages to past, present, and future policy. Responding to the growing demand from communities for redress, states have increasingly relied on transitional justice mechanisms—such as truth commissions—to engage in acts of performative morality as they seek to contend with their own histories of violence. In doing so, states often employ a politics of indifference, extending morality only as far as necessary to pacify the immediate demands for redress and justice. Although these mechanisms are most notably utilized in a transition to democracy,[3] they can and do exist where forms of democracy are already in place. Reacting to generations of Indigenous activism and resistance, settler colonial states—who continue to superimpose their own form of democracy over existing Indigenous democracies and democratic futures—have sought to balance Indigenous demands for justice with their own supposed international humanitarian reputations. To achieve this semblance of balance, Canada and the United States have upheld transitional justice mechanisms with a fervour unseen in preceding decades.

Within the field of transitional justice, apologies, compensation payments, revisions of national histories, commemoration, and truth and reconciliation commissions are often touted as facilitating justice. This promise of justice was initially appealing to Indigenous nations, who have consistently advocated for respect of their self-determination in the face of ongoing colonial violence. However, when utilized in colonial contexts, settler states have often manipulated the idea of justice in order to quell the demands of Indigenous nations without relinquishing power or seriously challenging their own imposed and presumed authority. Instead, settler states relegate violence to the past—simultaneously denying the present and lived experiences of coloniality that Indigenous peoples contend with daily and advancing narratives of victimhood and deficiency that facilitate the continued intervention in Indigenous lives and on Indigenous lands and waters.

Since the 1970s over forty truth commissions have emerged in states across the world,[4] although their use in what is now North America is a more recent phenomenon. As a function of transitional justice, they seek unity and a common future as their goals. In this movement to envision a common future, truth and reconciliation commissions were initiated in Canada and the state of Maine to address the savage removal of Indigenous children from vibrant Indigenous nations. The very existence of these two commissions must be understood as tied to the labour and strength of Indigenous survivors in pressing for truth telling. Yet, despite the apparent responsivity to calls for truth telling, these commissions were ultimately constrained by limited mandates that reduced injustice and harm to a single colonial policy, which silenced the experiences of ongoing colonialism, continued displacement from our territories, and the disruption of our relationships. Considering how Indigenous peoples are impacted by the emerging realities of transitional justice, we must ask: How can these mechanisms advance decolonization when they simultaneously reframe Indigenous experiences in the politics of distraction?[5] This chapter traces the emergence of these two commissions and draws together their similarities despite their differences in scale. I then map the performativity of reconciliation and postulate that while these truth and reconciliation commissions emerge from Indigenous peoples' calls for justice, they produce a robust discourse that takes on a life of its own and is mobilized to distract from the hard work of respecting Indigenous self-determination in all capacities.

Trajectory of Elimination: "The Indian Problem," Genocide, and Indigenous Children

Settler colonial states have remained intent on concealing not only their histories of colonization but the present and ongoing colonial violence

meted out within their imposed borders. They contend that the dismantling of various colonial empires in Africa and Asia after the Second World
War marked the near end of colonialism. This fallacy is further sustained
by the inability of the United Nations to contemplate decolonization for
Indigenous nations within the Special Committee on Decolonization.[6] The
realities of ongoing colonialism remain persistent as Indigenous peoples
resist and push back against settler states' active attempts to fashion their
own legitimacy through Indigenous erasure. To shift attention from their
own illegality, settler colonial states actively engage in revisionism. This can
be heard in the oft-referenced statement, "We also have no history of colonialism,"[7] made in 2009 at the G20 Summit by former Canadian prime
minister Stephen Harper—one year after issuing a formal apology to Survivors of Indian Residential Schools—or in the more recent fear mongering
by President Trump over immigration. This revisionism is fundamental to
state-driven reconciliation, and essential to maintaining settler colonial national myths of benevolence and stewardship of justice and human rights.

Despite these moves for revisionism, enduring indigeneity[8] is tied in an
unbroken thread between past, present, and future, and a testament to the
active resistance to an ongoing colonial assault. Some relationships, such as
those honoured in early Treaties, were intended to be built on respect, peace,
and a nation-to-nation dialogue. However, as Cody O'Neil also points out
in this volume, some of these relationships have been marked by fraudulent
and coerced negotiations, as well as by various settler colonial attempts to
end the so-called Indian problem that was standing in the way of capitalist expansion and territorial control. From the spread of disease, to forced
removal and displacement, Indigenous peoples have been continually resisting
attempts at genocide. Deeply embedded in these trajectories of erasure[9]—
aimed at usurping Indigenous political authority and ending Indigenous
sovereignty—are colonial policies that target the heart and future of our
communities: our children.

Although in existence for decades prior, in 1883 the Canadian government formally adopted the Indian Residential School system as a federal
policy, which operated until the last school closed in 1996. Over 150,000
Indigenous children across the country were violently removed from their
families, communities, and territories. Testimony reveals that these schools
were rampant with abuse of all kinds. Children faced corporal punishment
if they were caught speaking their language, became victims of sexual and

other forms of violence, were subjected to unauthorized nutrition experiments,[10] and endured the devaluing and complete debasement of Indigenous ways of being and knowing. The policy has resulted in various manifestations of intergenerational trauma, and, according to the Truth and Reconciliation Commission of Canada,[11] constitutes cultural genocide.[12]

Following the trajectory of elimination, the United States has also been implementing policies targeting Indigenous children for over a century. This targeting was viewed as an expedient solution to end Indigenous sovereignty, known as the "Indian problem." The shared colonial motivations cannot be lost here as the Indian Residential School system in Canada was, in fact, modelled after Indian Boarding Schools in the United States, and specifically the Carlisle Indian Industrial School in Pennsylvania spearheaded by Captain Richard Henry Pratt. The guiding principles of these schools to "kill the Indian in the man" can be seen as a miniscule departure from earlier mentalities that "the only good Indian is a dead one,"[13] as their desired outcomes similarly sought the end of indigeneity and sovereignty either through actively gunning down Indigenous people or by assimilating them into the settler colonial body politic.

Where colonial states found that the boarding/residential schools were not successful in extinguishing Indigenous nations, both Canada and the United States pursued the removal of Indigenous children through child welfare. In the United States this emerged out of a federal termination policy to close Indian Boarding Schools and to transfer the care of Indian children to the states.[14] Following this logic, as Margaret Jacobs asserts: "If fostering Indian children proved cheaper than institutionalization, adoption provided the ultimate fiscal solution for states and the federal government."[15] Colonial states quickly moved to rip children away from their families, erasing their identities and adopting them out to predominantly white families. This has become known as the Sixties Scoop in Canada, and the Indian Adoption Project in the United States. As Jacobs notes, at the same time that the Indian Adoption Project—a joint project between the Child Welfare League of America and the Bureau of Indian Affairs—was placing Indigenous children into non-Indigenous out-of-state homes, they simultaneously "worked to increase the numbers of Indian children that state agencies placed with non-Indian families within their states," and moved to decrease tribal jurisdiction over child welfare to speed up adoption processes.[16]

Responding to demands that were increasingly mobilized during the American Indian Movement, the United States Congress passed the Indian Child Welfare Act (ICWA) in 1978. The passage of this act is a celebration of resistance and survival, as well as a signal from the federal government of a move to respect tribal sovereignty. At its core, the ICWA was intended to "protect the best interests of Indian children and to promote the stability and security of Indian tribes and families."[17] In recognizing the ties between communities and their children, the Act affirmed a tribe's jurisdiction over their Indigenous children, creating federally recognized priority placement preferences to ensure the continued survival of Indigenous communities.

The Indian Child Welfare Act and its implementation are a strong assertion of self-determination. However, despite the achievement of passing the ICWA, not all states successfully implemented the Act or improved relationships with Indigenous nations. The state of Maine, home to the Passamaquoddy, Penobscot, Micmac, and Maliseet—collectively known as the Wabanaki—in particular continued to remain out of compliance with the ICWA years after its inclusion in state law. A 1984 report noted that the state of Maine was one of the top ten states in the country for placing Indigenous children into foster care,[18] and the rates for Wabanaki child removal remained more or less unchanged from those prior to the passage of the ICWA.

During the 1990s in Maine, a disproportionate number of Maliseet children continued to be removed from their homes and placed in foster care with other families, most of whom were non-Indigenous.[19] A 1999 Federal Pilot Review found the state to be out of compliance with the ICWA and, in particular, that there was a need to focus primarily on "outreach to the tribes and improved implementation of the ICWA,"[20] as some caseworkers found it too "challenging to have the tribe involved."[21] This relentless removal of Wabanaki children continued for decades, and it was found that Wabanaki children were 5.1 times more likely than non-Indigenous children to enter state care between 2000 and 2013.[22] The trajectory of elimination through child removal also continued in Canada during this same period, and it is now openly acknowledged that there are currently more Indigenous children in child welfare than at the height of the residential schools era.[23]

The Indian Child Welfare Act Work Group—a coalition between tribal child welfare workers and Maine state child welfare workers—formed to address the issues of non-compliance following the 1999 Federal Pilot Review. Despite the strides made by the ICWA Work Group to improve compliance—which included state-wide training for child welfare workers on the importance and implementation of the ICWA—a 2009 case review conducted by the Maine Office of Child and Family Services (OCFS) in collaboration with the Wabanaki tribes found that state caseworkers still needed to improve their engagement with tribal caseworkers.[24] The situation remained volatile when in 2010 the Maine Human Rights Commission found "reasonable grounds to believe that Maine OCFS, and one of its caseworkers, discriminated against a Penobscot member because of her 'race, ancestry and national origin.'"[25] It was becoming clear that deep, systemic change would be needed in order to fully implement the Indian Child Welfare Act and to truly respect Wabanaki self-determination.

In the Pursuit of Truth and Justice

Colonialism has not merely held a people in its grip, it seeks to assert its power and control in all spaces. As Franz Fanon notes, it does so "by a kind of perverted logic, it turns to the past of the oppressed people, and distorts, disfigures, and destroys it."[26] For generations this has manifested in the silencing of Indigenous histories and the marginalization of present Indigenous realities. Leanne Simpson notes that the oppressive extension of imperialism and the subjugation of Indigenous peoples have left many trapped individually and collectively in the victimry of the colonial assault.[27] In moving out of this cycle, Linda Tuhiwai Smith notes that "decolonization must offer a language of possibility, a way out of colonialism,"[28] and in the final report of the South African Truth and Reconciliation Commission, Desmond Tutu eloquently stated: "There can be no healing without truth."[29]

Truth commissions have been looked to as an important vehicle for illumining dark chapters of history and long-denied experiences. Yet, as a mechanism of transitional justice, truth commissions have also become a tool by which states signal a distinct break from the past, create legitimacy for institutions tainted by the legacy of authoritarian rule, and emphasize the ways that the new government is committed to protecting and respecting the rights of its citizens.[30] Given that truth commissions are committed to establishing and upholding the rights of citizens, one would assume that their utilization in colonial contexts would also necessitate an embrace of Indigenous rights of self-determination. However, as a function of transitional justice, their principles are guided by goals of national unity and state legitimation. In the adoption of these mechanisms, settler colonial governments avert public scrutiny by emphasizing their own difference from previous governments that may have appeared more genocidal, effectively crafting an image of a lesser of two evils. The privileging of national unity silences Indigenous voices who do not subscribe to state citizenship because they understand themselves to be self-determining nations whose existence extends far before and beyond that of the Canadian or American state. Although truth and reconciliation commissions can, in theory, offer a possibility for change through their victim-centred focus and the affirmation of non-repetition, we must be critical of their capacity to truly honour and advance Indigenous futurity given that their objective is to affirm state systems.

The movement for redress demands that we reflect on the ways in which Western justice mechanisms are limited in their ability to provide justice for Indigenous nations. Often, when settler states have approached redress for injustices, those injustices are so far in the past that traditional Western conceptions of justice, such as prosecution, are not always possible. Moreover, where these mechanisms are possible, the judiciary is a function of the colonial system that has been forced upon Indigenous nations,[31] and remains impeded in its ability to fundamentally question the authority and interests of a state that brought it into existence. Indigenous peoples are continually reminded of this as we seek justice from a system not designed for us.[32] Further, the judiciary has been unable to expand to address the interconnected and long-standing impacts of the injustice, or to work to reunify and regenerate our families and communities.[33]

In contrast, truth commissions are designed to provide "justice" on a more restorative basis aimed at healing the community as a whole instead of prosecuting individuals. In this context, through its victim-centred focus, truth can become a form of social empowerment in which survivors of violence are given the space to reclaim their lives and move to understand the nature of their subjugation.[34] As givers of testimony, individuals rupture silences about colonial policies of assimilation and oppression, giving voice to long-denied or stifled experiences.[35] In situating our experiences within the language of trauma, there is, as Dian Million notes, a direct "connect[ion] to a promise for justice, since it locates blame for historical acts of colonization to present conditions in Indigenous lives."[36] The promise of justice and the creation of opportunity for Indigenous peoples and communities to truly represent themselves and their histories in the face of ongoing colonialism are a powerful experience, particularly because settler governments denying our ability to represent ourselves is a strategy by which they have attempted to eliminate us. By giving testimony, there is an opportunity for Indigenous peoples to reclaim our history, which, Smith notes, is a critical step in the decolonial process.[37] In her words, the power of reclaiming our history is "not simply about giving an oral account or a genealogical naming of the land and the events which raged over it, but a very powerful need to give testimony to and restore a spirit, to bring back into existence a world fragmented and dying."[38]

Establishing the Parameters of Truth in Canada

In the early 2000s, the Canadian justice system became bogged down with tens of thousands of lawsuits against the government and the churches that ran residential schools. The system was facing the largest class action lawsuit in Canadian history. As a result, the Indian Residential Schools Settlement Agreement officially came into effect in 2007 and represented a multifaceted approach intended to provide a semblance of justice. This layered agreement included Common Experience Payments, an Independent Assessment Process, and commemoration activities, and established the mandate for the Truth and Reconciliation Commission of Canada (TRC), which officially began its work in 2009.

Granted a one-year extension in 2014 due to the federal government's failing to hand over legally mandated documents,[39] the Canadian TRC heard testimony from across the country in both community hearings and national events for six years. Although established through a Western court, the TRC was guided by a Survivors' Committee and other Indigenous Elders and Knowledge Keepers. With their guidance, the commission made a conscious effort to create space for Indigenous peoples, and to honour Indigenous traditions, ceremonies, ways of being, and knowledges.[40] The commission offered several different avenues for sharing testimony, including a Sharing Panel in front of all or a select number of TRC commissioners, a Sharing Circle facilitated by an Elder, or private statement gathering. In addition to hearing testimony, the commission also gathered extensive information from Canadian government and church records regarding the administration of residential schools.

In June 2015 the Truth and Reconciliation Commission of Canada held its closing ceremony in Ottawa and issued ninety-four Calls to Action. The complete multi-volume *Final Report* was released on 15 December 2015.

Approaching Justice in Dawnland
Discussions of a truth and reconciliation commission in Maine as the best avenue to, as Esther Attean et al. state, create "recognition and acknowledgement of the past"[41] emerged through the work of community members, tribal child welfare workers, and state child welfare workers—those individuals who were working on the front lines of child welfare. Growing out of this grassroots initiative, the Maine Wabanaki-State Child Welfare Truth and Reconciliation Commission (hereafter Maine Wabanaki TRC) was brought into being through a collaborative agreement signed by the five Wabanaki chiefs and the governor of the State of Maine, Paul LePage. Following the Declaration of Intent—signed in 2011—the commission was formally seated in February 2013. This commission was given a twenty-seven-month mandate "to uncover and acknowledge the truth, create opportunities to heal and learn from that truth, and collaborate to operate the best child welfare system possible for Wabanaki children . . . [with a] focus on the period from passage of the 1978 Indian Child Welfare Act (ICWA) to the authorization of the Mandate. This investigation will also include information that contributed to the passage of the ICWA in order to put understanding of the truth in a proper context."[42]

In marked contrast to other truth commissions globally, including the Truth and Reconciliation Commission of Canada, the Maine Wabanaki TRC moved to give ownership and control of the process back to each community. Grounded in ethical Indigenous research methodologies, the commission's research was guided by Wabanaki peoples through every step of the process. For example, the commissioners and research coordinator structured an outline for statement gathering and sought input from each of the five Wabanaki communities (Maliseet, Micmac, Passamaquoddy at Motahkomikuk, Passamaquoddy at Sipayik, and Penobscot). The result was a process that genuinely looked different within each community and made a conscious effort to be responsive to each community's desires and needs.

Understanding the centrality of our relationality, the commission sought to honour the importance of building relationships and trust by holding a welcoming event within each community. These events focused on getting to know one another through visiting and sharing a meal, instead of on gathering statements. Outside of these welcoming events, statement gathering was organized in partnership with Maine Wabanaki REACH—a cross-cultural collaboration that advances Wabanaki self-determination—who worked to provide community organizing and support for communities throughout the work of the Maine Wabanaki TRC, and helped to guide the Maine Wabanaki TRC in ways that would be the most beneficial for Wabanaki communities. On several occasions over the course of the Maine Wabanaki TRC's mandate, the research coordinator, a commissioner, and occasionally a few statement gatherers would travel back to communities to hear Wabanaki stories—formally called "statement gathering"—at the request of Wabanaki peoples. Similar to the Canadian TRC, the Maine Wabanaki TRC also conducted document-based research within the state archives and with the Department of Health and Human Services. In June 2015 the Maine Wabanaki TRC held its closing ceremony and offered fourteen recommendations within its *Final Report*.

The Possibility and Hope of Truth in Canada and Maine
Both the Canadian TRC and the Maine Wabanaki TRC were born of the labour and strength of Indigenous peoples in calling for truth telling and justice. For too long Indigenous experiences have been stifled under the guise of the supposed good intentions of the settler colonial state, and the denial of our collective experience has become a barrier to healing and change. For generations we have not been the final arbiters of our own stories in national discourse. The promise of justice facilitated through our truth telling pushes back against ongoing colonialism and its continued attempts at erasure. As previously mentioned, the movement to deny Indigenous self-representation has sought to remove us from discourse while the state simultaneously pursues our physical erasure from our homelands/waters. These moments of reclaiming stand as powerful markers of our continued resistance and resurgence.

Although constricted by mandates that reduced injury to a single colonial policy—residential schools and child welfare policies, respectively in the two TRCs—there was a degree of agency in how each of these commissions met the terms of their mandates. Given that mechanisms are often driven by hegemonic society and reflect hegemonic culture, it is essential that justice initiatives implemented for Indigenous communities predominantly reflect

the world views and beliefs of those communities. Settler colonial governments' continued refusal to acknowledge the historical roots of the conditions
still in existence today have simultaneously denied our claims to humanity,
to having a history, and, for some, to a sense of hope.[43] Reversing this means
centring Indigenous ways of being and knowing in a way that creates space
for Indigenous peoples, as well as affords control and ownership of the process
to Indigenous communities. Anything less than this is yet another colonial
injustice and a wrongful assertion of power.

In privileging and centring Indigenous epistemology and ontology, the
Canadian TRC and the Maine Wabanaki TRC placed emphasis most strongly
on hearing the truths of the Indigenous peoples they were working with. By
focusing on their stories, these two truth commissions sought to transfer
ownership of that specific history from the settler state to Indigenous peoples
and created a new oral history record. Constructing a place for continued
learning and dialogue, both of these commissions established archives to
preserve these stories in perpetuity, which can be viewed as a limited and
momentary rebalancing of the unequal power structures that have allowed
settler thinking and colonial denial to persist.

Within the complex operations of these commissions—which certainly
had nuanced and varied reception within Indigenous nations and among the
settler public—the centring of Indigenous voices has undeniably created new
space for the celebration of survival. Testimony shared in these forums offers
a moment to celebrate strength, courage, and survival, in which, in the words
of Teresa Godwin Phelps, "pain is acknowledged by an official body that is
not, [in theory,] constrained or controlled by the official state."[44] For some,
the opportunity to engage with a truth commission, to be heard and vali-
dated, can be positive and provides a significant avenue for healing.

Truth at the Expense of Justice

Despite their relative agency in meeting the terms of their mandates, truth
commissions addressing violence in settler colonial contexts too often engage with truth in problematic ways. They do so by reducing harm to singular past policies—whose foundations in historical and ongoing genocidal
settler colonial logic often escape those who engage with the TRC. Truth becomes constructed as within the past, devoid of connection to ongoing colonial territorial theft and violence in ways that potentially foreclose future

discussions of redress and justice. These instances of reconciliation become strangled by state mandates and restrictions that hinge on and advance the notion of *truth as justice,* where the ability to speak to specific violence is viewed by the public as the fulfillment of justice, without any change to the colonial structures that continue to facilitate violence. In these spaces, as Audra Simpson notes, "the cost of justice is pain, and its value is set within a market of sympathy."[45] Our victimization and pain become the truth that is sought rather than justice, thereby constructing what I refer to as the "spectacle of victimization": an authoritative forum for settler consumption of Indigenous stories of victimization, and the reproduction of the very formations of colonial power that we seek freedom from.

As the bodies emboldened to seek the truth, truth and reconciliation commissions craft themselves as the singular sovereign authority in the revision of collective history. By seeking particular details focused on wrongdoing, the complexity of Indigenous experiences is erased in order to advance an overarching narrative of right and wrong, of victim and perpetrator. While testimony in these spaces is upheld for its ability to shed light on a supposed "dark chapter of history," the pivotal focus on violence simultaneously demands a reconfiguration of Indigenous experiences within the confines of victimhood, where all aspects of indigeneity are spectacularly tied to colonial violence devoid of resistance. For example, in Rosemary Nagy and Emily Gillespie's 2015 media analysis about truth and reconciliation in Canada, they note that reporting was primarily framed around "stories of abuse, forgiveness, and healing."[46] While it would be a failure to negate understandings of how our experiences as Indigenous peoples include our survival through colonial violence, a narrative that focuses predominantly on abuse overstates the power of the colonial state and limits our agency and strength by marginalizing stories of our resistance. The reconstruction of our stories within the confines of victimhood temporally disconnected from the present creates a distance between the settler as consumer and Indigenous stories for their consumption. An example of this consumptive distancing is most visceral when Audra Simpson described how, at a TRC event in Victoria, people "ate popcorn and hotdogs, and cried with [those who told their stories]."[47]

In its construction the spectacle of victimization forces a confrontation of complicity and a redefinition of settler colonial national myths—such as those about benevolence and stewardship of justice and human rights—as it emphasizes experiences of violence. Yet, these windows of confrontation are only briefly embodied in TRC events, as the emphasis on settler passivity[48] allows for a self-congratulatory quick progression through guilt and shame in the consumption of victimized indigeneity. As Simpson stresses, a theatre is created for Canadians and Americans "to sit within and watch as their history is resorted . . . and repaired for them,"[49] yet there is no real demand for active engagement. Faced with momentary discomfort, the construction of truth as an entity of the past is a deliberate tactic to allow settlers to distance themselves from complicity and to occupy a space of absolution, while simultaneously laying the burden of labour on Indigenous peoples to become "reconciled, or perhaps reintegrated (or 'conciled'/ integrated) into Canadian society," as Kim Stanton asserts.[50] This performativity structures the discourse of reconciliation, prevents substantial change to the colonial relationship, and instead moves to reproduce colonial power.

According to Courtney Jung, these state-endorsed initiatives of reconciliation, including apologies, truth commissions, and reparations, "are designed in part to allow the government and the dominant (settler) society to finally say to [Indigenous] peoples 'OK, now we're even,'"[51] while simultaneously assuaging any settler and state responsibility and guilt for past and current abuses. These mechanisms seek to remove the legitimate justice demands of Indigenous peoples as a challenge to the legitimacy of the settler colonial nation.[52]

In the Canadian context the explicit examination of the residential school system set Indigenous experiences within the confines of the past. While the TRC produced a robust *Final Report* that drew attention to the linkages between current experiences and the legacies of the past, that reality is often something that escapes many settlers bearing witness to the TRC process.[53] "Reconciliation" has since been picked up and mobilized in ways that are not deeply informed by or connected to the breadth of the TRC *Final Report* or its vision for the future, making reconciliation's current manifestations potentially dangerous. Further, any connections to current experiences are framed as symptomatic of the residential school system, not of the wider experiences of colonialism and the multiplicity of genocidal attempts. This structuring allows the Canadian settler colonial government to seamlessly co-opt the narrative. Similarly, the Maine Wabanaki TRC had a limited mandate that could not reflect on the breadth of the colonial experience, although there was a marked attempt to draw attention to this in their final report. In both cases, these restricted framings allow settlers to believe that once the issues identified by these commissions are addressed and, it is hoped, rectified, the colonial process is over, injustice is resolved, and everyone can move on. Yet, colonial violence persists and can be seen in the high numbers of missing and murdered Indigenous women, girls, and Two-Spirits; in the criminal-ization of Indigenous peoples for their presence on the land and water; in the continued savage removal of Indigenous children from their commu-nities; and the list goes on. Each violence is ultimately linked back, not to the removal of Indigenous children through residential schools or through child welfare practices, but to the colonial process that has been intent on Indigenous erasure from our territories. In order for there to be an informed connection between reconciliation, truth, and justice, we must understand these practices as part of a larger ongoing colonial trajectory of elimination.

Within this structured public discourse, any discussion of topics related to our understandings of self-determination and relationships to our terri-tories are silenced in a deliberate attempt to erase challenges to the assumed sovereignty of the colonial state. For settler colonial nations whose authority over territory is imposed, it is not profitable to continue addressing injustice or to draw attention to the legitimate justice demands of Indigenous nations. Affirming the self-determination of Indigenous nations beyond conceptions of self-government would create uncertainty, and it is believed that this could negatively impact government-approved projects in the extractive industry. Beyond this, as Sheryl Lightfoot notes, Canadian national identity focuses on two important features: "Canada's image as a global steward of human rights; and multiculturalism."[54] To genuinely address the breadth of ongoing colonialism and violence would bring into question national identity—a dilemma that settler colonial governments have no intention of truly address-ing because justice for that violence would require a relinquishment of power.

Given the emphasis that transitional justice mechanisms place on the commitment to protecting and respecting the rights of its citizens, one would assume that when these mechanisms are used to address violence commit-ted against Indigenous peoples, the respect and protection of rights would include genuine self-determination and the ability to live and govern ourselves as we see fit. Instead, these mechanisms become co-opted by settler colonial-ism and unambiguously advance national unity while seeking to absorb our subjugated bodies into multiculturalism. These kinds of projects not only marginalize peoples who do not subscribe to the colonial state citizenship, but they actively silence the nationhood movement among Indigenous peoples and deny true expressions of self-determination unmitigated by state author-ity.[55] How can these projects contribute to decolonization when they seek to deny Indigenous nationhood and actively promote the maintenance of the state and colonial intervention into Indigenous lives and on Indigenous lands and waters?

The breadth of the colonial experience goes beyond single instances of violence; it has been a drawn-out assault manifesting in numerous laws and policies aimed at our erasure from the land/seascape. The danger of a state-driven reconciliation paradigm is that it allows for settler states to relegate all injustice to one specific instance, and, by seeking the truth of that instance, wrongfully claim that justice has been achieved. In doing so the mobiliza-tion of truth and reconciliation through these mechanisms denies current and ongoing injustices as well as further claims for restitution. The encapsu-lation of injustice to residential schools, or to Wabanaki experiences in the child welfare system, silences the complexities and roots of our experiences. The packaging of injustices into a neat box that the state government is able to deal with makes true justice for our communities impossible.

The Convergence of Recognition and Reconciliation: Social Inclusion and Ongoing Injustice

The creation of truth and reconciliation commissions in Canada and Maine has created a public space for Indigenous peoples to give voice to their expe-riences with colonial injustice, whether that be residential schools or child welfare. While there are marked differences in their operations due to their individual scales—one addressing reconciliation on a national level, the oth-er confined to the boundaries of a state—it remains undeniable that their existence has been important for Indigenous nations as we move to heal at the individual, family, and community levels. At the same time Indigenous peoples must hold the duality of the mechanism's promise of justice and the physical and material impacts of consuming victimized indigeneity. Con-siderations of the extent to which these commissions have altered Indige-nous-settler relationships will likely continue to proliferate in academic dis-course for the next few years. While the healing that has occurred on more personal levels is integral to building healthy communities, it is not the only necessity for our nationhood.

Healing is a critical step along a decolonizing pathway, but it does not force or fully advance the substantial systemic change that is required for true justice and decolonial relationality. The government of Canada has strategically framed the Canadian TRC and its Calls to Action as the full embodiment of justice and its commitment to improved relations between Indigenous and non-Indigenous peoples. However, watching this enactment of reconciliation unfold has only illuminated the new ways the Canadian government is reformulating an assimilative policy through the inclusion of indigeneity within a multicultural Canadian identity. As Glen Coulthard notes in *Red Skin, White Masks,* "reconciliation politics" have converged with a slightly older "politics of recognition," advocating that institutions recognize and accommodate Indigenous cultural difference as an important means of reconciling the colonial relationship between Indigenous peoples and the state.[56]

The celebration of cultural difference, and subsequently the creation of spaces to celebrate that difference, is a substantial component of the recommendations made by the Canadian TRC. For example, an entire section of the Calls to Action focuses on language and culture with the affirmation in Call 14.1 that "Aboriginal languages are a fundamental and valued element of *Canadian culture and society*" (my emphasis).[57] Through this affirmation, indigeneity—as expressed through language—is disassociated from Indigenous nations and encapsulated within Canadian society, and subsequently positioned to form a part of Canadian national identity. This is not to say that recommendations about language revitalization are not important but to draw attention to the danger and harm of attempting to remove Indigenous languages as an integral part of our nationhood and into a Canadian multicultural identity. In this context the creation of spaces to celebrate cultural expressions of indigeneity is a mechanism by which Indigenous peoples, through multiculturalism, are brought into the fold of Canadian society.

The rhetoric of the inclusion discourse in Canada is exceptionally prevalent in the municipal affirmations of reconciliation. Following the Canadian Truth and Reconciliation Commission's National Events, cities across Canada began proclaiming a "Year of Reconciliation." Among these are Vancouver, Toronto, Edmonton, Calgary, Winnipeg, and, in 2017, Victoria. During the Alberta National Event in 2014, Edmonton Mayor Don Iverson committed to three projects, including "creating more opportunities for Aboriginal

cultural events."[58] It is through these initiatives that our indigeneity becomes
relegated to sole instances of cultural performance (soft rights) and disassociated from our self-determining authority over our territories (hard rights).[59]
The reduction of indigeneity to cultural performance is of fundamental
benefit to the nation state because it does not seek to challenge the imposed
authority of the Canadian state over Indigenous peoples, and our sovereignty
and self-determination.

The reconciliation paradigm's emphasis on the accommodation or
"inclusion" of Indigenous cultural difference embodies a regeneration of
assimilation that seeks to further the state's multicultural policy.[60] Beyond
this objective the recognition and accommodation of cultural difference
are also advanced as an avenue for settler capitalistic benefit. The increasing
number of declarations of a "Year of Reconciliation" can be understood not as
a deep honouring of a new relationship with Indigenous peoples—grounded
in respecting Indigenous self-determination and the return of stolen lands—
but as a move that stimulates tourism through the creation of an attractive
civic profile. Addressing the topic of "reconciliation" has become an industry
in itself with the dramatic increase of funding opportunities to expression
in the arts. Yet, these funding bodies constrain the narrative of reconciliation[61] by solely focusing on residential schools, as evident in *Going Home
Star* by the Royal Winnipeg Ballet, or by crafting the dialogue through artis-
tic consumption.

Vancouver, British Columbia, has become one of the most well-known
examples of its creation of a civic profile by using Indigenous designs throughout the 2010 Winter Olympics and subsequently through its declaration of
a "Year of Reconciliation."[62] This has advanced the most blatant form of
consumption at the expense of Indigenous nationhood. The exploitation of
indigeneity in this context further erases Coast Salish people from their territories as—in the words of Dylan Robinson and Keren Zaiontz—"indigeneity
from elsewhere is imported as a permanent local art installation"[63] in
Kwakwaka'wakw/Tlingit Corrine Hunt's *Truce* sculpture, in using her design
on the Olympic medals, or in using the Inukshuk as a symbol for the 2010
Olympic games. The city's efforts can be seen as compliant with Call to
Action 91—"We call upon the officials and host countries of international
sporting events such as the Olympics, Pan Am, and Commonwealth games
to ensure that Indigenous peoples' territorial protocols are respected, and
local Indigenous communities are engaged in all aspects of planning and

participation in such events"[64]—despite the fact that they resulted in no structural change for the Musqueam, Skwxwú7mesh, Tsleil-Waututh, or Líl̓wat peoples on whose territory the Olympics were hosted. Using indigeneity for capitalistic opportunity further alienates and dispossesses Indigenous peoples from our lands and waters by erasing our distinct nationhood, and instead incorporating a pan-Indigenous culture under the umbrella of "Canadian" to enrich the identity of the nation state.

Initiatives like these do not create spaces that honour our self-determination. Instead, they create spaces where we are *afforded the opportunity* to live "Indigenously" through our culture, and nothing else, precisely because it is palatable and does not challenge the assumed authority of the settler state. When Indigenous peoples become strictly imagined through the advancement of our soft rights—cultural rights such as those embodied in our languages, songs, prayers, and art—we are removed as a challenge to settler access to our relations, to our territories. Yet, what this particular advancement of rights fails to conceptualize is that our culture is deeply tied to our relationality with kin in the physical places we call home. Structuring reconciliation as embodied in initiatives of education and opportunities for cultural events, without the hard work of respecting our self-determination to govern and be in relationship with our territories, leads to feigned reconciliation. It allows settlers to believe, as suggested in a "Declaration of Action" at the TRC Final Event in Ottawa, that: "We are committed to supporting the fulfillment of the vision of Aboriginal peoples, to building a fairer and more just country... we will work, each in our own way, and together, towards achieving the goal of reconciliation and in the end, *a much stronger, more inclusive Canada*" (my emphasis).[65]

The extent to which non-Indigenous peoples and the Canadian government have fallen in love with the performativity of reconciliation should speak volumes to the inability of its current formulation to advance decolonization and self-determination. As scholars like Eve Tuck and K. Wayne Yang and Paulette Regan have stressed, decolonization is inherently unsettling,[66] and cannot be achieved by attempting "to maintain as much comfort or privilege as possible."[67] Instead, as Art Manuel asserts: "[The government and Canadian people] do not really seem to understand the concept, but they truly love that word. Everything is reconciliation. When they join a round dance, they call that reconciliation. When their eyes tear up in discussing our poverty, that is reconciliation. At the same time, when they are denying our constitutional rights, they call that reconciliation of Aboriginal title with Crown title. In fact, every new plan to steal from us is called reconciliation."[68] The alteration of Indigenous peoples' vision to live freely as self-determining nations into a state-building project of inclusion within the settler state framework only advances the colonial relationship under the guise of "justice." This discourse furthers the state's and settlers' imposed authority over Indigenous peoples and does not represent anything even remotely close to self-determination or justice. What is needed is not social inclusion, or a bringing of Indigenous peoples into the folds of Canadian society through multiculturalism. As it is currently envisioned by the state, reconciliation will not solely achieve decolonization.

The politics of recognition have also permeated the process surrounding the Maine Wabanaki TRC. Within the context of Wabanaki relations in Maine, Governor Paul LePage continually used "recognition" as a bargaining chip in his assertions of state authority over Wabanaki peoples. In April 2013 Governor LePage threatened to withdraw support from the Maine Wabanaki TRC[69] if the Passamaquoddy community "didn't stand down on their claim to authority over tribal members' right to harvest elvers."[70] Although the governor had no authority to disband the independent work of the Maine Wabanaki TRC, that did not discourage him from attempting to use the commission in the politics of distraction, or from making threats on more than one occasion. Later that April LePage again threatened to withdraw support from the TRC due to his disapproval of one of the selected commissioners.[71] By recognizing certain injustices only when Wabanaki tribes are toeing the party line of imposed state authority, the state perpetuates a violent colonial relationship. This exploitation of the Maine Wabanaki TRC as a bargaining chip effectively denies the ongoing injustices faced by these communities. It forces Wabanaki people to consider trading some rights for others, depending on what the state considers most valuable.

Colonial Attempts to Reconceptualize Relationality as Absent of Our Homelands/Waters

The Truth and Reconciliation Commission of Canada's ninety-four Calls to Action covered an expansive set of topics, including improvements to child welfare, the justice system, education, health care, and calls to support language revitalization. While, if enacted, they would certainly represent moves of tangible improvement in Indigenous lives, these Calls to Action must simultaneously be held as half-measures toward decolonization due to their attempts to reconceptualize Indigenous relationalities. The primary focus on correcting the socio-economic disparities between Indigenous peoples and settlers is inherently tied to Canada's attachment to its multicultural identity.[72] Their connection to a policy of multiculturalism, and, by extension, assimilation, does not seek improvement for the benefit of Indigenous self-determination but for an improved global image. This emphasis on improving socio-economic conditions for Indigenous nations simultaneously silences the place-based existence of Indigenous peoples. Our relationality—with each other, with our territories, and with other beings over time—remains fundamental to our nationhood and self-determination. Yet, instead of insisting on the restitution of stolen lands, the discussion of reconciliation and territoriality is framed within the context of economic development and "sustainability."

Although the TRC may have asserted, "reconciliation between Aboriginal and non-Aboriginal Canadians, from an Aboriginal perspective, also requires reconciliation with the natural world. If human beings resolve problems between themselves but continue to destroy the natural world, then reconciliation remains incomplete,"[73] their capacity to envision this moves in the opposite direction. Within the pages of their *Final Report* volume devoted to reconciliation, the TRC notes that in its view, "sustainable reconciliation on the land involves *realizing the economic potential of Indigenous communities* in a fair, just, and equitable manner that respects the rights of their self-determination" (my emphasis).[74] The structuring of reconciliation within the scope and bounds of capitalistic exploitation furthers primitive accumulation (defined by Coulthard as "the violent transformation of non-capitalist forms of life into capitalist ones").[75] Given the Canadian state's manipulated definition of self-determination,[76] framing "sustainable reconciliation" through relationships based in economic potential allows the state to selectively deny self-determination when a nation's decisions do not align with "national interest."[77] This particular framing of reconciliation can be understood as a direct extension of the Canadian judiciary's contemplation of reconciliation—the reconciliation of Aboriginal rights and title with imposed Crown sovereignty—and moves away from understanding our relationality—and the responsibilities stemming from those relationships—as essential to our understandings of self-determination.

The discourse of social inclusion, as discussed in the context of Canada's deliberate consumption of indigeneity, is somewhat more silenced in the State of Maine following the completion of the Maine Wabanaki-State Child Welfare Truth and Reconciliation Commission. However, the denial of self-determination and the furthering of primitive accumulation are not. Wabanaki communities in Maine continue to deal with the ramifications of the 1980 Maine Indian Claims Settlement Act,[78] which emerged from an out-of-court settlement that "awarded $81-million to the Passamaquoddy Tribe, the Penobscot Nation, and the Houlton Band of Maliseet. The tribes reacquired 300,000 acres of land—almost all of it went to the Passamaquoddy and Penobscot—and the Houlton Band of Maliseets received federal recognition and a small portion of that money."[79]

The Maine Indian Claims Settlement Act (MICSA) was the product of the demand to handle unsettled title and land claim issues within the State of Maine. In a process that was divisive across the state and within communities, the final agreement granted significantly less than what should have been awarded to Wabanaki communities. Even with the MICSA, confrontations over jurisdiction continue. In 2012 the Penobscot Nation filed a lawsuit against the state, who was trying to run roughshod over their relationality with what is now known as the Penobscot River case. The Penobscot firmly pressed the state that "its reservation includes the water in the river because of the tribe's sustenance fishing rights."[80] Beyond this, the case is grounded in Penobscot self-determination, authority, and their stewardship over the health and well-being of the river—each firmly rooted in maintaining the vibrancy and health of Penobscot relationalities.

One year after the case was filed against the State of Maine, municipalities along the Penobscot River pushed back against Penobscot self-determination by intervening in the case. Growing out of fear mongering that the Penobscot would somehow restrict access to the river, the surrounding municipalities were granted intervener status, and, according to Judy Harrison in the *Bangor Daily News*, moved to support "the state's contention that the reservation included the islands but not the water. The municipalities claimed that a ruling in the tribe's favor would give it control over water quality on the river and allow the tribe to impose stricter rules than the state does on municipal discharges into the river."[81] The case reached a verdict in December 2015, which ruled against the Penobscot Nation and their sovereignty and

self-determination. The decision came a mere six months after the completion of the Maine Wabanaki TRC mandate.

The structural containment and redefinition of relationality within the
state's approach and mobilization of reconciliation affirms underlying colonial fantasies of our erasure. The mobilization of the settler colony's embrace
of reconciliation understood only as interpersonal healing and cultural expression seeks to remove Indigenous nations as a challenge to colonial fantasies of
entitlement and legitimacy. When nations are continually resisting against
colonial violence to assert their authority, rights, and responsibilities in their
territories, the work of justice and envisioning new relationships is impossible. As Leanne Simpson notes, "as reconciliation becomes institutionalized,
I worry our participation will benefit the state in an asymmetrical fashion,
by attempting to neutralize the legitimacy of Indigenous resistance."[82] Any
mechanism that distills violence and injustice to one specific set of experiences, and privileges the assertion of colonial power over Indigenous peoples,
only silences and neutralizes our responsibilities and everyday acts of resurgence[83] by disseminating a limited truth and creating an illusion that justice
has been served.

Redefining Justice and Freedom as Relational

The mobilization of truth and reconciliation by the settler colonial state
forces us to question their capacity to creatively build and envision decolonial Indigenous futures. Mechanisms that emerged from the resistance of
Indigenous peoples have been picked up and manipulated by the state in
order to advance the state's own objectives and reproduce the very config-
urations of colonial, racist, and patriarchal state power that we sought to
push back against. This manipulation stands in stark contrast to the hopes
we carried when we shared our stories in these spaces. While it would be
fallacious to suggest that TRCs can *only* result in the reproduction of colonial power, there remains a concern that our participation will benefit
the state in an asymmetrical fashion. Given this, we must remain conscious
of the tensions in a truth commission's promise of justice, and the tangible
repercussions of advancing narratives of victimization and the redefinition
of Indigenous relationality as devoid of our responsibilities with all life in
our territories. The colonial manipulation of processes such as truth and
reconciliation commissions—which hold importance in the healing of our

nations—suggests that we must remain critical of the emancipatory potential of these bodies when they work within state-sanctioned legal and political structures. As Leanne Simpson stresses, the state has become adept at
"manipulat[ing] the processes that maintain settler colonialism to give the
appearance that the structure is changing."[84]

There is an undeniable importance that these truth commissions hold
for our communities; after all, they are born of the love of our kin for our
relations and a determination to envision beautiful futures of freedom for
our nations. I have been privileged to be asked to hold some of these stories
and to bear witness to multigenerational resistance and strength. In those
moments and through relations continually built, I see the centrality that
our stories have in our healing. The sharing of these stories has moved deep
healing in individuals, between family members, and within communities.
This is the pivotal work of the TRCs—in the ways they have created space
for us to hear stories between relations and to move toward healing in our
own communities. Esther Altvater, co-director of Maine Wabanaki REACH,
stresses this most eloquently:

> It's not about making white people feel welcome, it's not about making
> you guys feel . . . it's not about you. It's about Sipayik . . . it's about my
> people feeling safe, and honoured, and listened to, and validated. So,
> there's that moment where you choose to have your voice. . . . And
> I knew all along in this process, just as there are competing interests
> with truth, healing, and change—sometimes they compete with each
> other. So does truth and reconciliation. Because, we knew from the
> beginning, that non-native people wanted to jump right into the
> reconciliation: "why can't we just all . . ." you know? . . . All through
> this process, you know since 2008, I have thought: "we should have just
> called it a truth commission," because reconciliation is not, it's not my
> goal really, I mean, the healing of my people is my goal.[85]

In holding the duality of these transitional justice mechanisms and
reflecting on their emancipatory potential, we must remain wary of their
capacity to advance decolonial futures, as they often result in minimal relinquishment of colonial power. Instead, as argued above, the mobilization of
truth and reconciliation reproduces the very structures of power we sought
to leave behind. In the silencing of our place-based responsibilities to our
relations, states are able to craft indigeneity as embodied in our soft rights,

while running roughshod over our hard rights to live as self-determining nations. The socio-political desire to centre discussions of the "good intent" of these commissions seeks to alleviate complicity and to move away from the tangible ramifications that come with consuming victimized indigeneity. These narratives of victimization allow colonial intervention to persist in Indigenous lives and on Indigenous lands and waters. These relentless interventions are evident in the continued savage removal of Indigenous children from vibrant nations and the violent exploitation of the land in the face of ongoing Indigenous resistance. As Aimé Césaire eloquently states, "the essential thing is that their highly problematic subjective good faith is entirely irrelevant to the objective implications of the evil work they perform as the watchdogs of colonialism."[86] Although these commissions were born of the love of Indigenous peoples, government manipulations and distortions of justice through their work amount to nothing more than, as Matt James says, "politics of distraction, yet another exercise of 'affirmative repair' or 'settler magic' aimed at staving off demands for the restitution of stolen lands."[87] Jeff Corntassel and Cindy Holder maintain that countering the politics of distraction requires "decolonization strategies centred on action via recovery of Indigenous homelands and regeneration of cultures and community."[88] Instead of allowing the reconciliation discourse, as it is currently embodied, to encapsulate justice for our communities, we must consider more active and responsive tactics of decolonization.

As we consider emancipatory pathways, the teachings of our nations hold the solutions. Decolonization and resurgence are liberatory precisely because they have a decentralized, grassroots focus that builds from our place-based understandings to embody our responsibilities and regenerate our relationality. As Simpson notes, "the only way not to be co-opted is to use our own legal and political practices to bring about justice."[89] The process begins with family and radiates out;[90] it is about connecting back to our stories, and taking them seriously.[91] When we conceptualize resurgence in relational ways, we direct our attention to what Gina Starblanket describes as the "significant role that our everyday interactions play in defining and pursuing our political objectives and priorities."[92] Grounding our liberation in resurgence allows for the continued creation of vibrant Indigenous futures that emerge from and honour our world views. It shifts the focus to our relationality with all of creation, not just the interpersonal. As Starblanket stresses: "because it is through our interactions with our environments that we learn the most about ourselves and those we share our existence with, our relationships have the biggest potential to act as sites of change and imagination."[93]

By fostering spaces for individual, familial, and community healing, the Maine Wabanaki-State Child Welfare Truth and Reconciliation Commission and the Truth and Reconciliation Commission of Canada *aid* in decolonization and *complement* ongoing resurgence work, but they will never solely represent justice or freedom for Indigenous nations. Freedom for our communities rests instead in the place-based resurgence work our nations have been engaging in. This can be seen in the work of Maine Wabanaki REACH,[94] or in community-responsive projects that are designed and implemented by Indigenous nations that seek to (re)vitalize our traditions. The hard work of decolonization is embodied in these various initiatives, such as Maine Wabanaki REACH's annual Healing Workshop, which began in 2014; language learning projects in nuučaańuł communities on the west coast of Vancouver Island; and community toolsheds and the revitalization of the kwetlal food systems by the Songhees First Nation, a Coast Salish community; and many other projects within communities across what is now referred to as North America. These projects are grounded in our relationality with all life in our territories and built on the knowledge that we know better than outsider "experts" what is best for us. As such, there is no prescriptive pan-Indigenous pathway to freedom; the strength to heal our respective communities comes from within.

Justice for colonial violence is about more than just rethinking national narratives that seek to uphold settler colonial notions of benevolence or stewardship of human rights, or decolonizing the settler mind.[95] True redress must result in structural change. Concrete restitution needs to include our lands and waters. Real justice means honouring our self-determination and building relationships from that place. Anything that moves away from this, that relegates our experiences to something solely of the past while denying the colonial realities of the present, merely reproduces the violence and colonial power structures we have sought liberation from.

Notes

1   This paper is born out of the love that grew through witnessing my family participate in the Truth and Reconciliation Commission of Canada, and through my experience as the research coordinator for the Maine Wabanaki-State Child Welfare Truth and Reconciliation Commission. I am forever grateful for the courage and strength of our relations in sharing their stories, and am humbled to have been asked to hold some of those stories. I hold my hands up to each of you; it is your courage and strength that continues to reverberate through our nations. It is your love and bravery that makes our work today possible.

   Throughout this process, I have been honoured to witness some of the healing that was sparked by both of these truth and reconciliation commissions. While healing certainly occurs outside of the spaces of a truth commission, I recognize that these bodies hold vital importance for some of our relatives in their healing. I acknowledge that healing is a journey that we can, and may, spend our whole lives on. There is no single moment that we can pinpoint where healing has occurred—where, by some strange manifestation, we can check a box that says we are healed and we can move on. I have witnessed the healing that has begun with the individual, and radiated out through our families, through our communities. I want to say λeekoo λeekoo (thank you) for sharing your journey and for your unconditional love. λeekoo λeekoo to my dear friends, relatives, supervisors, colleagues, editors and reviewers who read this piece, and provided generous and kind feedback. It is my hope that the reflections here continue to illuminate the importance these mechanisms hold for our people, while also drawing attention to the critical work that must continue as we resist colonial violence, and work to decolonize.

2   See Weitz, *A Century of Genocide;* Totten, Parsons and Charney, *Century of Genocide.*

3   De Brito, "Introduction."

4   International Center for Transitional Justice, "Truth and Memory."

5   Jeff Corntassel and Cindy Holder—drawing on Andrew Woolford's work on affirmative repair—postulate that the "politics of distraction" moves to shift the discourse away from the restitution of Indigenous homelands and resources, and instead to grounded justice within political/legal rights–based processes that advance affirmative repair and ultimately reward colonial injustices. (See Corntassel, Chaw-win-is, and Holder, "Who's Sorry Now?," 472.) By extension, in their utility of the politics of distraction, states seek to promise justice that is grounded in their own reproduction of colonial power, instead of the structural change that is necessary for decolonized relationality.

6   United Nations Special Committee on Decolonization, "United Nations and Decolonization."

7   Ljunggren, "Every G20 Nation."

8   Kauanui, "'Structure, Not an Event.'"

9   See, for example, Wolfe, "Settler Colonialism."

10 See Mosby, "Administering Colonial Science."

11 TRC, *Honouring the Truth,* 1.

12 There is widespread debate within the field of genocide studies about the parameters of genocide. Many scholars refer to the definition laid out in the UN Convention on the Prevention and Punishment of the Crime of Genocide, which enshrined aspects of Raphaël Lemkin's understandings of the term. Yet, what was omitted from this document was Lemkin's description of

"genocide" as targeted at the cultural foundations of a nation—a process by which destruction of those foundations disallowed that nation to make further contributions to the world by way of its traditions, practices, and national psychology. It is evident that Lemkin believed the implications of this cultural destruction were just as grave as those of physical destruction.

The complexities of using the term "genocide" cannot go without saying. While the Commission made a positive move in naming cultural genocide, the qualification of "cultural" undoubtedly lessens the severity of the term in the minds of many people. The focus on the cultural destruction that occurred within these spaces, while truly devastating, seems to shift focus and attention away from the reality that many lives were lost both with the walls of residential schools and after children returned to their communities. It is also undeniable that the decision to frame residential schools as "cultural genocide" was a deliberate negotiation of the political realities in which we presently exist. To assert that residential schools constituted genocide without qualification would bring further legal action against the Canadian government, something that was prohibited as a part of Schedule N, "The Mandate," of the Indian Residential Schools Settlement Agreement. There were undoubtably concessions that were made when deciding to use the term "cultural genocide" instead of "genocide" without qualification. It is important to note that, for some people, these concessions were too huge, and the reduction of the colonial assault to "cultural genocide" attempts to erase and reframe the totality of Indigenous experiences into something palatable to Canadians that—in conjunction with the emphasis on pastness—does not challenge the Canadian national identity.

13 Adams, *Education for Extinction*, 52.

14 Jacobs, "Habit of Elimination," 196.

15 Ibid., 197.

16 Ibid., 198.

17 National Indian Child Welfare Association, quoted in Maine Wabanaki-State Child Welfare Truth and Reconciliation Commission, *Beyond the Mandate*, 15.

18 Maine Wabanaki-State Child Welfare Truth and Reconciliation Commission, *Beyond the Mandate*, 25.

19 Attean et al., "Truth, Healing and Systems Change," 20.

20 Maine Wabanaki-State Child Welfare Truth and Reconciliation Commission, *Beyond the Mandate*, 31.

21 Johnson, "Statement by Bobbi Johnson," 42.

22 Maine Wabanaki-State Child Welfare Truth and Reconciliation Commission, *Beyond the Mandate*, 25.

23 Bennett, "Bennett: 'More Children.'"

24 Attean et al., "Truth, Healing and Systems Change," 21.

25 Ibid.

26 Ibid.

27 Simpson, *Dancing on Our Turtle's Back*, 15.

28 Smith, *Decolonizing Methodologies*, 204.

29 Tutu, "Foreword by Chairperson," 4.

30 Wilson, "Justice and Legitimacy," 200.

31 Barkan, *Guilt of Nations*, 179.

32 In Canada, one only needs to consider the trial of Gerald Stanley or Raymond Cormier to see the ways in which the Canadian justice system has been unable to provide a semblance of justice for Indigenous peoples.

33 Corntassel, Chaw-win-is, and T'lakswadzi, "Indigenous Storytelling," 140.

34 De Brito, "Introduction," 25.

35 Angel, "Before Truth," 200.

36 Million, *Therapeutic Nations,* 93.

37 Smith, *Decolonizing Methodologies,* 31.

38 Ibid., 29–30.

39 For more information on this, see TRC, *Honouring the Truth,* 27–29.

40 TRC, *Final Report,* vol. 6, *Reconciliation,* 162–65.

41 Attean et al., "Truth, Healing and Systems Change," 22.

42 Maine Wabanaki-State Child Welfare Truth and Reconciliation Commission, *Commission Mandate.*

43 Smith, *Decolonizing Methodologies,* 4.

44 Phelps, *Shattered Voices,* 55.

45 Simpson, "Reconciliation and Its Discontents."

46 Nagy and Gillespie, "Representing Reconciliation," 8, 22.

47 Simpson, "Reconciliation and Its Discontents."

48 The construction of the passive settler role in reconciliation has been affirmed throughout these processes. In Canada this was most clearly established in the 2008 apology by former prime minister Stephen Harper to Indian Residential School Survivors, where Harper suggested that the pathways forward were based on a "knowledge of our shared history" (Stephen Harper, *Statement of Apology to Former Students of Indian Residential Schools,* 11 June 2008, https://www.aadnc-aandc.gc.ca/eng/1100100015644/1100100015649).
    However, this position was asserted again in November 2017 when Justin Trudeau stood before hundreds in Happy Valley-Goose Bay to apologize to residential school Survivors in Newfoundland and Labrador. He spoke through teary eyes about the strength of Indigenous Survivors in sharing their stories, while simultaneously upholding this truth telling as the embodiment of national justice and solidifying the passive role of non-Indigenous Canadians to merely "confront the hard truths as a society" (Justin Trudeau, "Remarks by Prime Minister Justin Trudeau to Apologize on Behalf of the Government of Canada to Former Students of the Newfoundland and Labrador Residential Schools," 24 November 2017, https://pm.gc.ca/eng/news/2017/11/24/remarks-prime-minister-justin-trudeau-apologize-behalf-government-canada-former). In the State of Maine, this position was affirmed by the lack of wider state attention to the work of the Maine Wabanaki TRC throughout the TRC process, and in the TRC emphasis on witness in educational events.

49 Simpson, "Reconciliation and Its Discontents."

50 Stanton, "Canada's Truth and Reconciliation Commission," 11.

51 Jung, "Canada and the Legacy," 231.

52 Woolford, *Benevolent Experiment,* 287.

53 See, for example, Rosemary Nagy and Emily Gillespie's article on media representations of the Canadian TRC: Nagy and Gillespie, "Representing Reconciliation."

54 Lightfoot, *Global Indigenous Politics*, 176.

55 See George, "Inclusion Is Just the Canadian Word."

56 Coulthard, *Red Skin*, 106.

57 TRC, *Final Report*, vol. 6, *Reconciliation*, 255.

58 Ibid., 211.

59 See Lightfoot, *Global Indigenous Politics*, for a more detailed understanding of soft and hard rights.

60 George, "Inclusion Is Just the Canadian Word."

61 Hill and McCall, "Introduction," 1–2.

62 See, for example, the highlighted aspects of Vancouver's Year of Reconciliation, which identify "artworks commissioned by the Public Arts Program" as fundamental. This, in conjunction with Mayor Gregor Robertson's proclamation (which again focused predominantly on residential schools), constrains the dialogue of reconciliation, as well as creates an avenue for capitalistic consumption: City of Vancouver, *Year of Reconciliation*.

63 Robinson and Zaiontz, "Public Art in Vancouver," 31.

64 TRC, *Final Report*, vol. 6, *Reconciliation*, 202.

65 Ibid., 219.

66 See Regan, *Unsettling the Settler Within*; Tuck and Yang, "Decolonization Is Not a Metaphor."

67 Barker, "From Adversaries to Allies," 322.

68 Manuel and Derrickson, *Reconciliation Manifesto*, 200–201.

69 Moretto, "Tribe Says LePage Threatened."

70 Elver harvesting has remained a contentious issue in the state of Maine. These elvers have been a part of sustenance for Passamaquoddy people, but have, over time, become a lucrative business for Mainers. The state of Maine has attempted to place restrictions on elver harvesting, including reducing the number of licences/permits that are issued. This has significantly impacted the Passamaquoddy ability to harvest for sustenance.

71 Cousins, "LePage Threatens to Pull."

72 Lightfoot, *Global Indigenous Politics*, 180.

73 TRC, *Final Report*, vol. 6, *Reconciliation*, 13.

74 Ibid., 207.

75 Coulthard, *Red Skin*, 8.

76 George, "Inclusion Is Just the Canadian Word."

77 Ibid. This chapter also draws attention to the reconciliation paradigm's envisioning of justice as embodied in interpersonal relationships. This deconstructs our relationality to all of creation, central in our teachings, and emphasizes a Western view of the land and waters as outside of society whose primary purpose is extraction and capitalistic development.

78 The Maine Wabanaki TRC did draw attention to the complexities of the Maine Indian Claims Settlement Agreement (MICSA) and a brief overview of the ramifications that are felt in Wabanaki communities. However, it was not the focus of the commission's work. Any evaluation of MISCA was not included as a recommendation.

79 Maine Wabanaki-State Child Welfare Truth and Reconciliation Commission, *Beyond the Mandate*, 55.

80 Harrison, "Judge Rules Against Penobscot."

81 Ibid.

82 Simpson, *Dancing on Our Turtle's Back*, 22.

83 Jeff Corntassel, in his article "Re-envisioning Resurgence: Indigenous Pathways to Decolonization and Sustainable Self-Determination," discusses the importance of everydayness in disrupting the physical, social, and political boundaries that are created by the colonial state in order to impede our actions in restoring our nationhood.

84 Simpson, *As We Have Always Done*, 46.

85 Esther Altvater, quoted in Mazo and Pender-Cudlip, *Dawnland*.

86 Césaire, *Discourse on Colonialism*, 55.

87 James, "A Carnival of Truth?," 189.

88 Corntassel and Holder, "Who's Sorry Now?," 472.

89 Simpson, *Dancing on Our Turtle's Back*, 24.

90 Barney Williams Jr., quoted in Corntassel, Chaw-win-is, and T'lakswadzi, "Indigenous Storytelling," 145.

91 Mack, "Hoquotist."

92 Starblanket, "Resurgence as Relationality," 30.

93 Ibid.

94 For more information, see http://www.mainewabanakireach.org.

95 Park, "Settler Colonialism."

Part Two

LEARNING AND HEALING

CHAPTER 5

TEACHING TRUTH BEFORE RECONCILIATION

ERICA JURGENS

I was not taught to physically mistreat or abuse Indigenous peoples, but I was not taught to respect them. I was informed that they were drunks who chose to live off welfare rather than work for a fair wage. Indigenous people were not proud people; they were a primitive culture attempting to usurp our new wave westernized philosophies. I had been always reminded that historically Canada did nothing wrong, and that the Indigenous tribes were merely attempting to extort more land out of the government in order to establish a lost art, a lost culture. Now, couple this mindset with the lack of education taught in schools concerning Indigenous history and it creates a foundation built on ignorance and misinformation.[1]

This was one non-Indigenous university student's response to a public panel on the role of universities in reconciliation. I have heard many others—both Indigenous and non-Indigenous—say similar things. We were not taught the true history of Canada. We were never told. Not in our homes, not in the media, and not in the schools.

My Experience of Learning about Residential Schools through RCAP

I am an Indigenous scholar and educator who did not learn about residential schools until I was almost forty. I knew that my grandparents had gone to residential schools, but I had no understanding of what these schools were or why they existed. I do not think my mother understood what residential

schools were, either. She once mentioned that my grandfather was supposed to be educated to be a priest at St. Mary's Mission Indian Residential
School in Mission, British Columbia. She believed that my grandmother
had learned to crochet at St. George's Indian Residential School in Lytton,
British Columbia. I had never spoken with my grandmother; she had passed
away after my parents moved to Manitoba. My grandfather, whom I did
meet, never spoke about his school experiences at any great length. I learned
about residential schools only when I went to university. The Royal Commission on Aboriginal Peoples (RCAP) had come out in 1996, and university programs were attempting to integrate aspects of the report into their
courses.[2] It was 1997 and I was in the first year of a Social Services program
and RCAP was in the recommended reading list for a residential school
research assignment. Through this assignment I learned how and why my
grandparents had ended up in residential schools. I was shocked.

One group in my class shared their research findings on the residential
school roundup. During a roundup the Indian agent and the Royal Canadian
Mounted Police (RCMP) would go into people's homes, carry out all children
deemed old enough for residential school, and haul them away in trucks. As a
mother of young children at the time, I could empathize in a deeply visceral
way with those parents who had lost their children to residential school.
I could visualize my grandfather as a boy being ripped out of his community and carted off to spend the rest of his childhood in an institution that
served more as prison than school. I was tremendously angry at Canada for
its treatment of my grandparents and my people. How could Canadians have
allowed this to happen? How could this history have become so forgotten?
Residential schools are part of Canada's history. Because of the Indian Act,
residential schools became part of my family's history. Yet, when the RCAP
report was released, I would not have been able to explain exactly what the
Indian Act was. My ignorance both appalled and shamed me: appalled to
realize the impact this unspoken history had on me and on my family; and
shamed because, much like the non-Indigenous university student quoted
above, through my ignorance of this history, I had blamed and judged my
people for the social despairs I witnessed around me.

The RCAP report made me aware of how I had been unconsciously influenced by a settler colonial historical narrative replete with misinformation.
I was living with historical amnesia about who my people were, what Canada
had done to them, and how we got to be where we are in Canadian society.

A few years after RCAP, on 7 January 1998, then Minister of Indian Affairs and Northern Development Jane Stewart delivered the federal government's response to RCAP in *Gathering Strength: Canada's Aboriginal Action Plan,* which included a $350 million healing fund and a "Statement of Reconciliation."[3] She noted that "the [RCAP] Commissioners directed us to examine the very core of how we have lived together in this country" over four stages of our relationship: as separate nations neither knowing of the other; at first contact; during the displacement and marginalization of First Nations, Inuit, and Métis peoples; and in the present day when "this generation [has the opportunity] to correct past wrongs and move forward in cooperative relationships once again."[4]

The RCAP Commissioners recommended that Canadians be educated about the actual history between Indigenous nations and the Crown. In its "Statement of Reconciliation," Canada promised to learn from the past, take responsibility, and work to establish a renewed relationship. Assurances were made, funds were set up, but, ten years after the report, little came to fruition and the RCAP report had been shelved and forgotten by many.[5]

Twenty-Three Years Later—Learning through the TRC

In 2015, almost twenty years after RCAP, the Truth and Reconciliation Commission of Canada (TRC) released its final report. Once more, young people and adults are learning about residential schools and their ongoing impacts, and, again, many people are going through the same responses of shock, anger, and shame. The TRC endorsed and built on RCAP recommendations to redress harms and restore the relationship between Indigenous nations and Canada. The RCAP called for a return to the terms of the original nation-to-nation agreements, stressing, "Promises ought to be kept. Undertakings ought to be fulfilled. Solemn commitments ought to be honoured."[6] The TRC defines "reconciliation" as an "ongoing process of establishing and maintaining respectful relationships," by which we can put things right and make tangible reparations that transform Canada.[7] Both the RCAP and TRC emphasized that history education is critical to reconciliation. The TRC notes, in its chapter "Education for Reconciliation," that "education must remedy the gaps in historical knowledge that perpetuate ignorance and racism."[8] We cannot transform Canada without discussing the past. This holds the key to what promises must be kept, what commitments must be honoured, and what undertakings must be fulfilled. The past is everyone's inheritance; you cannot just forget it and push forward. The past holds some ugly history; it cannot be undone and tidied up and fed back to us as something more palatable. The past must be told truthfully so we can understand what reparations need to be made to achieve genuine reconciliation. Genuine reconciliation must recognize Indigenous peoples as peoples with their own histories.

Undoing the Primitive—Acknowledging Indigenous Histories

One critical thing to acknowledge and recognize is that Indigenous peoples had and continue to have a historiography. Having a historiography means we had methods for recording history. We had literacies. James Niigaanwewidam Sinclair points out that Indigenous literacies were recorded in many ways.[9] Indigenous literacies are expressed on rock as petroglyphs and pictographs; expressed through rocks as inukshuks, medicine wheels, and transformer stones; expressed with trees as a metaphor, or beings, or in utilitarian ways as birchbark scrolls. Some Indigenous nations use parchment to record the winter count and some nations used beads and shell to create wampum belts to record agreements. Our ceremonies of renewal are not merely cultural. They are an Indigenous way of analyzing the past through reiteration. Our ceremonies remind us that the past is the present and the present is the future. Our literacies were expressions of a history extending beyond our first contact with settlers. Indigenous historiographies must be resurrected and remembered.

Presently, Indigenous and settler histories are incomplete. Too often, Indigenous histories are mentioned only in relation to contact and within settler history told from the settler perspective. It is an issue of what Patrick Wolfe described as "split tensing" whereby the settler situates the Indigenous as dead or dying and the settler as constructing and progressing.[10] And this presents a twofold problem: one is the erasure of Indigenous history and the second is the singular story of Canadian nation building. The first problem is that the historiographies of Indigenous nations are severely impeded by the colonial project, which included residential schools, a project of assimilation that continues in present-day educational systems. Within schools millennia of Indigenous histories remain forgotten, positioned as bygone relics, as prehistory, or as folktales and thereby deemed irrelevant. The impact of this has been so powerful that even many Indigenous people see themselves ahistorically, without the knowledge of their own equally valued histories.

The second problem is embedded within the Canadian imaginary. Cree scholar Dwayne Donald describes this imaginary as "the socio-cultural mythology of newcomers to North America that is guided by the 'dream' of easily accessible resources and unfettered economic growth that will make them rich, successful, and thus happy. This 'dream' originated during the high colonial era and has largely been maintained to the present (albeit in altered forms) as a guiding vision of the good life."[11] When history is talked about only in the imaginary of settlement, it leaves everyone with historical amnesia. History then becomes a mistelling, where one dominant historical narrative of pioneers and homesteading is told, and Indigenous nations are largely left out. This mistelling has come to the fore since the TRC placed the spotlight on residential schools. The Elders who fought to obtain the Indian Residential Schools Settlement Agreement brought the TRC into being. Indeed, survivors, Elders, and Knowledge Keepers used their testimony and teachings to pierce through this historical amnesia and speak truth to power. This begs the question: What other narratives have been missed, dismissed, or forgotten?

Where does the truth lie today? How do we correct any misinformation? What is the role of schools? The TRC believes that everyone needs to learn that the history on this continent began long before European contact.[12] They propose that education is the key.[13] They note that schools need to pay attention to history education in particular and should present Indigenous peoples as peoples who belonged to nations that have a "rich linguistic and cultural heritage"; they should teach students "what it means to have inherent rights" and they should teach a mindful historiography that includes a contact narrative that shows how Indigenous nations negotiated with European nations "with integrity and good faith."[14]

In this chapter I present a three-part line of reasoning. Part 1 is an erratum to Canadian history in order to right our understanding of a nation-to-nation relationship. I present two examples of Indigenous history that illustrate a key point: we have forgotten our original nation-to-nation relationships. I share what I have learned from the history of the Aterihwihsón:sera Kaswenta (the Two-Row Wampum Belt). I share the story of Deskaheh, a Haudenosaunee, who, on behalf of his people, upheld Indigenous nationhood and resisted assimilation. As I make a case for the rewriting of our distorted settler colonial historiography, I posit some hard and painful truths that must be discussed. Indigenous and non-Indigenous peoples must see the connection between the acts of the colonial past and the acts of settler colonialism today in order to truly understand the necessary reparations and restitution going forward.

In Part 2 I argue we need to deconstruct the official record of Canada's past. We need to challenge the notion that Canada did nothing wrong. We need to tell the story of settler colonialism. We need to describe what settler colonialism was and what it is. We need to search out the stories we were *not* told so we can reconstruct a fulsome and truthful historical consciousness. I identify some narratives that need to come to the fore. Media has helped to bring some of these issues forward and this is important, but in terms of educating, schools bear the greatest responsibility in transforming our historical consciousness, particularly in the areas of understanding settler colonialism.

In Part 3 I discuss the steps needed to provide the restitution and redress to set schooling systems on the right path for the work they need to do. Transforming educational institutions is essential because they play a critical part in shaping how children come to know themselves. I propose a Two-Row model of educational restitution and redress. I offer concrete solutions as inspired by Elders who called for Indian control of Indian education and by the TRC's Call to Action to adopt and implement the United Nations Declaration on the Rights of Indigenous Peoples.

Part 1: History Erratum—(Re)Righting the Nation-to-Nation Relationship

Much work needs to be done to repair our historical amnesia. Currently, we are not taught to recognize seventeenth- and eighteenth-century First Nations chiefs as statesmen who conferred with European sovereigns, to think of Indigenous civilizations as nations, or to perceive Indigenous peoples as cosmopolitans.[15] Few of us learn about the international trade agreements the Haudenosaunee made with the Netherlands in the early seventeenth century[16] and with Great Britain throughout the eighteenth century.[17] KAIROS, a Canadian ecumenical network, surveyed provincial/territorial curricula on their implementation of TRC Call to Action 62(i), which calls for school curricula to include coverage of Indigenous history, treaties, and residential schools from kindergarten to grade twelve. In the 2015 "Education for Reconciliation Report Card," KAIROS found that only two provinces, Alberta and Saskatchewan, had most of the elements embedded in the curriculum and implemented in classrooms.[18] In their 2018 "Education for Reconciliation Report Card," KAIROS found improvements across most provinces but noted many provinces needed to do more work on implementing Indigenous historical content into the curricula.[19] The Canadian Broadcasting Corporation (CBC) keeps an update on Canada's progress in implementing each of the ninety-four Calls to Action.[20] As of April 2019 ten have been completed.[21]

We also need a new foundation. We need to understand the true historical background to situate a reconciliation discourse in its proper context.[22] For example, what does Prime Minister Trudeau mean when he calls for a nation-to-nation relationship between Indigenous and non-Indigenous peoples?[23] I think that to find common ground and to answer this question, we all need to be educated about the original nation-to-nation relationships Indigenous nations had with various European nations from the 1600s to the late 1800s.[24] Through correcting the historical narrative, we can learn what Indigenous self-governance is. In this chapter I specifically refer to the Haudenosaunee (as they know themselves) or Iroquois (as Canadians are taught to know them) who are made up of six nations: the Mowhawks, Oneidas, Onondagas, Cayugas, Senecas, and Tuscaroras.[25] The Haudenosaunee have maintained their political identity as an Indigenous nation, have resisted Canada's attempts to subsume them, and always remind Canada who the newcomers truly are. Haudenosaunee laws are *sui generis*: that is, their origins are unique to the Haudenosaunee Nations and are held within the Haudenosaunee Confederacy.

Aterihwihsón:sera Kaswenta: Two-Row Nation-to-Nation Relationships
The Haudenosaunee Confederacy have always governed through a system of covenant. The covenants were usually made for some purpose (i.e., trade agreements, alliances, or resolutions). The Haudenosaunee Confederacy Council was established 1,000 years before European contact.[26] The Haudenosaunee formalized these covenants into Guswenta (wampum belts), which functioned like handwritten records or legal documents.[27]

One belt is the Aterihwihsón:sera Kaswenta, also known as Tekanit Teyothata'tye Kaswenta, Teioháte, Kaswenta, or the Two-Row Wampum.[28] The first of these wampum belts was with the Dutch in 1613.[29] The Dutch agreed to honour Haudenosaunee law.[30] Tuscarora scholar Richard W. Hill has done extensive work to revive the knowledges contained within the Six Nations wampum belts. He explains that "the metaphorical imagery of the Two-Row Wampum is that the Dutch ship is now tied to the Haudenosaunee canoe, floating together on the River of Life. Our peoples became linked to one another. In fact, our leaders state that our children and grandchildren will be related to one another (meaning that we are to treat each other like family as called for in the Great Law). Yet they will not try to steer each other's vessel respecting one another's sovereignty and will use the good mind (rationality) to resolve any difficulties that may arise."[31]

Britain used wampum belts to seal their agreements. One was a Two-Row Wampum in 1664,[32] and the second, the Silver Covenant Chain in 1677.[33] The British governors assured the Haudenosaunee that the silver chain links would never tarnish and the covenants were everlasting. Each nation agreed that when one nation required the help of the other, that nation was to metaphorically "shake the Covenant-Chain."[34] Britain shook the Covenant Chain often. Britain shook the chain for support with King William's War in 1689.[35] They shook the chain for help in the Seven Years' War in 1748[36] and again in 1775 during the American Revolution. The last time Britain shook the Covenant Chain was for the First World War. Three hundred and fifty Haudenosaunee from the Six Nations of the Grand River responded, because, as Mohawk Ronald Lowry pointed out, "we came over with the United Empire Loyalists from the United States. Our treaties are with the Crown, so, when the Crown calls, you go."[37]

Haudenosaunee Resistance: Chief Deskaheh Shakes the Covenant Chain
Chief Deskaheh (Levi General) is an important twentieth-century historical figure in both settler Canadian history and in Indigenous peoples' history. In the early 1920s Deskaheh was chosen by the Haudenosaunee Council to represent the Confederacy's concerns relating to Canada's actions against their people. After the First World War, the Dominion of Canada was lobbying the League of Nations for admission.[38] Canada was making strong moves to break all the previous treaties Indigenous nations had with Britain[39] and to appropriate First Nations lands.[40] The Haudenosaunee protested and asserted their inherent sovereignty as nations.[41]

The Haudenosaunee decided to shake the Covenant Chain. Chief Deskaheh went to Europe in 1921 and again in 1923 to call for the sovereign rights of his nation to be upheld in accordance with the international agreements made with Britain in 1677.[42] His intent was to shake the Covenant Chain and remind the British monarchy of its nation-to-nation relationship.[43]

When Chief Deskaheh made his first visit to Britain in 1921 to meet with King George V to petition for the recognition of Six Nations sovereignty and to stop Canada's imposition of the Indian Act, he was blocked by Winston Churchill, secretary to the colonies.[44] Canada grieved to the League of Nations, claiming that the Dutch (who were sympathetic) were interfering with domestic matters[45] and, with the support of Britain and the United States, persuaded the League of Nations to refuse to hear Deskaheh's case.[46] Chief Deskaheh then began working with the Swiss to gain protection for the Haudenosaunee under the International Office for the Protection of Native Races.[47] Canada responded by dissolving the Haudenosaunee Council of Chiefs,[48] seizing every wampum belt held by the Haudenosaunee Council, and installing an "elective system" as prescribed by the Indian Act.[49] Historian Andrea Lucille Catapano reveals that "punishment of the Six Nations community even extended to the children for numerous youngsters were 'picked up off the road' without informing their parents and sent to residential schools in this tense time following the installation of the elected council."[50]

The Haudenosaunee historiography counters the benign nation-building historiographies and the truth illuminates why there is the political contestation between Indigenous nations and the Canadian state today.

Part 2: The Need to (Re)write the Settler-Colonial Historiography

Retelling the story of Indigenous-settler relations to include multifaceted stories of Indigenous treaty making shifts Canada's overall historiography. Today, Indigenous historiography makes visible many settler colonial atrocities, spanning 150 years in some provinces and up to 500 years elsewhere.[51] It is an unsettling truth telling that must occur. Indigenous and non-Indigenous peoples alike need to learn about the effects of Canadian settler colonialism, past and present, before we can truly build the respectful relationship necessary for reconciliation.

Since the release of the TRC's *Final Report*, Canadians are learning about the horrors of residential schools through the media. And information through the media can contribute to helping Indigenous people challenge the colonizing narratives most of us were taught. But we cannot leave this edification to the media only. The 2016 Environics survey, titled "Canadian Public Opinion on Aboriginal Peoples," found that "40 percent of those aware of Indian residential schools had not read or heard anything about the TRC" and "fully 57 percent who had heard of the Commission were unable to recall anything specific about its recommended Calls to Action."[52] People must become better educated. The TRC points out there is much more colonial history that we still need to reconcile. This history includes the pass system, which imprisoned Indigenous peoples on reserves; the anti-potlatch law, which criminalized Indigenous cultural practice; the prohibition on legal counsel for Indians; the scalping bounties placed on Indigenous peoples;[53] the starvation of the Plains peoples;[54] the biomedical experiments on children in residential schools;[55] the forced sterilization of Indigenous women;[56] and the biopolitics behind the state-created "Status" Indian.[57] One Canadian analysis, "Re-assessing the Population Impacts of Bill C-31," forecasts there will be no more Status Indians born within five generations.[58] The report notes, "Although Bill C-31 has no 'sunset' clause, new registrations are likely to effectively cease as a consequence of 'extinction' of the eligible population."[59] Can we truly have a discussion about reconciliation when the government is counting down the years to Indigenous extinction? How are we educating ourselves on these issues? I argue that schools must bring these discussions into the curriculum.

School curricula over the decades have tried to push incriminating aspects of Canadian history as far from the public memory as possible, and research into this, according to Anne Godlewska, Jackie Moore, and C. Drew Bednasek, finds that these historical omissions are neither "passive [nor] haphazard but a profoundly purposive and wilful ignorance."[60] Furthermore, many educators resist teaching about Canada's existing settler colonialism. In her thesis research, Jordan Watters found that many teachers actively avoid class discussion on politics, racism, or issues impacting Indigenous peoples today.[61] These findings are similar to Susan Dion's, who describes a school stance "informed simultaneously by what teachers know, what they do not know, and what they refuse to know."[62] Although research indicates this resistance is pervasive, we do not discuss it or address it. However, we do see the consequences. Failing to have a critical discourse about present-day impacts of settler colonialism has entrenched racial stigmatization against Indigenous peoples and results in education systems organized around an ideology of cognitive and cultural imperialism.[63] We must change this. Anti-racism scholar Dr. Howard C. Stevenson maintains that we stay locked in racial stress when we avoid talking about the "elephant in the room."[64] The omissions within Canadian historiography have left a large and growing elephant in the schoolhouse. With each year, each decade, each century, the elephant gets bigger.

Moving toward a Critical Historical Consciousness in Schools
Many schools have tried additive strategies to Indigenize the curriculum through the addition of cultural content. Mi'kmaw education scholar Marie Battiste notes that additive strategies often have no connection to a "history, politic, or community [of] significance."[65] For example, adding in some general Indigenous cultural content through storybooks, food, crafts, or events can be too superficial to be meaningful. Battiste and Sheelagh McLean call this the "add and stir" approach.[66] Of course, the core idea of reconnecting young people with their culture is a vital one; as authors Tracey Carr and Brian Chartier in this volume can attest, it is closely tied to healing. But rather than transforming education, the additive approach merely tries to make it more bearable for Indigenous students. This approach implies that the political underpinnings of the system are too entrenched to effect any real reform, and we end up with what Ron Scollon calls "institutional unresponsiveness."[67] Indigenous scholars emphasize that the status quo must be disrupted and that educators must discuss settler colonialism, Eurocentrism, racism, gender violence, and white supremacy in their classrooms.[68]

Asking critical questions about current issues regarding Canada and Indigenous peoples in the classroom can help us see how our past impacts our present. For example, we can ask: Why is it that Canada ranks twelfth nationally[69] on the United Nations Human Development Index, yet Indigenous nations within Canada are ranked seventy-eighth?[70] Why is it that Indigenous children are overrepresented in child welfare apprehensions,[71] in the criminal justice system,[72] and in poverty?[73] Teachers and students need to make the connections between the institutionalized violence against Indigenous peoples in residential schools in the past and the connected abuses and deaths in the present-day foster care system, the health care system, the reservation system, and in the justice system. Working toward reconciliation means the classroom discourse must centre on unpacking these issues underpinning the continual reproduction of harms against Indigenous peoples.

When we do not educate to get to the root of the Canadian problem, we foreclose opportunities to come to a true understanding of our past. Instead, we situate Indigenous peoples as being deficient and argue for "closing the gap" strategies. Anti-racism scholar George J. Sefa Dei argues that these types of framings are embedded within "deeply ingrained" and "socially constructed ideologies of race" that constitute daily acts of "educational violence" when our circumstances are not examined within a framework of critical historical consciousness.[74] Political scholars David Bedford and W. Thom Workman point out that this results in a number of intersectional losses for all people in Canada, such as "the loss of a sense of its historical constitution, the loss of ability to recognize its historical contingency, and the loss of capacity to imagine alternative ways of living."[75]

Developing a critical historical consciousness can go a long way toward fostering a possible space for reconciliation. Daniel S. Friedrich asserts that "anyone, but especially students, can draw from history in order to become better people."[76] Through a genuine and honest discourse, we can deconstruct our present historiography with a critical lens. This will help us decide who we want to be and how we should reconcile. Education and schools can and should be pivotal places for deconstructing myths, imagining a different future, and paving the way toward restitution and redress. This is the work that all schools can do immediately. To bring educational restitution and redress, however, involves making space for Indigenous-run schools to operate alongside provincial schools—a Two-Row model of education.

Part 3: A Two-Row Model for Educational Restitution and Redress

The TRC clearly recognizes the importance of education, placing its Legacy Calls to Action on education near the top of the list. The TRC had to issue Calls to Action to remedy the limitations, barriers, and gaps that exist in the current on-reserve/off-reserve education systems. However, we could resist this compartmentalization that defines Indigenous peoples through an on-reserve or off-reserve classification. Mi'kmaw legal scholar Pam Palmater points out that "every Indigenous person in this country lives on their traditional territories or the traditional territory of someone else."[77] She deepens this conceptual shift, noting "the fact that we are no longer defining or limiting ourselves to our reserve communities and really thinking about what is nationhood, our jurisdiction extends on or off artificially created reserves . . . [and] artificially created provincial borders, and [this] expands and strengthens our jurisdiction, like it would with any nation."[78] In his evidence to the Standing Committee on Canadian Heritage, Chief Gerald Antoine from the Liidlii Kue First Nation described his nation, the Dene, as "part of a large linguistic family that spans from Alaska and the Northwest Territories through southern Alberta to the northern territories of Mexico."[79] Blaire Gould, director of programs and services at Mi'kmaw Kina'matnewey, in her evidence to the Standing Committee on Canadian Heritage, asserted, "As a Mi'kmaw, I know no boundaries. My territory spans four provinces. I think that's very important in the step of recognizing who we are as language groups. I represent speakers in New Brunswick, Prince Edward Island, Newfoundland and Quebec."[80]

We also need to envision a comprehensive Indigenous education system that makes space for Indigenous peoples to enact Indigenous education sovereignty. Cree scholar Onowa McIvor points out that there is "no comprehensive support system in Canada to develop, implement and support [Indigenous] immersion education from preschool to grade 12."[81] As I examine how we might enact the TRC Calls to Action, I envision what an Indigenous model of education can look like if state-enforced distinctions between on-reserve and off-reserve schools were removed. I focus on how we can enact Indigenous sovereignty and self-determination in relation to developing our own educational systems in a comprehensive manner that honours reconciliation.

Reconciliation must include restitution and redress. "Restitution" is the act of restoring what has been taken away and "redress" is the act of making things right. The TRC points to the United Nations Declaration on the Rights of Indigenous Peoples (UNDRIP) as the framework for reconciliation in Canada. The Canadian government has stated that it intends to adopt and implement UNDRIP.[82] Adopting and implementing UNDRIP will ensure that Canadian laws are consistent with principles and values with regard to Indigenous peoples that are expressed in the Constitution, including the recognition and affirmation of Treaty and Aboriginal rights, including the rights to self-determination and self-governance in education. The United Nations has declared that Indigenous peoples have the "right to control their education systems and institutions providing education in their own languages in a manner appropriate to their cultural methods of teaching and learning."[83] This statement is the benchmark for all educational reforms within Canada. The United Nations declaration supports the development of Indigenous curricula. The United Nations declaration supports Indigenous rights to have Indigenous schools in urban centres, in cities and villages, and in First Nations, Inuit, and Métis communities. Ideally, reconciliation would see Canada and the provinces legislate UNDRIP and leave us to work the rest out according to our Indigenous legal traditions of negotiation.[84]

Creating Space for Indigenous-Run Schools: Bringing UNDRIP *into the Canadian Framework*

Several UNDRIP articles have relevance for Indigenous education in Canada. Specifically, Article 8(1) states, "Indigenous peoples and individuals have the right not to be subjected to forced assimilation or destruction of their culture." This article requires educators to assess the impacts of curricula in shaping Indigenous identity. In Canada this means implementing Article 8(2) by redressing cultural genocide and creating "effective mechanisms" within school systems for First Nations, Inuit, and Métis to "regain their integrity as distinct peoples" and, as outlined in UNDRIP Article 13(1), include schools in which we can "revitalize, use, develop and transmit to future generations their histories, languages, oral traditions, philosophies, writing systems and literatures." This requires more than simply including an Indigenous perspective here or there within a Canadian curriculum; it calls for developing Indigenous education models. It means enacting Article 14(1), which states, "Indigenous peoples have the right to establish and control their educational systems and institutions providing education in their own languages, in a manner appropriate to their cultural methods of teaching and learning." The UNDRIP framework would see Canada and the provinces working with Indigenous peoples to establish the bills, laws, and funding structures to support First Nations, Inuit, and Métis to develop "distinct political, economic, social and cultural institutions" (Article 5) and determine their own membership (Article 6 and Article 9). These articles provide the framework of Indigenous rights that Canada must redress for reconciliation to occur. There have been some bills introduced in the Senate and the House of Commons that can, if passed, create pathways for reconciliation and redress in education. These are Bill C-262 and Bill C-91.

On 4 April 2016, Romeo Saganash introduced Bill C-262, an Act to ensure that the laws of Canada are in harmony with the United Nations Declaration on the Rights of Indigenous Peoples (United Nations Declaration on the Rights of Indigenous Peoples Act). The process has been lengthy, and the Bill failed to gain Senate support.[85] It had been noted that if Bill C-262 did not make it to third reading before Parliament dissolved for the October 2019 election, it would be a dead bill.[86]

The revitalization of Indigenous languages is a critical component of Indigenous education. In its *Legacy* volume, the TRC notes that "the practice of Aboriginal languages was a pre-existing, distinctive, and continuous practice that should be recognized as an existing Aboriginal right under section 35(1) of the Constitution Act, 1982."[87] So far, Canada has reneged on funding promises, and has "treated Aboriginal languages as a minor part of a larger governmental portfolio devoted to all matters of Canadian heritage."[88] Legislation could create space for permanent funding. Legislation could also bring First Nations, Métis, and Inuit languages into equal status with English and French as the language of instruction within schools. Without legal backing the monies do not flow correctly. The TRC noted in 2009 that the language funding in Nunavut was forty-four dollars per capita to support Inuit languages for Inuit peoples in Nunavut and $4,000 per capita to support French languages for francophones living in Nunavut.[89]

Since 2009 there have been three attempts to move an Indigenous language bill through the Senate. All three attempts were made by Senator Serge Joyal, who named the Bill as an Act for the advancement of the Aboriginal languages of Canada and to recognize and respect Aboriginal language rights. He introduced it first as Bill S-237 on 28 May 2009.[90] It never moved. He introduced it again as Bill S-229 on 9 June 2015.[91] It never moved. And he introduced it as Bill S-212 on 3 December 2015, and it made it to second reading on 1 December 2016.[92] It never moved to third reading. Instead, everything moved to the start position again and a different bill was introduced into the House of Commons. On 5 February 2019, Prime Minister Trudeau announced that Bill C-91, an Act respecting Indigenous languages (Indigenous Languages Bill), had been introduced into the House of Commons. Because of its late introduction, it was moved precipitously in the House. This Bill went through three readings in the House of Commons and three readings in the Senate before it became law in June 2019.[93] The government wanted to get this done before the October 2019 election.[94] In his brief Amos Key, director of the First Nations Language Program at the Woodland Cultural Centre, shared that his "greatest fear for Bill C-91 is that it will 'die on the order paper', when the next election is called."[95] Bill C-91, however, has some issues. Bill C-91 appears to have more constraints in it than did Senator Joyal's Bill, and a number of concerning omissions. Senator Joyal's Bill S-212 has only twelve articles, yet it articulated ten commitments to "support" Indigenous governments and Indigenous languages.[96] Bill C-91 has fifty articles. "Support" is mentioned only four times in direct relation to Indigenous languages. Thirty-seven articles are dedicated to outlining the bureaucratic structure that will have "the control and the management of the Office and all matter connected with it."[97] The Indigenous think tank the Yellowhead Institute has critiqued the Bill and pointed out some issues that must be resolved: (1) There is no declaration of Indigenous languages as official languages; (2) responsibilities are not defined; (3) there is no legislated accountability; (4) there is no fiscal infrastructure and there is no direct link to the wording of the UNDRIP or to Bill C-262.[98] Is a poor Bill better than no Bill? It is hard to say. The general hope is that now that Bill C-91 is law (and if Bill C-262 had become law), we would have some legal mechanisms to begin to work for reconciliation.

What Could This Look Like for Indigenous Education?
There are several ways these Bills could have an impact on Indigenous education. First, Canada could restructure how it funds Indigenous education. Presently, Canada uses an on-reserve/off-reserve framework and funds on-reserve First Nations and Inuit schools. The provinces fund public schools. In 1996 Canada capped spending on First Nations schooling. Canadian economist Don Drummond explains that "for every dollar the province would spend, the First Nations schools were only getting 70 cents."[99] That cap was in place for over twenty years and the deficit has been cumulative. In 2016 Pamela Palmater accounted a twenty-billion-dollar shortfall in the First Nations K–12 funding stemming from the funding cap.[100] Her recommendation was that Canada redress this shortfall in the form of a block reimbursement.[101] This restitution could go a long way toward building the infrastructure needed for Indigenous peoples to build their own capacity and control their own educational institutions.[102]

Second, Canada could legislate a permanent funding structure providing equitable funding to First Nations, Inuit, and Métis. Sol Sanderson, senator in the Federation of Sovereign Indigenous Nations, has developed a policy framework for decolonization and implementing the UNDRIP.[103] In September 2017 Sanderson made a presentation to the Standing Senate Committee on Aboriginal Peoples outlining how to enact this policy. He proposes establishing separate jurisdictions such as a First Nations Finance Administration Act.[104] He also proposes a First Nations fee on all resource development and suggests the same jurisdiction and fee structure be offered to the Inuit and to the Métis.[105] These two steps of jurisdiction and creating a permanent fiscal structure embody the principles of reconciliation by providing legal space and stable funding. Then First Nations, Inuit, and Métis could create their own schools that can become the sites of Indigenous language and cultural revival. This would redress the impacts of linguicide and cultural genocide stemming from residential schools and halt the continuation of these harms.

Indigenous educational jurisdiction would create the legal space for the inclusion of Indigenous pedagogies, values, and cultural practices in all levels of schooling. This would make room for Indigenous language immersion schools, schooling models that are aligned to the cultural practices of Indigenous peoples, and schools that are inclusive to the spiritual practices of Indigenous peoples. Sanderson points out that this means existing federal and provincial jurisdiction would be transferred over to specific Indigenous government structures.[106] This would create the structure for a Two-Row education system. The TRC calls upon us to stop trying to make Indigenous students fit into Eurocentric institutions and to transform the system instead. For greater changes to take place in primary, secondary, and post-secondary systems, we need to release our attachment to the status quo and bravely move toward creating fundamental changes that will, at first, be disruptive.

What I propose here is founded on the premise that Canada has kept its reconciliation promises, and has legislated First Nations, Inuit, and Métis jurisdiction and funding into the Constitution. Then the focus can be on building Indigenous capacity. By "Indigenous capacity," I mean education by Indigenous people, with Indigenous people, for Indigenous people. There are many areas of capacity building, but my discussion point is on preschool to secondary education. This capacity building begins with starting language immersion schools, by working with Indigenous educators to develop local curriculum resources, and by ensuring that culturally fluent Indigenous staff are hired to support this development.

I propose that the ideal system would be within a centralized hub, where early childhood, elementary, and secondary programs are either housed in one large building or located in an area where all buildings are within walking distance to each other. A centralized system will pull together a critical mass of Indigenous staff, allowing them to build capacity and hone their pedagogical capacities in a specialized curriculum content. These hubs would also be practicum sites to draw in those Indigenous post-secondary students seeking culturally relevant workplace experiences, so in time we would have a full capacity of language teachers, curriculum resource developers, generalist teachers, counsellors, and support workers. We could build communities of practice with Indigenous scholars and Indigenous researchers. These hubs also would be sites for resource development and serve as centralized resource centres. At full capacity there would be enough Indigenous teachers and community workers to provide intercultural bridging throughout a school division, to establish Indigenous educational networks intraprovincially and interprovincially and even between countries. This model is an Indigenous model that would foster genuine cross-cultural discourse and ensure the diffusion of authentic Indigenous resources. This model would take us back to the more respectful relationships exemplified by the Two-Row Wampum and the Silver Covenant Chain.

Shaking the Covenant Chain

As Indigenous peoples provide evidence to the Standing Senate Committee on Aboriginal Peoples regarding the Indigenous Languages Act, they are, in essence, shaking the Covenant Chain. Many point to Indigenous-run schools as key to reconciliation. The Two-Row Wampum is a perfect conceptual expression of how Indigenous-run schooling can exist alongside non-Indigenous schooling systems. It is this form of nation-to-nation agreement that needs to be restored so reconciliation can begin and we can educate our children as people who can think and speak in the language of their nations. Taehowehs (Amos Key Jr.), director of the First Nations Language Program in Six Nations, discussed the concept of Indigenous civilizations in his brief regarding Bill C-91, a concept that, when fully realized, could "remove the tarnish and strengthen the 'Honour of the Crown' in their relations with Indigenous Peoples."[107]

I see the TRC's Call to Action 43, "to fully adopt and implement the United Nations Declaration on the Rights of Indigenous Peoples as the framework for reconciliation,"[108] as our first act of reconciliation. The UNDRIP is the resounding of Chief Deskaheh's call in 1921 to respect the Two-Row Wampum agreement. The Survivors who did the heavy lifting to expose the history of residential schools have also shaken the Covenant Chain. They have signalled to Canadians that there is a problem: Canada has allowed the Silver Covenant Chain to tarnish and has ignored its principles.

The principles embedded in the metaphor of the Covenant Chain are those of Peace, Equity, and Continuity.[109] Peace—when one has caused harm to another, those harms must be remedied in accordance with these principles. Equity—the promise to treat one another with honesty, integrity, and decency in order to maintain our peace. Continuity—the covenant is long-standing and inviolable. The TRC's Calls to Action shake the Covenant Chain to remind us that truth must come before reconciliation. The United Nations Declaration on the Rights of Indigenous Peoples is the road map to remedying past harms, stopping present ones, and preventing harm in the future. I close with the words of Richard W. Hill, who, in picking up the work of his Haudenosaunee ancestors, declares, "We are shaking our end of the Chain and awaiting their response. We have great faith that the hard work of our ancestors will not go to waste."[110]

Notes

1   McMorrow, "Reckoning with the Role."

2   RCAP, *Report*.

3   TRC, *Final Report*, vol. 1, *The History, Part 2*, 559.

4   Indian and Northern Affairs Canada, "Address by the Honourable Jane Stewart Minister of Indian Affairs and Northern Development on the occasion of the unveiling of Gathering Strength— Canada's Aboriginal Action Plan," 7 January 1998. https://www.aadnc-aandc.gc.ca/eng/11001000 15725/1100100015726.

5   Assembly of First Nations, *Royal Commission on Aboriginal People*.

6   RCAP, *Report*, vol. 1, *Looking Forward*, 6.

7   TRC, *Honouring the Truth*, 16.

8   TRC, *Final Report*, vol. 6, *Reconciliation*, 117.

9   Sinclair, "Indigenous Literacies Throughout Time."

10 Wolfe, "Settler Colonialism," 2.

11 Donald, "Homo Economicus," 1.

12 TRC, *Final Report*, vol. 6, *Reconciliation*, 119.

13 Ibid., 117.

14 Ibid., 119.

15 Oosterom, "Kings of the New World."

16 Belanger, "The Six Nations," 32.

17 Ibid., 34.

18 KAIROS, "Report Card."

19 KAIROS, "Winds of Change."

20 CBC, "Beyond 94."

21 Ibid.

22 TRC, *Final Report*, vol. 6, *Reconciliation*, 119.

23 Trudeau, "Statement by Prime Minister."

24 Belanger, "Six Nations of Grand River," 31.

25 *We Are the Haudenosaunee*, 10 September 2015, https://www.youtube.com/ watch?v=2DofTnRhm5o.

26 Johnston, "First Nations and Canadian Citizenship," 350.

27 Richard W. Hill, "The Original Archive Wampum Belts Pt. 1" (video of presentation to the Aboriginal Curatorial Collective, 30 May 2016), https://www.youtube.com/watch?v=1sYb-5Fm4xhI (accessed 19 January 2017).

28 Hill, *Talking Points on History*.

29 Hill, "Linking Arms."

30 Venables, *The 1613 Treaty.*

31 Hill, "Linking Arms," 19.

32 Colden, *History of the Five Indian Nations,* vol. 1.

33 Belanger, "The Six Nations of Grand River," 32.

34 Richard H. Hill, "Nation to Nation: 05 Richard W. Hill, Sr. (Linking Arms and Brightening the Chain: Building Relations Through Treaties)," Smithsonian National Museum of the American Indian, https://www.youtube.com/watch?v=JAFWDg05CQ8.

35 Blake et al., *Narrating a Nation,* 102.

36 Williams Jr., "Linking Arms Together."

37 Summerby, "Native Soldiers," 8, 44, n.18.

38 McConnell, "Towards Constitutional Independence."

39 Smith, *Strange Visitors,* 192.

40 Belanger, "Six Nations of Grand River," 35.

41 Hill, *The Clay We Are Made Of,* 226.

42 Monture, *We Share Our Matters,* 116–17.

43 Deskaheh, *Chief Deskaheh Tells Why.*

44 Grace Li Xiu Woo, "Canada's Forgotten Founders: The Modern Significance of the Haudenosaunee (Iroquois) Application for Membership in the League of Nations," Grand River Country, Home of the Six Nations (blog), http://grandrivercountry.org/legal-case-reviews/canadas-forgotten-founders/#_ednref19 (accessed 10 March 2019).

45 Belanger, "Six Nations of Grand River," 39.

46 Ibid.

47 Catapano, "Rising of the Ongwehonwe."

48 Ibid., 283.

49 Ibid., 282.

50 Ibid., 292.

51 Hill, *500 Years.*

52 Environics Institute, *Canadian Public Opinion on Aboriginal Peoples.*

53 Paul, *First Nations History,* 112–29, 155–60.

54 Dashchuk, *Clearing the Plains,* 100–121.

55 Mosby, "Administering Colonial Science."

56 Stote, *Act of Genocide.*

57 Palmater, *Beyond Blood.*

58 Clatworthy, *Re-assessing the Population Impacts,* 42.

59 Ibid., 33.

60 Godlewska, Moore, and Bednasek, "Cultivating Ignorance of Aboriginal Realities."

61 Watters, "Reproducing Canada's Colonial Legacy," 87–88.

62 Dion, *Braiding Histories,* 179.

63 Battiste, *Decolonizing Education*, 137.

64 Green Meadow, "Promoting Racial Literacy in Schools by Dr. Howard C. Stevenson," video of presentation, 16 December 2015, https://www.youtube.com/watch?v=CK222rNY5bQ (accessed 6 July 2016).

65 Battiste, *Decolonizing Education*, 78.

66 Battiste and McLean, *State of First Nations Learning*, 7.

67 Scollon, *Human Knowledge*, 17–18.

68 Cannon and Sunseri, *Racism, Colonialism, and Indigeneity.*

69 United Nations Development Programme, "Human Development Indices."

70 Manuel and Derrickson, *Reconciliation Manifesto*, 78.

71 Edwards, "Fighting Foster Care."

72 Canada, Public Safety Canada, "Examining Aboriginal Corrections."

73 Britton and Blackstock, *First Nations Child Poverty.*

74 Dei, "Rereading Fanon."

75 Bedford and Workman, "Whiteness and the Great Law," 27.

76 Friedrich, *Democratic Education,* 4.

77 Paikin, *A Commonwealth of Aboriginal Peoples.*

78 Ibid.

79 Standing Committee on Canadian Heritage: Bill C-91: Evidence, Number 148, 28 February 2019, 11, https://www.ourcommons.ca/Content/Committee/421/CHPC/Evidence/EV10357840/CHPCEV148-E.PDF.

80 Standing Committee on Canadian Heritage: Bill C-91: Evidence, Number 144, 21 February 2019, 3, https://www.ourcommons.ca/Content/Committee/421/CHPC/Evidence/EV10334448/CHPCEV144-E.PDF.

81 Standing Senate Committee on Canadian Heritage: Bill C-91: Evidence, 21 February 2019, https://www.ourcommons.ca/Content/Committee/421/CHPC/Evidence/EV10334448/CHPCEV144-E.PDF.

82 Hill, "Canada Endorses United Nations."

83 United Nations, *United Nations Declaration.*

84 TRC, *Final Report*, vol. 6, *Reconciliation*, 12, 38, 45–79.

85 House of Commons, Private Member's Bill: C-262: An Act to ensure that the laws of Canada are in harmony with the United Nations Declaration on the Rights of Indigenous Peoples (Parliament of Canada: LEGISinfo), https://www.parl.ca/LegisInfo/BillDetails.aspx?billId=8160636&Language=E (accessed 3 January 2020).

86 KARIOS, Urgent Action: Ask Senators to Pass Bill C-262, the Declaration, https://www.kairos-canada.org/what-we-do/indigenous-rights/pass-bill-c262 (accessed 4 March 2019).

87 TRC, *Final Report*, vol. 5, *Legacy*, 113.

88 Ibid., 124.

89 TRC, *Honouring the Truth*, 156.

90 Senate, Senate Public Bill S-237: An Act for the Advancement of the Aboriginal Languages of Canada and to Recognize and Respect Aboriginal Language Rights, Parliament of Canada: LEGISinfo, https://www.parl.ca/LegisInfo/BillDetails.aspx?Language=E&billId=8064056&View=3 (accessed 4 March 2019)

91 Senate, Senate Public Bill S-229, https://www.parl.ca/LegisInfo/BillDetails.aspx?Language=E&billId=8064056&View=3.

92 Senate, Senate Public Bill S-212: Status of the Bill, https://www.parl.ca/LegisInfo/BillDetails.aspx?Language=E&billId=8064056&View=0

93 Canada, *Guide to the Canadian House*, 11. https://lop.parl.ca/About/Parliament/GuideToHoC/pdf/guide_canadian_house_of_commons-e.pdf (accessed 3 March 2019).

94 Brake and Troian, "Canada Unveils Indigenous Languages."

95 Amos [Taehowehs] Key, Re: Bill C-91 An Act Respecting Indigenous Languages, Brief to the Standing Committee on Canadian Heritage, 27 February 2019, https://www.ourcommons.ca/Content/Committee/421/CHPC/Brief/BR10367384/br-external/KeyJrAmos-e.pdf.

96 Senate of Canada, Bill S-212: An Act for the advancement of the aboriginal languages of Canada and to recognize and respect aboriginal language rights, first reading, 9 December 2015, http://www.parl.ca/Content/Bills/421/Private/S-212/S-212_1/S-212_1.PDF.

97 Minister of Canadian Heritage and Multiculturalism, Bill C-91: An Act respecting Indigenous languages, 8, working copy, 1 April 2019, http://www.parl.ca/Content/Bills/421/Government/C-91/C-91_2/C-91_2.PDF.

98 Karihwakeron Tim Thompson, "Strengthening the Indigenous Languages Act—Bill C-91," Yellowhead Institute, 27 February 2019, https://yellowheadinstitute.org/2019/02/27/strengthening-the-billc-61/#1551198789991-d5245198-004a.

99 Porter, "First Nations Students."

100 Palmater, "Trudeau's Promises."

101 Ibid.

102 The Standing Senate Committee on Aboriginal Peoples: Bill C-91: Evidence: 2, 3, and 4 April 2019. https://sencanada.ca/en/committees/appa/TranscriptsMinutes/42-1.

103 Sanderson, "Building a Path."

104 Senate, Proceedings of the Standing Senate Committee on Aboriginal Peoples: Study on the New Relationship Between Canada and First Nations, Inuit and Métis Peoples, 19–20 September 2017, Issue No. 25, 25:11, https://sencanada.ca/en/Content/SEN/Committee/421/appa/25cv-e.

105 Ibid., 25:10.

106 Ibid., 25:11.

107 Amos Key Jr., Brief to: Department of Canadian Heritage Standing Committee: Re: Bill C-91, 27 February 2019, https://www.ourcommons.ca/Content/Committee/421/CHPC/Brief/BR10367384/br-external/KeyJrAmos-e.pdf.

108 TRC, *Calls to Action*, 191.

109 Bioneers, *Chief Oren Lyons—The Roots of American Democracy*, 19 December 2014, https://www.youtube.com/watch?v=Gs0EK1z9xhc (accessed 27 January 2017).

110 Hill, "Linking Arms," 19.

CHAPTER 6

LEARNING AND RECONCILIATION FOR THE COLLABORATIVE GOVERNANCE OF FORESTLAND IN NORTHWESTERN ONTARIO, CANADA

MELANIE ZURBA AND JOHN SINCLAIR

In northwestern Ontario conflicts between First Nations and forestry companies that receive licences from the Ontario Ministry of Natural Resources (OMNR at the time of this study; now the Ministry of Natural Resources and Forestry) have occurred for generations.[1] Furthermore, the degradation of land and separation of local Indigenous people from land-based activities have caused a shift in livelihoods, as well as various forms of transgenerational trauma.[2] Racial divides continue to exist in northwestern Ontario, which have been punctuated at times by conflict and violence.[3] Structural forms of oppression dictated through top-down decision making in the resource sector have also persisted within forest governance systems in the region, such as those of the OMNR, and have inhibited meaningful First Nations participation in forestry, forest management, and forestry policy making.[4] These ongoing issues underscore the need for new forest governance approaches that incorporate learning and reconciliation and that are capable of affecting existing forest management institutions.[5]

Recognizing this need, parties have recently attempted new transitional models of governance, guided by collaborative principles. Newer models are often driven by the desire for "peace in the woods," a term coming from people involved in forest governance.[6] However, in considering the meaning of equity and reconciliation, it is important to understand whether the desire for peace in the woods actually denotes a desire for a governance system inclusive of culturally relevant transitional justice mechanisms,[7] or if it simply denotes the absence of direct conflict between First Nations communities and forest companies.[8] Unlike other countries where transitional justice emerged following an end to genocides, armed conflicts, and mass human rights violations, Canada's need for reconciliation centres on settler colonial practices that still exist today.[9]

Our chapter's first objective is to explore structural shifts in forest governance and the potential for reconciliation from the perspective of people involved in forestry in northwestern Ontario. Our second objective is to consider how understanding the learning occurring alongside structural changes in governance can become a possible mechanism for transitional justice and a pathway to reconciliation. Given the issues outlined above, we apply Jonathan Jansen's "post-conflict pedagogy" to consider the structural changes in forestry governance.[10]

The Context for Collaboration and Reconciliation Processes in Northwestern Ontario

The Indigenous peoples of Treaty 3 territory are Anishinaabe (Anishinaabek, plural form) and speak Anishinaabemowin.[11] "Anishinaabe" is an autonym for "Ojibway," and is part of the Algonquin language group—one of the largest Indigenous language groups in North America. The area designated as Treaty 3 covers 55,000 square miles (14,244,935 hectares) of land, encompassing a large part of northwestern Ontario, as well as a small portion of southeastern Manitoba (Figure 6.1). The Grand Council of Treaty #3 is a governance umbrella for the Anishinaabe people, led by the grand chief, with a current membership of twenty-eight First Nations communities. It has a vision of "advancing the exercise of inherent jurisdiction, sovereignty, nation-building, and traditional governance with the aim to preserve and build the Anishinaabe Nation's goal of self-determination," and did not give up the right to traditional self-governance in the signing of the Treaty in 1873.[12]

Figure 6.1. Study area including Treaty 3 lands, Treaty 3 First Nations, and local cities and political borders. Map design by Weldon Hiebert.

The negotiation of Treaty 3 took place at the Northwest Angle of Lake of the Woods. The practice of treaty making in Canada is grounded in the Royal Proclamation of 1763, which states that treaties would be made if "Indian" nations were "inclined" to part with their land.[13] However, Treaty 3 First Nations did not share this interpretation of the treaties. Instead, they understood the treaties as the establishment of a sharing relationship—one that was expected to be reciprocal.[14] This understanding was recorded in the Paypom Treaty, a series of notes taken by Treaty 3 First Nations recording the treaty-making process. The Paypom Treaty is important because, according to the Grand Council of Treaty #3, there is "no single document that covers all of the terms and agreements known as Treaty #3."[15] With regards to resources, the Paypom Treaty outlines how families would be supported in agriculture and would be free to hunt and harvest wild rice, as well as how minerals discovered on "Indian" lands would "be to the benefit of the Indians."[16] There is no mention of forests, or of ceding lands.

Forests have, however, been the centre of industry in this part of northwestern Ontario and have shaped the economy, allocation of lands, and relationships between First Nations and settler populations since colonization.[17] The local forestry industry formally began in the late 1870s to early 1880s with the Keewatin sawmills. With the arrival of the Canadian Pacific Railway in Kenora in 1882, the forestry industry subsequently experienced a boom. In the following decades, several pulp and paper companies developed mills in the Kenora region, especially in the second half of the twentieth century. However, the economic downturn that occurred in the housing industry around 2005 marked a significant shift in development and in the regional forestry economy. The closure of wood-processing plants, along with the direct conflicts occurring over forestry, was the catalyst for changes in the forest tenure system that would bring First Nations into decision-making processes.[18]

With forest tenure modernization, the OMNR and the remaining forest industries operating in the area began to seek out collaborative governance models, which eventually took shape according to partners' interests and ideals.[19] These changes to the conditions under which forest land could be managed allowed some decentralization of forest governance in northwestern Ontario and created the opportunity for partnerships between forestry companies and First Nations. This, in turn, gave First Nations the opportunity to engage in forest decision-making processes in a more substantive way than they had been previously engaged.[20]

In addition to changes in thinking about how forest tenures, Kenora itself has begun to shift in the past decade toward becoming more aware of the need to understand their treaty relationship, reconcile differences, and move toward a common vision.[21] "Common ground," or *Wassay Gaa Bo* in Anishinaabemowin, is now used as both a formal and informal way of speaking of this awareness in the community.[22] This desire for "common ground" may not be completely unanimous, but it is strong enough to have created momentum for a number of like-minded community initiatives.[23] For example, the Common Ground Research Forum (CGRF) was a five-year community–university research alliance project supported by the Social Sciences and Humanities Research Council of Canada. Established in 2009 as the "social action research" component of the common ground movement, it brought together the University of Manitoba, the University of Winnipeg, the City of Kenora, three First Nations, the Grand Council of Treaty #3, and other community organizations.

Despite these recent shifts in forest governance structure, conflicts persist on the land and in Canadian courtrooms, resulting in clashes among First Nations, foresters, and local law enforcement.[24] This includes the clear-cutting dispute in Grassy Narrows territory, which is the longest-standing protest over forestry in the history of Canada.[25] Racism in the region has also been strongly linked to colonization and to development struggles relating to the protection of the environment. Differing visions for economic development between First Nations and the settler community in northwestern Ontario have caused significant rifts and have perpetuated racism based in the belief that First Nations attitudes on resource development might affect settler livelihoods (i.e., employment in the forestry sector).

Against this backdrop an important Indigenous resurgence movement is also happening across Canada and in northwestern Ontario. "Resurgence" is currently defined by Indigenous peoples, activists, and scholars in Canada and across the globe as a deeply connected and culturally driven process guiding the future of Indigenous rights, recognition, and relationships with other nations.[26] Leanne Simpson describes "resurgence" as resistance born out of strength, survival, culture, and relationships among a people, and argues that resurgence is both a political movement and an Indigenous philosophy with its own theoretical, methodological, and pedagogical foundations that centre Indigenous cultural knowledge, laws, governance systems, and land-based ways of teaching and learning.[27]

Indigenous resurgence, among the Anishinaabe peoples of Treaty 3, has been expressed through several actions, such as the Grassy Narrows anti-clear-cutting protest and water walks.[28] It is also expressed through participation in the Idle No More movement,[29] which swept across Canada starting in December 2012 with the slogan: "Turn the tables. Self-determination, not termination."[30] The Idle No More movement continues across Treaty 3 territory and has been connected to other land-based actions (Figures 6.2 and 6.3), such as the forty-year commemoration of the Anicinabe Park Occupation, a solidarity walk/dance for the Elsipogtog First Nation in Nova Scotia protesting shale gas exploration, and protests of the TransCanada Energy East pipeline project.[31] The Treaty 3 Idle No More movement continues to have Internet platforms, including a presence on the Idle No More official webpage and an Idle No More–Kenora / Treaty 3 Facebook page.[32]

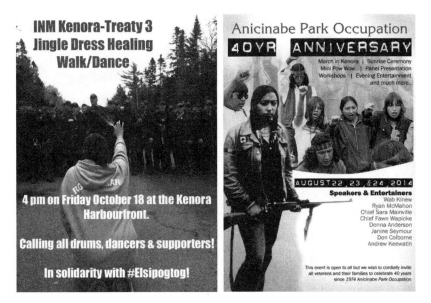

Figure 6.2. Facebook invitation to the Idle No More Kenora–Treaty 3 Jingle Dress Healing Walk/Dance. Reproduced with permission from the Idle No More–Kenora Facebook page, 2015.

Figure 6.3. Poster for the Anicinabe Park Occupation forty-year anniversary. Reproduced with permission from Treaty 3 Facebook page, 2015.

Our Conceptual Framework

Our conceptual framework for "structural reconciliation"—a governance process occurring within established institutions resulting in structural changes that promote equity and relationship building between Indigenous and non-Indigenous peoples—could also be applied to regions outside of northwestern Ontario. Drawing on a diverse body of literature, we begin by defining and differentiating between key terms and concepts, exploring the tensions that exist between conceptualizations of resurgence and reconciliation. We then follow by explaining our pedagogical approach in the context of resurgence and reconciliation.

We adopt Sue Crawford and Elinor Ostrom's definition of institutions that are shaped by structures, rules, norms, and shared strategies affecting human actions and physical conditions.[33] This broad definition is useful for recognizing that institutions may be formally enshrined entities, such as government agencies, or more loosely structured community groups involved in some form of collective action.[34] We use Jan Kooiman's definition of governance as "the totality of interactions, in which public as well as private actors participate, aimed at solving societal problems or creating social opportunities."[35] We draw on the works of Alexander Conley, Margaret Moote, and others who define "collaboration" (in governance) as a process involving communicative action where autonomous parties work toward mutually favourable outcomes.[36]

It is important to frame our analysis of cross-cultural collaborative governance systems that purport to give First Nations greater decision-making powers in the broader context of concepts of reconciliation and resurgence. We note that the concept and practice of reconciliation are widely critiqued by those who argue that reconciliation is a state-sanctioned process that ultimately supports the neocolonial status quo and is used as a state tool to quell internal conflict and uprisings.[37] More recently, Kiera Ladner explores the tensions between reconciliation and resurgence discourse to argue that the "importance of [Indigenous] songs, ceremonies, and stories goes far beyond discourses of anti-assimilation, decolonization, and resurgence, as they provide a basis for meaningful, transformative reconciliation."[38]

Reconciliation, as we understand it, is an ongoing and dialectic process that works toward establishing and maintaining mutually respectful relationships between Indigenous and non-Indigenous peoples into the future.[39] This relational way of thinking about reconciliation is consistent with the Truth and Reconciliation Commission (TRC) of Canada's view of reconciliation.[40] Moreover, as Paulette Regan notes, the Commission's final report concludes, "Reconciliation is . . . contingent on the land-based resurgence of Indigenous cultures, languages, knowledge systems, oral histories, laws, and governance structures."[41] Others note the importance of local contexts and everyday relationships in practices of resurgence and reconciliation. John Borrows says, "State-driven processes . . . can never create or replace the importance of resurgence and reconciliation in the hearts, minds, and actions of people living in more local contexts."[42] Weaving together these conceptual threads establishes a foundation for framing learning and collaboration as platforms for working against oppression.

Mindful of Gina Starblanket and Heidi Kiiwetinipinesiik Stark's caution that "while being committed to the regeneration of a relational way of being is relatively straightforward at a theoretical level, enacting this commitment in our day-to-day lives gives rise to many complex questions and contradictions," we now turn to these in the context of our pedagogical approach.[43] One of the most difficult questions to answer is whether collaboration can truly be a preliminary step toward reconciliation, or if it is simply "settling" in the absence of full sovereignty. We do know that if structural reconciliation is part of new collaborative governance systems, then those systems should be working to decolonize and rebuild authentic relationships, and not simply create new forms of colonial oppression.[44] A move toward structural reconciliation would also be a move toward the reciprocal relationship that Treaty 3 First Nations believed they were entering in 1873.

Learning is necessary for transforming oppressive institutions into ones that reflect greater equity in capacity and decision making.[45] Furthermore, the act of learning makes it possible to explore the different and shared meanings held within a society.[46] Looking at learning provides an opportunity to understand *how* structures are being transformed.[47]

However, a critical analysis of learning must reflect the context of the society in which the learning is taking place.[48] This is especially true for cross-cultural learning, since it includes different ways of knowing.[49] Learning is therefore integral to developing equitable and collaborative governance systems, and examining how people learn under these circumstances can provide important insights into understanding the emergence of structural and other forms of reconciliation.[50] Learning through collaborative governance therefore creates an ideal lens for understanding, and a possible pathway toward, structural reconciliation—a lens that we operationalize in this chapter's case study.

Jonathan Jansen's "post-conflict pedagogy" is a uniquely contextualized framework for examining learning in settings that are transitioning away from racial divides and structural oppression,[51] as it was developed through Jansen's experience as the first Black dean at the (predominantly white) University of the Free State in post-apartheid South Africa, and was used to guide reconciliation processes in the educational setting. Note, we do not use the terminology of post-conflict learning to imply conflict no longer exists. Rather, we believe that Jansen's post-conflict pedagogy provides important insights into learning that is directed toward collaboration and reconciliation.[52]

The attributes of Jansen's post-conflict pedagogy include: (1) the need to establish risk-accommodating environments; (2) the disruption of received knowledge; (3) the significance of pedagogical dissonance; (4) the reframing of victors and victims; (5) the acknowledgement of brokenness; (6) the acknowledgement of the power of "indirect knowledge"; (7) the value of demonstrative leadership; (8) the importance of listening; and (9) the importance of hope.

Indirect knowledge is made up of the culturally embedded world views passed down in a society, including through colonial relations. Examining indirect knowledge allows us to understand *what* is known (e.g., notions of difference and/or superiority) and *how* people hold to views in relation to people considered "Other." This indirect knowledge is deeply emotionally embedded and may often take shape as "racial exclusivity," "racial supremacy," and "racial victimization." This part of Jansen's post-conflict pedagogy is reinforced by other calls for the application of decolonizing pedagogy in Indigenous/settler learning environments, such as Regan's "unsettling pedagogy of history and hope," which engages both intellect and emotion toward unlearning racism and creating the connectivity required for meaningful reconciliation.[53]

In cross-cultural learning environments, the indirect knowledge held by different groups can come into conflict with one another. A post-conflict pedagogy is one that acknowledges this, wherein teachers and leaders are prepared to be emotionally engaged, forthcoming, and compassionate about the need to bring learners together within the "learning commons." This is described as overcoming dissonant knowledge toward crossing the "allegorical bridge," wherein learning facilitators guide learners to break free of their indirect knowledge and find common humanity with Others.

Jansen describes this kind of "brokenness" not as a weakness but rather as a requirement; it is essential to dissolving the "us vs. them" world view and the notion of Others. Jansen uses reflexivity and the power of personal narratives to work with indirect knowledge, which is often intimate, partial, or emotional and is grounded in human experiences and interactions, and his nine key elements relating to the post-conflict pedagogy help us understand learning's potential to transform relationships and bring institutions closer to structural reconciliation.

Research Approach and Methodology

The research presented here is a qualitative case study conducted within the Common Ground Research Forum (described in the section above). We selected the case study based on the following three criteria: (1) it was an example of an existing cross-cultural collaboration for governing land resources; (2) it was viewed locally as a leading example of such collaboration; and (3) there was interest from the main organizations involved in learning as a catalyst for ongoing collaboration. The case study was further chosen through semi-structured interview consultations with key informants, selected based on their various roles and extensive experience in regional consultation or collaboration in the context of resource management: a local historian and private consultant for First Nations, four managers with the Ontario Ministry of Natural Resources, and two managers with the Grand Council of Treaty #3.

Our case study focused on Miitigoog General Partner Inc., which involves local First Nations and industry partners. In Anishinaabemowin, Miitigoog is the forest itself. The corporate entity of Miitigoog is a collaborative endeavour established in 2010. It holds a Sustainable Forestry License (SFL) for the 1.2 million-hectare Kenora Forest. Miisun, the management company for Miitigoog, was formed to oversee Miitigoog's SFL and to direct the management activities in southern portions of the Whiskey Jack Forest (under contract from the OMNR, which continues to hold the SFL). SFLs are administered through the OMNR through the 1995 Crown Forest Sustainability Act on a five-year renewable basis.

In-depth, semi-structured interviews were conducted (n=43) with those involved in collaborative governance (i.e., Miitigoog board members and OMNR managers), along with community leaders, Elders, and people working for the companies on the ground. Informed consent was received from all participants, who could also choose the amount of anonymity within the study (i.e., to be quoted or have their statements synthesized into the larger pool of data).

Interviews were recorded and transcribed verbatim, and were analyzed with the assistance of Atlas.ti computer-assisted qualitative data analysis software (CAQDAS). Axial and selective coding were derived from the conceptual framework and applied to the data. Primary codes were *governance structure(s)* and *learning*. Secondary codes related to Jansen's post-conflict pedagogy (reframing of victors and victims, indirect knowledge, etc.). Emergent themes were also translated into codes that were applied to the interview data.

By matching participants' responses with the conceptual framework describing *governance structure(s)* and the attributes of Jansen's post-conflict pedagogy, we were able to shed light on the effects of collaborative governance and learning on structural reconciliation. The following two subsections under the main title "Results" follow the data analysis and coding structure according to *governance structure(s)* and *learning*, according to the two respective objectives of this chapter.

Results

Collaborative Governance through the Miitigoog Partnership

Miitigoog represents a significant shift in forest tenure, from licences held by forestry companies to licences held in partnership between forestry companies and First Nations in northwestern Ontario.[54] The Miitigoog Shareholder Agreement describes the company structure as well as the types of shareholders, their roles, and the terms of their shares. *Class A Common Shares* are unlimited, are redeemable and retractable, and are to be issued only to the First Nations Trust, a partnership of First Nations that have individual claims to the Kenora and/or Whiskey Jack forests. The original members of the First Nations Trust are Wabaseemoong Independent (a.k.a. Whitedog) Nations, Naotkamegwanning (a.k.a. Whitefish Bay) First Nation, and Ochiichagwe'Babigo'ining (a.k.a. Dalles) Ojibway Nation. The First Nations Trust has since expanded to include three other First Nations: the Ojibways of Onigaming First Nation and of Northwest Angle #33, and the Anishnabeg of Naongashing.

Class A shares must at all times be equal in number to *Class B Common Shares*. These shares belong to the larger industry partners that hold Forest Resource Planning Facility licences issued by the Minister of Natural Resources. *Class C Common Shares* are issued to those who have overlapping licences for the Kenora Forest, namely those companies represented by the Kenora Independent Loggers Association.

During initial negotiations, the partners determined that there would be an equal (50/50) number of shareholders with board-level decision-making authority between First Nations and industry. The OMNR does not have decision-making authority within Miitigoog; however, they would often join board meetings to provide guidance and to ensure their legal obligations were being met.

Zurba, Diduck, and Sinclair investigated the structural nature of Miitigoog's governance system and found that the partnership represented a significant shift in power sharing by the OMNR.[55] It was evident, for example, that changes in forest tenure policy made it possible for partners from First Nations to engage in substantive decision making. However, that substantive decision making was also highly influenced (some promoting and some hindering) by the norms, values, and principles guiding Miitigoog as a collaborative agreement. Miitigoog was institutionally mapped (i.e., relationships were visually depicted in terms of power and influence), and lessons were drawn from investigating the Miitigoog governance structure at different stages of its development, from concept to fully functioning organization. This led to the determination that despite certain shortcomings, Miitigoog as a partnership represented collaboration at the board level, while the OMNR remained in a position of power, since they had the ability to change tenure policy in the future.

Participants who had been involved in initiating Miitigoog commented on the structural shift in governance following tenure reform. Partners from First Nations talked about collaboration as being something that would bring positive change to their communities through greater decision-making power, opportunities to develop their workforce and infrastructure, and the ability to participate more broadly in the governance of their territory. However, despite some of the positive perspectives on how Miitigoog was bringing First Nations into decision making, new members of the First Nations Trust cited a significant learning curve, which may indicate an existing structural imbalance within the Miitigoog board as it continues to take on new members:

> Participant (P) 034: There's a big learning curve, even for myself. People around [the Miitigoog board] are not totally familiar how it operates. I'm probably more involved in this process than the chiefs are. I don't know how much of a learning curve it is for them. . . . The people on the other side of industry I believe are taking advantage of [the learning curve]. That's why I say it's [referring to collaboration] not there yet.

The learning curve presents a (perhaps temporary) disadvantage that mostly relates to unfamiliarity with forest policy, as well as with the board's existing norms, values, and interpersonal dynamics. Some new First Nations Trust members expressed positive attitudes about collaboration and felt they could obtain the learning required to work within the board. Others said that they were not sure if they could reach a working capacity because of the constraints that come along with also being in leadership within a First Nation (i.e., having to balance multiple projects and other responsibilities).

For industry partners Miitigoog meant changes to the relationship between forestry companies and First Nations, often framed as promoting "peace in the woods." The following quote from an industry board member illustrates some of the context for this term:

> P 036: On the woodlands side, [Miitigoog] is probably one of the leading ways of doing business because of 50 percent of the board being Aboriginal involvement and trying to stay relevant. The most important thing was, wherever the forests are to be logged and reforested, whatever bands were involved in those areas the ultimate best way for us to operate was with their full involvement. It would be economic development for those reserves, and peace in the woods for all of us, both sides.

Industry participants used the term "peace in the woods" on a few occasions, often in relation to the ability to do business on the land (e.g., extract resources, do construction work of various forms) with First Nations community buy-in, and without direct conflicts or protests. Striving for and creating peace in the woods, therefore, was one of the outcomes sought, at least by industry, through collaboration.

First Nations board members talked about collaboration as a way to change forest governance without using adversarial actions, such as legal battles, protests, and blockades. Grassy Narrows was cited as an example several times by industry and First Nations collaborators (and the OMNR) as the type of adversarial relationship that was unfavourable and counteractive to collaboration. However, collaborators from First Nations also empathized with Grassy Narrows and talked about the importance of their struggle for autonomy and decision-making power over their traditional territory (First Nations Trust participants 013 and 034).

Structural equity can also be evaluated in terms of the day-to-day management and kinds of opportunities available for people from the collaborating First Nations. The data show that there was a significant change in direction of the day-to-day management of the Kenora Forest and portions of the Whiskey Jack Forest as directed by the First Nations Trust from the management previously conducted solely through the forestry companies.

Through Miisun, Miitigoog's management company, participants indicated that First Nations were ready to exercise agency in the implementation of forest management plans. However, the design of such plans remains primarily in the hands of the OMNR, and the only First Nations people working for Miisun were Anishinaabe liaisons. All forest managers had been previously employed by large forestry companies and were from the settler community. The board of the First Nations Trust made this decision based on a desire to have a robust management system for the forest. Several Miisun staff reflected on this and said that more people from First Nations in forest management would be more equitable, but that this would take a long time because the amount of training involved in obtaining certification as a forest manager.

Some Anishinaabe participants reflected more broadly when asked about collaborative governance and reconciliation. A manager from Grand Council of Treaty #3 referred to the United Nations Declaration on the Rights of Indigenous Peoples (UNDRIP) as an important articulation of how consultation should take place (P 003). OMNR managers often spoke about their "duty to consult and accommodate First Nations," passed down to them through the federal government, but did not reference UNDRIP or any other types of articles. An Anishinaabe liaison working at Miisun shared their perspective on reconciliation and its connection to colonization, and how the treaty was meant to guide a relationship between peoples:

> P 033: The Treaty is just a document that guides a relationship. It is a living historical document and you need more than one party to make a Treaty. Because we did sign onto the Treaty, we know the spirit and intent of [what] the Treaty is. This is what I was negotiating for the Grand Council. I can talk about those aspects. So, we had the constitutional lawyers involved from time to time, and even when they worked with management positions they said they talked about the Treaty aspect of doing business with First Nations. To me, Indians don't come from the Treaty. We were already a people, we had systems in place, we had our own governance in place and we had our own trade initiatives in place.

These thoughts reflect the broader political environment that guides many of the dynamics between settler institutions and First Nations. The participant raises the point that First Nations governance exists outside of the treaty relationship. A few participants also talked about the Great Earth Law, the traditional governance system of the Anishinaabe. The Grand Council of Treaty #3 is currently rearticulating the Great Earth Law so that it can work alongside contemporary Anishinaabe governance. It is not known exactly how the newly articulated Great Earth Law will take shape, but it will likely affect collaboration and be part of the long-term process of structural reconciliation.

The consensus among those who initiated Miitigoog is that the board was collaborative and that participation was meaningful and egalitarian, despite conflict. Many Miitigoog board members stated that conflict was a necessary part of getting to agreements with mutually favourable attributes. Several board members explained that there were times when perspectives were understood only when they were expressed with passionate disapproval, and said that communication improved when people would return to the boardroom after such episodes. However, this was not the feeling for some of the newer board members joining Miitigoog. The same First Nations Trust board member who concluded that collaboration "was not there yet" said he felt that industry was not looking for meaningful participation from First Nations:

> P 034: I think industry thinks it's business as usual, just because they have some brown faces on the board.

"Post-conflict Learning"
The data on Miitigoog's governance activities indicates that this collaborative process reflects several of Jansen's key principles for post-conflict pedagogy.[56] Within this pedagogy Jansen describes the importance of creating a "risk-accommodation environment" where learners feel as if they can express their full range of thoughts and emotions without fear of retribution. In particular, data show that during Miitigoog's creation, OMNR managers played a particularly strong role in bringing people to the table, and in bringing them back to the table to resolve conflicts and find solutions that were mutually agreeable.

The risk-accommodating environment at Miitigoog board meetings was structurally maintained through an independent chair, which board members often cited as important for maintaining an environment where grievances could safely be put forward. The chair was responsible for keeping meetings on track according to the mutually agreed-upon terms, including that Miitigoog board members could air their complaints and challenge positions as long as they did so in a respectful manner.

This was also conducive to the "disruption of received knowledge," which Jansen identifies as a key quality of learning. This disruption explores and constructively confronts circumstances that had previously been the cause of oppression (in this case, forest governance) and strongly connects to the transformation of indirect knowledge. It is a central quality of pedagogical strategies that challenge colonial forms of knowledge.

Pedagogical dissonance, much like the disruption of received knowledge, was also present and a significant component of formal engagement within Miitigoog. For example, the independent chair encouraged board members to comment on how board-level decision making and on-the-ground management processes were advancing. Many board members said they encountered and/or presented viewpoints that were not mainstream, were contentious, and/or required navigating conflicting points of view to come to a decision that reflected greater equity and meaning. One OMNR manager described the kinds of conflicting feelings, experiences, approaches, and perspectives that emerge during natural resources-based negotiations:

> P 008: I [bring up feelings] so that everybody understands how each other feels and can respond accordingly when an issue comes up. . . . "Okay, what are your expectations, and what are your expectations?" There's commonality amongst all of them. Sometimes we just don't realize it, or forget.

The statement indicates that pedagogical dissonance was indeed encouraged during the initiation stage of Miitigoog, and, importantly, became part of the eventual principles and norms for formal engagement that were established for ongoing collaboration, in part through the independent chair.

While certain aspects of Jansen's framework were works in progress at Miitigoog (e.g., new board members' ability to bring forth pedagogical dissonance when they felt they had a large learning curve to overcome), other aspects were more strongly evident and were important for keeping parties at the table to continue the learning and shared governance processes. For example, through formal engagement and informal experiences, people from industry, First Nations, and the OMNR had many opportunities to learn about each other personally. This relates to the "reframing of victors and victims," the next important component in Jansen's pedagogy.

In emancipatory research, there is a tendency to focus exclusively on victims. With regards to the control over forests in northwestern Ontario, the institutions of industry and the OMNR would be labelled the "victors" and First Nations the "victims." However, Jansen's post-conflict pedagogy puts forward the argument that the labels of victors and victims both need to be reframed.[57]

In the context of settler/Indigenous relations as it relates to forest management, the victor/victim identity binary relates to colonizer/colonized identities (and any notions of superiority/inferiority that might be attached). However, these need to be broken down to create a level playing field for collaboration.[58] Relating to the workplace, participants talked about their roles in supporting the different needs of Indigenous and non-Indigenous staff members, and how this sometimes posed challenges. This included working through scheduling issues by paying special attention to the needs of First Nations communities (e.g., different holidays and bereavement times) and developing new communication strategies to learn what workers from First Nations communities needed to participate in employment (e.g., transportation and training).

While there were many changes that supported a shift in discourse away from victors and victims (e.g., the 50/50 decision making of the Miitigoog board), many of the challenges continued. Managers and workers experienced difficulties with communication, and many of those involved in collaboration still felt as though barriers existed between communities and the industry organizations (i.e., *Class B* shareholders) that made up the Miitigoog board:

> P 009: When I first got here and I'd go around to the communities the first thing I'd hear is five hundred years of hatred. "This is what you've done to me." So, you just sit there, you listen, you learn from it.

Jansen explains that the acknowledgement of brokenness, a concept grounded in a person's compassion and acceptance of the human journey, can be burdensome.[59] However, it provides a foundation for understanding why people bring forward painful conversations relating to the past. It also emphasizes the importance of working with the (sometimes transgenerational) trauma when relationship building, and potentially in collaborations. Several industry managers reflected that their learning processes included acknowledging brokenness, both within themselves (e.g., a feeling of living in a fractured society) and within communities due to the history of colonization (e.g., the dispossession of lands and poverty within communities). While participants felt that the acknowledgement of brokenness was exceedingly important, they also talked about the difficulty of putting their awareness into practice in the work environment. The following industry manager spoke of this in terms of having compassion for the people from Wabaseemoong Independent Nations struggling to work in the forest industry:

> P 011: You know, you're taking on all of the aspects and all of the problems of the community, which is poverty, drug addiction, solvent abuse, alcohol. You have all of the issues, which is quite explainable. . . . You have a thousand people in a community and no work. What are you going to do during the day? Like yourself, if you had nothing to do. If you don't give people a future or a purpose. We're all the same in that respect. Who do you turn to?

The acknowledgement of brokenness may seem like a type of victimization when used toward the Other, but instead it is meant to contribute to the reframing of victors and victims by bringing compassion into the structural process.[60]

Among the first collaborators, Other identities did start to shift once relationships were formed and trust was established. Several of the original Miitigoog board members indicated that this shift was a product of having a safe space to discuss not only the emerging collaboration but also some of the broader issues relating to past relationships between industry and First Nations in the region. Following these discussions the collaborators became unified in moving toward their common goal of shared forest governance, which all the partners wanted in the long term. This is not to say that the deeply embedded ideas of the Other disappeared; instead, indirect knowledge was continuously challenged as participants worked toward decolonizing their attitudes within the collaborative space created by the Miitigoog partnership.

The people involved in Miitigoog had several opportunities to bring indirect knowledge to the surface for discussion, mainly through informal relationship building. One First Nations Trust participant talked about how informal experiences led to friendships and trust (a major break from the notions of difference and/or superiority often associated with indirect knowledge) and what that meant when it came to building collaboration:

> P 015: Yeah, I've worked with guys from Weyerhaeuser and Miisun and they're my fishing buddies now. I come out here to fish with them. They come out there to fish with me. . . . Some of the [industry people] that had become my friends I know that they wouldn't lie to me just to cut more trees. I think it's when you build that friendship—if there's something that they don't like and I don't know about then they'll tell me.

This comment also speaks to the more open and reliable communication that comes with building meaningful relationships. An industry partner emphasized reciprocity as something that needs to extend over long periods of time if indirect knowledge is to be broken down enough to affect generational change:

> P 011: [Learning about culture] is something that's handed down through generations. That's not something that's learned overnight. I'm always wanting to learn, and the nice thing is that they're learning to teach. Whether it's bringing me closer to their beliefs, whether it's upbringing or religious. It's the understanding of their culture.

Such comments reflect how formal processes (e.g., ceremony) as well as informal experiences can give insight into Indigenous peoples' values and beliefs.

Jansen also cites "leadership" as being a key quality of learning together to eventually build cross-cultural post-conflict institutions.[61] Even though the OMNR played a strong role in initiating collaboration between First Nations and industry, leadership was also evident at the board level. The founding members of Miitigoog were leaders within their communities and companies. These individuals were mutually cited as being critical to its success, and the ability to work together toward a shared vision was referred to time and time again by several participants as an important leadership characteristic.

However, one industry participant said that he felt that First Nations community leadership (i.e., chiefs and councillors) became less important once collaboration was established as an entity of its own, and other industry partners also expressed similar thoughts:

P 024: Regardless of what happens over time with change in councils and changes in chiefs, it's key that [Miitigoog] is a good business model so it can move forward and it can flourish. Under whatever the current leadership is, although it is extremely important to get the initiative off the ground and get it moving, but over time when the business flourishes then existing leadership doesn't remain as important as they see how the business is set up and how it works. It is important to keep some separation between the politics and the business of a community.

Most participants from the Miitigoog board referred to the "importance of listening" within their formal processes, which is Jansen's second-last core principle. Two of the industry partners (024 and 032) emphasized that listening and being patient were two of the most important things they had learned about collaboration. In general there was an appreciation for hearing different perspectives, and rigid attitudes toward learning and decision making were virtually absent from the data.

Finally, and perhaps most essential to learning in a post-conflict setting, is what Jansen refers to as "the importance of hope." Hope comes from the cumulative learning and integration of all the attributes already discussed in this section.[62] Hope is also a reflection of holistic learning, and indicates strength of process and strength of relationship with those who are engaged.[63] Those who started Miitigoog shared a common hope that this form of collaboration would take them in the right direction, bringing about positive change for local communities and setting a good business model for industry.

This hope was, however, tempered by some of the newer First Nations Trust members, labourers, and managers from the Grand Council of Treaty #3. One Miisun worker described being hopeful, but he was also aware that collaboration is deeply embedded in the colonial system:

P 028: I'm hopeful [about relationships and collaboration] all the time no matter what, but at the same time that's going against a traditional process that's already been made between government and municipalities, contractors, all the employees, basically the public and that's been in effect for longer than you and I have been alive.

Discussion

Viewed through the lens of our conceptual framework and pedagogical approach, we are able to shed light on Miitigoog with regards to structural reconciliation. The data above pertaining to governance reveal that collaboration through Miitigoog did result in structural shifts (i.e., 50/50 decision making at the board level, and management decision making by First Nations through Miisun), which can be considered conciliatory in light of previous forest governance structures in northwestern Ontario.

Applying Jansen's post-conflict pedagogical model to this specific case study provided further insight into how reconciliation could be fostered through collaboration. While some of the components were strongly acknowledged (e.g., the acknowledgement of brokenness and the importance of listening), and others had only begun to take root (e.g., the disruption of indirect knowledge), different qualities of learning created a pathway for navigating and improving relationships between parties and individuals, and all attributes of Jansen's pedagogy were observable within the Miitigoog governance system.

The steep learning curve for new members to the First Nations Trust also indicates that there is much work to be done to make collaborative governance meaningful for the next generation of participants. Power imbalances based on held knowledge, therefore, will need to be worked through for participation and learning to become further aligned with structural reconciliation.

One thing to consider is that the Miitigoog board can be described as what John Gaventa calls an "invited space."[64] This type of shared space is based on dynamic relationships, which include constant struggles for legitimacy.[65] Gaventa highlights that the dynamic in a shared space is often influenced by the capacity of participants, and that power in these situations may belong to the "already empowered elite" (in this case, the founding members of Miitigoog).[66] Within this space alternative arguments to land use could be presented, but needed to fit within the mandate of Miitigoog (i.e., continued forestry) if they were to have any effect on forestry practices. More "radical," traditionally Indigenous, or resurgent perspectives therefore did not manifest in this case. It is reasonable to speculate that First Nations people with perspectives more directed toward resurgent forms of self-governance remained outside of these collaborations, at least partially because participating could have potentially negative implications for other community-based resurgence actions. Furthermore, participating could be viewed as a form of cooptation that replicates colonial relations, rather than decolonizing or transforming them.

However, the structural shifts with regards to decision-making authority meant that First Nations were playing a more central role in decision making. First Nations involved in Miitigoog entered into collaborative governance by choice as a way of bringing benefits to their respective communities. Nevertheless, one could quite rightly argue that the advantage of joining Miitigoog is that it provided best-case scenarios (which are often associated with collaborative governance, because of the innate connections between collaboration and compromise in any negotiation process)[67] but few opportunities to fully express land rights and self-determination, especially as Treaty 3 First Nations never ceded their land.

It is also important to consider the scope of the case study and our application of structural reconciliation. If we reflect on Miitigoog as an entity that operates for the Kenora SFL, we can assert that structural reconciliation has happened specifically through changes in participation, decision making, and learning at the board level, with such reconciliation being limited from advancing further due to the top-down decision-making authority of the OMNR. However, if we consider the entire forest governance system in northwestern Ontario as being a dynamic system that affects the multitude of actors involved (e.g., First Nations, the OMNR, municipalities, etc.), then we can more appropriately consider collaboration to be a first step rather than an accomplished goal. There will need to be many more meaningful relationships built to guide participants down the long path toward land-based structural reconciliation.

Through Jansen's pedagogical framework it was possible to contextualize learning as it related to the Other. New types of relationships were formed both structurally (i.e., formalized collaboration) and personally, creating unique opportunities for partners to explore further how they considered one another and their roles in the partnership agreement and in the sharing of resources more broadly.[68] However, aspects of Jansen's pedagogy, such as the reframing of victors and victims, cannot be fully realized if structural barriers are maintained, such as the overarching authority of the OMNR. Therefore, the use of Jansen's framework is limited by the context of forestry in northwestern Ontario, since major structural damage has not occurred in the way that it did for educational institutions in post-apartheid South Africa. Useful additions to Jansen's framework could also include pedagogical approaches that are explicitly decolonizing. Despite this limitation, the influence of several elements of Jansen's post-conflict pedagogy on the learning occurring through collaborative governance in Miitigoog indicates that this framework has applications to natural resources and land-based governance systems that are cross-cultural and are in a process of transition.

Forest policy in northwestern Ontario through shared SFLs could also be considered a step closer to reflecting the relationship set forth by Treaty 3; however, much remains to be achieved with regards to Indigenous sovereignty and authority over traditional territories.[69] Structural shifts, along with significant barriers that prevent the full assertion of First Nations governance, means that Miitigoog could be described as a socio-political space with a new kind of forestry agenda (i.e., inclusive of First Nations decision making) but a forestry agenda nonetheless. Miitigoog was largely conceived of and led by government and industry people who influenced the formation of the collaborative governance systems to complement state and industry objectives. As such, it could be criticized as a system that legitimizes state claims to land and structurally ensures "continued access to Indigenous peoples' lands and resources by producing neocolonial subjectives that coopt Indigenous people into becoming instruments of their own dispossession."[70]

The argument regarding state legitimization runs parallel to other arguments about the effects of state-centric reconciliation rhetoric on long-term relationship building between Indigenous and non-Indigenous peoples. Coulthard argues that such state-centric rhetoric can hinder decolonization and relationship building, because it is based on colonial interpretations of reconciliation and does not recognize or promote Indigenous cultural practices that are grounded in self-recognition.[71] As Rachel George argues in this volume, a limited gesture of redress (as some may interpret Miitigoog's shared governance structure) can be used to "quell" Indigenous peoples' discontent stemming from much larger issues the state is eager to ignore. Cody O'Neil also points out in this volume that settler governments' capitalist economies would be severely threatened if they were to relinquish significant control over Indigenous lands and labour. This is consistent with the continued overarching authority of the OMNR.

Therefore, recognition of sovereignty and community-driven concepts for reconciliation and decolonization will be essential in the next steps for enhancing meaningful governance outcomes for First Nations. The TRC framed reconciliation as contingent on Indigenous self-determination, as does the United Nations Declaration on the Rights of Indigenous Peoples. While this is and will remain a difficult issue for resource-rich areas such as northwestern Ontario, recognizing Indigenous self-determination would support the long-term goals of structural reconciliation in northwestern Ontario and beyond.

Conclusion

The Miitigoog governance structure represents a considerable shift away from previous forest management arrangements, which did not create space for collaboration in the form of equal partnerships and shared decision making among First Nations governments, colonial governments, and industry. Using a conceptual framework for structural reconciliation and Jansen's post-conflict learning, our data reveal that learning-oriented collaborative governance within the Miitigoog partnership is promoting relationship building and reconciliation. Most of the elements of Jansen's framework were prominent in the learning data; and most of these were found within formal settings, such as boardrooms, and connected to people's roles in governance as facilitators, managers, and community people. This learning, however, did not appear to spread past the Miitigoog board, and the OMNR remained in a position of authority.

It is yet to be fully determined if this collaboration will create lasting opportunities for structural reconciliation. Partners will be required to continue to build trust and reciprocity,[72] and structural forms of oppression will continuously need to be confronted and assessed. The provincial government, through the OMNR, has the power to review Miitgoog as an effective model for collaboration and renew the SFL every five years. Regardless of how Miitigoog's success is measured, however, the top-down authority of the OMNR makes Miitigoog vulnerable to shifts in the political landscape and resulting policy at the provincial level.

This study illustrates how exploring governance structures and learning can help us understand what drives reconciliation in the context of relationships regarding land and resources. The study also illuminates how learning and reconciliation can be either enhanced or confined by the power of the state, and how learning and reconciliation will go only so far without further devolution of authority and the recognition of Indigenous governance systems and approaches to reconciliation. Our findings echo many of the findings of the Truth and Reconciliation Commission of Canada regarding the importance of making space for Indigenous knowledge, governance systems, and laws that foster reconciliation.[73]

Acknowledgements

We would like to thank the study participants for sharing their perspectives so generously. We would like to extend a special thank you to Daniel Wemigwans for his extra guidance on the Miitigoog partnership and how to follow the correct cultural protocols. Your candidness about your experiences working together is at the heart of this project. We would also like to thank the reviewers and editors for their assistance with this final product.

The CGRF is a Community-University Research Alliance supported by the Social Sciences and Humanities Research Council of Canada (SSHRC 833-2008-1007). The research was also supported through a SSHRC doctoral scholarship.

Notes

1 Willow, "Conceiving Kakipitatapitmok"; Zurba, "Building Common Ground."

2 Tobias and Richmond, "'That Land Means Everything.'"

3 Anderson and Robertson, "'Bended Elbow' News.'"

4 Wyatt et al., "Collaboration between Aboriginal Peoples."

5 Ibid.; Lane and Hibbard, "Doing It for Themselves."

6 Hayter, "'The War in the Woods'"; Jackson and Curry, "Peace in the Woods."

7 Lundy and McGovern, "Whose Justice?"

8 Höglund and Kovacs, "Beyond the Absence of War."

9 Nagy, "Scope and Bounds."

10 Jansen, *Knowledge in the Blood*.

11 Government of the Anishinaabe Nation in Treaty #3, "Grand Council Treaty #3."

12 Government of the Anishinaabe Nation in Treaty #3, "About."

13 Canada, Indian and Northern Affairs Canada, "Highlights from the Report."

14 Grand Council of Treaty #3, "We Have Kept Our Part."

15 Grand Council of Treaty #3, "Paypom Treaty."

16 Ibid.

17 Hunt, "Indigenous Lands Management."

18 Zurba and Trimble, "Youth as the Inheritors"; Zurba, Diduck, and Sinclair, "First Nations and Industry."

19 Zurba, Diduck, and Sinclair, "First Nations and Industry."

20 Ibid.

21 Wallace, "Grassroots Community-based Peacebuilding."

22 Robson et al., "What's in a Name?"; Wheeler et al., "Place-Based Inquiry's Potential."

23 Wallace, "Grassroots Community-based Peacebuilding," 75.

24 Willow, "Conceiving Kakipitatapitmok"; Willow, *Strong Hearts*.

25 Ibid.

26 Simpson, *Dancing on Our Turtle's Back;* Corntassel, "Re-envisioning Resurgence"; King, *Inconvenient Indian;* Coulthard, *Red Skin*.

27 Simpson, *Dancing on Our Turtle's Back*, 148.

28 Willow, "Conceiving Kakipitatapitmok"; Willow, *Strong Hearts*; Thompson, "First Nations Demonstrate against Federal Bills Outside Kenora MP's Office," *Kenora Daily Miner and News*, 11 December 2012; Thompson, "Grassy Narrows Youth Lead Demonstrations in Kenora," *Kenora Daily Miner and News*, 7 November 2013; Idle No More, "Anishinaabe Water Walk."

29 Idle No More, "The Story."

30   Ibid.

31   Idle No More, "Kenora Family Day."

32   Idle No More, "Idle No More Kenora."

33   Crawford and Ostrom, "Grammar of Institutions."

34   Ostrom, *Evolution of Institutions.*

35   Kooiman, *Governing as Governance,* 4.

36   Conley and Moote, "Evaluating Collaborative Natural Resource"; Ross, Buchy, and Proctor, "Laying Down the Ladder."

37   Henry, "From Reconciliation to Transitional Justice"; Matsunaga, "Two Faces"; Coulthard, *Red Skin.*

38   Ladner, "Proceed with Caution," 251.

39   Arbour, "Economic and Social Justice."

40   TRC, *Honouring the Truth,* 3.

41   Regan, "Reconciliation and Resurgence," 213.

42   Borrows, "Earth-Bound," 66.

43   Starblanket and Stark, "Towards a Relational Paradigm," 200.

44   Coulthard, *Red Skin,* 22.

45   Keen, Brown, and Dyball, *Social Learning;* Zurba, "Leveling the Playing Field."

46   Merriam, Caffarella, and Baumgartner, *Learning in Adulthood;* Kroth and Cranton, "Transformative Learning through Storytelling."

47   Mezirow, "Contemporary Paradigms of Learning"; Taylor, "Transformative Learning Theory."

48   Cranton, *Understanding and Promoting;* Gozawa, "Cultural Complex and Transformative"; Tisdell, *Exploring Spirituality and Culture.*

49   Davidson-Hunt and Berkes, "Learning as You Journey."

50   Olsson et al., "Shooting the Rapids"; Zurba, "Leveling the Playing Field," 134–35.

51   Jansen, *Knowledge in the Blood.*

52   Ibid.

53   Regan, *Unsettling the Settler Within,* 19–53.

54   Zurba, Diduck, and Sinclair, "First Nations and Industry."

55   Ibid.

56   Jansen, *Knowledge in the Blood,* 260.

57   Ibid., 30.

58   Regan, *Unsettling the Settler Within.*

59   Jansen, "Bearing Whiteness."

60   Jansen, *Knowledge in the Blood,* 271.

61   Ibid., 269.

62   Ibid.

63   O'Sullivan, "Emancipatory Hope."

64 Gaventa, "Toward Participatory Governance."

65 Ibid.

66 Ibid.

67 O'Leary and Vij, "Collaborative Public Management."

68 Fisher-Yoshida, Geller, and Schapiro, *Innovations in Transformative Learning.*

69 Simpson, "Land as Pedagogy."

70 Coulthard, *Red Skin,* 156.

71 Ibid.

72 Zurba et al., "Building Co-management."

73 TRC, *Honouring the Truth.*

Part Three

RESEARCHING

CHAPTER 7

WHAT DOES RECONCILIATION MEAN TO NEWCOMERS POST-TRC?

CATHY ROCKE AND RÉGINE UWIBEREYEHO KING

Truth and reconciliation commissions are, Priscilla Hayner notes, "bodies set up to investigate a past history of violations of human rights in a particular country—which can include violations by the military or other government forces or by armed opposition forces,"[1] and supplement legal prosecutions to promote societal healing and reconciliation.[2] According to Darryl Robinson,[3] truth and reconciliation commissions are established in order to give voice to victims, build comprehensive records of events and causes, provide societal acknowledgement, facilitate compensation for victims, initiate reconciliation, and propose recommendations for the future. Beginning in 2009 the Truth and Reconciliation Commission of Canada (TRC) pursued the mandate of gathering written and oral histories of residential school Survivors and establishing recommendations for reconciliation between Indigenous peoples and other Canadians. As outlined in the Indian Residential Schools Settlement Agreement (IRSSA), "reconciliation" is defined as "an ongoing individual and collective process [that] will require commitment from all those affected including First Nations, Inuit and Métis former Indian Residential School (IRS) students, their families, communities, religious entities, former school employees, government and the people of Canada. Reconciliation may occur between any of the above groups."[4]

Canadians have divergent perspectives about the TRC. For instance, Colleen Sheppard[5] classifies them in two: (1) those who assume that Canada is a post-conflict country, where the harmful conflict has stopped, and suggest that acknowledgement, apology, and related forgiveness and compassion will suffice; and (2) those who assume that Indigenous people continue to be harmed and thus suggest structural and systemic change in the existing relationship between Indigenous and non-Indigenous people. Jean Paul Lederach argues that the catalyst for reconciliation requires both a relationship and encounter between the parties, but also requires us to look beyond the "mainstream international political traditions, discourse, and operational modalities . . . to find innovation."[6]

The definition of reconciliation in the IRSSA encompasses perspectives of both individual healing and structural change. However, the paths toward reconciliation within the Canadian context remain contested. For example, despite numerous long-standing Treaties between different Indigenous groups and the government of Canada, the majority of Canadians continue to believe that Treaties "are not more than outdated contracts"[7] and as such can be breached. In Canada the distortion of history within the grade school curriculum has also long been debated. Frances Henry and Carol Tator argue that the history curriculum within Canadian schools "often exhibits a dominant-culture bias that expresses itself in the way history texts are written" and that there is resistance to "look beyond the study of British, American, and European history."[8]

This lack of knowledge of Indigenous peoples and their history in Canada extends to new immigrants to Canada. Dialogue groups held in Vancouver in 2010 among First Nations, urban Indigenous, and immigrant communities identified that participants had developed stereotypes of each other based on what Zool Suleman calls the "erasure of histories"[9] of both Indigenous and immigrant communities. The TRC's Calls to Action 93 and 94 specifically insist on including a more comprehensive history of Indigenous peoples in the information kit, citizenship test, and Oath of Citizenship for newcomers to Canada.[10] Although newcomers constitute an important part of the Canadian fabric, it remains unclear how newcomers perceived the TRC, understood its meaning, and viewed their role in it. This chapter presents the findings of a pilot research project that sought to explore newcomers' current understanding of reconciliation and perceptions on the kind of reconciliation that would work for the Canadian context.

Study Site and Participants

The present study was conducted in Winnipeg, Manitoba. The city of Winnipeg represents a unique site for this study because of the nature of the formation of its current population and the steps that have been made toward reconciliation between Indigenous and non-Indigenous citizens.

Increasingly, Indigenous people have been making Winnipeg their home. The United Way of Winnipeg notes that "between 1996 and 2001, the Aboriginal population grew by 21.9% (10,005 people)" and "between 2001 and 2006, the Aboriginal population increased by 22.7% (12,630 people)."[11] By 2011 Statistics Canada identified that within Canada, the Metis population is highest in the city of Winnipeg with 46,325 individuals.[12]

Over the last two decades, Manitoba has also seen an increase in its refugee and immigrant populations. Since 2000, 150,000 people have immigrated to the province of Manitoba, with the majority of these newcomers settling in the city of Winnipeg.[13] Most of these new immigrants entered Canada under the economic class category (79.2 percent),[14] but in 2014 Manitoba received the highest number of refugees in its history.[15] Since then, the number of regugees has continued to climb. Similar to many other newcomers, many refugees who arrive in Winnipeg first resettle within inner city neighbourhoods, where they live in close proximity with the urban Indigenous population.[16] For many in the Indigenous and refugee communities who live in poverty, the Winnipeg's inner city is one of the only neighbourhoods where they can find affordable housing and have easy access to public transportation. The pervasive racism within Winnipeg[17] against Indigenous people and some racialized newcomers (those newcomers who arrive in Canada from non–Western European countries) also drives some residents to choose the inner city to be in closer proximity to similar community members.[18]

Study Objectives

The researchers had the opportunity to engage newcomers in conversation regarding their understanding of the TRC in the Canadian context and to determine what they perceive to be their role in the reconciliation process. Parvin Ghorayshi,[19] and John Gyepi-Garbrah, Ryan Walker, and Joseph Garcea[20] explored similar themes in their studies. However, our study occurred subsequent to the release of the TRC's *Final Report* with an overall goal to understand how newcomers understood processes of reconciliation and the Canada TRC Calls to Action and their implementation. The objectives of this pilot study were to: (1) determine how newcomers understand reconciliation with Indigenous peoples since the release of the TRC's *Final Report* in order to inform how to move forward with reconciliation efforts; and (2) articulate examples of reconciliation actions that may strengthen mutual respect and harmony between Indigenous people and newcomers. The objectives of this research are supported by one of the Calls to Action within the TRC report, which identified the need to "advance understanding of reconciliation" and the "urgent need for more dialogue between Aboriginal peoples and new Canadians."[21] It is our hope that this pilot study's research findings will help inform future reconciliation efforts between Indigenous peoples and newcomers.

Methods

This qualitative research was exploratory in nature. We recruited research participants with the help of a research assistant using a snowball approach, which is a "non-probability sample" in which each person interviewed may suggest additional people to interview.[22] The specific research assistant was chosen based on her connections within the newcomer community. The research assistant initially suggested a number of participants and then a few of the participants suggested other individuals from the newcomer community.

We recruited participants from different parts of the world with the hope of gaining rich data from diverse perspectives. Research participants represented a number of countries, including Eritrea, Ethiopia, Mali, Kenya, Rwanda, El Salvador, Colombia, Argentina, Philippines, China, Nepal, India, Kurdistan/Iraq, Ukraine, Germany, and Scotland. Of the twenty-three research participants, twelve were female and eleven were male, ranging from twenty-five to sixty-five years of age, with 78 percent of the research participants between thirty and fifty-five years of age. In-depth interviews were conducted with fifteen individuals (N=15), seven males and eight females. In addition, two focus groups, formed according to gender, were conducted with eight participants (four females and four males). In consultation with the research assistant, both researchers decided to divide the focus groups according to gender. This decision was based on the perception that this would allow for free-flowing discussion unencumbered by any gender dynamics that exist in some newcomer communities. The majority of research participants were university educated (96 percent), and 74 percent have lived in Canada for fifteen years or less. Of the research participants who responded, 52 percent were economic immigrants and 26 percent were refugees.[23]

The same interview guide was used for both the individual interviews and the focus group discussions (see Appendix for list of questions). In keeping with the research objectives, research participants were asked to respond to questions that reflected their understanding of the TRC in the Canadian context and helped to determine what they perceive to be their role in collaborating with Indigenous people in the reconciliation process. The questions used in the interview guide sought to determine participants' understanding of reconciliation in general, the history of Indigenous peoples in Canada, the TRC, their role in reconciliation with Indigenous people, and examples of conflict resolution and reconciliation processes that might help reconcile the relationship between Indigenous and non-Indigenous peoples. Ethics approval was obtained from the Psychology/Sociology Research Ethics Board at the University of Manitoba before the data collection.

Data from the individual interviews and the focus groups were audiotaped and transcribed for analysis. Data were analyzed using thematic analysis, which identifies, analyzes, and reports patterns (themes) within data.[24] The two researchers analyzed the data first separately, then together, by comparing the identified themes and quotes that helped to explain them. They obtained consensus on the main themes outlined in the findings section.

Findings

The findings presented in this chapter focus on the responses newcomers had about their understanding and role in the TRC in relation to the different identities they occupy as newcomers in Canada. Some participants did not view reconciliation as an issue that concerned them because they did not perceive themselves as part of the past wrongs in Canada. Others perceived themselves as Canadians and thus as part of the solution to the wrongs done by other Canadians. A third group, who originated from formerly colonized countries, felt they shared similar past experiences of colonialism and needed to ally themselves with Indigenous peoples in order to overcome the consequences of the destruction caused by colonialism.

It Is Not My Fight!

Several participants responded that they did not view the current conflict between Indigenous and non-Indigenous peoples as their fight:

> What have I done wrong to Aboriginal population? Nothing. So there is no need to talk about reconciliation then, from my understanding. But perhaps we should be able, because we are all part of this society, we should be able to work together to be able to build a strong society together, and to do that . . . we have to respect each other, we have to value the culture and the values of each culture, each population.

> I don't think there is a need for reconciliation because if we're talking about reconciliation that means something must have happened in the past between the Aboriginal community and the newcomers . . . the new Canadians, there is no past history between the two of them.

> I don't think we have any conflict that needs the reconciliation.

> I kind of disagree on this word reconciliation between the Aboriginal and the newcomer, I think it should be between government and Aboriginal people—newcomers they don't know because we never fought we don't need to reconcile with them. So we need education, listen, the newcomers need education on how, why they are there . . . new immigrants doesn't need to reconcile with them, but we just need more information about them, or they need more information about . . . our culture, our language . . . but the reconciliation word itself—the government and the First Nation[s], they should reconcile.

These research participants did not see a need for reconciliation with Indigenous peoples, as they were not part of the past wrongs inflicted on Indigenous peoples. However, they were aware of the mistreatment of Indigenous people in their midst and agreed that they owed them respect and honour regardless of wherever and whenever they arrived in this country. Although racialized newcomers may not perceive the need to reconcile with Indigenous peoples, many are empathetic to the conditions of Indigenous people and do wish to build coalitions between their respective communities.[25] Ravi DeCosta and Tom Clark observe that this perspective was more apparent within the more recently arrived newcomer populations.[26]

A Shared Canadian Identity

Some research participants admitted that although they did not do anything wrong to Indigenous people, since they have become Canadians, they share with other Canadians the responsibility to make things better by participating in the reconciliation process with Indigenous people:

> I believe I didn't contribute anything in the history to have it done that way. But if I don't understand, though I am a latecomer, I can continue the damage that started [a] long time [ago] if I am not aware. I can be part of the person who's oppressing if I'm not aware. Without knowing you can be an accomplice.... I don't want to fall into the wrong history, I want to be a participant of a good and vibrant society and that is by involving myself, participating myself in the reconciliation process because I am Canadian.

> There's a conflict and we need reconciliation so that we can have [a] more positive future or more peaceful future. For the newcomers I still think there is need for reconciliation although they might not have been involved in historic things and things in the past processes that [resulted] in oppression of Aboriginal people, but still I think there's a need for communication and for interaction.

Along with needing to participate in reconciliation processes, these participants acknowledged that choosing not to engage in these processes serves only to perpetuate the continued oppression of Indigenous people within Canadian society. Robinder Kaur Sehdev argues that it is imperative that newcomers recognize their implication in the colonial project against Indigenous peoples in Canada.[27]

Becoming Allies

Several research participants did not feel that the need for reconciliation was the primary issue, but rather there was a need to work together as allies based on the similar history of colonization:

> We were also victims of colonization from the countries where we came from.

> I am connected with them through colonization ... I recognize the suffering ... we are more close than different.

If you look at the history of these people there is so much in common,
you know. If you look at the colonial history most newcomers . . . come
from places where they have suffered the same type of injustices . . .
there is a lot of commonalities that could easily lead to solidarity.

Equating the immigrant to the colonizer would be taking away from
the strength that we can find from each other as outsiders because what
we were subjected to is very similar [to what] the Aboriginal people
[were] subjected to.

Most of the newcomers have experienced the same problems the
way Aboriginal people are experiencing now. That is why we left our
countries as refugees, so one group comes, oppresses the other ones, this
group moves out, goes outside. The same problem Aboriginal people
face we face the same, so we should really find a common ground
whereby we can understand each other. We don't want Aboriginal
[people] thinking that we the newcomers are coming to take their
jobs, to take everything. We want them to receive us as people who are
coming in really to have an input to contribute towards the economy of
this country, we don't want them to see us as afraid that we are coming
to take their jobs and everything.

My argument would be the immigrant was not an enemy in the
first place. So you don't [need] reconciliation. . . . I don't think the
immigrants were part of that process . . . immigrants are so busy
trying to survive here and sort their issues out that if they're stepping
on the toes of the Aboriginal people it's not with that deliberate
intention . . . because they think they are equally as victimized as the
Aboriginal people.

Past studies on the relationship between newcomers and Indigenous
people and their perceptions of one another concur that there is a general-
ized lack of knowledge about each other[28] and a significant distance between
these two groups.[29] According to Ghorayshi there are "layers of separation"[30]
between Indigenous people and newcomers in Winnipeg, despite the fact
that they live in the same neighbourhoods. Even though some newcomers
share a common history of colonialism, racism, and socio-economic difficulties,[31] this can also result in strained relationships between newcomers and
Indigenous people, especially when there is competition for scarce resources

(e.g., housing).[32] However, Maria Wallis, Lina Sunseri, and Grace-Edward Galabuzi maintain that colonization and racialization could be "one juncture from which to build an honest dialogue and form solidarity,"[33] as the common experiences of exclusion stemming from colonial forces may provide a way to examine the intersectionality of displacements of Indigenous people and refugees.[34]

Overall, despite the different perspectives participants had about reconciliation, all of them strongly emphasized the need to form relationships with Indigenous people:

> I think that it's very important to—there should be connection between newcomer immigrant[s] and Aboriginal people.

> I mean maybe it's not reconciliation, it's just meeting there—having these new relationships forged that are coming from a place of understanding.

The emerging research supports these findings by showing the importance of interaction and understanding of each other's cultures and the creation of shared spaces that can allow open dialogue.[35]

Lack of Information

Beyond the above varying perspectives, all participants agreed that there is a general lack of information provided to newcomers on the history of Canada and Indigenous peoples, specifically during their orientation before and upon their arrival in Canada. When they arrive in Winnipeg, newcomers are often shocked by the conditions in which Indigenous people live, including the issues of homelessness, alcoholism, and general poverty they observe in the inner city of Winnipeg. This first impression and the lack of information that most newcomers have about the history of Indigenous peoples in Canada often make the first encounter a negative one. As a result this reinforces negative stereotypes that newcomers develop about Indigenous people. A few participants offered examples from their own experiences:

> I have a friend . . . first time . . . to Canada and I take him from the airport, take him to the McDonald's. And there was one Aboriginal guy he told me . . . and my friend, "Give me a burger, give me a burger!" So he say, "We don't have anything" [and] he told to my friend, "Go back

to your country!" You know . . . straight from the airport he was hungry and he said to me, "You told me on the way, Friendly Manitoba!"

On the street a gentleman asked me for coins, he had a cup, and I was really startled, and I was shocked. I never thought a white person would beg so I gave him money.

Some participants added that these stereotypes and prejudice can be reinforced by some of the people who welcome newcomers:

I went to an entry program and we were actually taught negative things about Native people . . . that you have to be careful you know, you have to look after yourself on the street, you might be attacked.

When you are a newcomer, the first impressions from other people is just telling you the wrong thing what they do . . . they told me is like they're drinkers and they just, they don't want to do anything, they just lazy and they just want to live off the government . . . nobody told me the history why they are that way, what happened to their parents, what happened to their brothers, what happened to—you know? Like for the older people who went through, right? As a newcomer I just came to a new country but I didn't know about the history.

Stereotypes, when you think Aboriginal [people] are always—first thing that comes to mind those people who are homeless, they drink a lot, they don't work, these are the stereotypes that has been posed to me when I first arrived in Canada . . . there's still fear in me . . . there's still lots that I don't know about them but I find once I got to know them they are actually good people.

As participants suggest, newcomers to Canada do not receive information or they receive only very superficial information about the true history of Canada. What they see and hear from those who came before them, or members of the mainstream, may reinforce stereotypes and prejudice against Indigenous people.

The Canadian government often provides a generally romanticized and sanitized representation of Canada, as demonstrated in the Citizen and Immigration Canada booklet entitled *Welcome to Canada: What you should know*. Research shows that the image Canadian politicians and immigration services portray ignores or sanitizes the history of Indigenous peoples.[36] This lack of comprehensive historical information about the Indigenous peoples of Canada may explain the vulnerability of newcomers to the existing stereotypes and prejudices about Indigenous people upon arrival. Some participants offered their observations:

> I think there's a very romanticized picture of Indigenous people . . . associate it with a very narrow-minded set of ideas about being connected with the environment, living a traditional lifestyle.

> With what's all going on and where I come from, a poor country and people live in really destitute situations and you come to Canada and you see people who live [in] more destitute situation than what you think . . . is sad, is very sad when everything is here like to make life better or the chances are there all the money is there. . . . I feel ashamed to call myself Canadian.

Others indicated that it is after this realization that they start challenging other newcomers, especially when the latter take the same misinformed attitudes and views toward Indigenous people. One participant explained how he challenges other newcomers through his work:

> I'm working with the newcomers and when they come here, so many times they tell me "oh these people, they are like this one, they are like this one" so I told them "sit down, cool down, do you know their history? Do you know their—" They say no, no, so now I try to tell them and they say "ooh okay," they understand now.

While this participant took it upon himself to stop the perpetual stereotypes, many refugees and immigrants do not have the opportunities to unlearn and intervene to make a difference in the relationship between Indigenous and newcomer communities.

Ways Forward

The concept of reconciliation often lacks clarity[37] because of the particular mix of political, cultural, and historical forces of the concerned country.[38] Tristen Ann Borer articulates two different perspectives on reconciliation: (1) an interpersonal perspective that is premised on healing relationships between individuals with the goal of living in harmony; and (2) the political perspective that seeks to change laws and institutions to create tolerance within society.[39] As TRC Chair and Commissioner Murray Sinclair stated during a CBC radio broadcast of *The House*, "reconciliation has been a difficult term to define . . . because it means different things in different contexts."[40] Colleen Sheppard also articulated the divergent perspectives many Canadians hold (quoted in this chapter's introduction) that appear to be rooted in our own history of colonialism.[41]

Understanding the different perspectives newcomers have about reconciliation with their Indigenous neighbours will help to guide the variety of initiatives needed to improve this relationship. As demonstrated by the data, this distance between Indigenous and newcomer communities can result in a number of different perspectives on the relationship. Our study's findings confirm the results of other studies and emphasize the importance of newcomers' having the opportunity for intercultural interactions and dialogue[42] to move toward reconciliation. Immigration policies also need to change to ensure newcomers receive a more accurate historical account of the Indigenous peoples of Canada.

To address the need for meaningful contact between newcomers and Indigenous peoples, several initiatives across Canada have started showing us the way.[43] For example, in 2010, the Vancouver Dialogues brought together First Nations, urban Indigenous, and immigrant communities in a series of dialogues and cultural exchanges.[44] In Winnipeg a community-based group called 13 Fires began hosting a conversation series beginning in 2015 that is focused on how different social issues in Winnipeg and Manitoba are impacted by racism.[45] Currently, assistant professor Cathy Rocke[46] is working within the newcomer and Indigenous community to help train intergroup dialogue facilitators, with plans to facilitate relationship building between Indigenous and newcomer citizens in the city of Winnipeg.

Several youth initiatives have also sought to bridge the divide between the Indigenous and non-Indigenous communities. Ka Ni Kanichihk (an Indigenous-led social service agency) in Winnipeg held anti-racism training with both newcomer and Indigenous youth[47] with positive results. Beginning in 2008 several non-profit organizations have worked together to bring youth from the Indigenous, newcomer, and Canadian-born communities for peace-building summer camps.[48] The Meet Me at the Bell Tower initiative,[49] started by youth activist Michael Champagne, seeks to build relationships between the Indigenous and non-Indigenous communities in a weekly gathering in the North End of Winnipeg.

To address the lack of comprehensive history about the different Indigenous peoples of Canada, several groups have developed booklets for newcomers providing more detailed information on this history. In 2014 the City of Vancouver developed a guidebook for newcomers with a more comprehensive history of the Indigenous peoples in Canada and more specifically the Indigenous peoples in British Columbia.[50] In Manitoba, Mennonite Central Committee (MCC) has developed a guidebook titled *Indigenous Peoples of Manitoba: A Guide for Newcomers,*[51] which they have distributed to many community organizations. At the time of writing, Immigration Partnership Winnipeg[52] is working to develop an Indigenous orientation manual for newcomers as one of their strategic priorities to "enhance bridges between the Indigenous and newcomer communties."[53] The ultimate goal is to have this manual become part of the welcome package for all newcomers to Manitoba.

In conclusion, our findings highlight the need for interpersonal contact between the Indigenous and newcomer communities along with the dissemination of the accurate history of the Indigenous peoples in Canada if reconciliation is to be achieved. As identified by Gordon Allport over sixty years ago,[54] contact and social interaction between different social identity groups can be a powerful process in breaking down stereotypes and eliminating prejudice. Since the release of the TRC's *Final Report,* there have been numerous initiatives to bring Indigenous and newcomer communities together. While future research will be needed to examine the effectiveness of these initiatives, many of them appear promising and should continue to be supported as pathways to reconciliation within Canadian society.

Appendix : Interview Questions

Opening/Transition Questions

- What does the word *reconciliation* mean to you?

- What do you know about the history of Aboriginal people in Canada?

- What can you tell me about the relationship between Aboriginal people and other Canadians?

- Have you heard about the recent Truth and Reconciliation Commission of Canada? And have you heard about any Truth and Reconciliation Commissions in other countries?

Key Questions

- What does reconciliation look like between new Canadians and Aboriginal peoples of Canada?

OR

- Do you think there is a need for reconciliation between new Canadians and Aboriginal peoples in Canada?

- Can you provide some examples of practical reconciliation efforts that you have seen or would like to see that would be helpful in the reconciliation between new Canadians, other Canadians and Aboriginal peoples of Canada?

- What role do you think you could play in this reconciliation process?

Alternative Probing Questions

- *If they do not feel they have any responsibility as they did nothing wrong*: Who then should apologize? Those who committed the crimes? Their descendants or the government?

- What kind of apology would make a difference to the conditions of Aboriginal people?

- Is there anything newcomers are benefiting from that was taken away from Aboriginal people?

Ending Question

- Is there anything else that you would like to add?

Notes

1   Hayner, "Fifteen Truth Commissions," 225.

2   Amstutz, *Healing of Nations.*

3   Robinson, "Serving the Interests."

4   Indian Residential Schools Settlement Agreement, *Schedule N,* 1.

5   Sheppard, *Indigenous Peoples in Canada.*

6   Lederach, *Building Peace,* 27.

7   Frideres and Gadacz, *Aboriginal Peoples in Canada,* 189.

8   Henry and Tator, *Colour of Democracy,* 201–2. See also Jurgens in this volume.

9   Suleman, *Vancouver Dialogues,* 8.

10 TRC, *Honouring the Truth,* 362.

11 United Way of Winnipeg, *Eagle's Eye View,* 40.

12 Statistics Canada, *Aboriginal Peoples in Canada: First Nations People, Métis and Inuit: National Household Survey, 2011,* http://www12.statcan.gc.ca/nhs-enm/2011/as-sa/99-011-x/99-011-x2011001-eng.pdf (accessed 30 July 2016).

13 Manitoba, Labour and Immigration, *Manitoba Immigration Facts: 2014 Statistical Report,* Winnipeg, 2014, https://www.gov.mb.ca/labour/immigration/pdf/mb_imm_facts_rep_2014.pdf (accessed 27 September 2016).

14 Ibid.

15 Ibid.

16 Madariaga-Vignudo, *More Strangers than Neighbours,* 1–90.

17 The issue of racism within Winnipeg was dramatically highlighted in the 22 January 2015 *Maclean's* article by reporter Nancy Macdonald which claimed that racism in Winnipeg was "at its worst" in comparison with other parts of Canada.

18 Ghorayshi, "Diversity and Interculturalism"; Macdonald, "Welcome to Winnipeg."

19 Ghorayshi, "Diversity and Interculturalism."

20 Gyepi-Garbrah, Walker, and Garcea, "Indigeneity, Immigrant Newcomers."

21 TRC, *Honoring the Truth,* 293, 360.

22 Rubin and Babbie, *Research Methods for Social Work,* 756.

23 Percentages reflect that not all research participants responded to the question.

24 Braun and Clarke, "Using Thematic Analysis," 79.

25 Harris-Galia, "Arctic Bayanihan."

26 DeCosta and Clark, "Exploring Non-Aboriginal Attitudes."

27 Sehdev, "People of Colour in Treaty."

28 Kasparian, "Introduction."

29   DeCosta and Clark, "Exploring Non-Aboriginal Attitudes."

30   Ghorayshi, "Diversity and Interculturalism," 95.

31   Gyepi-Garbrah, Walker, and Garcea, "Indigeneity, Immigrant Newcomers."

32   Madariaga-Vignudo, *More Strangers,* 1–90.

33   Wallis, Sunseri and Galabuzi, *Colonialism and Racism,* 3.

34   Chung, "Relationship between Racialized Immigrants."

35   Ibid.

36   Henderson and Wakeham, "Colonial Reckoning."

37   Beresford and Beresford, "Race and Reconciliation"; Blackburn, "Producing Legitimacy"; Borer, "Truth Telling"; Regan, *Unsettling the Settler Within.*

38   Huyse and Salter, *Traditional Justice and Reconciliation*; Teitel, "Law and Politics."

39   Borer, "Truth Telling," 32–33.

40   *The House,* "Interview—Justice Murray Sinclair," hosted by Evan Solomon, CBC Radio, 28 May 2015, http://www.cbc.ca/radio/thehouse/interview-justice-murray-sinclair-1.3093941 (accessed 1 October 2016).

41   Sheppard, "Indigenous People in Canada," 3–4.

42   Ghorayshi, "Diversity and Interculturalism"; Gyepi-Garbrah, Walker, and Garcea, "Indigenity, Immigrant Newcomers."

43   Chung, "Relationships Between Racialized Immigrants."

44   Suleman, "Vancouver Dialogues."

45   Upcoming events can be found on 13 Fires Facebook page: https://www.facebook.com/13FiresWPG.

46   "Community Members Challenged to Address Racism in Winnipeg," http://news.umanitoba.ca/community-members-challenged-to-address-racism-in-winnipeg/ (accessed 30 September 2016).

47   Gyepi-Garbrah, Walker, and Garcea, "Indigenity, Immigrant Newcomers."

48   Burns, Williams, and Pankratz, *Youth Peacebuilding.*

49   CBC News, "Meet Me at the Bell Tower Turns 1 Year Old: Weekly Movement Aims to Stop Violence in Winnipeg's North End," CBC News, 16 November 2012, http://www.cbc.ca/news/canada/manitoba/meet-me-at-the-bell-tower-turns-1-year-old-1.1270422 (accessed 30 September 2016).

50   Wilson and Henderson, *First Peoples.*

51   Reynar and Matties, *Indigenous Peoples of Manitoba.*

52   Immigration Partnership Winnipeg (IPW) is hosted by the Social Planning Council of Winnipeg, which works to improve the settlement and integration of newcomers in Winnipeg. The development of the orientation manual is only one of several initiatives being undertaken by the IPW in their plans to improve the relationship between the Indigenous and newcomer communities. Further information can be found on the website: http://spcw.mb.ca/action/local-immigration-partnership/.

53   Immigrant Partnership Winnipeg, *2016–19 Strategic Plan Report,* 6.

54   Allport, *Nature of Prejudice.*

CHAPTER 8

HEALING FROM RESIDENTIAL SCHOOL EXPERIENCES

Support Workers and Elders on Healing and the Role of Mental Health Professionals

TRACEY CARR AND BRIAN CHARTIER

This chapter describes a research project in Saskatchewan with former students of Indian Residential Schools (IRSs) and their families. The specific aim of the project was to understand, from the perspectives of former students and their families, what they need in order to heal from residential school experiences, and to examine the role of mental health professionals in the healing process.

Background

Our interest in the topic of residential schools began before the Truth and Reconciliation Commission of Canada (TRC) and before the Indian Residential Schools Settlement Agreement (IRSSA). Dr. Tracey Carr's introduction to the IRS legacy occurred several years ago when she was involved with the Big Sisters program. The mother of her Little Sister attended residential school, where she suffered severe and multiple abuses and subsequently experienced long-term impacts. These impacts had profound effects on her children and have continued to influence her children's children. Part of Tracey's motivation to understand healing among residential school survivors and their families arises from this direct experience as witness to the ongoing negative consequences of IRS. In her current role as a lecturer in psychology, she carries on the work of conveying to undergraduate students the importance of the IRS context to contemporary experiences.

Dr. Brian Chartier has witnessed the consequences of IRS in a clinical setting. As a clinical psychologist, Brian has been conducting confidential assessments for the Independent Assessment Process (IAP) related to the IRSSA for ten years, and has documented the devastating impact of residential schools in his clinical work.

Both of us had these "bystander" experiences with residential school impacts in common. However, it was Brian's experience as a psychology professor that ultimately led to this project.

As part of course requirements, the psychology department at the University of Saskatchewan presents regular seminars on wide-ranging topics for psychology graduate students from each of its program streams. When Brian led the graduate seminar, he chose to introduce the IRSSA by providing students with links to the TRC, the IRSSA, and several other residential school–related websites prior to the actual presentation. He then instructed small groups of students to propose a research project on residential schools, including objectives, methods, ethics, and collaboration with Indigenous communities.

The results were unexpected, to say the least: every single group focused their hypothetical projects on the impacts of monies received (i.e., IRSSA compensation) on IRS survivors and their families, and only one of the six groups acknowledged it was important to involve Indigenous communities in research. Despite access to relevant information, the students did not appear to recognize some of the fundamental issues about the impacts of residential schools, the need for healing and reconciliation, and research approaches that included Indigenous communities.

After the seminar the two of us discussed what had happened and, more importantly, what had not happened. It was concerning to see how students had conflated financial compensation with healing and had failed to outline respectful research approaches with Indigenous communities. The outcome of the seminar, coupled with our previous experiences with former IRS students, fuelled our research interests in understanding healing among former IRS students.

Although there are studies of the long-term negative impacts on former
IRS students,[1] and the subsequent effects on their families,[2] the literature on
healing from the impacts of residential schools is relatively scant.[3] The work
of Gwen Reimer et al., published by the Aboriginal Healing Foundation,
is notable for its focus on the healing effects of the "common experience"
payment. They recognized the residual, almost accidental "healing" from
being forced to identify and cope with what had happened in the past. In this
context healing included the release of guilt at being bad parents, addicts, and
abused and abusers, as well as accepting that what happened in the IRS was
not their fault. However, we felt that an important component of reconciliation was to understand more about that healing process beyond Reimer et
al.'s work, to assess what survivors needed to heal from their experiences at
IRS, and to explore the potential role of mental health professionals in assist-
ing IRS students in their recovery.

Research Purpose

The aim of our research was to understand what healing meant to former
IRS students, to gather information on what they need to heal, and to explore the role of mental health professionals in meeting those healing needs.
To reflect a respectful research approach with Indigenous populations, we
began our work by relying on our established research partnership with an
Indigenous agency.[4] The Marguerite Riel Centre in Melfort, Saskatchewan,
houses one of Saskatchewan's Resolution Health Support Programs (RHSPs)
where support workers and Elders provide emotional and cultural support
to former IRS students and their families. With the assistance of Marguerite
Riel Centre, we conducted a pilot study of semi-structured, one-to-one interviews with ten former IRS students, and listened to their perspectives on
what healing meant for themselves, their families, and their communities.

The details of the pilot study are reported elsewhere,[5] but it is important to note that the former students we interviewed continued to report
long-lasting impacts of the IRS and, in particular, a loss of identity. They
identified education as a turning point in their lives, and described their
personal healing practices, which involved a blend of spirituality and religion
and the central role of forgiveness. Reconnecting with Indigenous culture
was important to healing. They spoke of the importance of changing the IRS
legacy for school attendees and for subsequent generations. These findings

suggested that healing was an important issue and that we had more to understand about what was needed to promote healing among former students.
These findings also led to our current study, the healing needs assessment
phase of the research.

For this study we wanted to gauge what former students and their families needed to move forward and specifically what resources they needed
from both within the Indigenous community and the non-Indigenous
community. Given our background, we had a particular interest in understanding what mental health professionals could offer former IRS students
and their families.

Method

We interviewed support workers and Elders in the Resolution Health Support Program (RHSP) in Saskatchewan during the fall months of 2015.
Support workers from this program provide emotional and cultural support
to former IRS students and their families, facilitate and coordinate other
support services, attend IAP hearings, and build larger networks of relationships.[6] Typically, support workers have attended residential school themselves and work to create a safe environment for former students to address
IRS-related issues. Because of their applied experiences, we considered support workers and Elders to be key informants in this study and well situated
to provide information on the healing needs of former IRS students.

We developed the interview guide together with members of the Melfort
RHSP to ensure it was as relevant as possible for the participants. Open-
ended interview questions asked about the role of mental health professionals,
non-Indigenous people, and the government in the healing process. Other
questions focused on the role of the band council, Indigenous communities
(including families), and the RHSP. Interviews were typically between sixty
and ninety minutes. They were audiotaped and transcribed, and themes were
derived using iterative thematic analysis.[7]

Beginning in Melfort we contacted other RHSP workers (i.e., potential
participants) using a snowball recruitment technique. For example, in the
first set of interviews, one participant was from another location. That then
became our next site for interviews, and so on. In total we contacted fourteen potential participants and eleven were interviewed. Of the three who did
not participate, we were unable to arrange interview times for two, and one

declined. Seven of the eleven participants were support workers, four were Elders, and all eleven worked with an RHSP in one of four Saskatchewan locations. All but one participant attended residential school. The majority of participants were women (n=6), and participant ages ranged between fifty-five and eighty years old.

Findings

We present our findings in two sections: "What It Takes to Heal" and "What Mental Health Professionals Can Do." The first section reflects what participants shared about their own healing experiences and their work with former IRS students. These experiences encompassed three themes: Connection to Culture, Support Programs, and Forgiveness. The second section describes participants' perceptions of the role of mental health professionals and the non-Indigenous community in healing from residential school impacts. These perceptions fell into two main themes: Understanding of Culture and Personal History, and Need for Continuity and Proper Diagnosis. In the following sections we provide representative participant quotes to illustrate each of the above themes.

What It Takes to Heal

A dominant theme in how participants described healing was Connecting with Culture. Many participants described the need to overcome drug and alcohol addiction in their communities, families, and themselves. Recovering from addiction often strengthened a renewed connection to culture.

After attempting to heal through church attendance, one participant described how he sought healing through his heritage:

> I was an addict and . . . I had to find ways to heal myself. And I couldn't find that healing in the churches. So I thought, I'm going to come back and learn about my heritage. Go back to my heritage and see if I can find healing in there and I did! I did. But I had to do a lot of travelling. I've got to do a lot of research! You know, talking to different Elders, going to different ceremonies, participating in ceremonies. In the sweat lodges, the sun dances, *fasting*. You know, fasting for knowledge. And learning about Creator. You know, learning about the creation belief.

Similar to other participants in this sample, he found recovery and healing by returning to Indigenous ceremonies and actively relearning his culture.

The second dominant theme was Support Programs. Such support programs took several forms: the RHSP itself, self-help groups, and sharing circles. As support workers, when participants listened with a commitment to confidentiality, they felt they could potentially empower former IRS students. As one participant stated: "I really pride myself in my ability to maintain confidentiality.... I sit with people and I listen ... I'm a good listener.... And I let people get to trust me ... I work to empower people. To help people to *empower* themselves." Another participant described the need for the RHSP to exist in all communities: "You know and I think if anything, there should be resolution health support and Elders, working specifically or supporting residential school survivors in *every* community ... I know in mine we don't have—in [community name] ... there's no support." Groups with a self-help focus were also fulfilling communities' healing needs: "We have a women's group out there and ... where I am now ... they have AA groups, NA groups, you know—that helps a lot too." Similarly, this participant identified the healing potential of family circles: "I think family circles help a lot. I've worked with family circles. I work with group circles. Like women's circles, men's circles, I think they help a lot ... [in] bringing ... that stuff out."

It appears that a group setting, whether with family, other former students, or people with comparable problems, may contribute to healing among former IRS students and their families.

The third key theme to the healing process was Forgiveness. Participants described how forgiving themselves and those who had harmed them was central to their healing efforts. The following participant articulated how forgiveness of herself and those who harmed her initiated her own ongoing process of healing:

> I had to deal with my issues. In order to go on, I had to forgive myself. Because that was one of the things that held me back for a long time—I hated myself and I hated my body.... To deal with that issue ... by *forgiving* I was able to go on. Those different things I took to help me heal and I'm still *healing* today. You'll never quit healing until you die. Because as an Elder I had to really dig deep ... inside, in my heart, and forgive the people that had harmed me. And also to forgive myself—that was the only way I could go on.

This participant characterized forgiveness as "amends": "[I] started making amends to myself with all the anger and bitterness that I had towards the world and to the white people."

Forgiveness as a path to healing was a two-way street in these participants' minds. They first had to acknowledge what had happened to them and the pain they had suffered. With this pain in mind, they then had to forgive themselves. Second, they had to forgive those people who had harmed them. Thus, healing for these participants involved connecting back to their cultural roots, engaging in support programs (such as the RHSP itself, self-help groups, and sharing circles), and being willing to forgive—but not necessarily forget—what had happened to them at IRS.

What Mental Health Professionals Can Do

Participants identified two main themes regarding what professionals could do: Understanding of Culture and Personal History, and the Need for Continuity and Proper Diagnosis.

Under the first theme, these RHSP workers and Elders noted how important it was for mental health professionals to gain knowledge and understanding about Indigenous culture, values, and spirituality. Participants noted a general lack of knowledge among mental health professionals regarding Indigenous people: "They need to learn more about us . . . they need to know our ways. Our culture . . . how we live . . . to know us."

In some cases, participants asserted that that lack of understanding manifested itself in the non-Indigenous community's unwillingness to believe that IRS experiences really happened. In response to the question about what non-Indigenous people could do to help, one participant stated: "Well, I guess they could support us. . . . But you know, a lot of our people never want the white [people]. They say, they don't understand us. Which is true! They don't understand us. So, like if there was a therapist that came or a counsellor that came to talk to you. 'No. I don't want to listen to them.' I've heard that! Because they don't understand us. They won't believe us. So how—how can the white community help us when they don't believe what happened to us?"

To reduce this lack of understanding, one participant encouraged non-Indigenous people to actively participate in Indigenous ceremonies and practices:

First thing they *need* to have an understanding of . . . the values of
Aboriginal people. Perhaps an understanding a little bit about the
spirituality of our people, ceremonial stuff. They need to understand—
know the protocols and perhaps they need to work with our Elders.
They need to, yeah! Come into our communities and maybe come to
Culture Camp or come to the vision quest time, when it's vision quest
time of the year and we have teachings for ten days at a time. And
then you can actually fast and things like that. Go to sweat lodge. Pipe
ceremony. Yeah, just come and get familiarized with how things are
done, what are the belief systems, right?

Other participants saw the need for mental health professionals to more
carefully examine their own personal and family histories. For example:
"I think they need to find out where they're coming from to begin with.
Look at their history . . . look at their family of origin issues. It's really hard
because mental health is mostly white professionals, you know."

These participants felt strongly that to be effective, mental health professionals not only had to be familiar with Indigenous culture, they also had to
experience Indigenous culture and be aware of how their own personal backgrounds could influence their opinions.

Lack of understanding among mental health professionals could also have
negative consequences such as labelling and misdiagnosis. Labelling, according to this participant, could direct therapy: "[They need to] see our people
as people . . . rather than as an Indian Residential School survivor. I think
that sometimes when we have those labels for people we have a mindset even
before we begin to work with them." If misdiagnosis occurred, this participant believed, improper treatment would ensue: "I think sometimes that
our people are diagnosed incorrectly . . . but sometimes our people are not
as fortunate and they get misdiagnosed and they get placed on medication
and then they stay there for forever and a day."

A final need participants identified was the lack of continuity regarding
the delivery of mental health programs in their communities: "We need to
have some kind of continuity in regards to the program delivery, in regards
to the kind of people who are working in our communities."

A final participant quote fits well with the theme of the "Pathways to
Reconciliation" conference in Winnipeg, June 2016, where we presented the
initial findings from the study. This participant characterized the importance

of coming to know one another—Indigenous and non-Indigenous people—
on a personal level: "We need to sit together. And we need to talk about that.
And you know what, we live in this world together. We need to get to know
one another. And if we don't ever get to know one another it doesn't matter—
all the research in the world you do . . . all the books you read. . . . It's for
naught. Because you won't have—you will never have that understanding."

   This participant is suggesting that reconciliation must involve personal
contact between Indigenous and non-Indigenous people, that reconciliation cannot be one-sided, and that reconciliation requires transformation.

Discussion

Links to the T RC's Calls to Action

These findings reflect and reinforce the T RC's Calls to Action. The first
main theme, Understanding of Culture and Personal History, is reflected in
the T RC's Call to Action 65, which calls upon "post-secondary institutions
and educators . . . to establish a national research program with multi-year
funding to advance understanding of reconciliation." This addresses the ongoing need to heal—First Nations, Inuit, and Métis people are still suffering.
Without further collaboration between researchers and communities, these
extensive needs may remain unheard and therefore unaddressed. Further,
authentic partnership in research can provide additional documentation of
the diversity of healing needs within Indigenous communities.

   A portion of Call to Action 57 noted the need for "skills-based training in
intercultural competency." A strong and distinct theme from our interviews
was participants' perceptions of the lack of cultural understanding among
mental health professionals. This finding intersects with Call to Action
23—the need for all levels of government to provide cultural competency
training for all health care professionals. Our findings indicate that intercultural competency must be based on relationship building and exposure
to Indigenous cultural practices, as this study shows that participants who
engaged in ceremonies and sought cultural teachings reported it helped them
heal from I R S impacts. These experiences illustrate the need to incorporate
Indigenous healing practices into treatments for former I R S students. Valuing
Indigenous healing practices is likely to promote healing.

   Under the second theme, the Need for Continuity and Proper Diagnosis,
the T RC also calls for the "availability of appropriate health services" (Call to

Action 19) to close health outcome gaps between Indigenous and non-Indigenous peoples. Our findings suggest that, currently, residential school survivors may not be receiving appropriate mental health services in their communities, either because of the mental health professionals' lack of cultural competency or because of the lack of funding. The TRC calls for "sustainable funding for existing and new Aboriginal healing centres" (Call to Action 21). The role for culturally competent mental health professionals in such centres could be to provide proper diagnosis and continuity of care.

Conclusion

In addition to reinforcing the significance of the role of cultural identity in healing from IRS impacts,[8] this study emphasizes the importance of forgiveness in healing. Even though forgiveness is sometimes equated with Christian values,[9] some participants in this study and in our pilot study perceived forgiveness as a necessary gateway to freedom from the past—an essential first step in an ongoing healing process.

Healing as an ongoing direction or journey is well documented in the literature,[10] and it was a dominant theme in our pilot study as well. Even with important projects such as the Truth and Reconciliation Commission, and ongoing struggles for justice, the effects on survivors and subsequent generations continue to be substantial and profound. They are not alone in this: the same holds true in other contexts, such as South Africa, the state of Maine, and Rwanda.[11] With such extensive ties to the broader history of colonization, we cannot expect healing to happen in a few days, a few months, or even a few years. While some supports are available to former students to help them move forward, considerable healing needs remain among families and communities, which will require ongoing, sustained, and adapted interventions, both individually and societally, given the profound effects of colonialization.

From our questions regarding the role of mental health professionals, we heard that there needed to be flexibility in the traditional clinical models of support. The people who support families and former IRS students, whether they are social workers, psychologists, or other counsellors, need to have an understanding of Indigenous values and cultures and of the history of residential schools and its impacts. The importance of relationships is already recognized in the clinical setting—however, with former students and families it may be necessary for the therapist or counsellor to extend their usual clinical techniques to include a more communal and culturally oriented model of healing. This point was highlighted by James Waldram (2008) in a report published by the Aboriginal Healing Foundation. For Waldram, it was essential for non-Indigenous therapists to become familiar with the Medicine Wheel and Indigenous ways of knowing and to mutually participate in cultural events.[12]

Our main lesson as researchers in this project has been the importance of relationships. As non-Indigenous researchers working with Indigenous groups and participants, it has been paramount to build relationships. One of the ways we have encouraged dialogue with participants and groups has been to openly share our previous experiences with people who have been affected by IRS. We have also relied on our reputation with the RHSP in Melfort to facilitate contacts with other sites. We need to continue to be aware that, as non-Indigenous researchers, we can be associated with a legacy of research exploitation of Indigenous people.[13] This means we will honour our promise to return our findings to our participants for their input and validation—the final phase of our research.

Implications

We return to what first spurred our interest in this research. As university teachers we recognize that the ultimate implication of this work is to educate university students at all levels about the importance of residential schools to the history of Indigenous peoples and the history of Canada. A failure to do so obscures the truth and distances us from reconciliation. In addition, another generation of mental health professionals who lack cultural competency may only add to the ongoing IRS impacts in Indigenous communities. A mandatory Indigenous Studies course in all universities, like the one implemented by the University of Winnipeg, could go a long way to reconcile the misunderstandings that we encountered in the graduate seminar that initiated our work. Moreover, such a course could also highlight the foundational work and research published by the Aboriginal Healing Foundation. The legacy of the foundation can be sustained despite the untimely cessation of federal government funding.

Our research embodies one pathway of many toward reconciliation. In relationship to each other—as the participant noted, "we live in this world together"—we can encourage and facilitate healing for former IRS students and their families.

Team Members / Acknowledgements

Our collaborators played an integral role in this project. First, a key collaborator was Joanne Yakowec, director of operations at Marguerite Riel Centre in Melfort, Saskatchewan. The centre houses several programs that serve Indigenous people, including the RHSP.

We were also fortunate to have had Dr. Jim Miller, professor emeritus of history from the University of Saskatchewan, as part of our team at the begining of our project. He has substantial expertise regarding the history of residential schools and is the author of *Shingwauk's Vision: A History of Native Residential Schools* and several other publications related to Indigenous peoples' history in Canada.

Our project received funding from the Collaborative Innovation Development grant (Saskatchewan Health Research Foundation).

Notes

1   Carr, Chartier, and Dadgostari, "'I'm Not Really Healed,'" 1; Bombay, Matheson, and Anisman, "Appraisals of Discriminatory Events," 80–81; Bombay, Matheson, and Anisman, "Impact of Stressors," 375–79; Elias et al., "Trauma and Suicide Behaviour," 1563–65; Gone, "Redressing First Nations Historical Trauma," 700.

2   Kirmayer, Tait, and Simpson, "Mental Health of Aboriginal Peoples," 3–7; Legacy of Hope Foundation, "Hope and Healing," 2; Morrissette, "Holocaust of First Nation People," 385–88; Miller, *Shingwauk's Vision,* 289–316.

3   Morrissette and Goodwill, "Psychological Cost of Restitution," 548–49; Pearce et al., "Cedar Project," 2189–90; Reimer et al., *Indian Residential Schools,* 43–55; Shewchuk, "Legacy of Residential School Abuse," 36; Wesley-Esquimaux and Smolewski, "Historic Trauma."

4   Waldram, *Aboriginal Healing,* 205–68.

5   Carr, Chartier, and Dadgostari, "'I'm not Really Healed,'" 1.

6   Waldram, *Aboriginal Healing,* 1–6.

7   Carr, *Healing Circle Continues,* 1.

8   Morrissette and Goodwill, "Psychological Cost of Restitution," 550–53; Pearce et al., "Cedar Project," 2189–90; Shewchuk, "Legacy of Residential School Abuse," 38.

9   Braun and Clarke, "Using Thematic Analysis," 86–93.

10   Waldram, "Transformative and Restorative Processes," 195–99.

11   Collins, McEvoy-Levy, and Watson, "Maine Wabanaki-State Child Welfare"; De la Rey and Owens, "Perceptions of Psychosocial Healing," 257; Staub et al., "Healing, Reconciliation."

12   Waldram, *Aboriginal Healing in Canada,* 205–68.

13   See O'Neil in this volume.

Part Four

LIVING

CHAPTER 9

BENDING TO THE PREVAILING WIND

How Apology Repetition Helps Speakers and Hearers Walk Together

PETER BUSH

We call upon church parties to the Settlement Agreement to develop ongoing education strategies to ensure that their respective congregations learn about the church's role in colonization, the history and legacy of residential schools, and why apologies to residential school students, their families, and communities were necessary.
—Call to Action 59 of the Truth and Reconciliation Commission of Canada

The Truth and Reconciliation Commission's Call to Action 59 highlights the church community's need for apology repetition: that is, for ongoing education regarding the apologies, and an invitation to reflect anew on what they did that requires apology.[1] Knowing what one's denomination did is to know what the church did in one's name; the sins of the collective are the sins of the individuals who make up the collective. Hearing of the churches' role in colonization and the residential school system once more invites the question: "Should we not again say, 'We are sorry'?"

Church apologies have been repeated in a variety of contexts: at national gatherings of the Truth and Reconciliation Commission of Canada (TRC); at school commemoration events; during hearings in the Alternative Dispute Resolution Process that preceded the Indian Residential Schools Settlement Agreement (IRSSA), and in the subsequent Independent Assessment Process itself,[2] where church representatives could speak if a Survivor asked them to do so; and at internal denominational gatherings when Indigenous issues are addressed. In these and other contexts, the words have been spoken aloud to former residential school students, their families, and communities.

Combining historical analysis and theological inquiry, this essay considers the ways apology repetition shapes the relationship between churches and Indigenous people so they might walk together. Just as the prevailing wind bends trees to lean in the same direction, so too does the repetition of apologies bend churches and Survivors, Indigenous people and settlers, toward reconciliation. The repetition of the apologies fuels the work of reconciliation, for speaking the apology anew can act as a renewal of the commitment to the serious action of reconciliation.

The word "church" is multi-layered. A narrow reading of "church parties" in Call to Action 59 might suggest that only the legally responsible church bodies need to do this work, yet the church signatories to the IRSSA have larger constituencies of church members. Some church members have little knowledge of their denomination's role in colonialism, others need reminding of the ongoing legacy of the schools, and still others need encouragement to keep walking the pathways to reconciliation.

In this essay, "the churches" are the four historic church denominations that operated residential schools and have issued apologies: the Anglican Church of Canada, the Presbyterian Church in Canada, the United Church of Canada, and those entities within the Roman Catholic Church in Canada who have issued apologies.[3] As church members seek to walk together with Indigenous people, recognizing the reasons for the apologies and repeating them exemplifies for the broader settler community how steps toward reconciliation may be taken.

"Apology repetition" in this essay does not mean a reciting of the exact words of the apologies originally given twenty or more years ago. Rather, as the churches have sought to show that the words of their original apologies were sincere, they have come to recognize new depths and enlarged meanings in their words, meanings not fully appreciated when first spoken. Reflecting on their church's apology in preparation for repeating them to Survivors and their families, church spokespeople gain deeper insight into the words, hearing them at a different point along the pathways to reconciliation.

Further, as research uncovers new truths about the relationship between Indigenous people and settlers, apology repetition takes this new information into account. For example, Ian Mosby's[4] research regarding the nutritional experiments in the schools was not available in the 1980s and 1990s when church apologies were first issued. Mosby discovered that a variety of government-funded experiments took place in some of the residential schools, which ranged from determining what was the least amount of food children needed to be able to study through to determining the impact of various additives in bread on the children's health. Anyone speaking apology following the publication of Mosby's article would be wise to reference the nutrition experiments in their words. Apology repetition builds on the original words with enhanced knowledge and insight. Knowing the spirit and intent of the original apology, the speaker improvises on the text in the same way a skilled musician improvises on an old standard, enriching the original.

The TRC commissioners defined reconciliation in the following way: "'reconciliation' is about establishing and maintaining a mutually respectful relationship between Aboriginal and non-Aboriginal peoples in this country. For that to happen, there has to be awareness of the past, acknowledgement of the harm that has been inflicted, atonement for the causes, and action to change behaviour."[5] Implicit in the definition is the recognition that Indigenous and non-Indigenous peoples in Canada are alienated from one another, and that that alienated relationship will become "a mutually respectful" one through the four-step process laid out in the definition. The steps described by the commissioners, this essay argues, share strong parallels to apology with its acknowledgement of the past and its desire to bring about restitution, coupled with a commitment to changed future behaviour.

A Brief History of the Churches' Apologies

The United Church of Canada was the first denomination to apologize.[6] Through the early 1980s, increased space and voice was given to Indigenous people within the United Church. Alberta Billy, a member of the Laichwiltach We Wai Kai Nation in British Columbia, challenged the church to apologize to Indigenous people within the church for the wrongs of colonialism.[7] Following a denomination-wide conversation, the Right Rev. Robert Smith presented an apology to a group of Indigenous leaders from the United Church in 1986.[8] While the apology named colonialism and the destruction of Indigenous culture, residential schools were not explicitly named.

The CBC TV's 1989 drama *Where the Spirit Lives*[9] and Manitoba Grand Chief Phil Fontaine's interview with Barbara Frum on CBC's *The Journal* in 1990[10] then brought the schools to national attention. A group of Roman Catholic bishops along with the superiors from some religious orders met in Saskatoon in March 1991, under the umbrella of the Canadian Conference of Catholic Bishops, to discuss how best to respond. Present also were observers from the Anglican, Presbyterian, and United churches.

The Saskatoon gathering sharpened the focus of the four historic churches. While the Canadian Conference of Catholic Bishops did not make a public statement, the apology by Rev. Doug Crosby of the Oblates of Mary Immaculate later in the year and many of the apologies by diocesan bishops are at least partially rooted in the Saskatoon gathering. Rev. Crosby, on 24 July 1991, was also the first church leader to issue an apology explicitly related to residential schools.[11] Primate Michael Peers of the Anglican Church of Canada, at the suggestion of an Anglican Church committee made up of both Indigenous and settler church members, presented an apology on 6 August 1993, at an Anglican Indigenous convocation at Minaki, Ontario. In June 1994 the General Assembly of the Presbyterian Church in Canada adopted the text of the Presbyterian confession. That fall, the moderator, the Rev. George Vais, presented the confession (apology) in Winnipeg to Grand Chief Phil Fontaine.

The Blackwater lawsuit launched by Survivors of the Port Alberni School instigated renewed conversations within the United Church about an apology specifically related to residential schools. In the early fall of 1998, a group of settlers from the United Church travelled to Port Alberni to listen to the Survivors' stories. This group put pressure on the church to apologize. At a hastily called news conference in Toronto on 27 October 1998, the Right Rev. Bill Phipps issued a second apology on behalf of the United Church of Canada, focused entirely on Indian Residential Schools.

The Roman Catholic Church, either as a national entity through the Canadian Conference of Catholic Bishops or as an international entity through the Pope, has not apologized for its part in the Indian Residential Schools system. This lack of an apology led to the Truth and Reconciliation Commission's Call to Action 58, which reads in part: "We call upon the Pope to issue an apology to Survivors, their families, and communities for the Roman Catholic Church's role in the spiritual, cultural, emotional, physical, and sexual abuse of First Nations, Inuit, and Métis children in Catholic-run residential schools." While the Pope has yet to issue an apology, a number of Roman Catholic bishops in Canada have issued apologies within their dioceses (regions).[12]

None of the denominations or bishops regarded their apologies as one-off events to be relegated to the pages of history. The apologies express the hope that Indigenous peoples and settlers might someday walk together. While apologies are not capable by themselves of transforming the connection between the two groups, the apologies are a starting point in the repair and renewal of the relationship.

The TRC's *Final Report* noted that Survivors "seldom mentioned the churches' apologies or healing and reconciliation activities."[13] The commissioners concluded that this silence was due to Survivors' waiting to see if the churches intended to live up to the words of the apologies, for "apologies mark only a beginning point on pathways of reconciliation; the proof of their authenticity lies in putting words into action."[14] This essay argues that apology repetition provides renewed motivation for "putting words into action."

Critiques of Apology and Apology Repetition

Indigenous critique of the various apologies issued in Canada by churches and the Government of Canada has focused largely on Stephen Harper's 11 June 2008 statement. However, some themes identified in these critiques apply equally to the church apologies.

The completeness of the apologies, from both the government and the churches, has been questioned. Ted Quewezance, who was the executive director of the Residential School Survivors of Canada at the time, summarized the groups' expectations for the government apology: a full, public accounting of and complete acceptance of responsibility for the residential school system.[15] A number of critics, including Thohahoken Michael Doxtater, have argued that the government and even the churches failed to meet this benchmark, noting that the choice of language in the apologies limits the responsibility being accepted.[16] As Matthew Dorrell argues, the apologies have sought to bring "closure rather than disclosure." By apologizing for the past injustices perpetrated in the residential schools, the statements have implied that the colonial project is now in the past, being largely limited to the residential school system—while, as many Indigenous persons and settlers would attest, the colonial project remains in place. From this perspective, the apologies potentially hamper the disclosure of the ongoing colonial project.[17]

A second cluster of critiques notes that the apologies may become an end rather than a beginning. While a great deal of work was required to achieve the apologies, as Taiaiake Alfred and Lorraine Flatfoot correctly note, the words of the apologies do not address other injustices such as inadequate housing, health care, and schooling, and neither do they protect Indigenous women and girls from violence and murder.[18]

Apology repetition, as framed in this essay, seeks to address some of this critique. Past apologies must not be allowed to be the final statements, defining the relationship between Indigenous people and settlers, but, rather, they must serve as tools for ongoing change and the restoration of Treaty relationships.

The Impacts of Repetition on Those Apologizing

Repeating apologies reminds the speaker and those they are speaking for that a wrong was done; the apology confirms a commitment to live differently now and in the future. The repeated apologies are a prevailing wind shaping settlers' attitudes and actions, bending them toward reconciliation.

In preparing its membership for the 1986 "Apology to Native Congregations," the United Church of Canada explored the "theology of apology." Apology has three stages: (a) knowing about the wrong done and recognizing the action as wrong; (b) feeling an aversion to "disliking" one's actions, be they personal or corporate, also known as guilt; and (c) willingly choosing to "disown" the sin and seeking to live a different way.[19] This framing is helpful in thinking about how apology repetition fuels reconciliation.

A Wrong Was Done

The churches' apologies were developed in response to hearing the stories of Indigenous peoples' experiences in residential schools. Leaders of the Presbyterian Church in Canada thought they had nothing to apologize for until they researched their archives and listened to Survivors' stories.[20] The United Church of Canada's 1998 apology was given after church members heard Survivors of the Port Alberni School tell their stories.

But as time passes, the immediacy of the stories fades, the horror of the events described seems less intense, and the voices of settler culture say, "It wasn't really that bad." These combine to minimize the wrong—i.e., the sin. Apology repetition reminds the speaker, and those they are speaking for, that the wrong was wrong. The repeated apology sharpens anew the recognition of the sin.

In the twenty-plus years since the apologies were first issued, children have become adults, young adults have become church leaders, and new people have joined the churches. Apology repetition confronts the new leaders, new members, and newly adult members with the wrong done by the church to which they belong. The repeated apology passes down the recognition of the wrong done from one generation of church leaders to the next. The United Church of Canada has ensured this remains true by making the 1986 and 1998 apologies part of the doctrinal standards of the denomination, weaving the apologies into the DNA of the church.

Immigrants from various parts of the world are also among the new members of Canadian churches. Cathy Rocke and Régine Uwibereyeho King's findings in their pilot study (see their chapter in the present volume) are consistent with my own experience with newcomer members: many have limited or even inaccurate information about Indigenous peoples and the legacy of the schools. In my conversations with recently arrived congregational leaders from Africa and the Middle East, I have found an eagerness to learn about the experience of Indigenous peoples and to understand the implications of the Treaties and other agreements between Indigenous leaders and the Government of Canada. While newcomers may see themselves playing different roles in reconciliation, Euro-Canadian churches have an opportunity to help Canada respond to the Truth and Reconciliation Commission's Calls to Action 93 and 94 regarding newcomers to Canada by involving newcomer church members in learning about the history and the future of Indigenous and settler reconciliation within the church.

Accepting Responsibility for the Wrong

Recognizing that wrong has been done may lead to statements of regret[21] but will not lead to apology until the speakers of the apology accepts responsibility: "I did wrong. We have sinned." Such statements could be described as experiencing guilt. Guilt is often dismissed by modern psychology as unhelpful, but as South African theologian John de Gruchy wrote at the end of apartheid, "guilt is a legal term indicating we are responsible for what we have done. Confessing guilt thus means taking responsibility for what is wrong and not shifting the blame somewhere else. Confessing guilt means acknowledging publicly and concretely that we have sinned against God and our fellow human beings."[22] Accepting one's guilt is central to apologizing for one's wrongdoing, and avoiding guilt leads to a limited apology.

Saying "I did wrong" not only acknowledges wrong was done, it unsettles our self-image as a person who is "good." This is important, as seeing oneself as a person with failings creates space for humility. Arrogant defensiveness is stripped away, to be replaced with "I am wrong, and you have helped me see the wrong as wrong." Further, using avoidance tactics like shifting blame to people in the past, contending "I was not there, I have nothing to apologize for," limits our capacity to take responsibility for the multigenerational harms created by our ancestors' past actions that are still impacting Indigenous communities today.

Through the act of apology, people see the one who has been hurt differently as well. The Presbyterian Church's statement says, "It is with deep humility and in great sorrow that we come before God and our Aboriginal brothers and sisters with our confession." In part the wrong was done because the church did not see the Indigenous students and parents as their "brothers and sisters." To call someone a brother or sister is to say that both they and the speaker are of equal worth. Colonizing views state the settler is "more equal" than the Indigenous person. The Presbyterian Church's apology frames a renewed relationship built in part on seeing each other as true equals.

Using first-person pronouns, "I" and "we," moves the wrong from being distant in space and time to being an ongoing wrong for which the speaker accepts responsibility. As successive generations of church members repeat the apologies, they are including both the wrong and the *impact* of the wrong in their acceptance of the responsibility, to continue to right that wrong in the present. The oral and aural repetition of the apologies using first-person pronouns transforms them from historic artifacts into living documents capable of challenging and transforming relationships in the present.

Naming the wrong and accepting responsibility for the wrongdoing are the first two steps. In the third step of repentance, which literally means to turn and travel a different road, the speaker is saying, "I no longer want to live that way." Repeating the apology reminds the speaker of their rejection of their former way of life. The ways of colonialism are deeply rooted in the settler. Unacknowledged racism surfaces only after the first layers have been removed. Apology helps the speaker of the apology shed those additional colonial layers, asking themselves, "Have I slid back into the patterns of colonialism I have said I am sorry for? Have I slid into patterns of arrogant control rather than the practice of humbly walking with?"

While serving on the board of a social service agency, I was confronted with how easily settlers can fall back into colonial patterns. The executive director was an Indigenous woman, and the organization had applied for a grant. Since the head of the granting agency, also a settler, knew me, he contacted me, suggesting a change to the project to be funded. I did not say, "You should call the executive director." Rather, I agreed the change should be made, and made it. Two male settlers, committed to reconciliation with Indigenous people, changed a plan written by an Indigenous woman without considering her authority on the issue, an action that stinks of colonialism. The executive director confronted me with my disrespectful actions and pointed to a copy of the Presbyterian Church's apology, asking, "When will the church live up to its apology?"

Thus, the apology serves as a powerful reminder—a mirror that shows those who have apologized all the flaws and blemishes they would rather forget. Apology repetition confronts settlers anew, even those of us committed to reconciliation. We can then see more clearly how easily the humility essential to reconciliation is overcome by the deeply rooted arrogance of colonialism.

Committing to a New Way: Walking Together

Acknowledging that wrong has been done and feeling sorrow and guilt for one's role in that wrongdoing are important steps in apology, but apology also invites the emergence of a new way of being. Apology is not just regret for the past; it is also a statement of what the speaker will do in the future. These actions should both focus on the past, seeking to make up for harms done, while also building toward the future. The TRC's Call to Action 61 highlights this dual focus. "Healing and reconciliation projects" along with "culture- and language-reconciliation projects" are needed because of the legacy of the residential school system, which sought to obliterate Indigenous languages and cultures. The word "revitalization" highlights a recovery of what existed before the wrong was done, the righting of past actions. "Education and relationship-building projects" together with "dialogues for

Indigenous spiritual leaders and youth to discuss Indigenous spirituality, self-determination, and reconciliation" have a future orientation, looking toward what might be and facilitating the hopes of youth.[23]

The churches' apologies make clear the churches' desire to behave differently in the future from what they did in the past. Bishop Rouleau's 1996 apology described the vision of the Roman Catholic diocese of Churchill-Hudson Bay: "What I long for most of all is a new covenant freed from the paternalism of our colonial heritage and grounded in renewed trust and solidarity."[24] The Presbyterian Church made the commitment: "With God's guidance our Church will seek opportunities to walk with Aboriginal peoples to find healing and wholeness together as God's people."[25] The apologies affirmed a commitment to the long walk toward reconciliation. As Anglican Bishop Michael Peers wrote to his fellow bishops, "An apology cannot be a one-time thing. It may need to be made on many occasions and in many circumstances. . . . We are at the beginning of a process that could take a long time and which is apt to be painful to all. But it is clearly the way towards reconciliation, and holds the promise of new life for the whole Church."[26]

Apology repetition reminds us of our motivation for starting this arduous journey in the first place, and the repeating of the apology rekindles that motivation. Apology repetition that does not lead to a renewed commitment to the hard work of reconciliation is but a repeating of empty words. Apology repetition, at its best, adds fresh vistas to the vision dreamed and hoped for, firing the imagination of the next generation of church leaders toward what could be. Apology repetition points to a new way of life, allowing people in a new time to make the choice to live into that new future.

The Impacts of Apology Repetition on Those Hearing the Words

The prevailing wind of apologies repeatedly shapes not only speakers but hearers as well. Oral apologies are also aural. This truism is central to the work of walking together, since, as authors Tracey Carr and Brian Chartier found in their work as mental health professionals (see their chapter in the present volume), forgiveness can play a strong role in the healing process. While forgiveness through apology is not guaranteed, and neither should it be demanded or expected, it nonetheless can be hoped for. Even if the words of apology are not fully trusted or accepted, they may kindle enough openness in the hearers for reconciliation to begin. Apology lives in hope that the hearer will also be transformed. Even as apology recognizes that hearers may not want to reconnect with the church as a member or adherent, apology offers a place where Indigenous people can articulate their hopes for what a mutually respectful relationship would be.

Holding the Speakers of Apology to Account

Apology repetition also gives permission to the hearers to hold the speaker to account. In the apology the speaker promises, "This is the new way I want to live. I am giving you permission to hold me accountable for living in ways that walk towards reconciliation." The churches' apologies set out terms that the hearers can use as benchmarks to determine whether or not churches are fulfilling their promises. The apologies are issued with no expectation of hearing the words "I forgive you." In fact, in the cases of the 1986 United Church apology, the Anglican Church apology, and the Presbyterian Church statement, the original hearers did not indicate acceptance of the apologies until years later. In all cases acceptance was withheld until the original hearers saw evidence of changed attitudes and actions in the churches.

The formal nature of most apology repetitions marks these moments as set apart from normal time, moments to be remembered and stories to be retold. As the apologies are spoken in communities where they have not been heard before, the circle of those holding speakers accountable for their words expands.

An example of holding accountability is the widespread knowledge that the Roman Catholic Church entities who were signatories to the Settlement Agreement did not contribute what was agreed to. The commitment was for $79 million in cash and in kind; following seven years of "best efforts," the various Roman Catholic entities combined had contributed $57.7 million in cash and in kind.[27] In this context apology repetition becomes a moment of being held accountable by hearers who ask, "Why should we believe the words spoken when the actions do not live out the promises of the words?" Apology repetition becomes a moment for accountability and reflection on whether the work promised by the apology is being fulfilled.

Call to Action 53 identifies the need for a National Council for Reconciliation to "monitor, evaluate, and report annually to Parliament and the people of Canada on the Government of Canada's post-apology progress on reconciliation to ensure the government accountability for reconciling the relationship between Aboriginal peoples and the Crown is maintained in the coming years."[28] In issuing this Call to Action, the TRC emphasized the need for ongoing accountability to reconciliation between the Government of Canada and First Nations, Inuit, and Métis peoples. Similarly, the churches have established their own accountability mechanisms. For example, the United Church of Canada's practice of presenting a plaque engraved with the church's two apologies to Indigenous communities they visit commemorates the moment when the apology was spoken. The plaque serves as a public reminder of the church's desire to be held accountable for its words.

New Ears to Hear in Apology Repetition

The school commemoration committee of Grand Council of Treaty #3 built stone markers, or cairns, in 2013 at the site of each of the residential schools operated in Treaty 3 territory. I was invited to speak on behalf of the Presbyterian Church at the dedication of the marker at the Round Lake site of Cecilia Jeffrey School on the edge of Kenora, Ontario.

The experience was humbling. The words I spoke were not a reciting of the church's 1994 statement. Ian Mosby's article had been published less than a month before, and Cecilia Jeffrey School was named as one of the schools involved in the experiments. I needed to acknowledge this hard truth, as well as make specific reference to the commemorative marker. Thus, my words, built on the Presbyterian Church's 1994 statement, incorporated new knowledge and events.

During the speeches drummers expressed their agreement with the words of speakers by sounding the drum. As I began to speak, members of the audience questioned what I was doing and others offered suggestions for what I should say. All in all, it was an interactive experience.

Following the formal presentations, which included three Survivors of Cecilia Jeffrey School telling their stories, a lunch was served, providing opportunity for informal conversation. One of those who had offered suggestions approached me, saying, "I'm sorry for heckling you, I didn't know what you were going to say. Thank you for your apology. I am still angry and hurt, but thank you for your words." Later, as I was preparing to leave, a couple in their forties approached me. The woman said, "His mother was a student at Cecilia Jeffrey, and when she received her common experience payment she also received a [printed] copy of the Presbyterian Church's apology. We read it and it was good. But hearing you speak the words aloud, hearing the words from a person, has made the words much more meaningful. Thank you." Both conversations reveal the importance of the words of the apology being spoken in person so new ears can hear them.

Diverse voices have suggested the apologies be spoken in every Indigenous community in the country. In this way the words of apology would be spoken to those who have been harmed in even the most remote communities and on lands from which the children were taken.

Urbanized settler attitudes and actions often imply that remote Indigenous communities are of secondary importance. Church representatives travelling to remote contexts to say "We are sorry" raises the importance of these often-overlooked communities. Paulette Regan highlights the dislocation experienced by urbanized Canadians when they visit remote and even rural communities: "The Hazelton feast hall in Gitxsan territory is a long way from the urban office towers where we can safely feel distanced from the victims of our benevolent peacemaking."[29] "Unsettling the settler," to use Regan's phrase, is possible through an ongoing practice of apology repetition, where settlers are exposed again to the impacts of colonialism not as abstract concepts but as the lived realities of individuals with whom the settler has met and engaged. Apology repetition on Indigenous territory, in remote contexts, in locations that unsettle the speaker, is transformative.

Conclusion

Apology repetition helps create a culture where reconciliation is an accepted way of life. At the Cecilia Jeffrey School Commemoration Event, the mayor of Kenora, David Canfield, said to me: "Saying 'I am sorry' takes courage; what you said took guts." When settlers hear other settlers apologize, it serves as an example they themselves might follow in their lives. The churches, in apologizing, accepted culpability for their own sins and those of the nation, providing a model to the wider settler community.

Acknowledging the wrong done and the speaker's responsibility for the wrong is not enough. There must be actions of atonement and a demonstration of the wrongdoer's commitment to walk the pathways of reconciliation. As the TRC commissioners note, "A just reconciliation requires more than simply talking about the need to heal the deep wounds of history. Words of apology alone are insufficient; concrete actions on both symbolic and material fronts are required. . . . In every region of the country, Survivors and others have sent a strong message, as received by this Commission: for reconciliation to thrive in the coming years, Canada must move from apology to action."[30]

Words do shape people's actions and attitudes. The stark beauty of trees shaped by the prevailing wind has captured the eye of many artists. The churches hope that in repeating the apologies and putting the words into action, not only settlers but also residential school Survivors, their families, and wider Indigenous communities will be shaped by the prevailing wind of apology repetition and bend toward walking together along the pathways to reconciliation.

Notes

1   Nicholas Tavuchis's *Mea Culpa: A Sociology of Apology and Reconciliation* stood virtually alone in 1991 as a scholarly writing about apology. The new millennium has seen an explosion of writing about apology. What follows is highly selective.

Tavuchis argues that apology is "first and foremost, a speech act" (*Sociology of Apology*, 22) deriving significance from being spoken in the presence of those violated or those impacted by the violation. Tone of voice, facial expression, word pacing, and body language are as much part of apology as the words themselves. Tavuchis argues that only through apology can the offense be dealt with. The words of apology open the way to forgiveness.

Theologian Miroslav Volf ("Social Meaning of Reconciliation") locates apology in the reconciliation of alienated peoples. Using the metaphor of exclusion and embrace to depict the community of love (reconciliation), Volf notes, "A genuine embrace cannot take place until the truth about transgressions between people has been told and justice is established. . . . The will to embrace includes the will to rectify the wrongs that have been done and to reshape the relationship according to what one believes to be true and just" (171). The embrace of reconciliation finds its first steps in the truth telling that is apology.

Danielle Celermajer's *The Sins of the Nation and the Ritual of Apologies* explores political apologies. She argues that the ritual processes accompanying political apologies create a collective experience that anticipates corporate acceptance of responsibility for past wrong actions.

The most extended analysis of the four historic churches' apologies is provided by Alain Durocher ("Between the Right to Forget and the Duty to Remember: The Politics of Memory in Canada's Public Church Apologies"). Durocher focuses on the involvement of Indigenous people in the drafting of the apologies, the ways in which victims' stories are acknowledged and shape the apologies, and how the public institutional apology is delivered in a personal way. Durocher notes the importance of former students and their family members' feeling the apology was for them.

Jeremy Bergen (*Ecclesial Repentance: The Churches Confront Their Sinful Pasts*) explores dozens of church apologies from around the world. His interests are largely theological as he asks the question: Why does it take so long for churches to recognize the sins in their past? He argues that the slowness "may be due to the church's willful blindness, or also due to the fact that discerning just where the church pointed to Christ and where it did not is a spiritual process that takes time. It takes prayer. It takes ears to hear and eyes to see" (171).

2   See TRC, *Final Report*, vol. 1, *The History Part 2, 1939–2000*, 551–79.

3   This list differs slightly from the Indian Residential Schools Settlement Agreement signatories, as some Roman Catholic entities that signed the agreement have not issued apologies.

4   Mosby, "Administering Colonial Science."

5   TRC, *Final Report*, vol. 6, *Reconciliation*, 3.

6   For more on the processes leading to the churches' apologies, see Bush, "Canadian Churches' Apologies."

7   Executive meeting, 19–22 March 1985, Minutes of the Executive and Sub-Executive, General Council, United Church of Canada (UCC), 122, #82-001, Box 35, File 1, United Church of Canada Archives (UCCA).

8   "Apology to First Nations Peoples," General Conference 1986, United Church of Canada.

9   *Where the Spirit Lives*, written by Keith Ross Leckie and directed by Bruce Pittman.

10   Phil Fontaine's disclosure of abuse at the Fort Alexander Residential School has been widely recognized as a significant event in raising the profile of the residential school issue.

11   App. 4 of TRC, *Honouring the Truth*, 378–94, has the text of most of the apologies referenced in this essay.

12   Among those who have issued apologies are the following. Archbishop Austin Burke, Archbishop of Halifax, preached sermons at St. Catherine's Church in Indian Brook, Nova Scotia (a Mi'kmaw congregation) (1992), and at Sacred Heart Church on the Millbrook Reservation, Nova Scotia, also a Mi'kmaw community (1993), which contained apologies for the church's role in the residential schools. Bishop Reynald Rouleau, OMI, Bishop of Churchill-Hudson Bay, attended a reunion of former students of Sir Joseph Bernier Day School and Turquetil Hall in Chesterfield Inlet, Nunavut, in 1996 and issued his second apology. At Alkali Lake, British Columbia, on 15 June 1998, Bishop Gerald Wiesner, Bishop of Prince George and an Oblate, presented an apology to a gathering of Indigenous people. Archbishop Gerard Pettipas, C. Ss. R., Archbishop of Grouard-McLennan in Alberta, sent an open letter to the Indigenous peoples of the Archdiocese on 28 April 2008, acknowledging the hurt caused by the church. Bishop Murray Chatlain, Bishop of Mackenzie-Fort Smith, on 27 May 2009, sent an official letter of apology to the Indigenous peoples of the diocese. See Bishops' Responses File, Authors files.

13   TRC, *Final Report*, vol. 6, *Reconciliation*, 101.

14   Ibid., 102.

15   Quewezance, "RSSC Welcome Apology."

16   Doxtater, "Apologia Canadiana Lessons," 10.

17   Dorrell, "From Reconciliation to Reconciling," 29–30.

18   See Alfred, *Wasáse*, 151–56; Flatfoot, "AHS Respond to Apology."

19   "Apology to Native Congregations," Study Guide, #94.161C Box 5, File 9, UCCA.

20   "I was naïve enough to believe that this [abuse] did not happen at the Presbyterian run schools." From notes provided to the author by Ian Morrison at an interview on 12 January 2012.

21 A statement of regret says, "I am sorry bad things happened to you." The speaker accepts no responsibility for the wrong done. An apology says, "I am sorry for the wrong I did to you. I will change my ways." Here the speaker accepts responsibility for the action and expresses a desire to change.

22 De Gruchy, "Confessing Guilt."

23 TRC, *Honouring the Truth*, 328.

24 Reynald Rouleau, "To the Former Students of Joseph Bernier Federal Day School and Turquetil Hall (1955–1969) – Chesterfield Bay," 18 January 1996.

25 "The Confession of The Presbyterian Church in Canada," The General Assembly of The Presbyterian Church in Canada, 9 June 1994.

26 Michael Peers to Archbishops and Bishops of the Anglican Church of Canada, 30 June 1993, Anglican Church General Synod Archives, General Synod 97-08, File 11.

27 For more details on the financial matters involved, see: https://www.theglobeandmail.com/news/politics/churches-escape-residential-school-settlement-obligations-in-wake-of-catholic-deal/article29767422/ (accessed 18 March 2019).

28 TRC, *Honouring the Truth*, 330.

29 Regan, *Unsettling the Settler Within*, 211.

30 TRC, *Final Report*, vol. 6, *Reconciliation*, 82.

CHAPTER 10

HOW DO I RECONCILE CHILD AND FAMILY SERVICES' PRACTICE OF CULTURAL GENOCIDE WITH MY OWN PRACTICE AS A CFS SOCIAL WORKER?

MARY ANNE CLARKE

How can Canada work for the Truth and Reconciliation Commission's call for reconciliation over the loss of First Nations children to the Indian Residential Schools (IRS) while First Nations children continue to be removed from their families and communities through child welfare? As a Child and Family Services (CFS) worker of more than thirty years, I am painfully aware that existing child welfare systems are not structured to achieve reconciliation. Rooted in the IRS system and mired in non-Indigenous bureaucracy, CFS today still perpetuates the very systems of settler colonialism, assimilation, and genocide that Canada purportedly condemns and apologized for in 2008.[1] It has become clearer and clearer to me over the years that it is not about simple tweaks of the system. Child welfare, in its current form, will never lead to true reconciliation for Indigenous children and families.[2]

As well as being a CFS worker, I am a PhD candidate in peace and conflict studies (PACS). I have come to ask myself: How then do I reconcile my actions as a child welfare worker with my studies and practice as a peace builder, when child welfare policies and practices continue to replicate the colonial structures of assimilation and cultural genocide that existed in the IRS system? How do I reconcile my desire for building peace through reconciliation with my work on the front lines of First Nations child welfare when I apprehend children from their homes and communities and place them with strangers? When I go into the office in the morning, I take a very deep breath and pray for the ability to face the pain and trauma of the families I am honoured to work with. I walk into the office knowing that while I have no control over whatever tragedies or urgent needs those families are facing, I am prepared to try to help them keep their children safe amid intergenerational trauma and pain.

Yet, too often, there are times when my hands are tied. I have had to apprehend children over the last thirty years because it was absolutely necessary for their life and safety; there was no other choice. But this raises a difficult question: Why were there no other viable options for these children and their families? And why is that still the case today? Why do Indigenous agencies and communities have to remove their children from their families, communities, languages, and lands to keep them "safe"?

Based on decades of experience, I do not believe we can achieve reconciliation within the existing colonial CFS system. The structural violence of not working with Indigenous leadership and of non-Indigenous micro-management within every level of child welfare must end if we are to stop the ongoing en masse removal of Indigenous children from their families and identities. For reconciliation to occur, this reactive European-based social work system brought to Canada through settler colonialism must be decolonized and transformed into proactive, community-specific systems based on the principle of Indigenous self-determination.[3] Indigenous communities already have the knowledge and abilities they need to manage and transform the child welfare system,[4] if only the federal and provincial governments "allow" traditional practices and provide the equitable resources required.

It can appear that the federal government may be starting to listen and work towards reconciliation. As of 1 January 2020, Indigenous governments have the opportunity to have their self-defined Indigenous family laws and corresponding services recognized through the federal government of Canada's Bill C-92, an Act respecting First Nations, Métis, and Inuit children, youth and families. However, there are multiple criticisms of its limitations. For example, there is no commitment to ensuring equitable or sufficient funding for First Nations CFS even though insufficient funding has been a primary denial of Indigenous rights,[5] along with overall insufficient on-reserve infrastructure and services; Indigenous family laws will only be respected if they meet the requirements outlined within the Act; neither is there recognition of First Nations rights to further self-determination in the care of their children and families[6] and the future of further self-determination depends on partisan federal politics.

Successful implementation of the Act will also require the support of the provinces and territories. Presently Quebec is attempting to overrule the Act and Manitoba is not yet definitive on how it will respond to it. Manitoba has stated its recognition of some of the opportunities available to Indigenous governments through the Act; however, it continues to structure its system in ways that continue its dominance over Indigenous governments, and it is still decreasing funds to Indigenous agencies. The challenge posed to Indigenous governments is if they will be "allowed" to provide care and safety for their own children in ways that are natural and inherent to their traditions, including their own languages and unique family systems, relationships, and roles and responsibilities. If not, the Act runs the risk of replicating some or all of the colonial violence that is found within the provincially mandated CFS. To have Eurocentric generic standards and policies is hardly Indigenous, traditional, or "customary."

This chapter is divided into four parts. First, I share my own motivations for assessing the child welfare system and demonstrate how, as a graduate student of PACS, I look at CFS from the perspectives of structural and cultural violence, colonization, and genocide—perspectives supported by the findings of the Truth and Reconciliation Commission (TRC). These external non-social work perspectives are necessary if Canada is to thoroughly examine how to prevent the ongoing assimilative losses of Indigenous children that began with the IRS system. In the second section, I trace the history of child welfare in Canada and Manitoba in particular, showing the progression from the IRS system to the challenges within child welfare today. Third, I look at the TRC's definition of "reconciliation" and identify critical elements of the reconciliation process that are lacking in the current child welfare system in Manitoba.

Despite these gaps, there are also stories of successful healing and community-specific initiatives that can guide our reconciliation work in the future. In my last section, I demonstrate how these examples can help guide transformation at all levels—individually, within families, within communities, within agencies, within leadership, and internationally—which is critical to breaking the destructive cycle of removing thousands of Indigenous children from their homes and depriving them of their birthright. While getting from here to there may seem like a daunting task, the more we understand what needs to be done as people commit to reconciliation, the faster we can effect real change.

Self-Positioning within Peace and Conflict Studies

As a practising Child and Family Services worker in Manitoba, I have a professional commitment to the safety and well-being of children. As a caregiver, mother, and grandmother, I also have my own personal commitments for providing safety for children. I have fostered children through CFS. I had to relinquish guardianship of my own son, as he had to become a permanent ward in care so that he could receive the specialized services he needed. My daughter, who chose me to traditionally adopt her, died of suicide in her placement while in the care of CFS. I have powerful professional and personal reasons for wanting to critically assess CFS. At the same time, as a graduate student of peace and conflict studies, I want to develop positive peace-building responses to the CFS system by fostering reconciliation.

This personal disclosure is consistent with the autoethnographic and Indigenous research methods I use in my work.[7] To understand my stories, it is necessary to have some understanding of my position within the world, my motivations, and my relationships with the many people to whom I am accountable. I am a Celtic Canadian woman, with a late Ininew partner. My children and grandchildren are Ininew, Anishinaabe, and Nakoda. I was formally and traditionally adopted into an Ininew-Anishinaabe family, who gave me both permission and a mandate to share what I have learned. This gives me multiple perspectives on colonization and reconciliation in Canada.

You should know, my position is not neutral. I have an agenda: to address the ongoing colonization in Canada, which now, thanks to the TRC, can lead into reconciliation. This does not mean that my perspective is the right one, merely that it is one of many.

I have front-line experience in how the system operates, as a CFS worker, as a client, and in management. Since child welfare operates within a cloak of confidentiality, many details cannot be shared. However, I share based on amalgamations of my personal experiences combined with as many external resources as possible; the truth needs to come forward.[8] The truth about child welfare is a prerequisite for reconciliation, and the truth is not pretty. At its best, CFS has deeply committed, capable workers who try to meet the needs of children and families within systems that too often are structured to break families apart. With the current reality of too few opportunities to prevent children from coming into care, there are only remedial changes and band-aid solutions.

No matter how hard I have tried within the system, in any of my roles, I hit brick walls. I needed to see everything from a different perspective. To gain new insights I turned to PACS—which can view child welfare as more than a form of social welfare intervention. PACS can identify child welfare as one aspect of colonial violence. According to pre-eminent PACS scholar Johan Galtung, "violence is present when human beings are being influenced so that their actual somatic and mental realizations are below their potential realizations."[9] Galtung's theory describes violence as "any physical, emotional, verbal, institutional, structural or spiritual behaviour, attitude, policy or condition that diminishes, dominates or destroys ourselves and others."[10] According to Galtung[11] violence is not natural or inevitable, and is based on three interacting forces—direct, structural, and cultural[12]—all of which can be found within CFS. Child welfare deals with the direct violence of child abuse and family every day; however, this chapter focuses on the systemic structural and cultural violence within the child welfare systems.

Structural violence exists when certain groups, classes, genders, nationalities, etc., have better access to goods, resources, and opportunities than others. This privilege and unequal advantage is built into the very social, political, and economic systems that govern societies, states, and the world.[13] The dehumanizing aspects of structural violence were well expressed when a mother whose children were in the care of CFS aptly said, "I am basically a file."[14] Structural violence within Canada's colonizing relationships with Indigenous peoples has been starkly identified by First Nations leaders and academics:

> There is no doubt that the colonizing processes in Canada are rooted in structural violence: For well over one hundred years, the policies of Canadian governments towards Aboriginal children were a major factor in the deterioration of Aboriginal cultures in Canada, and often resulted in the suffering and abuse of Aboriginal children. Aboriginal people have a justified concern about the deterioration of their families, communities, values and customs as a result of the policies that were adopted by Canadian governments, first in the residential schools and later in the child welfare system.... Past government policies however continue to have intergenerational effects, and many Aboriginal parents

and communities now face great challenges in caring adequately for their children.

An obvious and important indicator of the deterioration in Aboriginal cultures and communities is that Aboriginal children are taken into the child welfare system in disproportionally large numbers— at least five times greater than the rate of non-Aboriginal children.[15]

CFS has been identified in this expert legal writing[16] as a form of structural violence rather than as the benevolent social remedy that non-Indigenous governments and some practitioners purport it to be. Those of us who are most affected by the structural violence of the systems are well aware of violence within CFS.

When violence, structural and/or direct, becomes ingrained within government and social systems, it becomes culturally imbedded as normal. This cultural violence occurs when direct and structural violence become "legitimized" within the very fabric of a society or system. Cultural violence is made up of the attitudes, beliefs, and assumptions that shape our sense of self and the world, perpetuating violence as "normal" or necessary to perpetuate systems, governments, and processes.[17] As Galtung says, "Cultural violence makes direct and structural violence look, even feel, right—or at least not wrong."[18] The removals of large proportions of Indigenous children is a form of colonization and cultural genocide as defined by the TRC in its *Final Report*, and is an example of how colonization within Canada has become normalized and accepted. The en masse removals of thousands of Indigenous children have become the accepted norm in Canada. This is cultural violence: just as Indian Residential Schools were once considered normal, the continuing removal of Indigenous children through CFS is so common it is considered a routine part of our culture today. It became acceptable for Manitoba to have the highest apprehension rate in Canada and one of the highest rates of children in care in the world,[19] with 90 percent of the children in care in Manitoba being Indigenous.[20]

The structural and cultural violence of colonialism continues when few people ask or challenge why the numbers of Indigenous children in care are so high. According to Jillian Taylor in a CBC News Manitoba report, "As of March 31, 2016, of the 10,501 children in care of Child and Family Services, 9,205 were Inuit, Metis or First Nations"[21] (88 percent) while Indigenous people comprise only 10.5 percent of Manitoba's population.[22] Today, people are only starting to question why Indigenous children come into provincial care because of poverty, Eurocentric structural and systemic reasons,[23] and a lack of sufficient infrastructures and resources on-reserve—indicators of colonial structural violence—and then lose their culture, language, identity, and lands. This cultural violence that normalizes the losses of Indigenous children allows structural violence through colonization to continue.

With these many forms of structural and cultural violence inherent to CFS, I can view CFS only as a cog in the wheel of colonization and cultural genocide. Child welfare is an extension of the assimilative colonization of the IRS. According to the TRC the schools were the first form of child welfare for First Nations: "In many ways, the schools were more a child-welfare system than an educational one. . . . Canada's child-welfare system has simply continued the assimilation that the residential school system started."[24] These child removals continue with more Indigenous children being taken away from their families, communities, languages, and lands through CFS today than at the height of the residential school system.[25]

Reconciliation is meant to replace this violence with peace; however, it is not a matter of simply tweaking a few bureaucratic shortcomings. Structurally and culturally imbedded violence requires structural and cultural transformation. For these reasons I aim to work for positive peace (i.e., structural and cultural transformation) through my academic studies and in my work with CFS. Reconciliation calls on all of us to promote positive, transformative peace if we are to move past the legacy of residential schools and their current incarnation in CFS.[26] To achieve the reconciliation that the TRC calls for, we need an in-depth understanding of the destructive impacts of child welfare systems on Indigenous children and families. Within policies presented as "protective," children are still being removed from their homes and Indigenous identities en masse. What are they truly being protected from? An explanation of how colonization has impacted Indigenous children and families shows the depth and extent of colonial control over Indigenous lives to the extent of structural and cultural violence.

Child Welfare in Manitoba: How We Got Here

Before colonization, First Nations societies had multiple ways of ensuring the safety and well-being of children and families in accordance with their own unique cultures. This has been documented by several First Nations, including northern First Nations in Manitoba who documented the deep value they had for children.[27] According to late Elder Frank Wesley, when the missionaries asked the Elders in northern Manitoba how to translate the word or notion of "sin" into Cree, the Elders knew of no such concept. After four days of ceremonies, the closest the Elders could translate "sin" was for people to not care for their children. Children were so highly valued that not caring for them was the very worst anyone could do.

In contrast colonization attempted to assimilate Indigenous social systems into radically different approaches to child rearing based on Christian religious beliefs, such as the notion that children were the property of their fathers and the introduction of physical punishment.[28] Ironically, physical discipline, which was rampant in the IRS, is now one reason for child welfare interventions. Removing children to force them to attend residential schools caused further trauma to the children, their families, and the functioning systems of their communities. This was not an accidental by-product but part of the broader intentional colonial project,[29] as communities were targeted once their land came into the sights of colonial enterprises.[30] When residential schools began to close, children were literally transported from the schools into foster care and group homes—simply switching institutions.

Manitoba has long been aware of its continuously high numbers of Indigenous children in care. During the Sixties Scoop, Manitoba was the leading province in putting Indigenous children up for adoption outside of the province until the mid-1980s. Provincial Judge Kimelman's 1982 report, *No Quiet Place,* led to a moratorium on out-of-province adoptions;[31] however, the practice of bringing First Nations children into provincial care and placing them far from their home communities, into Winnipeg and other areas, continued.[32] Manitoba First Nations leadership lobbied to manage their own child welfare services on-reserve. Chiefs and communities worked hard to develop a system whereby their own children could at the very least remain within their communities. In the early 1980s they seemed to succeed: Manitoba First Nations signed tripartite agreements with the federal and provincial governments to allow First Nations communities to provide for the welfare of their own children, particularly on-reserve, through their own child welfare agencies.[33]

When I began my work on-reserve in the 1980s, it was an incredible opportunity to learn from Elders, community leaders, and families. We did not follow standard social work or child welfare practices as dictated by the province. Instead, the communities developed their own best practice methods with continuous consultation through local child care committees who knew the family's needs best. Child care concerns were brought forward quickly, and we sat down with the many family members and their supports to figure out—from a strength-based perspective—how to best take care of the children in that community according to the teachings and directions from the Elders and community members. It was not perfect, but it worked as we did not lose children to outside placements. We exerted First Nations sovereignty and self-determination by enacting traditional practices with accountability to the communities first and foremost. Manitoba's Aboriginal Justice Inquiry (AJI) in 1991 recognized the effectiveness of these First Nations agencies by noting that in the hands of Indigenous agencies, these changes were "remarkable"[34] and that the progress was nothing less than "tremendous."[35]

While the AJI's final recommendations went unacted upon throughout the 1990s, they were resurrected in 1999 through the Aboriginal Justice Implementation Commission (AJIC)[36] to decide how to implement the AJI in contemporary times. The AJIC documented the need for services for Aboriginal youth, and in 2001 the AJIC recommended that federal, provincial, and First Nations leadership further develop the tripartite political agreements for Aboriginal agencies. To be consistent with the AJI (1991), the 1996 Royal Commission on Aboriginal Peoples (RCAP),[37] and the Manitoba Framework Agreements Initiative that laid out detailed plans for self-determining child welfare and other departments,[38] there was a Memorandum of Understanding signed in 2000 and a 2001 CFS Protocol agreement for representatives from Manitoba, Canada, First Nations, and Metis to enter into an agreement to develop a new child welfare system.[39]

The 2003 Child and Family Services Authorities Act[40] provided the legal basis for the Aboriginal Justice Inquiry-Child Welfare Initiative (AJI-CWI), which was rolled out in 2005.[41] Its mandate was to create a jointly coordinated child and family services system that recognized "the distinct rights and authorities of First Nations and Metis peoples and the general population to control and deliver their own child and family services province-wide; that is community-based; and reflects and incorporates the cultures of First Nations, Metis and the general population respectively."[42] With over half of First Nations people living off-reserve, one of the AJI-CWI's major goals was to allow First Nations child welfare services to provide services to their members off-reserve. And, for the first time, the Manitoba Metis Federation was given the authority to provide services for its people.

In true colonial style the stated vision and mission in the AJI-CWI of Indigenous and provincial and federal governments working in partnership were not to become a reality.[43] Soon after the AJI-CWI rolled out, there was the tragic death of Phoenix Sinclair, an Indigenous five-year-old girl, and the provincial government immediately re-exerted its power and control over Indigenous child welfare—even though the poor child had been under the care of non-Indigenous Winnipeg CFS agency. Through its reactionary "Changes for Children Initiatives,"[44] beginning in 2006, and then through the 2013 Hughes Inquiry, *The Legacy of Phoenix Sinclair*,[45] some additional funds were provided to Indigenous agencies, since it was recognized that they were highly understaffed. There were also some generic programs developed in Winnipeg.

However, Indigenous child welfare agencies' and authorities' ability to be self-determining was decreased due to enforced micro-managing by the provincial and federal bureaucracies, and with the removal of First Nations political authority, such as not using the AJI-CWI Leadership Council that was mandated through the CFS Authorities Act.[46] First Nations and Metis political leadership was incorporated into the AJI-CWI structure through the Leadership Council, which has had its power increasingly diminished and currently is not even meeting. This can be why the Assembly of Manitoba Chiefs (AMC), Manitoba Keewatinowi Okimakanak (MKO), and the Southern Chiefs Organization (SCO) interpret the province as intending to assume control of child welfare without Indigenous leadership involvement.[47]

In addition, both First Nations authorities that had been created in conjunction with First Nations leadership were taken over by the province, and most First Nations agencies fell under the direct control of their authorities who were under provincial control.[48] Thus, the province has extended its reach, even onto reserves that are federally funded. Agencies and authorities must implement provincial standards over community-based practices in order to prevent further removals of agency directors or to come under a Section Four Review, whereby the authority assumes control under the province's watchful eyes.[49]

In the twenty-first century, cultural assimilation occurs due to provincial and federal control over front-line child welfare case management, and over the provincial standards and funding methods that control every movement of

First Nations CFS systems, agencies, and workers, which has led to grossly high numbers of Indigenous children in care in Manitoba. In 2004, pre-AJI-CWI, 83 percent of Manitoba's 5,782 children in care were Aboriginal.[50] In 2011 approximately 85 percent of children in care in Manitoba were Aboriginal,[51] and in 2014 the number climbed to approximately 87 percent. As mentioned earlier, CBC reported that as of March 2016 the equivalent of 88 percent of Manitoba children in care were Indigenous,[52] while Indigenous people comprise only one-tenth of Manitoba's population.[53] The actual numbers and the proportions of Indigenous children in care in Manitoba continue to climb.

The federal government's lack of funding for essential services on-reserve,[54] and Manitoba's simultaneous failure to adjust its child welfare standards to recognize this,[55] are key reasons why First Nations children have been removed from their communities. Even with the implementation of Jordan's Principle services that attempt to provide services to First Nations children comparable to those for non–First Nations children, many First Nations children are still coming into CFS care and being removed from their families and communities, not because of abuse or parental neglect but often because of poverty or simply to survive and to receive services that are otherwise not available at home. Often, this is for children with medical and developmental needs that cannot be met on-reserve due to the lack of, or insufficient, medical and educational services on-reserve. This is well documented by the 2016 Canadian Human Rights Tribunal, which found Canada to be violating human rights by not providing equal or equitable services to First Nations children. Currently, there is no documentation in Manitoba of exact numbers or proportions. However, it is common knowledge in the agencies that it is a significant proportion of their children in care who are transferred to Winnipeg. My own son was unable to live in his community due to his disabilities, and, even within the city, ended up coming into the care of child welfare to receive the services he required. Thus, the dearth of services for children with developmental challenges extends even off-reserve, leading to increased numbers of children in care.

When children on-reserve come into care, too many are forced to leave their community because reserve houses do not meet the housing requirements for foster children. The federal government, which is responsible for housing funds, has not provided housing that meets the provincial standards.[56] Details that do not meet the standards, such as the square footage per child within bedrooms, the sizes of windows, and the numbers of people living in the houses, often lead to a lack of on-reserve foster care placements, which results in children being sent away from their extended families, communities, languages, and lands. Children are often placed far away with strangers who have no knowledge of their lives, and they are left lost, alone, and forced to assimilate into other people's ways of life. The similarities to residential schools are self-evident.

A serious front-line challenge is the amount of micro-managed processes that workers must follow in order to attempt to meet the needs of the children and families for whom they are responsible. For example, at last count in one agency, there were over sixty-six different forms for children in care, which often asked for the same or similar information, albeit in different, non-interchangeable formats. These include intake forms, a number of different assessment forms (both the provincially standardized Structured Decision Making® model as well as agency-determined assessments that better culturally assess the families),[57] multiple court documents, and forms for every interaction with a child in care. In addition, there are social histories and daily contact notes that, like the other forms, must be completed both in hard copy and on the provincial Child and Family Services Information System (CFSIS) database; the federally funded children also have to have their information entered onto a different database, none of which are formatted for interchangeability.

To access even a single specific service for a child in care, not only is all the regular documentation required but also additional forms along with multiple levels of approval, *prior* to the child's receiving the services. The process involves the case manager who, together with the child and/or their family/ foster family, does the first needs assessment for additional services. This additional funding, the Special Support Services Rate (SSSR), must then be approved at the supervisor level, then by the agency's SSSR committee, which is consistent with the checks and balances required for good social work practices to help ensure that the agency is providing appropriate and sufficient resources to the child and their caregiver. However, even after being vetted by the case manager, the supervisor, and the SSSR committee (which consists of multiple management team members, including case specialists, foster care workers, financial workers and the director of the agency or the delegate), northern First Nations agencies must then submit this rate to the Northern Authority for further approval.

While the agency-level approval process is necessary, these additional approval steps ultimately place the power with the provincial government, through their control of the Northern Authority. At the Northern Authority a single employee with no case management experience or training decides yes or no to the rate, or may choose to decrease it. Highest needs children must then be further approved within the provincial Child Protection Branch before the child can access the services they require.[58] The ramifications can be devastating. Each child's services within northern First Nations agencies, both off- and on-reserve, are put on hold when they enter care until this multi-tiered Special Rates approval process is completed. This leaves children and/ or their care providers at risk—including serious risk—as they go without services or supports for at least weeks, and usually months.[59]

This is my greatest challenge as a social worker with CFS: working within a system that is not able to help me or other workers to respond on behalf of our families. Instead of supporting our work with children and families, the system is in fact our greatest barrier. Every single day there are CFS workers who go home with pounding headaches from banging their heads against the walls of bureaucracy and the structural violence of colonization. How can I as a social worker possibly reconcile these experiences with peace building for reconciliation?

This disconnected decision making is one of the central reasons I argue that our existing CFS systems cannot simply be tweaked but must be transformed. Bureaucrats who have never met the child and do not understand the community circumstances are making decisions based on finances that will have long-lasting impacts on that child, rather than based on the community-specific child's needs. The structural violence of colonialism is found in the front line and also in the political realm. Not only are the Indigenous CFS agencies and their workers being made powerless through stripping them of their rights and responsibilities to provide their expertise within community contexts, they have effectively been removed from any political self-determination that Indigenous agencies require to be Indigenous. This violates not only the principles set out in the AJI-CWI but also their inherent Indigenous rights, which are recognized in the 2007 United Nations Declaration on the Rights of Indigenous Peoples (UNDRIP)[60] and the treaties along with the 1982 Canadian Constitution,[61] which states in Section 35 that it recognizes Aboriginal and Treaty rights. Where can we find hope for reconciliation?

Restoring Respect as a Means of Reconciliation

"Reconciliation" has become a common term, and yet, what exactly does it mean? The Truth and Reconciliation Commission's *Final Report* defines "reconciliation" as "an ongoing process of establishing and maintaining *respectful* relationships" (my italics).[62] "Respect" is a key concept throughout the *Final Report*, mentioned 162 times. Yet, what is "respect"? In a study of Cree and Ojibway understandings of "respect," Annette Browne identified certain common characteristics: "The features of respect reflected ethical values related to equality, inherent worth, and the uniqueness and dignity of the individual."[63]

Let's examine how these terms apply to child welfare in Manitoba today. Is there *equality*? No, since on-reserve First Nations children are funded at 60 percent of the rate of other children for all services.[64] Is recognition of the children's *inherent worth* possible when the children are denied basic services and human rights? How are Indigenous children and families' *uniqueness and dignity* as Ininew, Anishinaabe, Anishininew, Dakota, or Dene (etc.) upheld when the provincial and federal governments are enforcing mass assimilation through provincial, Eurocentric CFS?

This enforced provincial bureaucracy leads to even more Indigenous children being placed away from their families, communities, and identities. According to Murray Sinclair et al., "In addition to these essentially political and rights-based arguments about the importance of cultural heritage, there is a growing recognition that the placement of Aboriginal children in non-Aboriginal homes has often been emotionally damaging to these children. The confusion and identity crises that are often experienced by Aboriginal children and adolescents who were apprehended by child welfare agencies and placed in non-Aboriginal foster homes and adoption placements is now widely documented. The separation of Aboriginal children from their families and communities results in cultural separation and has often had profound long-term psychological consequences."[65] Individually, separating Indigenous children from their families, assimilating them into other cultures, causes harm, and so how can mass assimilation affirm the dignity of individuals when it not only violates human rights but is a form of genocide, as per the TRC?[66] Obviously, we are not yet at a place of respect and equality when it comes to Indigenous children and families.

In addition to respect the TRC *Final Report* also defines other necessary aspects of reconciliation: "A critical part of this process involves repairing

damaged trust by making apologies, providing individual and collective reparations, and following through with concrete actions that demonstrate real
societal change."[67] Clearly, there are reasons that trust has been damaged when
it comes to Indigenous children. Non-Indigenous people and governments
need to recognize the ongoing nature of assimilation and cultural genocide
to start repairing that trust and follow through with real societal change;
however, the truths of Indigenous families' experiences and needs are still
being questioned or denied.

The First Nations chiefs' organizations (AMC, MKO, and SCO) have
attested to the ways in which the CFS system is continuing the damage of
assimilation and genocide, but they have been ignored and denied. Multiple
AMC resolutions identify in detail the ways CFS is not meeting their needs
and state their position for how to improve services.[68] In 2005, three years
after MKO's 2002 initially optimistic Statement of Intent regarding the
AJI-CWI, their tone changed from one asserting their jurisdiction in initiating processes in the coming AJI-CWI to one of responding to the concerns
that were quickly becoming evident within the AJI-CWI system. This led to
a call for restoration of First Nations jurisdiction over CFS in 2008.[69] By 2010
they called for a total review on the AJI-CWI process.[70] MKO then stated
their inherent authority over CFS in Resolution #2010-08-08, framed within
the context of the treaties, the Canadian Constitution, and even within the
global sphere, and clearly stated their dissatisfaction with the management
and board of the Northern Authority and the violations against Manitoba's
own CFS Act and CFS Authorities Act.[71]

MKO also provided direction in its 2011–12 Annual Report as to how
northern CFS agencies should provide for children and families, saying that
northern First Nations children need to be raised and cared for within their
traditional family roles and family heritage and with Elders: "In the process of
learning our family history we uncover our past, understand our present and
shape our future. This was the way of our people from time immemorial."[72]
In 2012 it appeared there was progress in northern First Nations leadership being able to exercise authority over their own child welfare with the
Northern Authority reporting directly to MKO chiefs at their Annual General
Assembly.[73] However, the following year, the province stepped in and dismantled the Northern Authority's board, which was its conduit to MKO. This
took place two years after the Southern Authority's board was dismantled.[74]

While the chiefs, through AMC, MKO, and SCO, have listened, the funding governments have not. It is like the residential schools all over again, where children and Survivors try to tell their stories, only not to be believed. Workers and administrators of Indigenous CFS agencies plead, beg, scream, and cry for the services required for the children and families we serve, knowing intimately these families' challenges as they struggle with multi-generational trauma due to colonization,[75] but too often, it is to no avail. If Indigenous and non-Indigenous governments and people are to begin working toward reconciliation, acknowledgement of the truth of people's current experiences is essential. This is why, as Paulette Regan discusses earlier in this volume, the Truth and Reconciliation Commission itself centred on oral history testimonies, public statements, and Honorary Witnesses, who would continue to speak these truths after the TRC concluded. Being heard and believed is the first step toward repairing that damaged trust.[76]

The second critical part of the reconciliation process is reparations. Canada's Human Rights Tribunal's (CHRT) 2016 decision found that Canada discriminates against First Nations children on reserves by failing to provide the same level of child welfare services that exist elsewhere. It is only after losing their nine-year battle against the rights of First Nations children that the federal government has begun to slowly start to comply with the CHRT decisions and directives. However, the complainant, the First Nations Child and Family Caring Society, continues to have to resort to the tribunal for orders of non-compliance with the decision, because of government inaction and continued denial of services. Yet, how can there be fair and just *reparations* for the loss of Indigenous children to the residential schools until our current truth about CFS is heard and believed? Sadly, the federal government has continued to challenge these truths and has been held in non-compliance with the tribunal's decision seven times.[77]

To know the truth, we must listen to people's experiences of pain, trauma, and devastation. The more stories are shared, either individually and/or collectively, the more the personal can become political.[78] Stories create connections and relationships within a group, as people discover that their individual experience is at least partially communal. Groups of people who have experienced similar trauma can then build a community base, power base, and knowledge base through the sharing of their stories.[79]

To restore and maintain respectful relationships, and to take *concrete actions* toward a *just* reconciliation, listening needs to occur within families.

and communities, with and within agencies, with and within governing organizations, and of course between Indigenous and non-Indigenous people, governments, and organizations. And listening costs nothing; we do not need funding, or administrators, or approvals. We simply need to listen to each other with our hearts.

We also need to listen to the silence: the silence of Indigenous children and youth whose voices were swallowed by the system, including those who felt they had no alternative but to kill themselves. Every child I know who died by suicide had tried desperately to be heard by someone, somewhere. They were either not heard or did not feel heard. What do their deaths mean? What does the silence of the empty spaces they inhabited tell us? My daughter's and the others' silence is deafening.

As my life goes on and a chair at meals sits empty of my girl, when she and others are absent from their graduation processions, when there are no children brought forth from them, the silence and emptiness become excruciatingly real. Their silence continues to reveal to me their stories, and they are not only part of the truths that we need to understand, they are at the heart of these truths. Nothing speaks louder than the silencing of their existence on this earth.

Transforming Child Welfare for Children and Families

Because of its roots in the IRS system, because of its entrenched inequalities that penalize Indigenous families, because of the demonstrated lack of colonial governments' willingness to listen to Indigenous leaders' call for change, and based on my own experiences, I am unable to see how we can achieve reconciliation within existing child welfare systems. I believe that the system needs to be replaced by self-directed initiatives that communities control, with an allocation of government funding and resources equitable to what non-Indigenous children and families receive, with additional resources for reparations for the violence.

This will provide healing opportunities for families to move past the intergenerational trauma caused by colonization. Right now the child welfare system is unable to do this because it is a negative, reactive system: child protective services are by law allowed to be involved only once a child is arbitrarily deemed to be at serious risk of abuse, neglect, or harm. Child welfare was not created and is not structured to prevent problems, merely to respond to them.

Child welfare is also recreating the IRS removals of the children under assimilative forms of removals, which leads to new and further traumas on top of the intergenerational effects of their grandparents' IRS traumas. Brenda Reynolds, the trauma consultant for the TRC and its liaison with Health Canada, spoke of the exponential impacts of colonial trauma when she said that many of the children who are in care today are "worse off" and suffering more than the children were at the Indian Residential Schools due to the exponential cumulative effects of the intergenerational traumas from the schools and child welfare.[80] It is highly concerning that a professional who was privy to the depths of the trauma of the Indian Residential Schools sees today's Indigenous children as suffering even more due to the cumulative traumas and losses of connection that they experience due to colonialism.

So where do we start? As Cindy Blackstock has said, "Children are the great hope of reconciliation. They know how to do it. We just need to follow their example."[81] The Carrier Sekani Tribal Council described self-government to the federal government: "The principle is simple. Only Indian people can design systems for Indians. Anything other than that is assimilation."[82] Simply put, the answers must come from within, self-determined by Indigenous peoples whose lives have been most affected by CFS.

Every First Nations community that I have lived in, worked in, or worked with has shown me that at the community level they view true "child welfare" (i.e., taking care of children) as preventive and holistic. In the traditional Indigenous practices that I have been a part of, children are equal participants within the circles of the families, communities, and lands, and social roles exist to prevent children from being harmed or neglected. When all aspects of these circles are working, children are not harmed but instead are respected and loved. Yet, through colonization, parts of the circles have been damaged, and the multigenerational trauma that each family experiences still places children at risk, primarily of neglect[83] and abuse from the unresolved prior experiences of their caregivers in residential schools and child welfare.[84]

Just as Erica Jurgens argues with education and Rachel George argues with resurgence (in the present volume), I argue with CFS: Indigenous communities have the knowledge and ability they need to preventively provide for their children and families, including the healing and decolonizing required. For example, many Indigenous teachings are still thriving today, including the widely known Anishinaabe Seven Sacred Teachings[85] and the Cree/Ininew Eight Sacred Teachings.[86] These teachings and principles were brought to life along with other cultural practices in the 1990s in the northern First Nations' program Meenoostahtan Minisiwin: First Nations Family Justice Initiative.[87] At the time all First Nations in northern Manitoba had the opportunity to participate in this program. It was developed by Awasis Agency, yet worked outside of CFS and its limited mandate.

Meenoostahtan Minisiwin focused on the root causes of family difficulties and on deep interventions that would strengthen families. Developed directly from the teachings of the Elders in each of the northern First Nations' communities, it had community-specific approaches to recognize the individuality of each First Nation and to most effectively help strengthen the family relationships that formed that community. Communication and listening were the primary methods of providing the families the opportunities to self-determine their healing paths, in balance with the protection needs of their children. Unlimited hours were spent reaching out to and listening to any and all family and community members who had an interest in the well-being of a child or family. Speaking in the language of their choice, Ininew, Dene, Anishininew, or English, families were encouraged to assess their own needs and to determine what they could use help with, rather than child welfare's approach of the agency identifying what the problems are and the family being required to follow the agency case plan, according to provincial legislation.

An underlying tenet was that the legal principle of "in the best interests of the child" can be effectively considered in First Nations only in relation to the family and community.[88] In mainstream social work and law, this principle often views children separately from their parents and families. In the Ininew, Anishininew, and Dene ways of northern Manitoba, the child can be understood only within his or her relationships with family, community, and lands.[89] For example, in one community, all the adults within a family would be involved in raising a child, such as the aunts and uncles and grandparents. In another community, when children were known to be at risk, the entire family would be brought to the land together for teachings and healing. There they would spend days or even weeks learning under supervision how to relate in healthy ways to each other and to the environment.

The most significant aspects about this voluntary program were that the services were in families' own Indigenous languages and that as many of the family members as possible were involved in trying to find ways to heal past and current traumas. According to those who developed and worked in the First Nations Family Justice program, the two greatest challenges were in helping people understand the unique nature of the program and in obtaining funding. Tragically, the pilot project's funding from the justice departments was limited and the program is no longer in existence.

Another transformative approach to child welfare is found in British Columbia's Spallumcheen Indian Band, which has a unique by-law approach that gives the band "exclusive jurisdiction over child welfare issues and the removal of a child from the care of a band family due to concerns over abuse or neglect."[90] Provincial involvement was eliminated, both politically and in its service provision. Through a Spallumcheen Indian Band by-law in 1980, which the federal and provincial governments recognized, British Columbia child welfare legislation has no authority over Spallumcheen children on- or off-reserve. While the band is funded by the federal government, the children's needs and protection are determined solely by the band through chief and council, who oversee the workers. It is both effective at keeping children safely within their community and politically consistent with their Indigenous right to care for their own children based on their own community's ways. It is also a one-of-a-kind arrangement that the federal government quickly eliminated as an option for other bands after its implementation, even though it has proven to be highly successful for over thirty years.[91]

For First Nations child care to be effective, First Nations' rights to care for their own children through politically self-determining means, as recognized in UNDRIP, need to be respected and maintained. Spallumcheen provides one example of how this can occur, although there are still some limitations, according to Chief Wayne Christian.[92] Even without political self-determination being recognized by the federal and provincial governments, community-specific opportunities such as northern Manitoba's Meenoostahtan Minisiwin provide the needed community-rooted approaches and, if strengthened, they can be interim steps to get from the colonial "here" to "there," with fully recognized self-determination for First Nations and other Indigenous peoples in Canada.

These are indicators that Indigenous peoples can provide care of their children that keeps their children safe within their communities, languages, and lands. If the colonial federal and provincial governments were to release their control and power over Indigenous peoples' relationships with their children and families and provide equitable resources and funding, Indigenous peoples in Canada could reverse the assimilative structural violence of the losses of thousands of their children.

How Do We Get from Here to There?

How do we get from *here*, where the *truth* is a place of ongoing and continuing structural violence, colonization, assimilation, and cultural genocide that is continuing the en masse removal of Indigenous children, to *there*, a place of *reconciliation* where Indigenous children and families are cared for by their own communities? It is my personal belief that within two generations, if everyone has the will, determination, and ability to work together, the child welfare system can be virtually eliminated. Obviously, there will still need to be many supportive services and resources in place for this happen. This includes services through health, education, and justice, and the development of infrastructure on-reserve, all of which need to be in place to help prevent children from coming into care for basic services. But it can happen, as there are examples such as Spallumcheen of Indigenous-controlled and -formed services that keep children safe within their communities and identities.

Based on Ininew, Anishinaabe, and other Indigenous teachings and peace-building methods, it is apparent that, to get from here to there, transformation needs to occur within every sphere: individually, within families, within communities, within agencies, within leadership, and within the international sphere.[93] *Individually*, speaking for myself, reconciliation is a process that begins with me. It is a never-ending journey of looking and listening and self-examination. What am I doing, and how am I doing it and living it? Am I watching and listening with an open heart and mind? Am I open to accepting the fact that even with a lifetime of truly sincere good intentions, I too am contributing to continuing colonization and genocide?

As a CFS worker there are times when my hands are tied, and I contribute to the removal of children when I must choose between the lesser of two evils to do my best with families. In full truth and honesty, I am unable to reconcile this within myself. I stand by every one of the many apprehensions I have had to do or be involved with in the last thirty years, because they were necessary for the life and safety of the children at that time and because there were no other options. I would hope that someone would step in and do the same thing if my children and grandchildren were in the exact same situations.

But why were there no other options for my son to receive services? Or for my daughter to stay alive within a CFS placement? I have yet to fully reconcile within myself my own inabilities to protect and provide for my children, let alone the thousands of other Indigenous children affected by CFS. It is because I cannot reconcile myself, or the child welfare system, that I advocate for moving completely away from such a reactive, oppressive system. I am experienced enough to know that we cannot replace CFS in one day; however, the work needs to begin immediately, even in small steps, to provide healing services rather than reactive punishing interventions. While I cannot reconcile myself to the existing child welfare system, I continue to practise social work to advocate for those small steps, to continue speaking for children and families, and to help amplify the truths of the people most affected by the systems. They must be heard and understood, so that any changes to child welfare do not simply morph into a "new" system that carries on the legacies of the IRSs.

Within *families* and *communities* I see us as parents, aunts, uncles, grandparents, making every single one of our decisions based on what's right for *all* the children within our families and communities, in all areas of our lives—economically, politically, socially, and more. True reconciliation in Canada's future depends on *all* children having safe and secure childhoods.[94]

Within *CFS agencies* we need to ask ourselves: Are we prepared to work ourselves out of our jobs? Are we open to decolonizing ourselves and our professional work, no longer turning to Eurocentric understandings of social work and instead using Bill C-92 to turn to Indigenous knowledge of traditional ways of keeping children and families safe and healthy? I envision us preparing ourselves to transition from our reactive jobs to roles as healers, as well as family and community builders. Within our daily work I see us standing up to funders and regulators to show them how their policies are destroying our children and families through the removals of thousands of Indigenous children, and providing the funders and regulators with alternatives for healing. We will need to be prepared to risk losing our jobs for standing with children and families seeking justice and basic rights. There will always be a lot of needs within communities due to generations of colonial policies that take direct aim at destroying Indigenous families and communities. Healing will need to take place over the next seven generations to help develop intergenerational resiliency in place of multi-generational trauma. Yet, instead of building bigger child protection agencies with more services for children in care, we should have our communities and agencies turn our focus to prevention and healing with families through non-CFS services whenever possible.

Within *leadership*, both Indigenous and non-Indigenous, we will need leaders who understand that Indigenous children have the need and the right to equitable services.[95] To respond to Canada's CHRT's 2016 decision and to meet the standards set out in the TRC and UNDRIP, leaders must make hard decisions about the priorities and distribution of funds, in all spheres. As Indigenous leaders' rights to self-determine their own communities, families, and children are recognized, the Elders' and communities' calls for care of services for children and families need to be heard.

This means making both micro community-level and macro countrywide choices that include the needs of Indigenous children, rather than continuing to exclude them from basic healing services. In Canada this means citizens holding leaders, governments, and the media accountable to put Indigenous children and families at the forefront of how Canada is and will be shaped. Only when Canada supports the rights and needs of Indigenous children can Canada assume a role *at the international level* as a true leader and defender of human rights. Within all of these spheres, we need to start the process of getting from here to there, even in the midst of contradictions.

Conclusion: Living within the Contradictions

For now, I exist extremely uneasily within the contradiction of working for CFS and living to build peace and strengthen Indigenous families to the point that it would entirely remove the need for child welfare services. I continue to work within child welfare to try to effect immediate, direct change for children and families. Yet, even in my current role of developing traditional community-based prevention services as alternatives to provincial CFS, the powerful grip of control from the CFS system continues to challenge communities' progress. I also further my PACS studies to understand the social and political forces that cause various forms of violence including settler colonialism, and to develop alternatives based within the structures of reconciliation and freedom from continuing colonization and cultural genocide.

This is my ongoing process: to work for transformation individually and collectively, personally and politically. As I continue to take my personal steps toward reconciliation, I am humbly and constantly aware that I cannot do it alone. Relationships with others and with the very colonizing forces that continue today are necessary to effect transformative reconciliation. But the more individuals do this, the more we become a collective whose impact will be profound if we are open to holistic transformation based on inherent Indigenous knowledges and practices.

Notes

1 Canada, "Statement of Apology to Former Students of Indian Residential Schools," https://www. aadnc-aandc.gc.ca/eng/1100100015644/1100100015649.

2 Blackstock, "Residential Schools"; Blackstock, "After the Apology"; Blackstock, "Social Movements and the Law"; Blackstock, "Understanding Reconciliation"; Trocmé, Knoke, and Blackstock, "Pathways to the Overrepresentation."

3 Hart, *Seeking Mino-Pimatisiwin.*

4 Awasis Agency, *First Nations Justice Institute*; York Factory First Nation, *First Nations Justice Initiative*; MacDonald, "Spallumcheen Indian Band By-Law."

5 Blackstock, "The Canadian Human Rights Tribunal"

6 Walqwan Metallic et al., "An Act Respecting First Nations, Inuit and Métis Children."

7 Kovach, *Indigenous Methodologies*; Wilson, *Research Is Ceremony;* Settee, *Pimatisiwin*; Lambert, *Research for Indigenous Survival*; Bochner and Ellis, "Personal Narrative"; Chang, "Autoethnography as Method."

8 In my professional experiences in CFS in Manitoba, there are personal experiences that cannot be corroborated by referencing through official sources for two reasons. One is the legislation of confidentiality (Manitoba CFS Act 1985) that the CFS system operates under; and the other is that the pace of CFS is so fast, in constant flux, that academic studies cannot keep up to the current circumstances.

9 Galtung, "Violence, Peace, and Peace Research," 168.

10 Quakers in the World, "Structural/Cultural/Direct Violence."

11 Galtung, "Violence, Peace, and Peace Research"; Galtung, "Cultural Violence"; Galtung, "Structural Theory of Imperialism"; Galtung, "Positive Peace."

12 Galtung, "Cultural Violence."

13 Galtung, "Structural Theory of Imperialism."

14 AMC, *Bringing Our Children Home.*

15 Sinclair et al., "Aboriginal Child Welfare," 199.

16 Note that, among others, this 2004 article was written by the future Chief Commissioner of the Truth and Reconciliation Commission (2015) and by Dr. Cindy Blackstock, executive director of Canada's First Nations Child and Family Services Caring Society, who spearheaded the Canadian Human Rights Tribunal challenge on behalf of First Nations children(2016).

17 Galtung, "Cultural Violence."

18 Ibid., 291.

19 Marni Brownell et al., "The Educational Outcomes of Children in Care in Manitoba," 85, http:// mchp-appserv.cpe.umanitoba.ca/reference/CIC_report_web.pdf.

20 AMC, *Keewaywin Engagement: Manitoba First Nations Child and Family Services Reform Final Report*, https://manitobachiefs.com/wp-content/uploads/2017/11/Final-FNCFS-Reform-Engagement-Report_September-2017.pdf.

21 Taylor, "'Ultimate Goal Is to Reduce.'"

22   Canada, Statistics Canada, "Aboriginal Peoples in Canada: Key Results from the 2016 Census," 25 October 2017, https://www150.statcan.gc.ca/n1/daily-quotidien/171025/dq171025a-eng.htm.

23   One example is the "Probability of Future Harm," a provincially standardized and enforced assessment tool that determines interventions for families. The Province of Manitoba enforces the use of this Eurocentric assessment tool that comes from the copyright holding "Wisconsin-based Children's Research Centre's Structured Decision Making" (SDM). It was developed for Wisconsin's criminal justice system. Even though many Indigenous agencies voiced their concerns and rejection of the tool's validity for their families, the provincial government enforces it through their standards and uses its implementation to assess the agencies' compliancy, which then determines their degrees of self-management away from their CFS Authority, and/or if the agency needs to be directly managed by the Authority.

24   TRC, *Final Report*, vol. 1, 138.

25   Obomsawin, *We Can't Make.*

26   TRC, *Final Report*; Galtung, "Positive Peace"; Fitz-Gibbon, *Positive Peace;* Blackstock, "Understanding Reconciliation"; Clarke and Byrne, "The Three R's."

27   Awasis Agency, *First Nations Justice Institute*; Bellefeuille et al., *Breaking the Rules*; York Factory First Nation, *First Nations Justice Initiative*; York Factory First Nation, *Mamowwechihatan Oskatisuk*; Wastesicoot, "Tapwetamowin."

28   Anderson, *Recognition of Being*; Wastesicoot, "Tapwetamowin."

29   Clarke and Byrne, "The Three R's."

30   Wolfe, "Settler Colonialism."

31   Manitoba, *No Quiet Place.*

32   Johnston, *Native Children.*

33   Clarke, "As a Social Worker"; Bellefeuille et al., *Breaking the Rules*; Awasis Agency, *First Nations Justice Institute.*

34   Manitoba, *Report of the Aboriginal Justice Inquiry*, 530.

35   Ibid., 531.

36   Chartrand and Whitecloud, *The Aboriginal Justice Implementation Commission Final Report.*

37   Canada, *Royal Commission on Aboriginal Peoples.*

38   Bennett, "Perspectives on Engaging"; Wastesicoot, "Tapwetamowin"; Wastesicoot, "Cultural Framework."

39   Bennett, "Perspectives on Engaging."

40   *The Child and Family Services Authorities Act*, CCSM 2002, c. C90.

41   There are four authorities that currently make up Manitoba's Child and Family Services system: the Metis Authority (two agencies), the First Nations Northern Authority (seven agencies), the First Nations Southern Authority (ten agencies), and the General Authority, for non-Indigenous children (four agencies).

42   Aboriginal Justice Inquiry – Child Welfare Initiative, "Mission Statement," http://www.aji-cwi.mb.ca/eng/joint_management_committee_mission.html.

43   MacDonald and Levasseur, "Accountability Insights"; Clarke, "As a Social Worker"; Bourassa, *Summary Review.*

44   Manitoba, *Changes for Children.*

45   Hughes, *Commission of Inquiry.*

46 First Nations and Metis political leadership was incorporated into the AJI-CWI structure through the Leadership Council, which is to be comprised of the Northern (Manitoba Keewatinowi Okimakanak) and Southern (Southern Chiefs Organization) Grand Chiefs, the president of the Manitoba Metis Federation, and provincial government representation.

47 AMC, *Bringing Our Children Home*.

48 Welch, "Profound Issues with Agencies"; Welch, "Indigenous Control a Myth."

49 Welch, "Profound Issues with Agencies"; Welch, "Indigenous Control a Myth"; Welch, "Awasis Director Forced Aside."

50 Bellringer, *Audit of the Child and Family Services*, 18–19.

51 Brownell, "Children in Care," 8.

52 Taylor, "'Ultimate Goal Is to Reduce."

53 Canada, "Aboriginal Peoples in Canada: Key Results from the 2016 Census."

54 Blackstock, "The Canadian Human Rights Tribunal."

55 Clarke, "As a Social Worker."

56 Canada, "Census in Brief. The Housing Conditions of Aboriginal People in Canada"; CBC News, "Manitoba First Nations Have Some of Worst Housing in Country, Report Says"; Fieldhouse and Thompson, "Tackling Food Security Issues"; University of Manitoba, "On-Reserve Housing."

57 Monias, Clarke, and Apetagon, "Understanding First Nation Practice."

58 Even children in care under federal funding must now have their special rates approved by the province prior to the federal government's releasing any dollars for that child.

59 Emergency supports can be put in for high needs children, but only temporarily, for no longer than thirty days, even though it takes far longer than that for the approval process to be completed.

60 United Nations, *United Nations Declaration*.

61 Canada, "Department of Justice—Final Report of the French Constitutional Drafting Committee"; Imai, *Annual Annotated Indian Act*.

62 TRC, *Final Report*, vol. 1, 28 (italics added).

63 Browne, "Meaning of Respect," 1.

64 Blackstock, "The Canadian Human Rights Tribunal"; Mansbridge, "Cindy Blackstock"; Blackstock, "Understanding Reconciliation."

65 Sinclair et al., "Aboriginal Child Welfare," 211.

66 MacDonald, "Five Reasons the TRC Chose."

67 TRC, *Final Report*, vol. 1, 28.

68 AMC, *Bringing Our Children Home*. Note: For resolutions from AMC, see: http://manitoba-chiefs.com/.

69 Resolution: 2008-05-09 was a "Call for a MKO Chiefs Assembly on Child and Family Services Devolution" to re-examine the effectiveness of the system, which led six months later to Resolution #2008-11-07, which called for the "Restoration of First Nation Jurisdiction over Child and Family Matters," http://www.mkonorth.com (accessed 2014).

70 Resolution #2010-03-06 was even more critical of the direction that NA and the AJI-CWI had gone, and went so far as to say, "BE IT FURTHER RESOLVED, The Chiefs in Assembly request for a total review on the AJI-CWI process and a preliminary report be tabled at the next Annual MKO General Assembly," http://www.mkonorth.com (accessed 2014).

71 http://www.mkonorth.com(accessed 2014); Clarke, "As a Social Worker."

72 Ibid.

73 Chief's Special Assembly in March 2012.

74 Welch, "Awasis Director Forced Aside."

75 Wesley-Esquimaux, "Intergenerational Transmission of Historic Trauma"; Wesley-Esquimaux, "Trauma to Resilience"; Linklater, *Decolonizing Trauma Work;* Volkan and Sinclair, *Bloodlines.*

76 Senehi, "Constructive Storytelling."

77 Metallic et al., "Act Respecting First Nations."

78 Ramanathapillai, "Politicizing of Trauma."

79 Senehi, "Constructive Storytelling."

80 Reynolds, "Keynote Address."

81 Mansbridge, "Cindy Blackstock."

82 As quoted in Canada, Parliament, House of Commons, Special Committee on Indian Self-Government, *Indian Self-Government in Canada*, 29.

83 Trocmé, Knoke, and Blackstock, "Pathways to the Overrepresentation"; Blackstock, Trocmé, and Bennett, "Child Maltreatment Investigations"; Wien et al., "Keeping First Nations Children"; MacLaurin et al., "A Comparison of First Nations."

84 Sinha et al., *Kiskisik Awasisak*; Awasis Agency, *First Nations Justice Institute*; York Factory First Nation, *Mamowwechihatan Oskatisuk*; York Factory First Nation, *First Nations Justice Initiative.*

85 While there are differences, the most common traditional Seven Sacred Teachings are: love, wisdom, respect, truth, humility, honesty, and courage.

86 Rudy Okemow shared the Cree Teachings in 2015. They were articulated at an Elder's Gathering at Frog Lake: Pimatisowin (life, trapping, hunting, camping); Pimachiwawin (looking after your-self/job life career); Manachiwawin (respect); Pastamowin (sin); Ocenahwin (respect of other: animal, bird, land); Mino opikayawaisawin (child care); Wakotowin (kinship); Tapatamowin (truth/faith).

87 Awasis Agency, *First Nations Justice Institute.*

88 Monias, Clarke, and Apetagon, "Understanding First Nation Practice."

89 Wastesicoot, "Tapwetamowin"; Bellefeuille et al., *Breaking the Rules*; Awasis Agency, *First Nations Justice Institute*; York Factory First Nation, *First Nations Justice Initiative.*

90 Sinclair et al., "Aboriginal Child Welfare," 240.

91 MacDonald, "Spallumcheen Indian Band By-Law." Information was augmented by personal experience while I was employed with Spalluncheen (1989 to 1991) and discussions with Chief Wayne Christian, 2015.

92 Information obtained by personal experience while I was employed with Spallumcheen (1989 to 1991) and discussions with Chief Wayne Christian, 2015.

93 Smith, *Decolonizing Methodologies*; Wilson, *Research Is Ceremony;* Monias, Clarke, and Apetagon, "Understanding First Nation Practice"; Wastesicoot, "Tapwetamowin."

94 Anderson, *Recognition of Being;* Wesley-Esquimaux, "Trauma to Resilience"; Sohki Aski Esquao and Wa Cheeh Wapuguunew Iskew, "Practising from the Heart."

95 Blackstock, "The Canadian Human Rights Tribunal."

CHAPTER 11

REPATRIATION, RECONCILIATION, AND REFIGURING RELATIONSHIPS

A Case Study of the Return of Children's Artwork from the Alberni Indian Residential School to Survivors and Their Families[1]

ANDREA WALSH

The repatriation of a collection of children's paintings created at the Alberni Indian Residential School (Alberni IRS) is an example of reconciliation in the contexts of Canadian cultural institutions and their collections, and their relationships with peoples whose lives and identities are deeply connected to these collections. The artworks were created at the Alberni IRS between the years 1959 and 1964 and the collection consists of seventy-five paintings. These paintings were repatriated to Survivors and their families in a Truth and Reconciliation Commission (TRC)–funded Commemoration Feast in the spring of 2013. The paintings were originally gifted to the University of Victoria (UVic) in 2008 as part of a larger collection of children's art by the family of Robert Aller. Robert Aller was a professional artist and an occasional volunteer art instructor at the Alberni IRS in the late 1950s through early 1960s. The work to locate Survivors who created the artworks as children and the details of repatriating the paintings to those people through the University of Victoria's Legacy Art Gallery were carried out by a group of Alberni IRS Survivors and staff, faculty, and students at UVic.[2]

The majority of the paintings gifted to U Vic in the 2008 Aller family gift were created by Ojibwe and Algonquin children. These children attended summer art camps that were organized by Aller and funded by the Department of Indian Affairs in the early 1970s. Prior to teaching at these camps, however, Aller taught as an occasional volunteer in two residential schools in Canada: the Alberni IRS in Port Alberni, British Columbia, and the MacKay IRS in Dauphin, Manitoba. Children who attended these two residential schools during the late 1950s and early 1960s created 134 paintings of the 700-plus included in the entire Aller Collection gift.[3]

A Gift of Art to the University of Victoria

My introduction to the collection of paintings saved by Robert Aller was through former U Vic Maltwood Art Gallery Director Martin Segger. Professor Segger was a lead on a Social Sciences and Humanities Research Council–funded Community University Research Alliance (CURA) project that involved a collaboration among myself, the Osoyoos Indian Band, and Osoyoos Museum. Our work focused on a collection of children's drawings from the Inkameep Day School created in the late 1930s and early 1940s. From his knowledge of this work, Professor Segger brought the Aller Collection of paintings to my attention, and the university proposed their availability for research and exhibition.

Two years later, in 2010, I was able to mount a summer term class in the U Vic Department of Anthropology on curating Indigenous art collections. This class provided students at U Vic the opportunity to work in a hands-on manner with the collection of paintings and the associated 2,000-plus-page personal archive of documentation and correspondence that accompanied the collection.

This documentation work by students revealed the names of the children who created the paintings as well as information about Mr. Aller's experiences as a volunteer art instructor at the school. That same year the TRC released a call for artists to submit contemporary artworks about residential school experiences and legacies. I contacted the TRC about the recently gifted collection of residential school art, and this call brought about a meeting with Justice Murray Sinclair, chair of the TRC, who was coincidentally travelling to U Vic to give a public lecture in October of 2011.

Figure 11.1. Students from Social Sciences work to document the 700-plus paintings collected by Mr. Robert Aller. Photograph courtesy of Andrea Walsh.

The Truth and Reconciliation Commission, Protocol, and Ceremony as Foundations for Repatriation

Between the fall of 2011 and 2012, I worked with Elders and Survivors from the Elders in Residence program through First Peoples House at U Vic to learn how we could respectfully use Salish protocols to ground our work with the paintings from residential schools in the Aller Collection. The Coast Salish Elders who guided this early work were Deb and Ron George and Victor Underwood and his wife, the late Joyce Underwood. We knew from the students' research that it was very possible that people who created the residential school paintings were alive, and that it was highly likely that they were unaware of the existence of the artwork or its location at the university. We also knew as part of these considerations that we would need to respectfully and ethically exercise cultural sensitivity in the event a person who created a painting was no longer alive.

It was decided by the Elders (three of whom were also residential school Survivors) that prior to any kind of academic or public engagement, Salish protocols and ceremonial work would be done to bless and cleanse the art and to strengthen those who would work with the paintings. This work took a few months over the winter to complete. In the late spring of 2012, we commissioned a traditional woven Salish blanket that we carried with us in March as we travelled northwest on Vancouver Island to Port Alberni. In

Port Alberni in a meeting room at the North Island College, we gifted the blanket to the chief of the Tseshaht First Nation, on whose traditional territory the Alberni IRS had operated. With guidance from Alberni IRS Survivor Patricia Watts and the late Ray Seitcher, we also met with Nuu Chah Nulth hereditary chiefs and cultural leaders. We explained what we knew about the paintings as part of their arrival at the university, and we asked for the leaders' permission to bring the paintings out in public at the TRC Regional Event in Victoria planned for mid-April 2012. The community leaders and chiefs granted us permission on the basis that such an event would have "all the right people" in attendance. These people, who included Survivors, their families, and communities from largely Vancouver Island and the lower mainland, might be able to help us to reconnect people with the paintings, and there would be cultural support for those who might be triggered by the artwork. At this meeting Elder and Alberni IRS Survivor Wally Samuel (Ahousaht First Nation) stepped forward as a project lead for the community to work with the UVic Elders and myself. At this time, too, Qwul'sih'yah'maht (Dr. Robina Thomas, School of Social Work, UVic) joined our collaboration. Our team was building with the strengths of individuals from both community and academic contexts.

TRC Commissioner Dr. Marie Wilson was present to witness our meeting with the chiefs and leaders on that day in Port Alberni and hear our request to bring the paintings to the Victoria Regional Event. After the meeting she invited me to join a circle of Honorary Witnesses to the Truth and Reconciliation Commission. I was inducted as an Honorary Witness at the 2012 Regional Event in Victoria, where I gave an address to 1,300 people who attended the final Call to Witness on the last day. I chose to speak about the paintings, our growing collaboration with Survivors and their families, and what our work together might mean when we reflected upon the work of reconciliation.

Bringing the Paintings out in Public and the Ceremony of Repatriation

At the April 2012 TRC Regional Event in Victoria, the Alberni IRS paintings were brought out in public for the first time in almost sixty years. The overwhelming response to the paintings created a desire by many Survivors who were at the event, or heard about it through social media, to start efforts to locate Survivors so that the paintings could be returned to them or their families. The process of locating Survivors took approximately a year and a half of concentrated work that was led by Survivors themselves, who activated their own social and familial networks of relations and communications. By 2013 we managed to locate approximately 90 percent of the people whose names were on the fifty paintings we exhibited. Importantly, not all those people whom we were able to contact and inform about the paintings wished to be part of the project, or even have their painting returned.

In the spring of 2013 we learned that monies were available from the TRC to hold "Commemorations," and we worked on behalf of the Survivors to secure $40,000 to hold a feast that would publicly return the paintings to Survivors. For four months we worked on arrangements to bring Survivors and their families back to Port Alberni (some were back in their home communities as far away as Prince Rupert and in remote locations along the central coast). On 30 March 2013, we held a feast at the Port Alberni Athletic Centre. At this event 80 percent of the paintings from the Alberni IRS collection were repatriated in a ceremony that included the family of Robert Aller and had over 400 witnesses. For this ceremony of return, we reproduced each painting onto archival paper with archival inks and placed the works into frames. These reproductions were given to Survivors in addition to their returned original painting(s). The reproductions were created because the original paintings were created on newsprint and have become fragile with age. Our thinking at the time was that Survivors could hang the reproduction in their home if they wished and keep the original work away from light in the acid-free envelopes we provided. At the ceremony of return, all the Survivors and/or their families accepted their original paintings and reclaimed their legal ownership. At the same time we returned the original, we handed each Survivor its framed reproduction. Unexpectedly, however, most of the Survivors stated their desire to have their painting stored at UVic and cared for by the university while retaining control over how it was cared for and seen. This turn of events began a unique kind of partnership with the university. A small number of Survivors and families decided to personally care for their original paintings, but they expressed a desire to collaborate on exhibtions in the future.[4] At the repatriation ceremony, the university and Survivors and/or their families signed an agreement that stated that the physical painting and all aspects of its ownership were transferred back to the Survivor/family. For the majority of Survivors who decided to have their painting stored at the university, another clause was included. This included specific instructions from the Survivor, if they wished to participate in future exhibitions with their painting that they be contacted, and if they consented to the publication of the image of the painting for academic/education purposes. Some Survivors also indicated who, in the event of their death, the university should contact about the continued care of the painting, or its return to that designated person, and, in the case of multiple paintings, persons.[5]

Figure 11.2. Family members of Robert Aller gift a reproduction artwork to the brother of the late Harry Wilson. The family has loaned back the artwork to the university for research and exhibition. Photograph courtesy of Andrea Walsh.

Figure 11.3. A few of the Survivors who participated in the repatriation ceremony have their picture taken with framed reproductions of their childhood paintings. Photograph courtesy of Andrea Walsh.

Stepping onto National Stages with the Story of Repatriation

In September of 2013 the Commissioners for the TRC asked us if we would bring the paintings to the National Event in Vancouver. We were invited to address the closing ceremony audience about our work in what they called a Gesture of Reconciliation. In the interim between the Commemoration Feast and the National Event, we discovered another twenty-five paintings from the school. We decided that instead of speaking about the work we had done, we would use the opportunity to publicly return a painting to a Survivor at the event. With over 1,000 witnesses, Survivors, and university faculty, students, and staff, in a short ceremony we returned to Mark Atleo of the Ahousaht Nation his childhood painting. We also used the National Event as an opportunity to educate the public about our work. Survivors and UVic students sat for three days to speak with people at the educational display. Over 4,000 people walked through this education event, and many of them stopped and discussed the paintings and spoke to Survivors about the repatriation project.

Figure 11.4. The return of Mark Atleo's childhood painting at the TRC National Event in Vancouver. September 2013. Photograph courtesy of Andrea Walsh.

Figure 11.5. One thousand witnesses to the repatriation of an Alberni IRS painting at the TRC National Event in 2013. Photograph courtesy of Andrea Walsh.

Figure 11.6. Chief Jeffrey Cook, Huu-ay-aht First Nation, and anthropology student Jesse Henderson set up the education booth at the TRC National Event in Vancouver. Photograph courtesy of Andrea Walsh.

In June 2015 Survivors and UVic faculty and students were asked to recount our repatriation story at the official closing of the TRC in Ottawa. On 1 June we presented our work at the Museum of History to the public as part of the official closing agenda of the TRC. For this four-day trip, seventeen people, consisting mostly of Survivors and their family members alongside UVic faculty and students, travelled to Ottawa as part of this story of repatriation and reconciliation.

While we were in Ottawa, the Canadian Museum of History requested that the story of the paintings' repatriation and the Survivors' narratives of residential school be officially recorded for inclusion in its new Canada Hall, which was opened to the public on 1 July 2017. The inclusion in the exhibition of Survivor paintings and recorded videos forms a feature component in this new exhibition that educates visitors about "reconciliation" in the wake of the legacy of the schools. It is expected that this exhibition at the Museum of History featuring the work of our collaboration between the university and Survivors will run for approximately twenty years.

Figure 11.7. Chuck August from the Ahousaht First Nation records his story about the return of his painting for the Canadian Museum of History. June 2015. Photograph courtesy of Andrea Walsh.

Figure 11.8. Survivor Gina Laing (Cootes) of the Uchucklesaht First Nation and Andrea Walsh outside Rideau Hall on the release of the TRC *Final Report,* 2 June 2015. We were invited to attend the private ceremony by the governor general, in attendance with Indigenous leaders, national party leaders, the prime minister, and the commissioners of the TRC to witness the conclusion of the Commission. Photograph courtesy of Andrea Walsh.

Figure 11.9. The entire group of travellers to Ottawa for the close of the TRC and release of the *Final Report*, as well as to work with the Canadian Museum of History. Photograph courtesy of Andrea Walsh.

Alberni IRS paintings have been collaboratively exhibited with the Legacy Gallery in Victoria (2013, 2017), Penticton Museum (2014), Alberni Valley Museum (2014/15), Emily Carr House (2015), University of British Columbia's Belkin Gallery (2015), and the Museum of Vancouver (2019). All of these exhibitions have had an educational component for students. School groups attend the exhibitions and Survivors from the repatriation project have given talks to students; and Survivors, faculty, and students have given lectures on residential schools and repatriation at various national and international conferences. In recognition of this work toward historical preservation and knowledge, Alberni IRS Survivors were awarded the Alberni Valley Heritage Award in 2015.

The story of the paintings has been reported through interviews with Walsh and Survivors on CBC Radio and television stations APTN and CBC. The record of the repatriation of the paintings forms part of the Executive Summary report of the TRC under "The Challenge of Reconciliation" and is featured in length in volume 6 of the TRC *Final Report* on Reconciliation. A photograph of three of the Survivors holding their repatriated paintings was featured on the front page of the *Globe and Mail* on 2 June when the *Summary Report* was officially released.

Figure 11.10. Front page of the *Globe and Mail* on the day of the TRC report release, featuring the photograph of three Alberni IRS Survivors with their returned paintings standing in the Great Hall of the Canadian Museum of History. Image courtesy of Andrea Walsh.

Critical Thoughts on the Process of Repatriating Children's Artworks to Survivors

Works of art created by children at Indian Residential Schools and Indian Day Schools are objects that often find themselves in the centre of critical conversations and actions pertaining broadly to colonial violence, representation, ownership and control, appropriation, and objectification. Cultural and educational institutions that hold such collections must go to extraordinary efforts to bring these objects to prominence in their agendas for reconciliation. Community/activist-based scholarship is an ideal mode of inquiry, and collaborations that seek partnerships between institutions and communities to address issues of social justice and reconciliation that can produce results that benefit Indigenous communities and museums are important but often in different ways. For Indigenous individuals and families, the meanings and value ascribed to objects held in museum collections are fathoms deeper than colonial records of acquisition and exhibition. In the specific case of the Indian Residential School and Indian Day School art collections, these collections of art represent the very people, relations, and ancestors who attended the schools. In many cases they are the only remaining traces of these childhoods.

The story of the repatriation of Alberni IRS artworks to Survivors and families is a success story in many ways, and it has provided us a way to reconsider the work we do in collections with communities connected to residential school legacies. Beyond the physical return of the paintings, the transfer of knowledge between Survivors and those of us at the university about the artwork's production and the connections between the works and individuals was seen to be of primary importance to our work. Part of this knowledge came in the form of information about people, events, and histories related to the artwork found in document archives created by the artist who worked with the children at the Alberni IRS, Mr. Robert Aller. Other archival research was conducted in provincial and national archives and cultural institutions' collections. As well, knowledge transfer regarding the paintings provided opportunities for the release and sharing of memories among Survivors, families, and communities, and, at times, it led to the physical reconnection of people. Through our work on exhibiting the residential and day schools art using methods of co-curation and collaboration, we have created contexts for knowledge from Survivors and former students to reach public audiences in direct ways.[6] We have worked diligently to prioritize a process of face-to-face relationship building over academic publication as the core of our work. Indeed, the concept of caring is at the heart of the work we do. In a 2015 plenary panel at the British Columbia Museums Association annual meeting, we presented our research methodology in a panel we titled "Taking Good Care: Curating Culturally Sensitive Collections." In this panel Survivors, UVic students, museum curators, and myself described our methodology of "caring for people" as the foundation for our work with material culture collections.

In the wake of the TRC, its report and Calls to Action, universities are uniquely positioned to make contributions to positive changes in the relationships between Indigenous peoples and Canada. On 27 November 2015, the *Globe and Mail* reported that Carolyn Bennett, in her former role as minister of Indigenous and Northern Affairs, stated, "Reconciliation is not an aboriginal issue; it is a Canadian issue," and "it is imperative that the country's leading cultural change institutions—the nation's universities—take up the challenge issued by Perry Bellegarde, national chief of the Assembly of First Nations, to 'do more to bring about a reconciliation in Canada.'"

The work of reconciliation in museums/galleries and cultural and educational institutions is an ongoing process.[7] It can be fraught with difficult and unsettling situations/issues for many people working in/through museums who have inherited the policies and practices created through kinds of colonial museology.[8] Reconciliatory work with collections intersects with Indigenous and institutional concepts and practices of preservation as well as control over cultural property.[9] Indeed, at times various agendas for reconciliation and preservation appear incommensurable.[10]

Since its onset, our work with the Alberni IRS paintings has been grounded by two Salish teachings expressed in Hul'qumi'num as *Natsu'maat* (We are all one or Everything is related) and Uy'skwuluwun (With a good heart and a good mind). These teachings were identified by Susa'meethl (Deb George) and Tousilum (Ron George) of Cowichan Tribes when we began work with Survivors and their families in 2012. Our efforts to ground our initiatives in these teachings engages with other projects that prioritize Indigenous research methodologies and ways of knowing.[11]

Collections and Relationships: Pathways Forward

In closing I would like to share three thoughts about the materiality of residential school art collections, and three thoughts about the relationships that are grounded in the concerns and issues that have arisen in our work.

The collections:

1. The material objects of the collections challenge the composition of typical ethnographic collections of Indigenous material culture in museums that are focused on adult-produced objects that have traditional use value in cultural practice and daily life. As they are pieces of newsprint paper with poster paint, they may be slotted into a category of lesser "value" than other objects. Our witnessing of the ways by

which people relate to the paintings, however, points to their historic importance for the recording of people's lives, and in some cases, they are seen as spiritual objects.

2. When the TRC archives were envisioned at the beginning of the Commission's work, they were imagined to include the documents of organizations and individuals who were associated with the running of the schools (teachers, administrators, governments, churches) as well as the recordings of Survivor testimonies and other gifts to the TRC through the ceremonial Bentwood Box that was present at regional and national gatherings.

    These collections of children's art compel us to acknowledge their existence as official records, as well as effective and affective objects.

3. Art collections as they exist today often come to light through estates of individuals who worked in the schools (mostly former teachers, medical staff, and administrators). Their identification as the property of these individuals begs questions about ownership and decolonial approaches to working with the collections. In the case of the Aller Collection, of which the Alberni IRS paintings were originally part, we have thought deeply about how and whether we can "decolonize" this collection of paintings through the attribution of individual ownership and intellectual property rights to Survivors, or that transferred to their families. By repatriating the paintings to Survivors and families, we dismantled the collection from the bounded collection it formed when it arrived at the university. However, in our ongoing work, we acknowledge the provenance of the paintings as part of their story and object biographies. It is curious to consider how this process of dismantling the collection strengthened our collective knowledge about the paintings as well as brought about unforeseen relationships between Survivors and institutions.

Our relationships:

When the university returned the paintings, with full and unqualified transfer of ownership (e.g., no proposed research was expected), and then in the context of the Commemoration Ceremony when Survivors stated they wished to walk the paintings back across the floor to be placed in UVic's care for preservation, relationships were formed. Our partnerships and collaborations for exhibition have been grounded by that day when it was understood that, through the paintings, the university and Survivors had entered into a relationship. The paintings have become material nodes through which ideas and histories flow. Placed in the context of exhibitions featuring Survivor-led tours or gallery talks with students and the public, the paintings have become sites of healing, according to the Survivors who speak about their work.

Our evolving relationship through the paintings can be tracked through exhibitions. The first exhibition we mounted in 2013 was titled *To Reunite, To Honour, To Witness.* The second major exhibition, held two years later, was titled *We Are All One.* The first exhibition's title reflects what we felt was the mandate of our work: to reconnect people with their paintings, to honour what they meant as objects in history, and then to consider what role audiences played in seeing the works in the era of the TRC. In hindsight the approach to this exhibition was very institutional and reflects the process of the gallery and public spectatorship more than the perspectives of Survivors and their stories, although this was the focus of the actual exhibition and text in the gallery. The second exhibition title reflects the deepening involvement in the Survivors' work regarding exhibiting their paintings, and the way they used the gallery space to deliver their specific messages to their audience.[12] Such direction came through their decision of the exhibition's title and its declaration—in giving Indigenous languages as part of the wall text, their colour choice for the walls, to the ways in which paintings were hung in groups to signify family relations and nations, to the counter-clockwise direction by which the paintings were viewed by the public. Education units for this second exhibition were also delivered by Survivors to students and public visitors.

As the paintings have come to be central to the refiguring of relationships between Indigenous communities and museums, between Canadians and their country's history of cultural genocide, between Survivors and their children as they share their stories through their art that they were not previously able to speak about, the story of the return of the paintings is easily bound within the concept and processes of "reconciliation." The challenge for us now, as we continue to be in relationship with each other, is to maintain the core principle of the paintings' repatriation: the paintings are the property of individuals and their stories are the cultural property of Survivors and their families. As objects that carry oral histories, they are owned and they carry knowledge. The challenge for those of us who work through Canadian cultural and educational institutions that exhibit artworks by Indigenous children will be to maintain their visibility and presence as the contributions of individuals to the unsettling and revisioning of Canada's history. We must push against any instances where the images and their stories may be appropriated as examples of Canada's reconciliation with Indigenous peoples.

Notes

1   This chapter was originally delivered as a presentation at the Ontario Museums Association's
     Indigenous Collections Symposium: Promising Practices, Challenging Issues, and Changing the
     System at Six Nations Polytechnic, Ohsweken and Woodland Cultural Centre, Brantford, 23–24
     March 2017.

2   When I refer to "we" or "us" in this story of repatriation, or "our" work, I am referring to a collec-
     tive of people from Alberni IRS Survivors, as well as staff, faculty, and students from UVic.
     I position myself as one of this team of individuals in a professional way as a visual anthropolo-
     gist/curator at UVic, guest curator with the Legacy Art Gallery, and Honorary Witness to the
     Truth and Reconciliation Commission. Through these various positions I am interested in deco-
     lonial approaches to refiguring relationships between Indigenous peoples and institutions through
     collections work and exhibitions. I locate myself personally in this work and in relation with
     other people in this project as a Canadian woman with Irish, British, Scottish, and Nlaka'pamux
     ancestries.

3   At the time of writing this chapter, a portion of the paintings from this larger collection are part
     of two other significant projects involving repatriation and reconciliation. Paintings from the
     original Aller collection at UVic were transferred to Laurentian University in 2014 with the inten-
     tion of creating a repatriation/exhibition project with communities from Manitoulin Island. In
     2019 this collaboration between Laurentian University and UVic received support to begin this
     work through the Social Sciences and Humanities Research Council of Canada's New Frontiers
     in Research Fund. UVic faculty, staff, and students are working with members of the MacKay
     Residential School Group, Inc. to return paintings to Survivors of the MacKay IRS and their fami-
     lies with the support of a Social Sciences and Humanities Research Council (SSHRC) Partnership
     Engage Grant.

4   Some of the Survivors who retained their originals in their care have given the Survivor/UVic
     collaboration their permission to digitally reproduce their artworks, but declined to participate in
     any exhibitions with the original works. Others have requested that no digital reproductions be
     made, and also declined participation in the project.

5   Since this agreement, the protocols and agreements regarding the care of the paintings have
     been further nuanced. As of 2015, some of the paintings are now housed at the Alberni Valley
     Museum at the request of the Survivors who live in the Alberni Valley and mid-Island communi-
     ties. After the exhibition *We Are All One*, the university and the Alberni Valley Museum drafted
     an MOU that the two institutions would work together on behalf of Survivors to care for their
     paintings and continue to provide the access and rights outlined in the original repatriation docu-
     ments of 2013.

6   Our work follows the precedent of community-engaged curatorial work in Canada as seen
     through the work of Heather Igloliorte (2012) to create public exhibitions focused on Inuit oral
     histories and experiences of residential schools.

7   See Czyzewski, "Truth and Reconciliation Commission"; Martin, Robinson, and Garneau, *Arts of
     Engagement*.

8   See Matthews, *Naamiwan's Drum*; Brown, *First Nations, Museums, Narrations*; Whittam, "'In a
     Good Way'"; Krmpotich, *Force of Family*; McTavish et al., "Critical Museum Theory"; Johnson,
     "Decolonizing Museum Pedagogies"; McCracken, "Community Archival Practice"; Allen and
     Hamby, "Pathways to Knowledge"; Watson, *Museums and Their Communities*.

9   See: Clavir, *Preserving What Is Valued*; Flynn and Hull-Walski, "Merging Traditional Indigenous Curation"; Alcock et al., "Developing Ethnic Research Practices"; Glass, "Return to Sender"; Laszlo, "Ethnographic Archival Records."

10   See: Angel, "Before Truth"; James, "Carnival of Truth?"; Martin, "Truth, Reconciliation, and Amnesia"; Niezen, *Truth and Indignation*; Stanton, "Canada's Truth and Reconciliation."

11   See: Smith, *Decolonizing Methodologies*; Castledon, Morgan, and Neimanis, "Researchers' Perspectives"; Lavallée, "Practical Application"; Ball and Janyst, "Enacting Research Ethics"; Wilson, *Research Is Ceremony*.

12   The exhibition *There is Truth Here: Creativity and Resilience in Children's Art from Indian Residential and Day Schools* (2017 Legacy Art Gallery, Victoria, and 2019 Museum of Vancouver) exhibited the Alberni IRS paintings alongside works by children who attended the MacKay IRS, the St. Michael's Indian Day School and the St. Michael's Indian Residential School, and the Inkameep Day School. The title of this exhibition reflected the focus on how art portrays particular kinds of truths of children's lives that were not recorded in TRC testimonies, and that the work is a profound example of the abilities that children displayed, as well as the knowledge they carried while surviving dire living conditions that were too commonly abusive. This title emerged through discussion with Survivors and Intergenerational Survivors about the value and meaning of art in exhibitions today.

CONCLUSION

SHERYL LIGHTFOOT

"Reconciliation is going to take hard work."[1] As one of the most power-ful closing statements of *Honouring the Truth, Reconciling for the Future: Summary of the Final Report of the Truth and Reconciliation Commission* (hereinafter TRC *Summary Report*), this is also an appropriate conclusion for this volume.

As the TRC *Summary Report* points out, there are multiple meanings of the term "reconciliation." Some scholarly and community voices have critiqued the very notion of "reconciliation" as deeply problematic, charging that these processes are intended as a renewed form of assimilative politics in Canada.[2] In my own work I have drawn the distinction between the competing visions of reconciliation: the Doctrine of Discovery interpretation, which involves the maintenance of liberal and colonial institutions; and the Indigenous interpre-tation of "reconciliation," which refers to a set of transformational politics.[3] The TRC was keenly aware of this debate. It thus chose to address this issue explicitly and deliberately early in the *Summary Report*. The TRC acknowl-edges that the interpretation of "reconciliation" as the return to a conciliatory state is an impossibility, as this has, for most Indigenous peoples, never existed in their relationship with Canada. The TRC was exceedingly clear that it in no way intended for "reconciliation" to mean maintenance of the status quo or a legitimation of existing colonial structures and institutions. Rather, the TRC, along with the authors of this volume, refer to reconciliation as a long-term, ongoing process that comes to terms with a difficult past and creates healthy and respectful relationships going forward into the future. Like the TRC itself, the authors in this volume soberly recognize the challenges of reconciliation, both the depth and breadth of work yet to be done, yet remain steadfast in their commitment that it *must* be done, and that it must be done in a transformational way.

With the TRC's finding that Canada committed cultural genocide against Indigenous peoples through the Indian Residential Schools (IRS) system, it is no longer possible for Canada to credibly claim to be a world leader in human rights protections unless it acknowledges this ugly history—a history that has left many lingering effects on Indigenous peoples and negative impacts on relations between Indigenous and non-Indigenous peoples—and makes fundamental changes to the nature of these relationships.

The TRC found numerous legacy impacts on Indigenous peoples, both on individuals and families but also on communities and cultures. The TRC exposed that the IRS system itself was made possible by the presumption of European supremacy, and then by its enactment through the governance structures and societal institutions that spawned from this presumption. A systemic problem therefore requires a systemic solution. Thus, the TRC found that not only do individuals need healing, along with their families and communities, but the entire system that made such a century-long policy a possibility is still largely in place and must be healed, must be radically transformed. As reflected in the TRC *Summary Report*, "Reconciliation is not about 'closing a sad chapter of Canada's past,' but about opening new healing pathways of reconciliation that are forged in truth and justice."[4] It is about dismantling the old systems and structures that are based on assumptions of European supremacy and creating new ones based in justice and mutual respect.

The TRC *Summary Report* includes ninety-four Calls to Action, which form the necessary actions that governments and institutions in Canada must take in our reconciliation journey. These ninety-four Calls include some that address the legacy effects of the IRS system, such as child welfare, education gaps, funding inequities, and loss of language and culture. The ninety-four Calls to Action also include some whose ultimate aim is to transform the country in order to restore or establish relations based in equality and mutual respect. Call 43 reads: "We call upon federal, provincial, territorial and municipal governments to fully adopt and implement the *United Nations Declaration on the Rights of Indigenous Peoples* as the framework for reconciliation in Canada."[5]

The TRC thus made several bold, transformative moves. First, the TRC *Summary Report* made the case that the IRS system was a policy of cultural genocide committed by Canada, thus forever dispelling the myth of peaceful settlement. It also brought this stain into full international view so that Canada's human rights reputation must now take Indigenous rights into account. Canada will now need to answer to the international community about its serious weaknesses in Indigenous rights; it can no longer hide behind its mythology. Second, the ninety-four Calls to Action took the bold step of linking the IRS system to wider doctrines of European supremacy and discourses of colonialism. Third, by embedding implementation of the UN Declaration on the Rights of Indigenous Peoples (hereinafter UN Declaration) into the ninety-four Calls to Action, the TRC created a road map for fundamental transformative change at all layers of Canadian government and society. In fact, the TRC linked reconciliation and implementation of the UN Declaration so tightly together that it is now simply impossible for one to support the TRC and not support full implementation of the UN Declaration. Rejecting full implementation of the UN Declaration would necessarily equate to a rejection of the TRC report. Reconciliation in Canada can only mean transformative change.

Linking Reconciliation to the UN Declaration on the Rights of Indigenous Peoples

The United Nations General Assembly passed the UN Declaration on the Rights of Indigenous Peoples on 13 September 2007, after thirty years of intense advocacy by Indigenous peoples' organizations from around the world in negotiation with states and international and non-governmental organizations. In the end 143 states voted in favour of the UN Declaration, eleven abstained, and four voted against: the United States, Australia, New Zealand, and Canada.[6] Each of these four issued statements immediately following the General Assembly vote to explain their negative positions. All four articulated that they had concerns about language, process, and collective rights, but especially they objected to the land rights and self-determination provisions in the UN Declaration, including the issue of free, prior, and informed consent.[7]

In the years immediately following the passage of the UN Declaration in the General Assembly, international and domestic moral and political pressure mounted on these four states and brought each of them to change their official position by 2010 to "support" or "endorse" the UN Declaration. Canada changed its position after Australia and New Zealand did so in 2009 and early 2010, but about a month ahead of the United States. Late on a Friday afternoon in November 2010, Indian and Northern Affairs Canada released a brief statement of endorsement on its website. The statement indicated that Canada did retain several caveats, exclusions, and qualifications on this endorsement, particularly regarding land rights; self-determination; and free, prior, and informed consent.[8]

The UN Declaration again became an issue during Canada's 2015 federal election, which began in mid-summer that year, right on the heels of the June TRC announcement of the *Summary Report* and ninety-four Calls to Action. Within weeks of the June TRC announcement, Liberal Party leader Justin Trudeau addressed the Assembly of First Nations 36th Annual General Assembly in Montreal. He noted that the TRC and the ninety-four Calls to Action serve as "an especially important conversation as we prepare to commemorate the 150th anniversary of Confederation. We need to recognize that ours was a nation forged without the meaningful participation of Aboriginal Peoples. . . . This commemoration stands as a reminder that much work remains. One hundred and fifty years on, we've yet to complete the unfinished business of Confederation."[9]

Trudeau continued, stating that there is an "urgent need for a renewed relationship between the federal government and Indigenous Peoples in Canada—one built on trust, recognition and respect for rights, and a commitment that the status quo must end." Trudeau promised an honourable and renewed nation-to-nation relationship, based on "recognition, rights, respect, co-operation and partnership . . . [and] rooted in the principles of the United Nations Declaration on the Rights of Indigenous Peoples." Later in the address Trudeau specifically mentioned that the Liberal Party's response to the TRC's ninety-four Calls to Action would start with implementation of the UN Declaration.

After winning the election in October 2015, Trudeau's mandate letter to Carolyn Bennett as incoming minister of Indigenous and Northern Affairs, which was made public in November 2015, again asserted Canada's new linked approach to the TRC and the UN Declaration. The prime minister directed that the relationship between Indigenous peoples and Canada must be renewed on a "nation-to-nation" basis because "no relationship is more important to me and to Canada than the one with Indigenous peoples." In particular the prime minister wrote: "I expect you to work with your colleagues and through established legislative, regulatory, and Cabinet processes to deliver on your top priorities: To support the work of reconciliation, and continue the necessary process of truth telling and healing, work with provinces and territories, and with First Nations, the Métis Nation, and Inuit, to implement recommendations of the Truth and Reconciliation Commission, starting with the implementation of the *United Nations Declaration on the Rights of Indigenous Peoples.*"[10]

In May 2016 Canada's Justice Minister Jody Wilson-Raybould and Indigenous Affairs Minister Carolyn Bennett went to New York to address the United Nations. Wilson-Raybould addressed the opening plenary in the General Assembly with a special statement on Canada's new position on the UN Declaration, the Indian Act, reconciliation, and the principle of free, prior, and informed consent (FPIC). In this statement, she indicated the need for Canada to reform the ways it conducts business with Indigenous peoples, and the central role that the UN Declaration should play in that reordering and renewal. She said:

> We need to find long-term solutions to decades-old problems as we seek to deconstruct our colonial legacy. Important to this work will be implementing the Calls to Action set out in the recent report of the Truth and Reconciliation Commission which considered the legacy of the Indian Residential schools.
>
> One of the significant challenges to this work is that although strengthening the nation-to-nation relationship is the goal, practically speaking the administration of Indigenous affairs in Canada is not organized around Indigenous Nations. For the most part, it is organized around an imposed system of governance. With respect to Indians this is through "bands," which are creatures of federal statute under the Indian Act. The Indian Act being the antithesis of self-government as an expression of self-determination.
>
> Simply put, we need to move beyond the system of imposed governance. . . . Tied to the fundamental work of Nation rebuilding and implementing the UNDRIP, one of the biggest legal questions we need to unpack is how to implement the concept of "free, prior and informed consent."
>
> The Declaration recognizes that Indigenous peoples have both individual and collective rights. Participation in real decision-making is at the heart of the Declaration's concept of free, prior and informed

consent—that Indigenous peoples must be able to participate in making decisions that affect their lives.[11]

The very next day, Indigenous Affairs Minister Carolyn Bennett issued a statement at the first working day of the United Nations Permanent Forum on Indigenous Issues (UNPFII). She stated—unequivocally—that her purpose in speaking at the UNPFII was to address Canada's position on the UN Declaration. She announced that Canada would hereafter be a "full supporter of the Declaration, without qualification."[12] Following loud applause and a standing ovation, she continued, "We intend nothing less than to adopt and implement the Declaration."

Implementing the UN Declaration

The UN Declaration represents the global consensus on the minimum standard ("the floor") for Indigenous peoples' rights that all states are obligated to recognize, protect, and uphold. It emphasizes the nationhood and self-determination of Indigenous peoples: their right to exist, to maintain and strengthen their cultures, and to protect and enhance their own traditions and institutions. As a human rights declaration, it prohibits state discrimination against Indigenous peoples, while also recognizing their collective right to remain distinct from their surrounding societies, to pursue their own visions of development, and to promote their full and effective participation in decision-making processes on issues that impact them.

As a human rights declaration, and not an international treaty or convention, the UN Declaration joins other important human rights declarations, such as the 1948 Universal Declaration of Human Rights, in articulating a global standard that all states are morally and politically obligated to respect as well as promote.

The UN Declaration challenges states and the international system to complete the postcolonial project, reclaim moral legitimacy, and restructure themselves along lines that promote justice, fairness, and human dignity for all. Walter Echo-Hawk argues that the Declaration is "planting the seeds of change" on the global level. He writes, "This harbinger of change asks every nation to restore the human rights of Native peoples that fell by the wayside during the colonial era. If that call is answered, the Declaration will someday be seen as the Magna Carta for the world's indigenous peoples. If implemented, those measures will change the world and fundamentally alter the way that humanity views some 350 million indigenous peoples who reside in over 70 nations."[13]

In the words of Onondaga Faithkeeper Oren Lyons, the UN Declaration was significant because "for the first time, we became human."[14] He is referring to the history of UN decolonization that, through the twin colonial doctrines of the Doctrine of Discovery coupled with the Salt Water Thesis, deliberately excluded Indigenous peoples from the human right of self-determination, which all other peoples enjoyed as an inherent aspect of their humanity.

The Doctrine of Discovery is "the theory that guided colonial practice" and state making in colonial and settler colonial contexts.[15] Its underlying assumption, according to Steve Newcomb, is that "Europeans were higher ... in intelligence than the Indians, and also suggests that the Europeans, by virtue of a 'superior' intelligence, possessed a higher position of power in relation to the lands of the [American] continent and in relation to the indigenous peoples living there."[16] As Vine Deloria Jr. (Standing Rock Sioux) wrote, "in practice, the theory meant that the discoverer of unoccupied lands in the rest of the world gained a right to the land titles as against the claims of other European nations."[17] Eastern Shawnee legal scholar Robert J. Miller also writes about property and other rights that Europeans claimed for themselves under the Doctrine of Discovery, which provided that "newly arrived Europeans immediately and automatically acquired property rights in native lands and gained governmental, political, and commercial rights over the inhabitants without the knowledge nor the consent of the Indigenous peoples."[18]

Furthermore, Indigenous peoples were specifically excluded from the UN decolonization project by the 1950s Salt Water or Blue Water Thesis, which asserted that only overseas territories, non-contiguous to the colonial power (i.e., located over "salt water"), were eligible for decolonization and self-determination, defined under the UN decolonization project as independent, sovereign statehood. While the UN Charter and the major human rights covenants each explicitly state that "all peoples have the right of self-determination," the question of who those "peoples" were, and who was therefore entitled to self-determination, remained undefined and subject to contentious politics. The Salt Water Thesis developed in response to efforts by some colonial powers, especially Belgium, to expand the scope of the UN Charter and thus the decolonization project to include Indigenous peoples. This effort was defeated by an unusual (by Cold War standards) coalition of the United States and its allies, along with the Soviet Union and its allies. The Salt Water Thesis was placed into a General Assembly resolution, which passed in 1960.[19] Thus, as the UN decolonization project proceeded over the next several decades, Indigenous peoples were left, as Chickasaw legal scholar James (Sa'ke'j) Youngblood Henderson describes, as "the unfinished business of decolonization."[20]

With the UN Declaration, Indigenous peoples finally enjoy human rights, including self-determination, on equal terms. As S. James Anaya, former UN Special Rapporteur on the Rights of Indigenous Peoples, observed,

> It is perhaps best to understand the Declaration and the right of self-determination it affirms as instruments of reconciliation. Properly understood, self-determination is an animating force for efforts toward self-determination—or perhaps, more accurately, conciliation— with peoples that have suffered oppression at the hands of others. Self-determination requires confronting and reversing the legacies of empire, discrimination, and cultural suffocation. It does not do so to condone vengefulness or spite for past evils, or to foster divisiveness but rather to build a social and political order based on relations of mutual understanding and respect. That is what the right of self-determination of indigenous peoples, and all other peoples, is about.[21]

As a standard-setting tool, the forty-six articles of the UN Declaration are intended to guide state action toward relationships with Indigenous peoples; they are based on justice and serve as a framework for mutual recognition and respect, with the self-determination of Indigenous peoples at its core. Anaya offered the following concrete suggestions for initial steps toward implementation:

> First, State officials as well as indigenous leaders should receive training on the Declaration on the related international instruments, and on practical measures to implement the Declaration. . . .
>
> Additionally, States should engage in comprehensive reviews of their existing legislation and administrative programmes to identify where they may be incompatible with the Declaration. This would include a review of all laws and programmes touching upon indigenous peoples' rights and interests, including those related to natural resource development, land, education, administration of justice and other areas.

On the basis of such a review, the necessary legal and programmatic
reforms should be developed and implemented in consultation with
indigenous peoples.

States should be committed to devoting significant human
and financial resources to the measures required to implement
the Declaration. These resources will typically be required for the
demarcation or return of indigenous lands, the development of
culturally appropriate educational programmes, support for indigenous
self-governance institutions and the many other measures contemplated
by the Declaration.

The United Nations system and the international community
should develop and implement programmes to provide technical and
financial assistance to States and indigenous peoples to move forward
with these and related steps to implement the Declaration, as a matter
of utmost priority.[22]

As the TRC *Summary Report* noted, "Studying the Declaration with a view
to identifying its impacts on current government laws, policy and behaviour
would enable Canada to develop a holistic version of reconciliation."[23] In
sum, the principle of self-determination must be integrated into the constitutional and legal framework of all layers of government in Canada as well as
civic institutions. Specifically, according to the TRC, this means repudiating
the Doctrine of Discovery in all areas of law and policy practice, recognizing and supporting treaties signed with Indigenous peoples, and revitalizing
Indigenous law and justice practices.

The authors of this volume collectively echo the sentiments of the TRC
and the principles of the UN Declaration on the Rights of Indigenous Peoples.
Reconciliation, for them, involves the four steps identified by the TRC:
(1) learning the truth of the past and the legacy conditions of present; (2)
acknowledging the harms done; (3) atoning for the causes; and (4) taking
actions to change behaviour in the present and the future. While healing
Indigenous individuals and communities is essential, reconciliation, these
authors argue, must involve both Indigenous and non-Indigenous peoples
at all levels and in all aspects of governance and society. Reconciliation must
emanate from and help support Indigenous agency and self-determination.
Most importantly, whether in government, educational institutions, health,
justice, child welfare, or civil society, reconciliation grounded in the UN

Declaration must be ongoing and transformative. As the closing statement
of the TRC *Summary Report* directs us,

> The way we govern ourselves must change.
> Laws must change.
> Policies and programs must change.
> The way we educate our children and ourselves must change.
> The way we do business must change.
> Thinking must change.
> The way we talk to, and about, each other must change.
>
> All Canadians must make a firm and lasting commitment to
> reconciliation to ensure that Canada is a country where our children
> and grandchildren can thrive.[24]

Reconciliation is not a destination but, rather, a difficult and necessary
journey we must all make together, far into the future.

Notes

1   TRC, *Honouring the Truth*, 364.

2   For examples, see Simpson, *Dancing on Our Turtle's Back*; Audra Simpson, "Interview with Audra Simpson: Reconciliation Needs to Be More than Permission to Maintain Status Quo," 25 March 2016, http://anthropology.columbia.edu/interview-audra-simpson-reconciliation-needs-be-more-permission-maintain-status-quo (accessed 16 July 2018).

3   Lightfoot, *Global Indigenous Politics*.

4   TRC, *Honouring the Truth*, 12.

5   Ibid., 244.

6   United Nations, Department of Public Information, 13 September 2007, *General Assembly Adopts Declaration on the Rights of Indigenous Peoples*, GA/10612, New York: United Nations, 2007.

7   See R. Banks, 2007, *Declaration on the Rights of Indigenous Peoples Explanation of Vote (New Zealand), 13 September 2007*, New York: United Nations; R. Hagen, 2007, *Explanation of Vote by Robert Hagen, U.S. Advisor, on the Declaration on the Rights of Indigenous Peoples, to the UN General Assembly, 13 September 2007*, New York: United Nations; H.R. Hill, 2007, *Explanation of Vote by the Hon. Robert Hill, Ambassador and Permanent Representative of Australia to the United Nations, 13 September 2007*, New York: United Nations; J. McNee, 2007, *Statement by Ambassador McNee to the General Assembly on the Declaration on the Rights of Indigenous Peoples, 13 September 2007*, New York: United Nations.

8   Indian and Northern Affairs Canada, Canada Endorses the United Nations Declaration on the Rights of Indigenous Peoples, 10 November 2010, http://www.ainc-inac.gc.ca/ai/mr/nr/s-d2010/23429-eng.asp (accessed 10 January 2011). Also see Chapter 4 in Lightfoot, *Global Indigenous Rights*, for how each of the four opposing countries engaged in a practice of "selective endorsement" of the UN Declaration.

9   Justin Trudeau, "Real Change: Restoring Fairness to Canada's Relationship with Aboriginal Peoples: Justin Trudeau's Remarks at the Assembly of First Nations General Assembly," Liberal Party of Canada, 7 July 2015, https://www.liberal.ca/justin-trudeau-at-assembly-of-first-nations-36th-annual-general-assembly/ (accessed 24 November 2016).

10 Justin Trudeau, Office of the Prime Minister, "Minister of Indigenous and Northern Affairs Mandate Letter," 13 November 2015, http://pm.gc.ca/eng/minister-indigenous-and-northern-affairs-mandate-letter (accessed 25 November 2016).

11 Jody Wilson-Raybould, Minister of Justice and Attorney General, "Address to United Nations General Assembly," New York, 9 May 2016. Author's personal notes.

12 Carolyn Bennett, 2016, "Announcement of Canada's Support for the United Nations Declaration on the Rights of Indigenous Peoples," speech, United Nations Permanent Forum on Indigenous Issues, New York, 10 May 2016. Author's personal notes.

13 Echo-Hawk, *In the Light of Justice*, 5.

14 Lyons, "Conversation."

15 Newcomb, *Pagans in the Promised Land*, ix.

16 Ibid., 78.

17 Deloria Jr., *Behind the Trail*, 86.

18 Miller, *Native America*, 1.

19 The Salt Water, or Blue Water, Thesis developed in opposition to efforts by some colonial powers (especially Belgium) to expand the scope of the UN Charter to include Indigenous populations. The thesis was placed into G.A Res. 1541 in 1960. The resolution stated that decolonization was required only for "geographically separate" territories administered by a colonial authority.

20 Henderson, *Indigenous Diplomacy*, 34.

21 Anaya, "Right of Indigenous Peoples," 196.

22 Anaya, "Agenda Item 4: The UN Declaration on the Rights of Indigenous Peoples."

23 TRC, *Honouring the Truth*, 244.

24 Ibid., 364.

ACKNOWLEDGEMENTS

Producing a co-edited volume of essays is truly a collaborative effort. Many hands have indeed made our work as co-editors much lighter. We have been honoured to work with everyone who helped bring this book to life. Our heartfelt thanks go to the following people. First and most importantly, to residential school survivors, whose courage, resilience, wisdom, and vision set all of us on pathways of reconciliation. Our Indigenous and settler authors for sharing their rich insights on concepts and practices of reconciliation in such a diverse range of settings. The anonymous peer review scholars whose suggestions for revisions improved the book immeasurably. We, of course, are responsible for its contents. The amazing staff at the University of Manitoba Press who guided us with their expertise, and provided valuable feedback and kind encouragement along the way: Jill McConkey, Glenn Bergen, Barbara Romanik, David Larsen, and Ariel Gordon. The National Centre for Truth and Reconciliation (NCTR) for funding support, and most especially a big thank you to Kaila Johnston, NCTR Acting Manager, Education, Outreach, and Public Programming, for co-ordinating the logistics of this project and keeping it all on track. Last, but certainly not least, our deep gratitude to Kelsey Hutton, independent copyeditor, for her keen eye, incisive analysis, and sharp but always respectful pen. Without each of you, this book would not have been possible. Miigwech!

BIBLIOGRAPHY

Primary Sources

Anglican Church of Canada General Synod Archives

Michael Peers to Archbishops and Bishops of the Anglican Church of Canada, 30 June 1993, General Synod 97-08, File 11, Anglican Church of Canada General Synod Archives.

United Church of Canada Archives

"Apology to First Nations Peoples," General Conference 1986, United Church of Canada.

"Apology to Native Congregations" Study Guide, #94.161C Box 5, File 9, United Church of Canada Archives.

Executive meeting, 19–22 March 1985, Minutes of the Executive and Sub-Executive, General Council, United Church of Canada (UCC), p. 122, #82-001, Box 35, File 1, United Church of Canada Archives (UCCA).

Reynald Rouleau, O.M.I., Bishop of Churchill-Hudson Bay, "To the Former Students of Joseph Bernier Federal Day School and Turquetil Hall (1955–1969)—Chesterfield Bay," 18 January 1996.

"The Confession of The Presbyterian Church in Canada," The General Assembly of The Presbyterian Church in Canada, 9 June 1994, http://presbyterian.ca/canadian-ministries/native-ministries/.

Secondary Sources

Aboriginal Affairs and Northern Development Canada. *The Community Well-Being Index: Report on Trends in First Nations Communities, 1981–2011.* Ottawa: Her Majesty the Queen in Right of Canada, represented by the Minister of Aboriginal Affairs and Northern Development, 2015.

Aboriginal Justice Inquiry: Child Welfare Initiative Site. 23 February 2017. http://www.aji-cwi.mb.ca/eng/.

Adams, David Wallace. *Education for Extinction: American Indians and the Boarding School Experience 1875–1928.* Kansas: University Press of Kansas, 1995.

Adams, Howard. *Prison of Grass: Canada from a Native Point of View.* Calgary: Fifth House, 1989.

Adams, Michael. "The Door to Reconciliation Is Truly Open." *Globe and Mail,* 8 June 2016. http://www.theglobeandmail.com/opinion/the-door-to-reconciliation-is-truly-open/article30339754/.

Alcock, Danielle, Jennifer Elgie, Chantelle Richmond, and Jerry White. "Developing Ethical Research Practices Between Institutional and Community Partners: A Look at the Current Base of Literature Surrounding Memorandums of Understanding in Canada." *The International Indigenous Policy Journal* 8, no. 4 (2017): 1–37.

Alfred, Taiaiake. *Wasáse: Indigenous Pathways of Action and Freedom.* 2nd ed. Toronto: University of Toronto Press, 2009.

Alfred, Taiaiake, and Jeff Corntassel. "Being Indigenous: Resurgences against Contemporary Colonialism." *Government and Opposition Government and Opposition* 40, no. 4 (2005): 597–614.

Allen, Lindy, and Louise Hamby. "Pathways to Knowledge: Research, Agency and Power Relations in the Context of Collaborations Between Museums and Source Communities." In *Unpacking the Collection: Networks of Material and Social Agency in the Museum*, edited by Sarah Byrne, Anne Clarek, Rodney Harrions, and Robin Torrence, 209–29. New York: Springer, 2011.

Allport, Gordon W. *The Nature of Prejudice*. Cambridge: Addison-Wesley, 1954.

Amstutz, Mark R. *The Healing of Nations: The Promise and Limits of Political Forgiveness*. Lanham: Rowman and Littlefield Publishers, 2005.

Anaya, S. James. *Indigenous Peoples in International Law*. Oxford; New York: Oxford University Press, 2004.

———. "The Right of Indigenous Peoples to Self-Determination in the Post-Declaration Era." In *Making the Declaration Work: The United Nations Declaration on the Rights of Indigenous Peoples*, edited by Claire Charters and Rodolfo Stavenhagen, 184–198. Copenhagen: International Work Group for Indigenous Affairs, 2009.

———. "Statement on the United Nations Declaration on the Rights of Indigenous Peoples, to the EMRIP." 15 July 2010.

———. "Agenda Item 4: The UN Declaration on the Rights of Indigenous Peoples. Statement of the Special Rapporteur on the Situation of Human Rights and Fundamental Freedoms of Indigenous People." Speech delivered at the Expert Mechanism on the Rights of Indigenous Peoples, Geneva, 15 July 2010).

———. "Statement by James Anaya, Special Rapporteur on the Rights of Indigenous Peoples on the Obligations of States to Implement the Declaration on the Rights of Indigenous Peoples." Speech, United Nations, New York, 18 October 2010.

Anderson, Mark C., and Carmen Robertson. "The 'Bended Elbow' News, Kenora 1974: How a Small-Town Newspaper Promoted Colonization." *The American Indian Quarterly* 31, no. 3 (2007): 410–40.

Anderson, Mark Cronlund, and Carmen Robertson. *Seeing Red: A History of Natives in Canadian Newspapers*. Winnipeg: University of Manitoba Press, 2011.

Angel, Naomi. "Before Truth: The Labours of Testimony and the Canadian Truth and Reconciliation Commission." *Culture, Theory and Critique* 53, no. 2 (2012): 199–214.

Angus Reid. "Canadians on Indigenous Issues: Focus on Reserves Final Survey Questionnaire – Post Pre-Test Feedback." 19 March 2018. http://angusreid.org/wp-content/uploads/2018/06/Canadians-on-Indigenous-Issues-Final.-March-20.pdf.

———. "Truths of Reconciliation: Canadians Are Deeply Divided on How Best to Address Indigenous Issues." 7 June 2018. http://angusreid.org/indigenous-canada/.

———. "Truth and Reconciliation: Canadians See Value in Process, Skeptical about Government Action." 9 July 2015. http://angusreid.org/aboriginal-truth-and-reconciliation/.

Anishinabek Nation. *The Soul Wounds of the Anishinabek People: The Psychological and Inter-generational Impacts of Indian Residential School*. North Bay: Anishinabek Nation, 2013.

Apuuli, Kasaija P. "Procedural Due Process and the Prosecution of Genocide Suspects in Rwanda." *Journal of Genocide Research* 11, no. 1 (2009): 11–30.

Arbour, Louise. "Economic and Social Justice for Societies in Transition." *International Law and Politics* 40, no. 1 (2007): 1–28.

Asch, Michael, John Borrows, and James Tully, eds. *Resurgence and Reconciliation: Indigenous-Settler Relations and Earth Teachings*. Toronto: University of Toronto Press, 2018.

Assembly of First Nations. "Assembly of First Nations National Chief Says 2015 Federal
    Budget a 'Missed Opportunity' for First Nations and Canada." Winnipeg: Assembly
    of First Nations. 21 April 2015. http://www.afn.ca/en/news-media/latest-news/
    assembly-of-first-nations-national-chief-says-2015-federal-budget-a-mi.

————. *Royal Commission on Aboriginal People at 10 Years: A Report Card*. Ottawa: Assembly of
    First Nations. http://www.turtleisland.org/resources/afnrcap2006.pdf.

Assembly of Manitoba Chiefs. *Bringing Our Children Home*. Winnipeg: Assembly of Manitoba
    Chiefs, 2014.

————. *Keewaywin Engagement: Manitoba First Nations Child and Family Services Reform Final
    Report*. Winnipeg: Assembly of Manitoba Chiefs, 2017. https://manitobachiefs.com/wp-con-
    tent/uploads/2017/11/Final-FNCFS-Reform-Engagement-Report_September-2017.pdf.

Attean, Esther Altvater et al. "Truth, Healing and Systems Change: The Maine Wabanaki-State Child
    Welfare Truth and Reconciliation Commission Process." *Child Welfare* 9, no. 3 (2012): 15–30.

Avruch, Kevin. "Truth and Reconciliation Commissions: Problems in Transitional Justice and
    the Reconstruction of Identity." *Transcultural Psychiatry* 47, no. 1 (2010): 33–49. doi:
    10.1177/1363461510362043.

Awasis Agency of Northern Manitoba. *First Nations Justice Institute: Mee-Noo-Stah-Tan Mi-Ni-Si-Win*.
    Winnipeg: Awasis Agency of Northern Manitoba, 1996.

Axworthy, Thomas. "In the North, Justin Trudeau Can Accomplish Great Things." *Toronto Star*, 6
    March 2016. https://www.thestar.com/opinion/commentary/2016/03/06/in-the-north-justin-
    trudeau-can-accomplish-great-things.html.

Backhouse, Constance. *Colour-Coded: A Legal History of Racism in Canada 1990–1950*. Toronto:
    University of Toronto Press, 2010.

Ball, Jessica, and Pauline Janyst. "Enacting Research Ethics in Partnerships with Indigenous
    Communities in Canada: 'Do It in a Good Way.'" *Journal of Empirical Research on Human
    Research Ethics* 3, no. 2 (2008): 31–51.

Bannerji, Himani. *The Dark Side of the Nation: Essays on Multiculturalism, Nationalism and Gender*.
    Toronto: Canadian Scholars' Press, 2000.

Barkan, Elazar. *The Guilt of Nations: Restitution and Negotiating Historical Injustices*. Baltimore: Johns
    Hopkins University Press, 2000.

Barker, Adam. "From Adversaries to Allies: Forging Respectful Alliances Between Indigenous and
    Settler Peoples." In *Alliances: Re/Envisioning Indigenous–non-Indigenous Relationships,* edited by
    Lynne Davis, 316–33. Toronto: University of Toronto Press, 2010.

Barria, Lillian A., and Steven D. Roper. "How Effective Are International Criminal Tribunals?
    An Analysis of the ICTY and ICTR." *The International Journal of Human Rights* 9, no. 3
    (2014): 349–68.

Bar-Simon-Tov, Yaacov, ed. *From Conflict Resolution to Reconciliation*. New York: Oxford University
    Press, 2004.

Bar-Tal, Daniel, ed. *Intergroup Conflicts and Their Resolution: A Social Psychological Perspective*. New
    York: Psychology Press, 2011.

Bar-Tal, Daniel, and Eran Halperin. "Socio-Psychological Barriers to Conflict Resolution." In
    Intergroup Conflicts and Their Resolution: A Social Psychological Perspective, edited by Daniel
    Bar-Tal, 217–40. New York: Psychology Press, 2011.

Battell-Lowman, Emma, and Adam J. Barker. *Settler: Identity and Colonialism in 21st Century Canada*.
    Winnipeg: Fernwood Publishing, 2015.

Battiste, Marie. *Decolonizing Education: Nourishing the Learning Spirits*. Saskatoon: Purich, 2013.

Battiste, Marie, and James (Sa'ke'j) Youngblood Henderson. *Protecting Indigenous Knowledge and Heritage*. Saskatoon: Purich Publishing, 2000.

Battiste, Marie, and Sheelagh McLean. *State of First Nations Learning*. Ottawa: Canadian Council on Learning, 2005. http://en.copian.ca/library/research/ccl/state_first_nations_learning/state_first_nations_learning.pdf.

Bedford, David, and W. Thom Workman. "Whiteness and the Great Law of Peace." In *Working Through Whiteness: International Perspectives*, edited by Cynthia Levine-Rasky, 25–42. Albany: State University of New York Press, 2002. http://www.sunypress.edu/pdf/60552.pdf.

Belanger, Yale D. "The Six Nations of Grand River Territory's: Attempts at Renewing International Political Relationships, 1921–1924." *Canadian Foreign Policy Journal* 13, no. 3 (2007): 29–46.

Belcourt, Christi. "Opinion." *Red Rising Magazine*. http://redrisingmagazine.ca/christi-belcourt-opinion/ (accessed 11 August 2016).

Bellefeuille, Gerard, Sydney Garrioch, and Frances Ricks. *Breaking the Rules: Transforming Governance in Social Services*. Thompson, MB: Awasis Agency of Northern Manitoba, 1997.

Bellringer, Carol. *An Audit of the Education of Aboriginal Students in the BC Public School System*. Victoria: Government of British Columbia, November 2015. https://www.bcauditor.com/sites/default/files/publications/reports/OAGBC%20Aboriginal%20Education%20Report_FINAL.pdf.

Bennett, Carolyn. "Bennett: 'More Children in Care Now than Height of Residential Schools." CBC, 27 October 2016. https://www.cbc.ca/news/politics/bennett-more-children-in-care-now-than-height-of-residential-schools-1.3823844.

Bennett, Marlyn L. "Perspectives on Engaging the Participation of First Nations Peoples in the Development of Child Welfare under Self-Government." Master's thesis, University of Manitoba, 2003.

Beresford, Quentin, and Marilyn Beresford. "Race and Reconciliation: The Australian Experience in International Context." *Contemporary Politics* 12, no. 1 (2006): 65–78. doi: 10.1080=13569770600704880.

Bergen, Jeremy. *Ecclesial Repentance: The Churches Confront Their Sinful Pasts*. Edinburgh: T and T Clark, 2011.

"Bernice King's Speech at the Walk for Reconciliation." *Reconciliation Canada*, 27 September 2013. http://reconciliationcanada.ca/staging/bernice-kings-speech-at-the-walk-for-reconciliation/.

Blackburn, Carole. "Producing Legitimacy: Reconciliation and the Negotiation of Aboriginal Rights in Canada." *Journal of the Royal Anthropological Institute* 13, no. 3 (2007): 621–38. doi: 10.1111/j.1467-9655.2007.00447.x.

Blackstock, Cindy. "Residential Schools: Did They Really Close or Just Morph into Child Welfare?" *Indigenous Law Journal* 6, no. 1 (2007): 71–78.

———. "The Canadian Human Rights Tribunal on First Nations Child Welfare: Why if Canada Wins, Equality and Justice Lose." *Children and Youth Services Review* 33, no. 1 (January 2011): 187–94.

———. "Social Movements and the Law: Addressing Ingrained Government-Based Racial Discrimination against Indigenous Children." *Australian Indigenous Law Review* 19 (2015–2016): 6–19.

———. "Understanding Reconciliation: Mere Co-Existence, New Foundation, or Mutual Celebration?" Presentation at Pathways to Reconciliation, Winnipeg, MB, June 2016. https://youtu.be/dr9sl2Su8h8.

Blackstock, Cindy, Nico Trocmé, and Marlyn Bennett. "Child Maltreatment Investigations among Aboriginal and Non-Aboriginal Families in Canada." *Violence Against Women* 10, no. 8 (1 August 2004): 901–16. https://doi.org/10.1177/1077801204266312.

Blake, Raymond, Jeffrey Keshen, Norman Knowles, and Barbara Messamore, eds. *Narrating a Nation: Canadian History Pre-Confederation.* Whitby: McGraw-Hill Ryerson, 2011.

Bochner, Arthur P., and Carolyn Ellis. "Personal Narrative as a Social Approach to Interpersonal Communication." *Communication Theory* 2, no. 2 (1992): 165–72.

Bombay, Amy, Kimberly Matheson, and Hymie Anisman. "The Impact of Stressors on Second Generation Indian Residential School Survivors." *Transcultural Psychiatry* 48, no. 4 (2011): 367–91. doi: 10.1177/1363461511410240.

Bomer, Randy, Joel Dworin, Laura May, and Peggy Semingson. "Miseducating Teachers about the Poor: A Critical Analysis of Ruby Payne's Claims about Poverty." *Teachers College Record* 110, no. 12 (December 2008): 2497–2531. https://blogs.nd.edu/poverty-cap/files/2012/07/TCRecord_Payne_Critique.pdf.

Borer, Tristan Anne. "Truth Telling as a Peace-building Activity: A Theoretical Overview." In *Telling the Truths: Truth Telling and Peace Building in Post-Conflict Societies,* edited by Tristan Anne Borer, 1–57. Notre Dame: University of Notre Dame Press, 2006.

Borrows, John. "Earth-Bound: Indigenous Resurgence and Environmental Reconciliation." In *Resurgence and Reconciliation: Indigenous-Settler Relations and Earth Teachings,* edited by Michael Asch, John Borrows, and James Tully, 66. Toronto: University of Toronto Press, 2018.

Bourassa, Carrie. *Summary Review of the Manitoba Child Welfare System for the Saskatchewan Child Welfare Review Report.* Regina: Saskatchewan Child Welfare Review Panel, 18 August 2010.

Brake, Justin, and Martha Troian. "Canada Unveils Indigenous Languages Bill to Fanfare, Criticism." APTN National News, 5 February 2019. https://aptnnews.ca/2019/02/05/canada-unveils-indigenous-languages-bill-to-fanfare-criticism/.

Braun, Virginia, and Victoria Clarke. "Using Thematic Analysis in Psychology." *Qualitative Research in Psychology* 3, no. 2 (2006): 77–101. doi: 10.1191/1478088706qp063oa.

Brehm, Hollie N., Christopher Uggen, and Jean-Damascène Gasanabo. "Genocide, Justice, and Rwanda's Gacaca Courts." *Journal of Contemporary Criminal Justice* 30, no. 3 (2014): 333–52.

Britton, Melisa, and Cindy Blackstock. *First Nations Child Poverty: A Literature Review and Analysis.* Edmonton: First Nations Children's Action Research and Education Service, 2015. https://fncaringsociety.com/sites/default/files/First%20Nations%20Child%20Poverty%20-%20A%20Literature%20Review%20and%20Analysis%202015-3.pdf.

Brooks, Roy L. *When Sorry Isn't Enough: The Controversy over Apologies and Reparations for Human Injustice.* New York: New York University Press, 1999.

Brown, Alison K. *First Nations, Museums, Narrations: Stories of the 1929 Franklin Motor Expedition to the Canadian Prairies.* Vancouver: University of British Columbia Press, 2015.

Browne, Annette J. "The Meaning of Respect: A First Nations Perspective." *Journal of Nursing Research* 27, no. 4 (Winter 1995): 95–109.

Brownell, Marni. "Children in Care and Child Maltreatment in Manitoba: What Does Research from the Manitoba Centre for Health Policy Tell Us, and Where Do We Go from Here?" Paper prepared for Phase III, Phoenix Sinclair Inquiry. Winnipeg, 2013.

Brownwell, Marni, et al. "The Educational Outcomes of Children in Care in Manitoba." Winnipeg: Manitoba Centre for Health Policy, June 2015. http://mchp-appserv.cpe.umanitoba.ca/reference/CIC_report_web.pdf.

Burnet, Jennie E. *Women in Africa and the Diaspora: Genocide Lives in Us: Women, Memory, and Silence in Rwanda.* Madison: The University of Wisconsin Press, 2012.

Burns, Phoebe, Kendra Williams, and David Pankratz. *Youth Peacebuilding Gathering 2008: Final Report.* Winnipeg: Final Report of Peacebuilding Project, 2008.

Burton, John W. *Conflict and Communication: The Use of Controlled Communication in International Relations.* London: Macmillan, 1969.

Bush, Peter. "The Canadian Churches' Apologies for Colonialism and Residential Schools, 1986–1998." *Peace Research: The Canadian Journal of Peace and Conflict Studies* 47, nos. 1, 2 (2015): 47–70.

Cajete, Gregory. *Native Science: Natural Laws of Interdependence.* Santa Fe: Clear Light Publishers, 2000.

Canada, Citizenship and Immigration. "Annual Report on the Operation of the Canadian Multiculturalism Act—2013–2014," Citizenship and Immigration Canada, http://www.cic.gc.ca/english/resources/publications/multi-report2014/3.asp (accessed 15 July 2016).

———. "Annual Report on the Operation of the Canadian Multiculturalism Act—2013–2014." http://www.cic.gc.ca/english/resources/publications/multi-report2014/3.asp.

———. *Welcome to Canada: What You Should Know.* Ottawa: 2013.

Canada, Government of. *Guide to the Canadian House of Commons.* https://lop.parl.ca/About/Parliament/GuideToHoC/pdf/guide_canadian_house_of_commons-e.pdf (accessed 3 March 2019).

———. *National Household Survey: Aboriginal Peoples in Canada: First Nations People, Métis and Inuit.* Ottawa: Statistics Canada, 2011. http://www12.statcan.gc.ca/nhs-enm/2011/as-sa/99-011-x/99-011-x2011001-eng.pdf.

———. *Report of the Royal Commission on Aboriginal Peoples.* 5 vols. Ottawa: Minister of Supply and Services Canada, 1996.

———. "Statement of Apology to Former Students of Indian Residential Schools." https://www.aadnc-aandc.gc.ca/eng/1100100015644/1100100015649.

———. "Suicide Prevention—First Nations and Inuit Health Canada." Health Canada: First Nations and Inuit Health. http://www.hc-sc.gc.ca/fniah-spnia/promotion/suicide/index-eng.php (accessed 24 January 2017).

Canada, Indian and Northern Affairs Canada. "Address by the Honourable Jane Stewart Minister of Indian Affairs and Northern Development on the occasion of the unveiling of Gathering Strength—Canada's Aboriginal Action Plan." 7 January 1998. https://www.aadnc-aandc.gc.ca/eng/1100100015725/1100100015726.

———. "Highlights from the Report of the Royal Commission of Aboriginal Peoples." https://www.aadnc-aandc.gc.ca/eng/1100100014597/1100100014637 (accessed 20 January 2017).

Canada, Justice. "Final Report of the French Constitutional Drafting Committee Responsible for Providing the Minister of Justice of Canada with a Draft Official French Version of Certain Constitution Enactments." 1 Dec 1990; modified 7 January 2015. https://www.justice.gc.ca/eng/rp-pr/csj-sjc/constitution/lawreg-loireg/index.html.

Canada, Parliament, House of Commons, Special Committee on Indian Self-Government. *Indian Self-Government in Canada: Report of the Special Committee.* Ottawa: 12–20 October 1983.

Canada, Public Safety Canada. "Examining Aboriginal Corrections in Canada." https://www.
    publicsafety.gc.ca/cnt/rsrcs/pblctns/xmnng-brgnl-crrctns/index-en.aspx (accessed 24
    January 2017).

Canada, Statistics Canada. "Aboriginal Peoples in Canada: Key Results from the 2016 Census."
    The Daily, 25 October 2017. https://www150.statcan.gc.ca/n1/daily-quotidien/171025/
    dq171025a-eng.htm.

————. "Census in Brief. The Housing Conditions of Aboriginal People in Canada." 25 October
    2017. https://www12.statcan.gc.ca/census-recensement/2016/as-sa/98-200-x/2016021/98-200-
    x2016021-eng.cfm.

Canadian Broadcasting Corporation (CBC). "Beyond 94, Truth and Reconciliation in Canada." 19
    March 2018. https://www.cbc.ca/news/indigenous/beyond-94-truth-and-reconciliation-1.4574765.

————. "Manitoba First Nations Have Some of Worst Housing in Country, Report Says." 1 February
    2016. https://www.cbc.ca/news/canada/manitoba/first-nations-housing-manitoba-1.3428743.

Cannon, Martin J., and Lina Sunseri, eds. *Racism, Colonialism, and Indigeneity in Canada: A Reader.*
    Don Mills: Oxford University Press, 2018.

Carr, Tracey. *The Healing Circle Continues: Phase II Evaluation of the Resolution Health Support
    Program for Residential School Survivors.* Melfort: Canadian Metis Heritage Corporation, 2009.

Carr, Tracey, Brian Chartier, and Tina Dadgostari. "'I'm Not Really Healed . . . I'm Just Bandaged
    Up': Perceptions of Healing among Former Students of Indian Residential Schools." *International
    Journal of Indigenous Health* 11, no. 2 (2017): 1–17. doi: 10.18357/ijih121201716901.

Carter, Linda E. "Justice and Reconciliation on Trial: Gacaca Proceedings in Rwanda." *New England
    Journal of International and Comparative Law* 14, no. 1 (2008): 41–55.

Cass, Loren. "Norm Entrapment and Preference Change: The Evolution of the European Union Position
    on International Emissions Trading." *Global Environmental Politics* 5, no. 2 (2005): 38–60.

Castleden, Heather, Vanessa Sloan Morgan, and Aelita Neimanis. "Researchers' Perspectives on
    Collective/Community Co-Authorship in Community-Based Participatory Indigenous
    Research." *Journal of Empirical Research on Human Research Ethics* 5, no. 4 (2010): 23–32.

Celermajer, Danielle. *The Sins of the Nation and the Ritual of Apologies.* Cambridge: Cambridge
    University Press, 2009.

Césaire, Aimé. *Discourse on Colonialism.* Translated by Joan Pinkham. New York: Monthly Review
    Press, 1972.

Chakravarty, Anuradha. "'Partially Trusting' Field Relationships Opportunities and Constraints of
    Fieldwork in Rwanda Post-conflict Setting." *Field Methods* 24, no. 3 (2012): 251–71.

Chang, Heewon. *Autoethnography as Method.* London: Routledge, 2008.

Chartrand, Paul, and Wendy Whitecloud, commissioners. *The Aboriginal Justice Implementation
    Commission Final Report.* Winnipeg: Aboriginal Justice Implementation Commission, 2001.
    http://www.ajic.mb.ca/reports/final_toc.html.

Check, Nicasius A. "Ethnicity and Arms Proliferation in the Great Lakes Region." *Africa Institute of
    South Africa,* briefing no. 43 (2011): 1–7.

Chief Oren Lyons—The Roots of American Democracy. Posted by Bioneers, 19 December 2014. Video,
    23.10. https://www.youtube.com/watch?v=Gs0EK1z9xhc.

Chiefs of Ontario. "Understanding First Nation Sovereignty." http://www.chiefs-of-ontario.org/faq
    (accessed 15 July 2016).

Chung, Melissa May Ling. "The Relationship between Racialized Immigrants and Indigenous Peoples in Canada: A Literature Review." Master's thesis, Ryerson University, 2010.

City of Vancouver. "Year of Reconciliation: June 2013–June 2014." City of Vancouver, 2017. http://vancouver.ca/people-programs/year-of-reconciliation.aspx.

Clark, Brad. "Framing Canada's Aboriginal Peoples: A Comparative Analysis of Indigenous and Mainstream Television News." *Canadian Journal of Native Studies* 34, no. 2, (2014): 41–64.

Clark, Ella Elizabeth. *Indian Legends of Canada*. Toronto: McClelland and Stewart, 1977.

Clark, Janine. "Learning from the Past: Three Lessons from the Rwandan Genocide." *African Studies* 68, no. 1 (2009): 1–28.

Clark, Phil. "Bringing the Peasants Back In, Again: State Power and Local Agency in Rwanda's Gacaca Courts." *Journal of Eastern African Studies* 8, no. 2 (2014): 193–213.

———. "Hybridity, Holism, and Traditional Justice." *The George Washington International Law Review* 39, no. 4 (2007): 765–837.

Clarke, Mary Anne. "As a Social Worker in Northern First Nations, am I also a Peacebuilder?" MA thesis, University of Manitoba, 2014.

Clarke, M.A., and S. Byrne. 2017. "The Three R's: Resistance, Resilience and Reconciliation in Ireland and Canada." *Peace Research: Canadian Journal of Peace and Conflict Studies* 49, no. 2 (2017): 105–132.

Clatworthy, Stewart. *Re-assessing the Population Impacts of Bill C-31*. Winnipeg: Four Directions Project Consultants, 2001. http://www.collectionscanada.gc.ca/webarchives/20071213113854/ainc-inac.gc.ca/pr/ra/rpi/rpi_e.pdf.

Colden, Cadwallader. *The History of the Five Indian Nations of Canada: Which are Dependent on the Province of New-York in America, and are the Barrier between the English and French in That Part of the World*. vol. 1. London: Lockeyer Davis, 1755.

Coleman, Sherry, and Howard C. Stevenson. "The Racial Stress of Membership: Development of the Faculty Inventory of Racialized Experiences in Schools." *Psychology in the Schools* 50, no. 6 (2013): 548–66. http://dx.doi.org/10.1002/pits.21693.

Collins, Bennett, Siobhan McEvoy-Levy, and Alison Watson. "The Maine Wabanaki-State Child Welfare Truth and Reconciliation Commission: Perceptions and Understandings." In *Indigenous Peoples' Access to Justice, Including Truth and Reconciliation Processes*, ed. Wilton Littlechild and Elsa Stamatopoulou, 140–69. New York: Institute for the Study of Human Rights, Columbia University, 2016. https://doi.org/10.7916/D8NC603B.

Conley, Alexander, and Margaret A. Moote. "Evaluating Collaborative Natural Resource Management." *Society and Natural Resources* 16 (2003): 371–86.

Corey, Allison, and Sandra F. Joireman. "Retributive Justice: The Gacaca Courts in Rwanda." *African Affairs* 103, no. 410 (2004): 73–89.

Cornell Law School. "Civil Rights." https://www.law.cornell.edu/wex/civil_rights (accessed 15 July 2016).

Corntassel, Jeff. "Re-envisioning Resurgence: Indigenous Pathways to Decolonization and Sustainable Self-Determination." *Decolonization: Indigeneity, Education and Society* 1, no. 1 (2012): 86–101.

Corntassel, Jeff, Chaw-win-is, and T'lakswadzi. "Indigenous Storytelling, Truth-Telling and Community Approaches to Reconciliation." *English Studies in Canada* 35, no. 1 (2009): 137–59.

Coulthard, Glen Sean. *Red Skin, White Masks: Rejecting the Colonial Politics of Recognition*. Minneapolis: University of Minnesota Press, 2014.

Cousins, Christopher. "LePage Threatens to Pull Support of Tribal Commission if Secretary of State is Involved." *Bangor Daily News* (Bangor, ME), 8 April 2013.

Craft, Aimée. "Neither Infringement nor Justification—The SCC's Mistaken Approach to Reconciliation." In *Renewing Relationships: Indigenous Peoples and Canada*, edited by Brenda Gunn and Karen Drake. Saskatoon: Native Law Centre, University of Saskatchewan, 2019.

Cranton, Patricia. *Understanding and Promoting Transformative Learning.* 2nd ed. San Francisco, CA: Jossey-Bass, 2006.

Crawford, Sue E.S., and Elinor Ostrom. "A Grammar of Institutions." *The American Political Science Review* 89, no. 3 (1995): 582–600.

Czyzewski, Karina. "The Truth and Reconciliation Commission of Canada: Insights into the Goal of Transformative Education." *International Indigenous Policy Journal* 2, no. 3 (2011).

D'Arcy, Paul. "No Empty Ocean: Trade and Interaction Across the Pacific Ocean in the Middle of the Eighteenth Century." In *Studies in the Economic History of the Pacific Rim*, edited by Sally Miller, A.J.H. Latham, and Dennis Flynn. London: Routledge, 1998.

Dashchuk, James. *Clearing the Plains: Disease, Politics of Starvation, and the Loss of Aboriginal Life.* Regina: University of Regina Press, 2013.

Dauge-Roth, Alexandre. "Testimonial Encounter: Esther Mujawayo's Dialogic Art of Witnessing." *French Cultural Studies* 20, no. 2 (2009): 165–80.

Davidson-Hunt, Iain. "Indigenous Lands Management, Cultural Landscapes and Anishinaabe People of Shoal Lake." *Environments* 3, no. 1 (2003): 21–41.

Davidson-Hunt, Iain J., and Fikret Berkes. "Learning as You Journey: Anishinaabe Perception of Social-Ecological Environments and Adaptive Learning." *Conservation Ecology* 8, no. 1 (2003): 5.

De Brito, Alexandra, Carmen González-Enriguez, and Paloma Aguilar Fernadez. "Introduction." In *The Politics of Memory: Transitional Justice in Democratizing Societies*, edited by Alexandra Barahona de Brito, Carmen González-Enriguez, and Paloma Aguilar Fernadez, 1–39. Oxford: Oxford University Press, 2001.

De Brouwer, Anne-Marie, and Sandra Chu. "The Men Who Killed Me." Citing Organization of African Unity, *Rwanda: The Preventable Genocide.* Addis Ababa, Ethiopia: OUA, 2000, para 16.20.

De Brouwer, Anne-Marie, and Etienne Ruvebana. "The Legacy of the Gacaca Courts in Rwanda: Survivors' Views." *International Criminal Law Review* 13, no. 5 (2013): 937–76.

DeCosta, Ravi, and Tom Clark. "Exploring Non-Aboriginal Attitudes towards Reconciliation in Canada: The Beginnings of Targeted Focus Group Research." In *Cultivating Canada: Reconciliation through the Lens of Cultural Diversity*, edited by Ashok Mathur, Jonathan Dewar, and Mike DeGagné, 327–40. Ottawa: Aboriginal Healing Foundation, 2011.

De Gruchy, John. "Confessing Guilt in South Africa Today in Dialogue with Dietrich Bonhoeffer." *Journal of Theology for Southern Africa* 67 (1989): 37–43.

Dei, George J. Sefa. "Rereading Fanon for his Pedagogy and Implications for Schooling and Education." In *Fanon and Education: Thinking Through Pedagogical Possibilities*, edited by George J. Sefa Dei and Marlon Simmons, 1–27. New York: Peter Lang, 2010.

De la Rey, Cheryl, and Ingrid Owens. "Perceptions of Psychosocial Healing and the Truth and Reconciliation Commission in South Africa." *Peace and Conflict: Journal of Peace Psychology* 4, no. 3 (1998): 257–70. doi: 10.1207/s15327949pac0403_4.

Deloria Jr., Vine. *Behind the Trail of Broken Treaties: An Indian Declaration of Independence.* Austin, TX: University of Texas Press, 1974.

Deskaheh, Chief. *Chief Deskaheh Tells Why He Is Over Here Again*. Kealeys Limited, 1923. http://
www.sfu.ca/~palys/ChiefDeskahehTellsUsWhyHeIsHereAgain1923.pdf (accessed 21 May 2016).

Deutsch, Morton. *The Resolution of Conflict: Constructive and Destructive Processes*. New Haven: Yale
University Press, 1973.

Deutsch, Morton, Peter T. Coleman, and Eric C. Marcus, eds. *The Handbook of Conflict Resolution:
Theory and Practice*. San Francisco: Jossey-Bass, 2006.

DiAngelo, Robin. "White Fragility." *International Journal of Critical Pedagogy* 3, no. 3 (2011): 54–70.

Dion, Susan. *Braiding Histories: Learning from Aboriginal Peoples' Experiences and Perspectives*.
Vancouver: University of British Columbia Press, 2009.

Dodson, Mick. "Towards the Exercise of Indigenous Rights: Policy, Power and Self-Determination."
Race and Class 35, no. 4 (1994): 65–76.

Donais, Timothy. *Peacebuilding and Local Ownership: Post-Conflict Consensus-Building*. London:
Routledge, 2012.

Donald, Dwayne. "Homo Economicus and Forgetful Curriculum: Remembering Other Ways to be a
Human Being." 2015. http://blogs.ubc.ca/inearthscare/files/2019/06/Donald-2012.pdf.

Dorrell, Matthew. "From Reconciliation to Reconciling: Reading What 'We Now Recognize' in the
Government of Canada's 2008 Residential Schools Apology." *English Studies in Canada* 35, no. 1
(Spring 2009): 27–45.

Doughty, Kristin. "Law and the Architecture of Social Repair: Gacaca Days in Post-Genocide
Rwanda." *Journal of the Royal Anthropological Institute* 21, no. 2 (2015): 419–37.

Doxtater, Thohahoken Michael. "The Apologia Canadiana Lessons for an Indian Boarding School
Apologia Americana." *Indigenous Policy Journal* 20, no. 3 (2013): 1–33.

Durocher, Alain. "Between the Right to Forget and the Duty to Remember: The Politics of Memory in
Canada's Public Church Apologies." PhD diss., Graduate Theological Union, 2002.

Echo-Hawk, Walter. *In the Light of Justice*. Golden: Fulcrum Publishing, 2013.

Edwards, Kyle. "Fighting Foster Care." *Maclean's*. https://www.macleans.ca/first-nations-fighting-fos-
ter-care/ (a10).

Ehle, John. *Trail of Tears, The Rise and Fall of the Cherokee Nation*. New York: Doubleday, 1988.

Elias, Brenda, et al. "Trauma and Suicide Behaviour Histories Among a Canadian Indigenous
Population: An Empirical Exploration of the Potential Role of Canada's Residential
School System." *Social Science and Medicine* 74, no. 10 (2012): 1560–69. doi: 10.1016/j.
socscimed.2012.01.026.

Environics Institute. *Canadian Public Opinion About Immigration and Multiculturalism*. Toronto:
Environics Institute for Survey Research, 2015.

———. *Canadian Public Opinion on Aboriginal Peoples*. Toronto: Environics Institute for Survey
Research, 2016.

Ephgrave, Nicole. "Women's Testimony and Collective Memory: Lessons from South Africa's TRC
and Rwanda's Gacaca Courts." *European Journal of Women's Studies* 22, no. 2 (2015): 177–90.

Farr, Robert M. *The Roots of Modern Social Psychology*. New York: Blackwell, 1996.

Fieldhouse, Paul, and Shirley Thompson. "Tackling Food Security Issues in Indigenous Communities
in Canada: The Manitoba Experience: Food Security in Indigenous Communities in
Canada." *Nutrition and Dietetics* 69, no. 3 (September 2012): 217–21. https://doi.
org/10.1111/j.1747-0080.2012.01619.x.

Fierens, Jacques. "Gacaca Courts: Between Fantasy and Reality." *Journal of International Criminal Justice* 3, no. 4 (2005): 896–919.

Fisher-Yoshida, Beth, Kathy D. Geller, and Steven A. Schapiro. *Innovations in Transformative Learning: Space, Culture and the Arts.* New York: Peter Lang Publishing, 2009.

Fleras, Augie. *The Politics of Multiculturalism: Multicultural Governance in Comparative Perspective.* New York: Palgrave Macmillan, 2009.

Flynn, Gillian A., and Deborah Hull-Walski. "Merging Traditional Indigenous Curation Methods with Modern Museum Standards of Care." *Museum Anthropology* 25, no. 1 (2001): 31–40.

Four Arrows. "Historical Notes on the League of Indian Nations." 19 October 2001. https://www. academia.edu/20546437/Deskaheh_The_League_of_Nations_and_the_League_of_Indian_Nations.

Frideres, James, and René R. Gadacz. *Aboriginal Peoples in Canada: Contemporary Conflicts.* Toronto: Prentice Hall, 2001.

Friedrich, Daniel S. *Democratic Education as a Curricular Problem: Historical Consciousness and the Moralizing Limits of the Present.* New York: Routledge, 2014.

Funkeson, Ulrika, Emilie Schröder, Jacques Nzabonimpa, and Rolf Holmqvist. "Witnesses to Genocide: Experiences of Witnessing in the Rwandan Gacaca Courts." *Peace and Conflict: Journal of Peace Psychology* 17, no. 4 (2011): 367–88.

Gaertner, Samuel L., John F. Dovidio, Phyllis A. Anastasio, Betty A. Bachman, and Mary C. Rust. "The Common Ingroup Identity Model: Recategorization and the Reduction of Intergroup Bias." *European Review of Social Psychology* 4 (1993): 1–26. doi: 10.1080/14792779343000004.

Galtung, Johan. "Cultural Violence." *Journal of Peace Research* 27, no. 3 (1 August 1990): 291–305. https://doi.org/10.1177/0022343390027003005.

———. "A Structural Theory of Imperialism." *Journal of Peace Research* 8, no. 2 (1971): 81–117.

———. "Violence, Peace, and Peace Research." *Journal of Peace Research* 6, no. 3 (1969): 167–91.

Gasibirege, Simon. *Lien entre Guérison du Traumatisme, Réconciliation et Développement. Cas du Rwanda: Deux Expériences qui Tentent de Retisser ce Lien et de le Consolider.* Kigali: Alert, 2009.

Gaventa, John. "Toward Participatory Governance: Assessing the Transformative Possibilities." In *From Tyranny to Transformation? Exploring New Approaches to Participation in Development,* edited by Samuel Hickey and Giles Mohan. New York: Zed Books, 2004.

Gellately, Robert. *Backing Hitler: Consent and Coercion in Nazi Germany.* New York: Oxford University Press, 2002.

George, Rachel Yacaaʔał. "Inclusion Is Just the Canadian Word for Assimilation: Self Determination and the Reconciliation Paradigm in Canada." In *Surviving Canada: Indigenous Peoples Celebrate 150 Years of Betrayal,* edited by Kiera L. Ladner and Myra J. Tait, 49–62. Winnipeg: Arbeiter Ring Publishing, 2017.

Ghorayshi, Parvin. "Diversity and Interculturalism: Learning from Winnipeg's Inner City." *Canadian Journal of Urban Research* 19, no. 1 (2010): 89–104.

Glass, Aaron. "Return to Sender: On the Politics of Cultural Property and the Proper Address of Art." *Journal of Material Culture* 9, no. 2 (2004): 115–39.

Gobodo-Madikizela, Pulma. *A Human Being Died that Night: A South African Woman Confronts the Legacy of Apartheid.* Boston: Mariner Books, 2003.

Godlewska, Anne, Jackie Moore, and C. Drew Bednasek. "Cultivating Ignorance of Aboriginal Realities." *Canadian Geographer* 54, no. 4 (2010): 417–40. http://dx.doi.org/10.1111/ j.1541-0064.2009.00297.x.

Goldhagen, Daniel. *Hitler's Willing Executioners: Ordinary Germans and the Holocaust.* New York: Random House, 1997.

Gone, Joseph. "Redressing First Nations Historical Trauma: Theorizing Mechanisms for Indigenous Culture as Mental Health Treatment." *Transcultural Psychiatry* 50 no. 5 (2013): 683–706.

Government of the Anishinaabe Nation in Treaty #3. "About." http://gct3.ca/about/mandate (a23).

———. "Grand Council Treaty #3." http://www.gct3.ca (a20).

Gozawa, Joanne. "The Cultural Complex and Transformative Learning Environments." *Journal of Transformative Education* 7, no. 2 (2009): 114–33.

Grand Council of Treaty #3. "The Paypom Treaty." Grand Council of Treaty #3. http://www.gct3.ca/wp-content/uploads/2016/02/paypom_treaty.pdf.

———. "We Have Kept Our Part of the Treaty." Kenora: Grand Council of Treaty #3, 2011.

Graybill, Lyn S. "Pardon, Punishment, and Amnesia: Three African Post-Conflict Methods." *Third World Quarterly* 25, no. 6 (2004): 1117–30.

Greenwood, Margo, Sarah de Leeuw, Nicole Marie Lindsay, and Charlotte Reading, eds. *Determinants of Indigenous Peoples' Health In Canada: Beyond the Social.* Toronto: Canadian Scholars' Press, 2015.

Groundwork for Change. http://www.groundworkforchange.org.

Gyepi-Garbrah, John, Ryan Walker, and Joseph Garcea. "Indigeneity, Immigrant Newcomers and Interculturalism in Winnipeg, Canada." *Urban Studies* 51, no. 9 (2014): 1795–1811.

Haile, Dadimos. "Rwanda's Experiments in People's Courts (Gacaca) and the Tragedy of Unexamined Humanitarianism: A Normative/Ethical Perspective." Discussion Paper, Institute of Development Policy and Management (IOB), University of Antwerp, 2008.

Hale, Charles R. "Neoliberal Multiculturalism." *PoLAR: Political and Legal Anthropology Review* 28, no. 1 (2005): 10–19.

Hamber, Brandon, ed. *Past Imperfect: Dealing with the Past in Northern Ireland and Countries in Transition.* Derry/Londonderry, Northern Ireland: INCORE/UU, 1998.

Hamber, Brandon, and Elizabeth Gallagher, eds. *Psychological Perspectives on Peacebuilding.* New York: Springer, 2015.

Harris-Galia, Rhose. "Arctic Bayanihan." In *Cultivating Canada: Reconciliation through the Lens of Cultural Diversity,* edited by Ashok Mathur, Jonathan Dewar, and Mike DeGagné, 193–201. Ottawa: Aboriginal Healing Foundation, 2011.

Harrison, Judy. "Judge Rules Against Penobscot Nation in Lawsuit over River Rights." *Bangor Daily News* (Bangor, ME), 16 December 2015.

Hart, Michael Anthony. *Seeking Mino-Pimatisiwin: An Aboriginal Approach to Helping.* Winnipeg: Fernwood Publishing, 2002.

Harvey, O. J., Jack B. White, William R. Hood, and Carolyn W. Sherif. *Intergroup Conflict and Cooperation. The Robbers Cave Experiment.* Vol. 10. Norman: University of Oklahoma Press, 1961.

Hauptman, Laurence M. *Seven Generations of Iroquois Leadership: The Six Nations Since 1800.* Syracuse: Syracuse University Press, 2008.

Hayner, Priscilla B. "Fifteen Truth Commissions 1974 to 1994. A Comparative Study." In *Transitional Justice. How Emerging Democracies Reckon with Former Regimes.* Vol. 1, *General Considerations,* edited by Neil J. Kritz, 226–61. Washington: United States Institute of Peace Press, 1995.

————. *Unspeakable Truths: Transitional Justice and the Challenge of Truth Commissions.* New York: Routledge, 2015.

Hayter, Roger. "'The War in the Woods': Post-Fordist Restructuring, Globalization, and the Contested Remapping of British Columbia's Forest Economy." *Annals of the Association of American Geographers* 93, no. 3 (2003): 706–29.

Henderson, James (Sa'ke'j) Youngblood. *Indigenous Diplomacy and the Rights of Peoples: Achieving UN Recognition.* Saskatoon: Purich Publishers, 2008..

Henderson, Jennifer, and Pauline Wakeham. "Colonial Reckoning, National Reconciliation?: Aboriginal Peoples and the Culture of Redress in Canada." *English Studies in Canada* 35, no. 1 (2009): 1–26.

————. *Reconciling Canada: Critical Perspectives on the Culture of Redress.* Toronto: University of Toronto Press, 2013.

Henry, Frances, and Carol Tator. *The Colour of Democracy.* 4th ed. Toronto: Nelson, 2009.

Henry, Nicola. "From Reconciliation to Transitional Justice: The Contours of Redress Politics in Established Democracies." *International Journal of Transitional Justice* 9 (2015): 199–218.

Hill, Brian. "Canada Endorses United Nations Declaration on the Rights of Indigenous Peoples." Global News, 9 May 2016. http://globalnews.ca/news/2689538/canada-endorses-united-nations-declaration-on-the-rights-of-indigenous-peoples/.

Hill, Gabrielle L'Hirondelle, and Sophie McCall. "Introduction." In *The Land We Are: Artists and Writers Unsettle the Politics of Reconciliation,* edited by Gabrielle L'Hirondelle Hill and Sophie McCall, 1–19. Winnipeg: Arbeiter Ring Publishing, 2015.

Hill, Gord. *500 Years of Indigenous Resistance.* Oakland: PM Press, 2009.

Hill, Richard W. "Linking Arms: The Haudenosaunee Context of the Covenant Chain." In *Mamow Be-Mo-Tay-Tah: Let Us Walk Together,* edited by Jose Zarate and Nora McMurtry, 17–29. Canadian Ecumenical Anti-Racism Network. Toronto: Canadian Council of Churches, 2009. http://www.ccforum.ca/wp-content/uploads/2-Spiritual-Quadrant-English.pdf.

————. *Talking Points on History and Meaning of the Two Row Wampum Belt.* Ohsweken: Deyohahá:ge: Indigenous Knowledge Centre, March 2013. http://honorthetworow.org/wp-content/uploads/2013/03/TwoRowTalkingPoints-Rick-Hill.pdf.

Hill, Sid. "My Six Nation Haudenosaunee Passport is not a 'Fantasy Document.'" *Guardian.* 30 October 2015. https://www.theguardian.com/commentisfree/2015/oct/30/my-six-nation-haudenosaunee-passport-not-fantasy-document-indigenous-nations.

Hill, Susan M. *The Clay We Are Made Of: Haudenosaunee Land Tenure on the Grand River.* Winnipeg: University of Manitoba Press, 2017.

Hirsch, Ben-Josef, Megan MacKenzie, and Mohamed Sesay. "Measuring the impacts of truth and reconciliation commissions: Placing the global 'success' of TRCs in local perspective." *Cooperation and Conflict* 47, no. 3 (2012): 386–403.

Höglund, Kristine, and Mimmi Söderberg Kovacs. "Beyond the Absence of War: The Diversity of Peace in Post-settlement Societies." *Review of International Studies* 36, no. 2 (2010): 367.

Hughes, Hon. Ted. *Commission of Inquiry into the Circumstances Surrounding the Death of Phoenix Sinclair.* 2013. http://www.phoenixsinclairinquiry.ca/.

Human Rights Watch. *Justice Compromised: The Legacy of Rwanda's Community-Based Gacaca Courts.* New York: Human Rights Watch, 2011.

Humphrey, Michael. "From Victimhood: Truth Commissions and Trials as Rituals of Political Transition and Individual Healing." *The Australian Journal of Anthropology* 14, no. 2 (2003): 171–87.

Hunt, S. "Ontologies of Indigeneity: The Politics of Embodying a Concept." *Cultural Geographies* 21, no. 1 (2013): 27–32.

Hunt, Sarah, and Cindy Holmes. "Everyday Decolonization: Living a Decolonizing Queer Politics." *Journal of Lesbian Studies* 19, no. 2 (2015): 154–72.

Huyse, Luc, and Mark Salter, eds. *Traditional Justice and Reconciliation after Violent Conflict: Learning from African Experiences*. Stockholm: International Institute for Democracy and Electoral Assistance, 2008.

Idle No More. "Anishinaabe water walk to unite Treat 3 people against Energy East Pipeline." 30 July 2105. http://www.idlenomore.ca/anishinaabe_water_walk_to_unite_treaty_3_people_against_energy_east_pipeline.

———. "Idle No More Kenora / Treaty 3 Territory." https://www.facebook.com/IdleNoMoreKenora (accessed 20 January 2017).

———. "Kenora Family Day: No Energy East." http://www.idlenomore.ca/kenora_family_day_event_no_energy_east (accessed 20 January 2017).

———. "The Story." http://www.idlenomore.ca/story (accessed 20 January 2017).

Igloliorte, Heather. "'We were so far away': Exhibiting Inuit Oral Histories of Residential Schools." In *Curating Difficult Knowledge: Violent Pasts in Public Places*, edited by Erica Lehrer, Cynthia Milton, and Monica Patterson, 23–40. United Kingdom: Palgrave Macmillan: 2011.

Ignatieff, Michael. "The Elusive Goal of War Trials." *Harper's Magazine*, 1 March 1997. https://harpers.org/archive/1997/03/the-elusive-goal-of-war-trials/.

Imai, Shin. *Annual Annotated Indian Act and Aboriginal Constitutional Provisions*. Toronto: Carswell, 2015.

Immigrant Partnership Winnipeg. *2016–19 Strategic Plan Report*. Winnipeg: Immigrant Partnership Winnipeg.

Indian Residential Schools Agreement. *Schedule N: Mandate for the Truth and Reconciliation Commission*. N.d. http://www.residentialschoolsettlement.ca/schedule_n.pdf.

Ingelaere, Bert. "Does the Truth Pass Across the Fire Without Burning? Locating the Short Circuit in Rwanda's Gacaca Courts." *Journal of Modern African Studies* 47, no. 4 (2009): 507–28.

———. "The Gacaca Courts in Rwanda." In *Traditional Justice and Reconciliation after Violent Conflict: Learning from African Experience*, 25–59. Stockholm: International Institute for Democracy and Electoral Assistance IDEA, 2008.

Inglis, Christine. "Multiculturalism: New Policy Responses to Diversity." *Management of Social Transformations* 4 (1995). http://www.unesco.org/most/pp4.htm#need.

International Center for Transitional Justice. "Truth and Memory." https://www.ictj.org/our-work/transitional-justice-issues/truth-and-memory (a20).

Jackson, Tony, and John Curry. "Peace in the Woods: Sustainability and the Democratization of Land Use Planning and Resource Management on Crown Lands in British Columbia." *International Planning Studies* 9, no. 1 (2004): 27–42.

Jacobs, Margaret. "The Habit of Elimination: Indigenous Child Removal in Settler Colonial Nations in the Twentieth Century." In *Colonial Genocide in Indigenous North America*, edited by Andrew Woolford, Jeff Benvenuto, and Alexander Laban Hinton, 189–207. Durham: Duke University Press, 2014.

James, Matt. "On Carnival and Context: A Response to Bridget Storrie." *International Journal of Transitional Justice* 9 (2015): 486-93.

———. "A Carnival of Truth? Knowledge, Ignorance, and the Canadian Truth and Reconciliation Commission." *International Journal of Transitional Justice* 6, no. 2 (2012): 182–204.

Jansen, Jonathan. "Bearing Whiteness: A Pedagogy of Compassion in a Time of Troubles." *Education as Change* 12, no. 2 (2008): 59–75.

Jansen, Jonathan D. *Knowledge in the Blood: Confronting Race and the Apartheid Past.* Stanford: Stanford University Press, 2009.

Johnson, Bobbi. "Statement by Bobbi Johnson collected by Meredith Eaton on June 27, 2014." Maine, 2014. Maine Wabanaki-State Child Welfare Truth and Reconciliation Commission: Statements, 42. https://digitalcommons.bowdoin.edu/maine-wabanaki-trc-statements/42.

Johnson, Kay. "Decolonizing Museum Pedagogies: 'Righting History' and Settler Education in the City of Vancouver." In *Adult Education, Museums and Art Galleries: Animating Social, Cultural and Institutional Change*, edited by Darlene Clover, K. Sandford, L. Bell, and K. Johnson, 129–40. Rotterdam: Sense Publishers, 2016.

Johnston, Darlene. "First Nations and Canadian Citizenship." In *Belonging: The Meaning and Future of Canadian Citizenship*, 349–67. Montreal: McGill-Queen's University Press, 2014.

Johnston, Patrick. *Native Children and the Child Welfare System.* Toronto: James Lorimer and Company, 1983.

Jones, Nicholas A., and Rob Nestor. "Sentencing Circles in Canada and the Gacaca in Rwanda: A Comparative Analysis." *International Criminal Justice Review* 21, no. 1 (2011): 39–66.

Jones, Robert, Daniel C., E.J. Dionne Jr., W. Galston, B. Cooper, and Rachel Lienesch. *How Immigration and Concerns about Cultural Changes Are Shaping the 2016 Election.* Washington: Public Religion Research Institute, 2016.

Joseph, Robert. "Chief Dr. Robert Joseph, O.B.C." *Reconciliation Canada.* 2015. http://reconciliation-canada.ca/about/team/chief-dr-robert-joseph/.

Jost, John. T., and Mahzarin R. Banaji. "The Role of Stereotyping in System Justification and the Production of False Consciousness." *British Journal of Social Psychology* 33, no. 1 (1994): 1–27. doi: 10.1111/j.2044-8309.1994.tb01008.x.

Jost, John T., Mahzarin R. Banaji, and Brian A. Nosek. "A Decade of System Justification Theory: Accumulated Evidence of Conscious and Unconscious Bolstering of the Status Quo." *Political Psychology* 25, no. 6 (2004): 881–919. doi: 10.1111/j.1467-9221.2004.00402.x.

Jost, John. T., Aaron C. Kay, and Hulda Thorisdottir, eds. *Social and Psychological Bases of Ideology and System Justification.* New York: Oxford University Press, 2009.

Judd, Charles M., and Bernadette Park. "Out-Group Homogeneity: Judgments of Variability at the Individual and Group Levels." *Journal of Personality and Social Psychology* 54, no. 5 (1998): 778–88. doi: 10.1037/0022-3514.54.5.778.

Jung, Courtney. "Canada and the Legacy of the Indian Residential Schools: Transitional Justice for Indigenous People in a Nontransitional Society." In *Identities in Transition: Challenges for Transitional Justice in Divided Societies*, edited by Paige Arthur, 217–50. New York: Cambridge University Press, 2011.

KAIROS. http://www.kairoscanada.org/what-we-do/indigenous-rights.

———. "Report Card: Provincial and Territorial Curriculum on Indigenous Peoples." KAIROS: Canadian Ecumenical Justice Initiatives. October 2015. http://www.kairoscanada.org.

———. "Winds of Change: Education for Reconciliation Report Card Summary." 18 October 2018. https://www.kairoscanada.org/what-we-do/indigenous-rights/windsofchange-report-cards.

Kasparian, Sylvia. "Introduction. Aboriginal Peoples: Canada's First Welcoming Community: Where Do Aboriginal-Immigrant Relations Stand Today?" *Canadian Issues* (Summer 2012): 3–8.

Kassam, Ashifa. "Canada Is Hailed for Its Tolerance But Is It Ready to Confront Its Racism?" *Guardian*, 12 July 2016. https://www.theguardian.com/world/2016/jul/12/canada-black-lives-matter-indigenous-people-muslims?

Kauanui, J. Kēhaulani. "'A Structure, Not an Event': Settler Colonialism and Enduring Indigeneity." *Lateral, Journal of Critical Studies Association* 5, no. 1 (Spring 2016).

Keen, Meg, Valerie A. Brown, and Rob Dyball. *Social Learning in Environmental Management: Toward a Sustainable Future.* New York: Routledge, 2005.

Kelman, Herbert C. "Experiences from 30 Years of Action Research on the Israeli-Palestinian Conflict." *Zeitgeschichtliche Hintergründe Aktueller Konflikte VII: Zürcher Beiträge zur Sicherheitspolitik und Konfliktforschung* 54 (1999): 173–97.

———. "Interactive Problem Solving: Informal Mediation by the Scholar-Practitioner." In *Studies in International Mediation: Essays in Honor of Jeffrey Z. Rubin*, edited by J. Bercovitch, 167–93. New York: Palgrave Macmillan, 2002.

———. "Israelis and Palestinians: Psychological Prerequisites for Mutual Acceptance." *International Security* 3, no. 1 (1978): 162–86.

———. "Reconciliation as Identity Change: A Social-Psychological Perspective." In *From Conflict Resolution to Reconciliation*, edited by Yaacov Bar-Simon-Tov, 111–24. Oxford: Oxford University Press, 2002.

———. "Reconciliation from a Social-Psychological Perspective." In *The Social Psychology of Intergroup Relations*, edited by Arie Nadler, Thomas E. Malloy, and Jeffery D. Fisher, 15–32. Oxford: Oxford University Press, 2008.

Kinew, Wab. *The Reason You Walk.* Toronto: Viking, 2015.

King, Martin Luther Jr. "I Have a Dream." 28 August 1963. https://www.archives.gov/press/exhibits/dream-speech.pdf.

King, Regine U. "Healing Psychosocial Trauma in the Midst of Truth Commissions: The Case of Gacaca in Post-Genocide Rwanda." *Genocide Studies and Prevention* 6, no. 2 (2011): 134–51.

King, Thomas. *The Inconvenient Indian.* Toronto: Doubleday Canada, 2012.

Kirkby, Coel. "Rwanda's Gacaca Courts: A Preliminary Critique." *Journal of African Law* 50, no. 2 (2006): 94–117.

Kirmayer, Laurence J., Caroline L. Tait, and Cori Simpson. "The Mental Health of Aboriginal Peoples in Canada: Transformations of Identity and Community." In *Healing Traditions: The Mental Health of Aboriginal Peoples in Canada*, edited by Laurence J. Kirmayer and Gail G. Valaskakis, 3–35. Vancouver: University of British Columbia Press, 2009.

Koch, Robert G. "George P. Decker and Chief Deskaheh." *The Crooked Lake Review* (blog), 1992. http://www.crookedlakereview.com/articles/34_66/54sept1992/54koch.html (accessed 22 October 2016).

Kohut, Tania. "Canada 9th Best Country to Live in: UN Human Development Index." Global News, 16 December 2015. http://globalnews.ca/news/2405032/canada-9th-best-country-to-live-in-un-human-development-index/.

Kombo, Eddah M. "Their Words, Actions, and Meaning: A Researcher's Reflection on Rwandan Women's Experience of Genocide." *Qualitative Inquiry* 15, no. 2 (2009): 308–23.

Kooiman, Jan. *Governing as Governance*. London: SAGE Publications Inc, 2003.

Kovach, Margaret. *Indigenous Methodologies: Characteristics, Conversations, and Contexts*. Toronto: University of Toronto Press, 2009. http://site.ebrary.com/lib/umanitoba/Top?id=10442459.

Krmpotich, Cara Ann. *The Force of Family: Repatriation, Kinship, and Memory on Haida Gwaii*. Toronto: University of Toronto Press, 2014.

Krog, Antjie. *Country of My Skull: Guilt, Sorrow, and the Limits of Forgiveness in the New South Africa*. New York: Three Rivers Press, 1998.

Kroth, Michael, and Patricia Cranton. "Transformative Learning through Storytelling." In *Stories of Transformative Learning*, edited by Michael Kroth and Patricia Cranton. Rotterdam, NL: Sense Publishers, 2014.

Kruglanksi, Arie W., and Wolfgang Stroebe. "The Making of Social Psychology." In *Handbook of the History of Social Psychology*, edited by Arie W. Kruglanski and Wolfgang Stroebe, 3–18. New York: Psychology Press, 2012.

Kubai, Anne N. "Between Justice and Reconciliation: The Survivors of Rwanda." *African Security Review* 16, no. 1 (2007): 53–66.

Kusch, Larry. "Liberal Convention Opens with Message of Reconciliation." *Winnipeg Free Press*, 26 May 2016. http://www.winnipegfreepress.com/local/liberal-convention-opens-with-message-of-reconciliation-381055181.html.

Ladner, Kiera. "Proceed with Caution: Reflections on Resurgence and Reconciliation. In *Resurgence and Reconciliation: Indigenous-Settler Relations and Earth Teachings,* edited by Michael Asch, John Borrows, and James Tully. Toronto: University of Toronto Press, 2018.

Lahiri, Karan. "Rwanda's Gacaca Courts: A Possible Model for Local Justice in International Crime?" *International Criminal Law Review* 9, no. 2 (2009): 321–32.

Lambert, Lori. *Research for Indigenous Survival: Indigenous Research Methodologies in the Behavioral Sciences*. Pablo, Montana: Salish Kootenai College Press, 2014.

Lambert, Veronica, Michelle Glacken, and Mary McCarron. "Employing an Ethnographic Approach: Key Characteristics." *Nurse Researcher* 19, no. 1 (2011): 17–21.

Lane, Marcus B., and Michael Hibbard. "Doing It for Themselves: Transformative Planning by Indigenous Peoples." *Journal of Planning Education and Research* 25, no. 2 (2005): 172–84.

Laszlo, Krisztina. "Ethnographic Archival Records and Cultural Property." *Archivaria 61: Special Section on Archives, Space and Power* (Spring 2006): 299–307.

Lavallée, Lynn F. "Practical Application of an Indigenous Research Framework and Two Qualitative Indigenous Research Methods: Sharing Circles and Anishnaabe Symbol-Based Reflection." *International Journal of Qualitative Methods* 8, no. 1 (2009): 21–40.

Lawrence, Bonita, and Enakshi Dua. "Decolonizing Antiracism." *Social Justice* 32, no. 4 (2005): 120–43.

Leckie, Keith Ross. *Where the Spirit Lives*. VHS. Directed by Bruce Pittman. Toronto: Amazing Spirit, Canadian Broadcasting Corporation, Mid-Canada TV, TV Ontario, 1989.

Lederach, Jean Paul. *Building Peace: Sustainable Reconciliation in Divided Societies*. Washington: United States Institute of Peace, 2007.

Legacy of Hope Foundation. *Tebatchimowin, Promoting Awareness of the History and Legacy of the Indian Residential School System*. Ottawa: Legacy of Hope Foundation, 2014.

———. "Hope and Healing: The Legacy of the Indian Residential School System." Ottawa: Legacy of Hope Foundation, 2014.

Lerner, Melvin F. *The Belief in a Just World: A Fundamental Delusion*. New York: Plenum, 1980.

Levine, John M. *Group Processes*. New York: Psychology Press, 2013.

Lewin, K. "Frontiers in Group Dynamics: Concept, Method and Reality in Social Science; Social Equilibria and Social Change." *Human Relations* 1 (1947): 5–41. doi: 10.1177/001872674700100103.

———. *Resolving Social Conflicts: Selected Papers on Group Dynamics*. Edited by Gertrude W. Lewin. New York: Harper and Brothers, 1948.

Lightfoot, Sheryl. *Global Indigenous Politics: A Subtle Revolution*. New York: Routledge, 2016.

Linklater, Renee. *Decolonizing Trauma Work: Indigenous Stories and Strategies*. Halifax: Fernwood Publishing, 2014.

Ljunggren, David. "Every G20 Nation Wants to Be Canada, Insists PM." Reuters, 25 September 2009. http://www.reuters.com/article columns-us-g20-canada-advantages-idUSTRE58P0 5Z20090926#zChpeZTEq2GBPlxg.97.

Loney, Shaun, with Will Braun. *An Army of Problem Solvers*. Winnipeg: Friesens, 2016.

Longman, Timothy. "An Assessment of Rwanda's Gacaca Courts." *Peace Review: A Journal of Social Justice* 21, no. 3 (2009): 304–12.

———. "Trying Times for Rwanda: Re-evaluating Gacaca Courts in Post-Genocide Reconciliation." *Harvard International Review* 33, no. 2 (2010): 48–52.

Lundy, Patricia, and Mark McGovern. "The Politics of Memory in Post-Conflict Northern Ireland." *Peace Review* 13, no. 1 (2001): 27–33.

———. "Whose Justice? Rethinking Transitional Justice from the Bottom Up." *Journal of Law and Society* 35, no. 2 (2008): 265–92.

Lyons, Oren. "Conversation." Berkeley: Earth Island Journal, 2015. http://www.earthisland.org/journal/index.php/eij/article/oren_lyons_onondaga/ edn.

McClaren, Peter. "White Terror and Oppositional Agency: Towards a Critical Multiculturalism." In *Multicultural Education, Critical Pedagogy, and the Politics of Difference*, edited by Christine Sleeter and Peter McLaren. New York: SUNY Press, 1995.

MacDonald, David. "Five Reasons the TRC Chose 'Cultural Genocide.'" *Globe and Mail*, 6 July 2015. http://www.theglobeandmail.com/opinion/five-reasons-the-trc-chose-cultural-genocide/article25311423/.

MacDonald, Fiona, and Karine Levasseur. "Accountability Insights from the Devolution of Indigenous Child Welfare in Manitoba." *Canadian Public Administration* 57, no. 1 (1 March 2014): 97–117. https://doi.org/10.1111/capa.12052.

MacDonald, John A. "The Spallumcheen Indian Band By-Law and Its Potential Impact on Native Indian Child Welfare Policy in British Columbia." *Canadian Journal of Family Law* 4 (July 1983): 75–95.

Macdonald, Nancy. "Welcome to Winnipeg: Where Canada's Racism Problem Is at Its Worst." *Maclean's*, 22 January 2015. http://www.macleans.ca/news/canada/welcome-to-winnipeg-where-canadas-racism-problem-is-at-its-worst/.

MacGinty, Roger. "Gilding the Lily? International Support for Indigenous and Traditional Peacemaking," In *Palgrave Advances in Peacebuilding: Critical Developments and Approaches*, edited by Oliver P. Richmond. Basingstoke: Palgrave, 2010.

McGregor, Catherine. "Aboriginal Inquiry: Lifting All Learners." Aboriginal Affairs and Northern Development Canada. http://inquiry.noii.ca/ (accessed 6 June 2013).

Mack, Johnny. "Hoquotist: Reorienting through Storied Practice." In *Storied Communities: Narratives of Contact and Arrival in Constituting Political Community*, edited by Hester Lessard, Rebecca Johnson, and Jeremy Webber, 287–307. Vancouver: University of British Columbia Press, 2011.

MacLaurin, Bruce, et al. "A Comparison of First Nations and Non-Aboriginal Children Investigated for Maltreatment in Canada in 2003." *CECW (Centres for Excellence for Children's Well-Being) Information*, no. 66E (2008).

McMorrow, Thomas B., "Reckoning with the Role of Universities in Reconciliation." RECONCILIATION SYLLABUS, a TRC-Inspired Gathering of Materials for Teaching Law. 31 May 2016. https://reconciliationsyllabus.wordpress.com/author/mcmorrowtb/.

McTavish, Lianne, Susan Ashley, Heather Igloliorte, Kirsty Robertson, and Andrea Terry. "Critical Museum Theory/Museum Studies in Canada: A Conversation." *Acadiensis: Journal of the History of the Atlantic Region / Revue D'histoire De La Region Atlantique* 46, no. 2 (2017): 223–41.

Madariaga-Vignudo, Lucia. *More Strangers than Neighbours: Aboriginal-African Refugee Relations in Winnipeg's Inner City*. Winnipeg: Manitoba Research Alliance, 2009. http://www.academia.edu/198376/More_Strangers_than_Neighbours_Aboriginal-African_Refugee_Relations_in_Winnipegs_Inner_City.

Maiangwa, Benjamin, and Sean Byrne. "Peacebuilding and Reconciliation through Storytelling in Northern Ireland and the Border Counties of the Republic of Ireland." *Storytelling, Self and Society: An Interdisciplinary Journal of Storytelling Studies* 11, no. 1 (2015): 85–110.

Maine Wabanaki-State Child Welfare Truth and Reconciliation Commission. *Maine Wabanaki-State Child Welfare Truth and Reconciliation Commission Mandate*. 29 June 2012. http://www.mainewabanakireach.org/maine_wabanaki_state_child_welfare_truth_and_reconciliation_commission.

Manitoba, Government of. *No Quiet Place: Final Report to the Honourable Muriel Smith, Minister of Community Services*. Review Committee on Indian and Metis Adoptions and Placements. Winnipeg: Manitoba Community Services, 1985.

———. *Report of the Aboriginal Justice Inquiry of Manitoba*. Public Inquiry into the Administration of Justice and Aboriginal People. Winnipeg: The Inquiry, Queen's Printer, 1991. http://www.ajic.mb.ca/volume.html.

Manitoba, Justice. "Manitoba Laws Child and Family Services Authorities Act." 2002. http://web2.gov.mb.ca/laws/statutes/ccsm/c090e.php.

Mann, Charles C. *1491: New Revelations of the Americas before Columbus*. New York: Knopf, 2005.

Mansbridge, Peter. "Mansbridge One on One: Cindy Blackstock." CBC, 13 February 2016. http://www.cbc.ca/player/play/2683617202.

Manuel, Arthur, and Grand Chief Ronald Derrickson. *The Reconciliation Manifesto: Recovering the Land and Rebuilding the Economy*. Toronto: James Lorimer and Company Ltd., 2017.

Martin, Keavy. "Truth, Reconciliation, and Amnesia: *Porcupines and China Dolls* and the Canadian Conscience." *ESC: English Studies in Canada* 35, no. 1 (2009): 47–65.

Martin, Keavy, Dylan Robinson, and David Garneau. *Arts of Engagement: Taking Aesthetic Action in and beyond the Truth and Reconciliation Commission of Canada*. Waterloo: Wilfrid Laurier University Press, 2016.

Matsuda, Mari J. "Looking to the Bottom: Critical Legal Studies and Reparations." *Harvard Law Liberties–Civil Right Law Review* 22 (1987): 362–97.

Matsunaga, Jennifer. "Two Faces of Transitional Justice: Theorizing the Incommensurability of Transitional Justice and Decolonization in Canada." *Decolonization: Indigeneity, Education and Society* 5, no. 1 (2016): 22–44.

Matthews, Maureen. *Naamiwan's Drum: The Story of a Contested Repatriation of Anishinaabe Artefacts.* Toronto: University of Toronto Press, 2016.

Matties, Zoe, and Anika Reynar. *Indigenous Peoples of Manitoba, a Guide to Newcomers.* Winnipeg: Mennonite Central Committee, 2015.

Mazo, Adam, and Ben Pender-Cudlip. *Dawnland.* DVD. Directed by Adam Mazo and Ben Pender-Cudlip, 2018. Boston, Massachusetts: Upstander Project.

Mercredi, Ovide. *My Silent Drum.* Winnipeg: Aboriginal Issues Press, 2015.

Merriam, Sharan B., Rosemary S. Caffarella, and Lisa M. Baumgartner. *Learning in Adulthood: A Comprehensive Guide.* San Francisco: John Wiley and Sons, 2012.

Mezirow, Jack. "Contemporary Paradigms of Learning." *Adult Education Quarterly* 46, no. 3 (1996): 158–72.

Mibenge, Chiseche. "Enforcing International Humanitarian Law at the National Level: The Gacaca Jurisdictions of Rwanda." *Yearbook of International Humanitarian Law* 7 (2004): 410–24.

Milgram, Stanley. "Behavioural Study of Obedience." *Journal of Abnormal and Social Psychology* 67, no. 4 (1963): 371–8. doi: 10.1037/h0040525.

Miller, James R. *Shingwauk's Vision: A History of Native Residential Schools.* Toronto: University of Toronto, 1996.

Miller, Robert J. *Native America, Discovered and Conquered: Thomas Jefferson, Lewis and Clark, and Manifest Destiny.* Westport: Praeger Publishers, 2006.

Million, Dian. *Therapeutic Nations: Healing in an Age of Indigenous Human Rights.* Tuscon: University of Arizona Press, 2014.

Mills, Charles. *The Racial Contract.* Ithaca: Cornell University Press, 1997.

Minow, Martha. *Between Vengeance and Forgiveness: Facing History After Genocide and Mass Atrocities.* Boston: Beacon Press, 1998.

———. *Breaking the Cycles of Hatred: Memory, Law, and Repair.* Princeton: Princeton University Press, 2002.

Molefe, T.O. "T.O. Molefe on Reconciliation Ideology." *SA Reconciliation Barometer Blog* (blog), 29 July 2014. https://reconciliationbarometer.org/?p=5874 (accessed 13 October 2015).

Monias, David, Mary Anne Clarke, and Rhonda Apetagon. "Understanding First Nation Practice in Child and Family Services." Presented at the National Indigenous Social Work Conference 2016, Winnipeg, MB, 2016.

Monture, Rick. *We Share Our Matters: Two Centuries of Writing and Resistance at Six Nations of the Grand River.* Winnipeg: University of Manitoba Press, 2014.

Moretto, Mario. "Tribe Says LePage Threated Passamaquoddy over Elvers during 'Enraged' Phone Call." *Bangor Daily News* (Bangor, ME), 2 April 2013.

Morgan, Anthony. "The Suffocating Experience of Being Black in Canada." *Toronto Star*, 31 July 2015. https://www.thestar.com/opinion/commentary/2015/07/31/the-suffocating-experience-of-being-black-in-canada.html.

Morrissette, Patrick J. "The Holocaust of First Nation People: Residual Effects on Parenting and Treatment Implications." *Contemporary Family Therapy* 16, no. 5 (1994): 381–92. doi: 10.1007/bf02197900.

Morrissette, Patrick J., and Alanaise Goodwill. "The Psychological Cost of Restitution: Supportive Intervention with Canadian Indian Residential School Survivors." *Journal of Aggression, Maltreatment and Trauma* 22, no. 5 (2013): 541–58. doi: 10.1080/10926771.2013.785459.

Mosby, Ian. "Administering Colonial Science: Nutrition Research and Human Biomedical Experimentation in Aboriginal Communities and Residential Schools, 1942–1952." *Histoire Sociale/Social History* 46, no. 91 (2013): 145–72.

Muehlmann, Shaylih. "How Do Real Indians Fish? Neoliberal Multiculturalism and Contested Indigeneities in the Colorado Delta." *American Anthropologist* 111, no. 4 (2009): 468–79.

Murithi, Tim, and Fanie du Toit. "Reconciliation as Framework for Preventing Conflict and Sustaining Peace." United Nations Development Programme. July 2015. http://us-cdn.creamermedia.co.za/assets/articles/attachments/62259_policy_document_inclusive_reconciliation_final_july_2015.pdf.

Nadler, Arie. "Post Resolution Processes: Instrumental and Socio-Emotional Routes to Reconciliation." In *Peace Education: The Concept, Principles, and Practices Around the World*, edited by Gavriel Salomon and Baruch Nevo. Mahwah: Lawrence Erlbaum, 2002.

Nadler, Arie, Thomas E. Malloy, and Jeffery D. Fisher, eds. *The Social Psychology of Intergroup Reconciliation*. Oxford: Oxford University Press, 2008.

Nadler, Arie, and Nurit Shnabel. "Intergroup Reconciliation: The Instrumental and Socio-Emotional Paths and the Need-Based Model of Socio-Emotional Reconciliation." In *Social Psychology of Intergroup Reconciliation*, edited by Arie Nadler, Thomas E. Malloy, and Jeffery D. Fisher. New York: Oxford University Press, 2008.

Nagy, Rosemary. "The Scope and Bounds of Transitional Justice and the Canadian Truth and Reconciliation Commission." *The International Journal of Transitional Justice* 7, no.1 (2012): 52–73.

Nagy, Rosemary, and Emily Gillespie. "Representing Reconciliation: A News Frame Analysis of Print Media Coverage of Indian Residential Schools." *Transitional Justice Review* 1, no. 3 (2015): 3–40.

Napoleon, Val, and Hadley Friedland. "Gathering the Threads: Developing a Methodology for Researching and Rebuilding Indigenous Legal Traditions." *Lakehead Law Journal* 1, no. 1 (2015): 16–44.

National Indian Brotherhood. *Indian Control of Indian Education*. National Indian Brotherhood, 1972. http://www.avenir-future.com/pdf/maitrise%20indienne%20de%20l'%C3%A9ducation%20ang.pdf (accessed 5 August 2016).

National Unity and Reconciliation Commission (Republic of Rwanda). "Rwanda Reconciliation Barometer." http://www.nurc.gov.rw/fileadmin/Documents/RWANDA_RECONCILIATION_BAROMETER.pdf (accessed 16 March 2016).

Neuffer, Elizabeth. "Kigali Dispatch: It Takes a Village." *The New Republic* 222, no. 15 (2000): 18–20.

Newcomb, Steve. *Pagans in the Promised Land*. Golden: Fulcrum Pub, 2008.

Niezen, Ronald. *Truth and Indignation: Canada's Truth and Reconciliation Commission on Indian Residential Schools*. 2nd ed. Toronto: University of Toronto Press, 2017.

Nylund, David. "Critical Multiculturalism, Whiteness, and Social Work." *Journal of Progressive Human Services* 17, no. 2 (2006): 27–42.

Obomsawin, Alanis. *We Can't Make the Same Mistake Twice*. Directed by Alanis Obomsawin. Film. Toronto: National Film Board of Canada, 2016.

"Occupied Canada: Indigenous and Black Lives Matter Activists Unite to Protest Violence and Neglect." Democracy Now. 20 May 2016. http://www.democracynow.org/2016/5/20/occupied_canada_indigenous_black_lives_matter.

O'Leary, Rosemary, and Nidhi Vij. "Collaborative Public Management: Where Have We Been and Where Are We Going?" *The American Review of Public Administration* 42, no. 5 (2012): 507–22.

Olsson, Per, Lance H. Gunderson, Steve R. Carpenter, Paul Ryan, Louis Lebel, Carl Folke, and Crawford S. Holling. "Shooting the Rapids: Navigating Transitions to Adaptive Governance of Social-Ecological Systems." *Ecology and Society* 11, no. 1 (2006).

Olwine, Brittany, A. "One Step Forward, But Two Steps Back: Why Gacaca in Rwanda is Jeopardizing the Good Effect of Akayesu on Women's Rights." *William and Mary Journal of Women and Law* 17, no. 3 (2011): 639–63.

"On Views of Race and Inequality, Blacks and Whites are Worlds Apart." Pew Research Center, 27 June 2016. http://www.pewsocialtrends.org/2016/06/27/on-views-of-race-and-inequality-blacks-and-whites-are-worlds-apart/.

"Ontario Library Service—North Conference 2015: Keynote: Reading Kanata as Canada." Posted by Ontario Library Service—North, 23 September 2015. Video, 1:22:15. https://www.youtube.com/watch?v=f8QOdzq-_dg.

Oomen, Barbara. "Donor-Driven Justice and Its Discontents: The Case of Rwanda." *Development and Change* 36, no. 5 (2005): 887–910.

Oosterom, Nelle. "Kings of the New World." *Canada's History*, 2016. https://www.canadashistory.ca/explore/first-nations-inuit-metis/kings-of-the-new-world.

Ostrom, Elinor. *The Evolution of Institutions for Collective Action: Political Economy of Institutions and Decisions.* New York: Cambridge University Press, 1990.

O'Sullivan, Edmund. "Emancipatory Hope: Transformative Learning and the 'Strange Attractors.'" In *Holistic Learning and Spirituality in Education: Breaking New Ground*, edited by John P. Miller, Selia Karsten, Diana Denton, Deborah Orr, and Isabella Colalillo Kates. New York: State University of New York Press, 2005.

Paikin, Steve. *A Commonwealth of Aboriginal Peoples.* TVO, 17 February 2016. Video, 17:51. http://tvo.org/video/programs/the-agenda-with-steve-paikin/a-commonwealth-of-aboriginal-peoples.

Palmary, Ingrid, Brandon Hamber, and Lorena Núñez, eds. *Healing and Change in the City of Gold: Case Studies of Coping and Support in Johannesburg.* New York: Springer, 2015.

Palmater, Pamela. *Beyond Blood: Rethinking Indigenous Identity.* Saskatoon: Purich Publishing, 2011.

———. *Indigenous Nationhood: Empowering Grassroots Citizens.* Winnipeg: Fernwood Publishing, 2015.

———. "Trudeau's Promises of 'Renewed Relationship' with First Nations Evaporated with Liberal Budget." rabble.ca (blog), 23 March 2016. http://rabble.ca/blogs/bloggers/pamela-palmater/2016/03/trudeaus-promises-renewed-relationship-first-nations-evaporat.

Park, Augustine S.J. "Settler Colonialism and the Politics of Grief: Theorising a Decolonising Transitional Justice for Indian Residential Schools." *Human Rights Review* 16, no. 3 (2015): 273–93.

Park, Bernadette, and Myron Rothbart. "Perception of Out-Group Homogeneity and Levels of Social Categorization: Memory for the Subordinate Attributes of In-Group and Out-Group Members." *Journal of Personality and Social Psychology* 42, no. 6 (1982): 1051–68. doi: 10.1037/0022-3514.42.6.1051.

Paris, Erna. *Long Shadows: Truth, Lies and History.* Toronto: Knopf Canada, 2000.

———. *The Sun Climbs Slow: International Criminal Court and the Struggle for Justice.* Toronto: Knopf Canada, 2008.

Pascoe, Bruce. *Dark Emu: Black Seeds: Agriculture or Accident?* Djugun: Magabala Books Aboriginal Corporation, 2015.

Paul, Daniel N. *First Nations History: We Were Not the Savages: Collision Between European and Native American Civilizations.* Winnipeg: Fernwood Publishing, 2006.

Pearce, Margo E., et al. "The Cedar Project: Historical Trauma, Sexual Abuse and HIV Risk Among Young Aboriginal People Who Use Injection and Non-injection Drugs in Two Canadian Cities." *Social Science and Medicine* 66, no. 11 (2008): 2185–94. doi: 10.1016/j. socscimed.2008.03.034.

Peetz, Johanna, Gregory R. Gunn, and Anne E. Wilson. "Crimes of the Past: Defensive Temporal Distancing in the Face of Past In-Group Wrongdoing." *Personality and Social Psychology Bulletin* 35, no. 5 (2010): 598–611. doi: 10.1177/0146167210364850.

Penal Reform International. *Eight Years On ... A Record of Gacaca Monitoring in Rwanda.* Glasgow: Bell and Bain, 2010. http://srsg.violenceagainstchildren.org/sites/default/files/consultations/ restorative_justice/presentations/nikhil_roy/Gacaca.pdf.

Phelps, Teresa Godwin. *Shattered Voices: Language, Violence and the Work of Truth Commissions.* Philadelphia: University of Pennsylvania Press, 2004.

Porter, Jody. "First Nations Students Get 30 Per Cent Less Funding than Other Children, Economist Says." CBC News, 14 March 2016. http://www.cbc.ca/news/canada/thunder-bay/first-nations-education-funding-gap-1.3487822.

Povinelli, Elizabeth A. *The Cunning of Recognition: Indigenous Alterities and the Making of Australian Multiculturalism.* Durham: Duke University Press, 2002.

Pozen, Joanna, Richard Neugebauer, and Joseph Ntaganira. "Assessing the Rwanda's Experiment: Popular Perceptions of Gacaca in Its Final Phase." *The International Journal of Transitional Justice* 8, no. 1 (2014): 31–52.

"President Barack Obama's Speech to Parliament." CBC News, 29 June 2016. http://www.cbc.ca/ news/politics/president-barack-obama-full-speech-parliament-1.3659229.

Probe Research. "Majority of Manitobans Believe Residential Schools were 'Cultural Genocide.'" Probe Research. 6 July 2015. http://news.probe-research.com/2015/07/majority-of-manitobans-be-lieve.html.

Proctor, Jason. "CBC-Angus Reid Institute Poll: Canadians Want Minorities to Do More to 'Fit In.'" CBC News, 3 October 2016. http://www.cbc.ca/news/canada/british-columbia/ poll-canadians-multiculturalism-immigrants-1.3784194.

"Promoting Racial Literacy in Schools by Dr. Howard C. Stevenson." Posted by Green Meadow Waldorf School, 16 December 2015. Video, 1:07.00. https://www.youtube.com/ watch?v=CK222rNY5bQ.

Quakers in the World. "Structural/Cultural/Direct Violence. Turning the Tide." Turning the Tides. Nonviolent Power for Social Change (Quakers), 2014. http://www.turning-the-tide.org/files/ Structural%20Cultural%20Direct%20Violence%20Hand-out.pdf.

Quattrone, George A., and Edward E. Jones. "The Perception of Variability within Ingroups and Outgroups: Implications for the Law of Small Numbers." *Journal of Personality and Social Psychology* 38 (1980): 141–52. doi: 10.1037/0022-3514.38.1.141.

Quewezance, Ted. "RSSC Welcome Apology but Expect More." *Windspeaker* 26, no. 4 (2008): 5.

Ramanathapillai, Rajmohan. "The Politicizing of Trauma: A Case Study of Sri Lanka." *Peace and Conflict: Journal of Peace Psychology* 12, no. 1 (2006): 1–18.

Razack, Sherene. "Introduction: When Place Becomes Race" In *Race, Space, and the Law: Unmapping a White Settler Society*, edited by Sherene Razack, 1–46. Toronto: Between the Lines, 2002.

Reconciliation Canada. "THE CANADIAN RECONCILIATION LANDSCAPE: Current
    Perspectives of Indigenous Peoples and Non-Indigenous Canadians." May 2017. http://
    reconciliationcanada.ca/staging/wp-content/uploads/2017/05/NationalNarrativeReport-
    ReconciliationCanada-ReleasedMay2017_3.pdf.

"Reconciliation and Its Discontents: Settler Governance in an Age of Sorrow." Posted by
    University of Saskatchewan, 22 March 2016. Video, 1:22:36. https://www.youtube.com/
    watch?v=vGl9HkzQsGg.

Regan, Paulette. "Reconciliation and Resurgence: Reflections on the TRC Final Report." In *Resurgence
    and Reconciliation: Indigenous-Settler Relations and Earth Teachings,* edited by Michael Asch, John
    Borrows, and James Tully, 209–27. Toronto: University of Toronto Press, 2018.

———. *Unsettling the Settler Within: Indian Residential Schools, Truth Telling, and Reconciliation in
    Canada.* Vancouver: University of British Columbia Press, 2010.

Reimer, Gwen, et al. *The Indian Residential Schools Settlement Agreement's Common Experience
    Payment and Healing: A Qualitative Study Exploring Impacts on Recipients.* Ottawa: Aboriginal
    Healing Foundation, 2010.

Reynolds, Brenda. "Keynote Address." Presentation at the Resolve Trauma Informed: Treatment,
    Intervention and Prevention Research Day, Winnipeg, MB, 20 October 2017.

Richmond, Oliver. "Peace during and after the Age of Intervention." *International Peacekeeping* 21, no.
    4 (2014): 509–19.

Rimé, Bernard, Patrick Kanyangara, Dario Paez, and Vincent Yzerbyt. "Social Rituals and Collective
    Expression of Emotion after a Collective Trauma." In *Restoring Civil Societies: The Psychology of
    Intervention and Engagement Following Crisis,* edited by Kia J. Jonas and Thomas A. Morton,
    177–91. Chichester: John Wiley and Sons, 2012. doi: 10.1002/9781118347683.ch10.

Robinson, Darryl. "Serving the Interests of Justice: Amnesties, Truth Commissions and the
    International Criminal Court." *European Journal of International Law* 14, no. 3 (2003): 481–505.

Robinson, Dylan, and Keren Zaiontz. "Public Art in Vancouver and the Civic Infrastructure of
    Redress." In *The Land We Are,* edited by Gabrielle L'Hirondelle Hill and Sophie McCall, 22–51.
    Winnipeg: Arbeiter Ring Publishing, 2015.

Robson, James P., A. John Sinclair, Iain J. Davidson-Hunt, and Alan P. Diduck. "What's in a Name?
    The Search for 'Common Ground' in Kenora, Northwestern Ontario." *International Journal of
    Public Participation* 9, no. 2 (2013): 1–22.

Ross, Helen, Marlene Buchy, and Wendy Proctor. "Laying Down the Ladder: A Typology of
    Public Participation in Australian Natural Resources Management." *The Australian Journal of
    Environmental Management* 9, no. 4 (2002): 205–17.

Royal Commission on Aboriginal Peoples. *Report of the Royal Commission on Aboriginal Peoples.* 5 vols.
    Ottawa: The Royal Commission on Aboriginal Peoples, 1996.

Rubin, Allen, and Earl R. Babbie. *Research Methods for Social Work.* Belmont: Brook/Cole, 2005.

Sanderson, Sol. "Building a Path to Reconciliation and Decolonization for Nation-to-Nation
    Government-to-Government Relations." Federation of Saskatchewan Indian Nations. 2016.
    http://www.nalma.ca/wp-content/uploads/2016/01/Policy-Documents-and-Implementation-
    Agreements-1Jan2016.pdf.

Saunders, Doug. "Why Black Canadians Are Facing U.S.-Style Problems." *Globe and Mail,* 16 July 2016.
    http://www.theglobeandmail.com/opinion/why-black-canadians-are-facing-us-style-problems/
    article30939514/.

Savage, Candace. *A Geography of Blood.* Vancouver: Greystone Press, 2012.

Schabas, William A. "Genocide Trials and Gacaca Courts." *Journal of International Criminal Justice* 3, no. 4 (2005): 879–95.

Schotsmans, Martien. "'But We Also Support Monitoring': INGO Monitoring and Donor Support to *Gacaca* Justice in Rwanda." *International Journal of Transitional Justice* 5, no. 3 (2011): 390–411.

Scollon, Ron. *Human Knowledge and the Institution's Knowledge: Communication in Patterns and Retention in a Public University, Final Report (October 1, 1980–December 31, 1981)*, 1981. https://eric.ed.gov/?id=ED213338 (accessed 27 January 2017).

Sehdev, Robinder Kaur. "People of Colour in Treaty." In *Cultivating Canada: Reconciliation through the Lens of Cultural Diversity*, edited by Ashok Mathur, Jonathan Dewar, and Mike DeGagné, 264–74. Ottawa: Aboriginal Healing Foundation, 2011.

Senehi, Jessica. "Constructive Storytelling in Intercommunal Conflicts: Building Community, Building Peace." In *Reconcilable Differences: Turning Points in Ethnopolitical Conflict*, edited by Sean Bryne and Cynthia L. Irvin, 96–114. West Hartford: Kumarian Press, 2000.

Settee, Priscilla. *Pimatisiwin*. Vernon: J Charlton Publishing, 2013.

Sheppard, Colleen. *Indigenous Peoples in Canada: Understanding Divergent Conceptions of Reconciliation*. Montreal: Institute for the Study of International Development Aboriginal Policy Study Papers, 2013. http://www.mcgill.ca/isid/files/isid/pb_2013_04_sheppard.pdf.

Sherif, Muzafer. *Experimental Study of Positive and Negative Intergroup Attitudes Between Experimentally Produced Groups: Robbers Cave Study*. Norman: University of Oklahoma Press, 1954.

———. "Superordinate Goals in the Reduction of Intergroup Conflict." *American Journal of Sociology* 63 (1958): 349–56. doi: 10.1086/222258.

Sherif, Muzafer, O.J. Harvey, B. Jack White, William R. Hood, and Carolyn W. Sherif. *Intergroup Cooperation and Competition: The Robbers Cave Experiment*. Norman: University Book Exchange, 1961.

Shewchuk, Diane. "The Legacy of Residential School Abuse." *BC Psychologist* (2012): 36–39. http://www.apadivisions.org/division-31/publications/articles/british-columbia/residential-school-abuse.pdf.

Shnabel, Nurit, and Arie Nadler. "The Role of Agency and Morality in Reconciliation Processes: The Perspective of the Needs-Based Model." *Current Directions in Psychological Science* 24 (2015): 477–83. doi:10.1177/0963721415601625.

Short, Damien. *Reconciliation and Colonial Power: Indigenous Rights in Australia*. Farnham: Ashgate, 2008.

Shrubb, Rebecca. "'Canada Has No History of Colonialism.' Historical Amnesia: The Erasure of Indigenous Peoples from Canada's History." Master's thesis, University of Victoria, 2010.

Simpson, Audra. *Mohawk Interruptus: Political Life Across the Borders of Settler States*. Durham: Duke University Press, 2014.

———. "Reconciliation and Its Discontents: Settler Governance in an Age of Sorrow." Lecture. University of Saskatchewan, 22 March 2016.

———. "Settlement's Secret." *Cultural Anthropology* 26, no. 2 (2011): 205–17.

Simpson, Leanne. *Dancing on Our Turtle's Back: Stories of Nishnaabeg Re-Creation, Resurgence and a New Emergence*. Winnipeg: ARP Books, 2011.

———. "Land as Pedagogy: Nishnaabeg Intelligence and Rebellious Transformation." *Decolonization: Indigeneity, Education and Society* 3, no. 3 (2014): 1–25.

———. "A Smudgier Dispossession Is Still Dispossession." *Active History.ca: History Matters* (blog), 11 January 2016. http://activehistory.ca/2016/01/a-smudgier-dispossession-is-still-dispossession/.

Sinclair, James Niigaanwewidam. "Indigenous Literacies Throughout Time." Video, Ontario Library Service—North Conference 2015: Keynote: Reading Kanata as Canada, 23 September 2015. https://www.youtube.com/watch?v=f8QOdzq-_dg (accessed 15 January 2017).

Sinclair, Murray, Nicholas Bala, H. Lilles, and Cindy Blackstock. "Aboriginal Child Welfare." In *Canadian Child Welfare Law: Children, Families and the State*, edited by Nicholas Bala, Michael Kim Zapf, R. James Williams, Robin Vogl, and Joseph P. Hornick. 2nd ed. Toronto: Thompson Educational Publishing, 2004.

Sinha, Vandna, Nico Trocmé, Barbara Fallon, Bruce MacLaurin, Elizabeth Fast, Shelley Thomas Prokop et al. *Kiskisik Awasisak: Remember the Children. Understanding the Overrepresentation of First Nations Children in the Child Welfare System*. Ottawa: Assembly of First Nations, 2011.

Smith, Keith D., ed. *Strange Visitors: Documents in Indigenous-Settler Relations in Canada from 1876*. North York: University of Toronto Press, 2014.

Smith, Linda Tuhiwai. *Decolonizing Methodologies: Research and Indigenous Peoples*. 2nd ed. London: Zed Books, 2012.

Sohki Aski Esquao [Jeannine Carriere], and Wa Cheeh Wapuguunew Iskew [Carolyn Peacock]. "Practising from the Heart: Living and Working in First Nations Communities." In *Walking This Path Together: Anti-Racist and Anti-Oppressive Child Welfare Practice*, 286–301. 2nd ed. Winnipeg: Fernwood Publishing, 2015.

Sosnov, Maya. "The Adjudication of Genocide: Gacaca and the Road to Reconciliation in Rwanda." *Denver Journal of International Law Policy* 36, no 2 (2008): 125–53.

Spallumcheen Indian Band. *A By-law for the Care of Our Indian children: Spallumcheen Indian Band By-law #3—1980*. Spallumcheen Indian Band, 1980. http://sp.fng.ca/fngweb/600_children_by-law_1980.pdf.

Stanton, Kim. "Canada's Truth and Reconciliation Commission: Settling the Past?" *The International Indigenous Policy Journal* 2, no. 3 (2011): 1–18.

Starblanket, Gina. "Resurgence as Relationality." In *Everyday Acts of Resurgence,* edited by Jeff Corntassel et al., 28–31. Washington: International Cry, 2018.

Starblanket, Gina, and Heidi Kiiwetinipinesiik Stark. "Towards a Relational Paradigm—Four Points for Consideration: Knowledge, Gender, Land, and Modernity." In *Resurgence and Reconciliation: Indigenous-Settler Relations and Earth Teachings,* edited by Michael Asch, John Borrows, and James Tully. Toronto: University of Toronto Press, 2018.

Starn, Orin. "HERE COME THE ANTHROS (AGAIN): The Strange Marriage of Anthropology and Native America." *Cultural Anthropology* 26, no. 2 (2011): 179–204.

Starzyk, Katherine B., Renee M. El-Gabalawy, Gregory D.B. Boese, and Katelin H. Neufeld. "Signs of Solidarity Among Minority Groups in Support of Reparations." Working Paper, Faculty of Personality and Social Psychology, University of Manitoba, Winnipeg, 2016.

Starzyk, Katherine B., Danielle Gaucher, Gregory D.B. Boese, and Katelin H. Neufeld. "Framing Reparation Claims for Crimes Against Humanity: A Social-Psychological Perspective." In *Reparations for Victims of Crimes Against Humanity: The Healing Role of Reparation*, edited by Jo-Anne M. Wemmers, 113–25. London: Routledge, 2014.

Staub, Ervin. "Justice, Healing, and Reconciliation: How the People's Courts in Rwanda Can Promote Them." *Peace and Conflict: Journal of Peace Psychology* 10, no. 1 (2005): 25–32.

Staub, Ervin, Laurie Anne Pearlman, Alexandra Gubin, and Athanase Hagengimana. "Healing, Reconciliation, Forgiving and the Prevention of Violence after Genocide or Mass Killing: An Intervention and its Experimental Evaluation in Rwanda." *Journal of Social and Clinical Psychology* 24, no. 3 (2005): 297–334. doi: 10.1521/jscp.24.3.297.65617.

Stote, Karen. *An Act of Genocide: Colonialism and the Sterilization of Aboriginal Women*. Winnipeg: Fernwood, 2015.

Suleman, Zool. *Vancouver Dialogues: First Nations, Urban Aboriginal and Immigrant Communities*. Vancouver: Social Policy, 2011. http://vancouver.ca/files/cov/dialogues-project-book.pdf.

Summerby, Janice. "Native Soldiers—Foreign Battlefields." Canada, Minister of Veterans Affairs, 2005. https://www.veterans.gc.ca/public/pages/remembrance/those-who-served/aboriginal-veterans/native-soldiers/natives_e.pdf.

Tajfel, Henri. "Experiments in Intergroup Discrimination." *Scientific American* 223 (1970): 96–102.

Tajfel, Henri, and John C. Turner. "The Social Identity Theory of Intergroup Behaviour." In *Psychology of Intergroup Relations*, edited by Stephen Worchel and William G. Austin, 7–24. Chicago: Nelson-Hall, 1986.

Tasker, John P. "Cap Leads to Steep Drop in First Nations Students Receiving Post-Secondary Support." CBC News, 12 September 2016. http://www.cbc.ca/news/politics/first-nations-cap-higher-education-1.3753021.

Tavuchis, Nicholas. *Mea Culpa: A Sociology of Apology and Reconciliation*. Stanford: Stanford University Press, 1991.

Taylor, Edward W. "Transformative Learning Theory." *New Directions for Adult and Continuing Education* 119 (2008): 5–15.

Taylor, Jillian. "'The Ultimate Goal Is to Reduce the Number of Children in Care': Indigenous Affairs Minister Overhaul of Manitoba CFS System Beginning with Meetings in 20 Communities." CBC News Manitoba, 27 March 2017. http://www.cbc.ca/news/canada/manitoba/manitoba-carolyn-bennett-child-welfare-1.4042484.

Teitel, Ruth. "The Law and Politics of Contemporary Transitional Justice." *Cornell International Law Journal* 38, no. 3 (2005): 837–62.

Teitelbaum, Stephanie, and R. Edward Geiselman. "Observer Mood and Cross-Racial Recognition of Faces." *Cross-Cultural Psychology* 28, no. 1 (1997): 93–106. doi: 10.1177/0022022197281006.

Thobani, Sunera. *Exalted Subjects: Studies in the Making of Race and Nation in Canada*. Toronto: University of Toronto Press, 2007.

Thomson, Susan, and Rosemary Nagy. "Law, Power and Justice: What Legalism Fails to Address in the Functioning of Rwanda's Gacaca Courts." *The International Journal of Transnational Justice* 5, no. 1 (2011): 11–30.

Tiemessen, Alana E. "After Arusha: Gacaca Justice in Post-Genocide Rwanda." *African Studies Quarterly* 8, no. 1 (2004): 57–76.

Tisdell, Elizabeth J. *Exploring Spirituality and Culture in Adult and Higher Education*. San Francisco: Jossey-Bass, 2003.

Tobias, Joshua K., and Chantelle A.M. Richmond. "'That Land Means Everything to Us Anishinaabe . . .': Environmental Dispossession and Resilience on the North Shore of Lake Superior." *Health and Place* 29 (2014): 26–33.

Totten, Samuel, William S. Parsons, and Israel Charney, eds. *Century of Genocide: Critical Essays and Eyewitness Accounts*. 2nd ed. New York: Routlege, 2004.

Towner, Emil. "Documenting Genocide: The 'Record of Confession, Guilty Plea, Repentance and Apology' in Rwanda's Gacaca Trials." *Technical Communication Quarterly* 22, no. 4 (2013): 303–85.

Trocmé, Nico, Della Knoke, and Cindy Blackstock. "Pathways to the Overrepresentation of Aboriginal Children in Canada's Child Welfare System." *Social Service Review* 78, no. 4 (1 December 2004): 577–600. https://doi.org/10.1086/424545.

Trudeau, Justin. Facebook, 9 August 2016. http://www.facebook.com/justinpjtrudeau.

Trudeau, Justin. "Statement by Prime Minister on Release of the Final Report of the Truth and Reconciliation Commission." Canada—Important Notices, 15 December 2015. http://www.pm.gc.ca/eng/news/2015/12/15/statement-prime-minister-release-final-report-truth-and-reconciliation-commission.

Trudeau, P.E. "Justice in Our Time [excerpt]." In *Ethical Issues: Perspectives for Canadians,* edited by Eldon Sofir. 3rd ed. Toronto: Broadview, 2009.

Truth and Reconciliation Commission of Canada. *Calls to Action.* Winnipeg: Truth and Reconciliation Commission of Canada, 2015. http://trc.ca/assets/pdf/Calls_to_Action_English2.pdf.

——— . *Canada's Residential Schools: The Final Report of the Truth and Reconciliation Commission of Canada. Volume One. The History. Part 1: Origins to 1939.* Montreal: TRC and McGill-Queen's University Press, 2015.

——— . *Canada's Residential Schools: The Final Report of the Truth and Reconciliation Commission of Canada. Volume One. The History. Part 2: 1939 to 2000.* Montreal: TRC and McGill-Queen's University Press, 2015.

——— . *Canada's Residential Schools: The Final Report of the Truth and Reconciliation Commission of Canada. Volume Three. The Métis Experience.* Montreal: TRC and McGill-Queen's University Press, 2015.

——— . *Canada's Residential Schools: The Final Report of the Truth and Reconciliation Commission of Canada. Volume Four. The Missing Children and Unmarked Burials Report.* Montreal: TRC and McGill-Queen's University Press, 2015.

——— . *Canada's Residential Schools: The Final Report of the Truth and Reconciliation Commission of Canada. Volume Five. The Legacy.* Montreal: TRC and McGill-Queen's University Press, 2015.

——— . *Canada's Residential Schools: The Final Report of the Truth and Reconciliation Commission of Canada. Volume Six. Reconciliation.* Montreal: TRC and McGill-Queen's University Press, 2015.

——— . *Final Report of the Truth and Reconciliation Commission of Canada. Volume One: Summary.* Lorimer: Halifax, 2015.

——— . *Honouring the Truth, Reconciling for the Future: Summary of the Final Report of the Truth and Reconciliation Commission of Canada.* Lorimer: Halifax, 2015.

——— . *Interim Report of the Truth and Reconciliation Commission of Canada.* https://www.falconers.ca/wp-content/uploads/2015/07/TRC-Interim-Report.pdf.

——— . "Our Mandate." http://www.trc.ca/websites/trcinstitution/index.php?p=7 (accessed 15 July 2016).

——— . *What We Have Learned: Principles of Truth and Reconciliation.* http://www.trc.ca/assets/pdf/Principles%20of%20Truth%20and%20Reconciliation.pdf.

Tuck, Eve, and K. Wayne Yang. "Decolonization Is Not a Metaphor." *Decolonization: Indigeneity, Education and Society* 1, no. 1 (2012): 1–40.

Turner, Dale. *This Is Not a Peace Pipe: Towards a Critical Indigenous Philosophy.* Toronto: University of Toronto Press, 2006.

Tutu, Desmond. "Foreword by Chairperson." In *South African Truth and Reconciliation Commission Final Report*, 1–23. Vol. 1. South Africa: Truth and Reconciliation Commission, 1998.

———. *No Future Without Forgiveness*. New York: Doubleday, 1999.

United Nations Development Programme. "Human Development Indices and Indicators: 2018 Statistical Update—Canada." http://www.hdr.undp.org/sites/all/themes/hdr_theme/country-notes/CAN.pdf (a10).

———. "Reconciliation as Framework for Preventing Conflict and Sustaining Peace." http://www.ijr.org.za/home/wp-content/uploads/2012/07/Policy-Document-Inclusive-Reconciliation-Final-July-2015.pdf (accessed 20 June 2016).

United Nations General Assembly. *United Nations Declaration on the Rights of Indigenous Peoples*. New York: United Nations, 2007.

United Nations Special Committee on Decolonization. "The United Nations and Decolonization." https://www.un.org/en/decolonization/index.shtml.

United Way of Winnipeg. *Eagle's Eye View: An Environmental Scan of the Aboriginal Community in Winnipeg*. 2nd ed. Winnipeg: 2010.

University of Manitoba. "On-Reserve Housing." University of Manitoba School of Architecture. n.d. http://www.umanitoba.ca/architecture/cp/app/sections/issues/other/housing/on_reserve.html.

Uvin, Peter, and Charles Mironko. "Western and Local Approaches to Justice in Rwanda." *Global Governance* 9, no 2 (2003): 219–31.

Venables, Robert W. *The 1613 Treaty*. http://honorthetworow.org/wp-content/uploads/2012/01/VenablesonTwoRow-1.pdf (accessed 19 January 2017).

Venter, Christine M. "Eliminating Fear through Recreating Community in Rwanda: The Role of Gacaca Courts." *Texas Wesleyan Law Review* 13, no. 2 (2007): 577–97.

Veracini, Lorenzo. *Settler Colonialism*. London: Palgrave Macmillan, 2010.

Vizenor, Gerald, ed. *Survivance: Narratives of Native Presence*. Lincoln: University of Nebraska Press, 2008.

Volf, Miroslav. "The Social Meaning of Reconciliation." *Interpretation* 54 (2000): 158–72.

Volkan, V.D., and C. Sinclair. *Bloodlines: From Ethnic Pride to Ethnic Terrorism*. New York: Farrar, Straus and Giroux New York, 1997.

Vowel, Chelsea. *Indigenous Writes, a Guide to First Nations, Métis and Inuit Issues in Canada*. Winnipeg: HighWater Press, 2016.

Wagner, Ulrich, Linda R. Tropp, Gillian Finchilescu, and Colin Tredoux. *Improving Intergroup Relations: Building on the Legacy of Thomas F. Pettigrew*. Malden: Blackwell Publishing, 2008. doi: 10.1002/9781444303117.

Walcott, Rinaldo. *Black Like Who? Writing Black Canada*. Toronto: Insomniac Press, 2003.

Waldorf, Lars. *Transitional Justice and DDR: The Case of Rwanda*. Research Unit International Centre for Transitional Justice, 2009. https://www.ictj.org/sites/default/files/ICTJ-DDR-Rwanda-CaseStudy-2009-English.pdf.

Waldram, James B., ed. *Aboriginal Healing in Canada: Studies in Therapeutic Meaning and Practice*. Ottawa: Aboriginal Healing Foundation, 2008.

———. "Transformative and Restorative Processes: Revisiting the Question of Efficacy of Indigenous Healing." *Medical Anthropology* 32, no. 3 (2013): 191–207. doi: 10.1080/01459740.2012.714822.

Wale, Kim. *Confronting Exclusion: Time For Radical Reconciliation: SA Reconciliation Barometer Survey: 2013 Report*. Cape Town: Institute for Justice and Reconciliation, 2013.

———. *Reflecting on Reconciliation: Lessons from the Past, Prospects for the Future*. Cape Town: Institute for Justice and Reconciliation, 2014.

Wallace, Rick. "Grassroots Community-based Peacebuilding: Critical Narratives on Peacebuilding and Collaboration from the Locality of Indigenous and Non-Indigenous Activists in Canada." PhD diss., University of Bradford, 2010.

Wallis, Maria, Lina Sunseri, and Grace-Edward Galabuzi. *Colonialism and Racism in Canada: Historical Traces and Contemporary Issues*. Toronto: Nelson, 2009.

Walqwan Metallic, Naiomi, et al. "An Act Respecting First Nations, Inuit and Métis Children, Youth and Families: Does Bill C-92 Make the Grade?" Toronto: Yellowhead Institute, 2019. https://yellowheadinstitute.org/bill-c-92-analysis.

Wastesicoot, Jennie. "A Cultural Framework for Cree Self-Government: Re-Tracing Our Steps Back." Master's thesis, University of Manitoba, 2004. https://mspace.lib.umanitoba.ca/xmlui/handle/1993/3831.

———. "Tapwetamowin: Cree Spirituality and Law for Self-Governance." PhD diss., University of Manitoba, 2015. http://primo-pmtna01.hosted.exlibrisgroup.com/primo_library/libweb/action/dlDisplay.do?vid=UMB&afterPDS=true&docId=UMB_MSPACE1993/30319.

Watson, Sheila, ed. *Museums and Their Communities*. New York: Routledge, 2007.

Watters, Jordan A. "Reproducing Canada's Colonial Legacy: A Critical Analysis of Aboriginal Issues in Ontario High School Curriculum." Master's thesis, Queens University, 2007.

Watts, Vanessa, and Hayden King. "TRC Report a Good Start, but Now It's Time for Action." *Globe and Mail*, 5 June 2015.

Weber, Cynthia. *International Relations Theory: A Critical Introduction*. New York: Routledge, 2009.

Weitz, Eric D. *A Century of Genocide: Utopias of Race and Nation*. Princeton: Princeton University Press, 2003.

Welch, Mary Agnes. "Awasis Director Forced Aside. Child Welfare Agency Probed." *Winnipeg Free Press*, 5 December 2009. https://www.winnipegfreepress.com/local/awasis-director-forced-aside-78587207.html.

———. "Indigenous Control a Myth: Three Agencies Overseen by Appointed Administrators." *Winnipeg Free Press*, 11 December 2015. http://www.winnipegfreepress.com/special/cracksinthe-system/indigenous-control-a-myth-361532481.html.

———. "Profound Issues with Agencies: Order Explains Why Minister Fired Board Overseeing CFS." *Winnipeg Free Press*, 2 June 2016. http://www.winnipegfreepress.com/local/profound-is-sues-with-agencies-367905941.html.

Wells, Sarah L. "Gender, Sexual Violence and Prospects for Justice at the Gacaca Courts in Rwanda." *Review of Law and Women's Studies* 14, no. 2 (2005): 167–96.

Wesley-Esquimaux, Cynthia C. "The Intergenerational Transmission of Historic Trauma and Grief." *Indigenous Affairs* 4, no. 7 (2007): 6–11.

———. "Trauma to Resilience: Notes on Decolonization." In *Restoring the Balance: First Nations Women, Community and Culture*, edited by Eric Guimond, Gail Guthrie Valaskakis, and Madeline Dion Stout, 13–34. Winnipeg: University of Manitoba Press, 2009.

Wesley-Esquimaux, Cynthia C., and Magdalena Smolewski. "Historic Trauma and Aboriginal Healing." Prepared for Aboriginal Healing Foundation, Ottawa, ON, 2004.

Wheeler, Mya J., A. John Sinclair, Patricia Fitzpatrick, Alan P. Diduck and Iain J. Davidson-Hunt. "Place-Based Inquiry's Potential for Encouraging Public Participation: Stories from the Common Ground Land in Kenora, Ontario." *Society and Natural Resources* (2016): 1–16. doi: 10.1080/08941920.2015.1122130 (accessed 20 January 2017).

White, Jerry P., Dan Beavon, and Nicholas Spence, eds. *Aboriginal Well-Being, Canada's Continuing Challenge*. Toronto: Thompson Educational Publishing, 2008.

Whittam, Julian. "'In a Good Way': Repatriation, Community and Development in Kitigan Zibi." *Anthropologica* 57, no. 2 (2015): 501–509.

Wibabara, Charity. *Gacaca Courts versus the International Criminal Tribunal for Rwanda and National Courts: Lessons to Learn from the Rwandan Justice Approaches to Genocide*. Baden-Baden: Nomos Verlagsgesellschaft, 2014.

Wielenga, Cori, and Geoff Harris. "Building Peace and Security after Genocide: The Contribution of the Gacaca Courts of Rwanda." *African Security Review* 20, no. 1 (2011): 15–25.

Wien, Fred, Cindy Blackstock, John Loxley, and Nico Trocmé. "Keeping First Nations Children at Home: A Few Federal Policy Changes Could Make a Big Difference." *First Peoples Child and Family Review* 3, no. 1 (2007): 10–14.

Williams, Alex. *The Pass System*. Toronto: Tamarack Productions, 2015.

Williams Jr., Barney. Quoted in Corntassel, Jeff, Chaw-win-is, and T'lakswadzi. "Indigenous Storytelling, Truth-Telling and Community Approaches to Reconciliation." *English Studies in Canada* 35, no. 1 (2009): 137–59.

Williams Jr., Robert A. "Linking Arms Together: Multicultural Constitutionalism in a North American Indigenous Vision of Law and Peace." *California Law Review* 82, no. 4 (July 1994): 981–1049. http://scholarship.law.berkeley.edu/californialawreview/vol82/iss4/8.

Willow, Anna J. "Conceiving Kakipitatapitmok: The Political Landscape of Anishinaabe Anticlearcutting Activism." *American Anthropologist* 113, no. 2 (2011): 262–76.

———. *Strong Hearts, Native Lands: Anti-clearcutting Activism at Grassy Narrows First Nation*. Winnipeg: University of Manitoba Press, 2012.

Wilson, Kory, and Jane Henderson. *First Peoples: A Guide for Newcomers*. Vancouver: City of Vancouver, 2014. http://vancouver.ca/files/cov/First-Peoples-A-Guide-for-Newcomers.pdf.

Wilson, Richard. "Justice and Legitimacy in the South African Transition." In *The Politics of Memory: Transitional Justice in Democratizing Societies*, edited by Alexandra Barahona de Brito, Carmen González-Enriquez, and Paloma Aguilar, 190–217. Oxford: Oxford University Press, 2001.

Wilson, Shawn. *Research Is Ceremony: Indigenous Research Methods*. Black Point: Fernwood Publishing, 2008.

Wing Sue, Derald. *Multicultural Social Work Practice*. Hoboken: John Wiley and Sons, 2006.

Wolfe, Patrick. "Settler Colonialism and the Elimination of the Native." *Journal of Genocide Research* 8, no. 4 (2006): 387–409.

———. *Traces of History: Elementary Structures of Race*. London and Brooklyn: Verso, 2016.

Wolters, Stephanie. "The Gacaca Courts." *African Security Review* 14, no. 3 (2005): 67–68.

Woolford, Andrew. "Genocide, Affirmative Repair, and the British Columbia Treaty Process." In *Transitional Justice: Global Mechanisms and Local Realities After Genocide and Mass Violence*, edited by Alexander L Hinton, 137–56. New Brunswick: Rutgers University Press, 2010.

———. *This Benevolent Experiment: Indigenous Boarding Schools, Genocide, and Redress in Canada and the United States*. Winnipeg: University of Manitoba Press, 2015.

Woolford, Andrew, Jeff Benvenuto, and Alexander Laban Hinton. *Colonial Genocide in Indigenous North America*. Durham: Duke University Press, 2014.

Wyatt, Stephen, Jean-François Fortier, David C. Natcher, Margaret A. Peggy Smith, and Martin Hébert. "Collaboration between Aboriginal Peoples and the Canadian Forest Sector: A Typology of Arrangements for Establishing Control and Determining Benefits of Forestlands." *Journal of Environmental Management* 115 (2013): 21–31.

York Factory First Nation. *First Nations Justice Initiative: Mee-Noo-Stah-Tan Mi-Ni-Si-Win*. York Factory First Nation, 1996.

———. *Mamowwechihatan Oskatisuk. A Social Development Framework*. York Factory First Nation, March 2003.

Zimmer, Markus B. "Rwanda's Gacaca Courts: An Innovative Experiment in the post-Genocide Pursuit of Criminal Justice." *International Journal for Court Administration* 6, no. 2 (2014): 1–2.

Zurba, Melanie. "Building Common Ground: Learning and Reconciliation for the Shared Governance of Forest Land in Northwestern Ontario." PhD diss., University of Manitoba, 2015.

———. "Leveling the Playing Field: Fostering Collaborative Governance Toward On-Going Reconciliation." *Environmental Policy and Governance* 24, no. 2 (2014): 134–46.

Zurba, Melanie, Alan P. Diduck, and A. John Sinclair. "First Nations and Industry Collaboration for Forest Governance in Northwestern Ontario, Canada." *Forest Policy and Economics* 69 (2016): 1–10.

Zurba, Melanie, and Micaela Trimble. "Youth as the Inheritors of Collaboration: Crises and the Factors that Influence Participation of the Next Generation in Natural Resource Management." *Environmental Science and Policy* 42 (2014): 78–87.

Zurba, Melanie, Helen Ross, Arturo Izurieta, Phillip Rist, Ellie Bock, and Fikret Berkes. "Building Co-management as a Process: Problem Solving through Partnerships in Aboriginal Country, Australia." *Environmental Management* 49, no. 6 (2012): 1130–42.

CONTRIBUTORS

Peter Bush, a Presbyterian minister, has served congregations in Flin Flon, Manitoba, Mitchell, Ontario, and Winnipeg. He has written extensively about the Presbyterian Church in Canada's involvement with Indian Residential Schools and served as a contract researcher with the Truth and Reconciliation Commission working on a project "How the Church got to Sorry." He has spoken words of apology on behalf of the Presbyterian Church at the sites of the Cecilia Jeffrey Indian Residential School and at the Regina Industrial School Cemetery.

Tracey Carr has extensive experience in program planning and evaluation and has worked with First Nations communities for the past ten years. Her work has comprised health services evaluation, health status reporting, and program evaluation in the Resolution Health Support Program for former students of Indian Residential Schools. Currently, she is a research associate in Community Health and Epidemiology at the University of Saskatchewan and teaches psychology at St. Thomas More College.

Brian Chartier, professor emeritus, St. Thomas More College, Saskatoon, Saskatchewan, was an associate professor of psychology from 1981 to 2018. Between 2005 and 2017, he conducted approximately eighty-five psychological assessments of former students of Indian Residential Schools as part of the Independent Assessment Process. He currently works in private practice.

Mary Anne Clarke is a Celtic-settler mother and grandmother of Indigenous children and as a social worker in First Nations, she has personally and professionally experienced the colonial violence found within Canada's Child and Family Services. As a PhD candidate in Peace and Conflict Studies at the Arthur V. Mauro Institute for Peace and Justice at the University of Manitoba, her goal is to disrupt the colonial power imbalances in Canada. Her front-line work and studies focus on strengthening community-based traditional family systems and corresponding forms of distinct First Nations family laws and Indigenous governments. Her commitment is broad-reaching reconciliation through deep structural transformation between the colonial society and Canadian governments, and Indigenous peoples and governments.

Aimée Craft is an Indigenous (Anishinaabe-Métis) lawyer from Treaty 1 territory in Manitoba. She is an associate professor at the Faculty of Common Law, University of Ottawa. Craft is the former director of research at the National Inquiry into Missing and Murdered Indigenous Women and Girls and the founding director of research at the National Centre for Truth and Reconciliation. Her book, *Breathing Life into the Stone Fort Treaty: An Anishinaabe Understanding of Treaty One* (2013) won the Eileen McTavish Sykes Award for Best First Book and the Margaret McWilliams Scholarly Book Award from the Manitoba Historical Society.

Rachel (yacaaʔał) George is nuučaańuł of Ahousaht and Ehattesaht First Nations. Residing on Treaty 6 territory in Edmonton, she is a lecturer in the Department of Political Science at the University of Alberta and a PhD candidate at the University of Victoria. Her doctoral research explores the emergence and efficacy of redress mechanisms—including truth commissions—in facilitating justice for Indigenous nations. In particular, she is interested in pathways to decolonization through resurgence and storied practice. Her teaching focuses on Indigenous politics, reconciliation, and resurgence. Prior to beginning her PhD, Rachel served as a research coordinator for the Maine Wabanaki-State Child Welfare Truth and Reconciliation Commission where she worked closely with Wabanaki communities to share their stories with the commission.

Erica Jurgens is of Stó:lō and Nlaka'pamux ancestry with family ties to Leq'á:mél, Seabird Island, and Lytton First Nations. She is a PhD candidate in Educational Technology and Learning Design at Simon Fraser University and holds a master's degree in Education: Leadership in Indigenous Education (Squamish Nation) from the University of British Columbia. Her research interests reflect the tenets of Article 13 of the United Nations Declaration on the Rights of Indigenous Peoples, which asserts: "Indigenous peoples have the right to revitalize, use, develop and transmit to future generations their histories, languages, oral traditions, philosophies, writing systems and literatures, and to designate and retain their own names for communities, places and persons" (United Nations 2008). She works to explicate Indigenous intellectualism, historiographies, narratives, and language. She has partnered with First Nations schools and educators to develop Indigenous learning designs where Indigenous theory and practice are both regenerative and generative.

Régine Uwibereyeho King is an associate professor in the Faculty of Social Work, University of Calgary. She has a PhD in Social Work and an MEd in Counseling Psychology and Community Development from the University of Toronto. She also has post-doctoral training in social aetiology of mental illness from the Centre for Addiction and Mental Health, University of Toronto. Her research interests focus on psychosocial processes involving survivors of organized and structural violence, who resettle in their former communities and those who become refugees in high income countries. Her local and international research projects build on many years of front life work experiences in community-based organizations serving the marginalized both in Canada and in Rwanda. She is a community-based researcher with special interests in narrative inquiry, oral history, and interpretive research methods. Dr. King is committed to social justice, human rights, non-violent practices, and healthy communities.

Sheryl Lightfoot is Anishinaabe, a citizen of the Lake Superior Band of Ojibwe, enrolled at the Keweenaw Bay Indian Community in Baraga, Michigan. She is an associate professor in School of Public Policy and Global Affairs, First Nations and Indigenous Studies and the Department of Political Science, and Canada Research Chair in Global Indigenous Rights and Politics, at the University of British Columbia. She is also senior advisor to the UBC President on Indigenous Affairs. Her book, *Global Indigenous Politics: A Subtle Revolution*, was published in May 2016 by Routledge Press in their "Worlding Beyond the West" critical international relations book series.

David B. MacDonald is from Treaty 4 territory, and is a full professor and the research leadership chair for the College of Social and Applied Human Sciences at University of Guelph. He has held faculty positions at the

University of Otago (New Zealand) and the Graduate School of Management (Paris, France). He has a PhD in International Relations from the London School of Economics. His work focuses on comparative Indigenous politics in Canada, Aotearoa (New Zealand), and United States. He has also worked extensively in the areas of international relations, American foreign policy, Holocaust and genocide studies, and critical race theory. He is the principal investigator (with co-researcher Sheryl Lightfoot) on multi-year Insight Grant through the Social Science and Humanities Research Council of Canada entitled "Complex Sovereignties: Theory and Practice of Indigenous-Self Determination in Settler States and the International System." He is a mixed race (Indian and white) political scientist whose mother is from Trinidad. He is the author of *The Sleeping Giant Awakens: Genocide, Indian Residential Schools, and the Challenge of Conciliation* (University of Toronto Press, 2019).

Benjamin Maiangwa completed a PhD in Peace and Conflict Studies at the Arthur V. Mauro Institute for Peace and Justice. He teaches Indigenous peacebuilding at the Mauro Institute, and researches conflicting ideas of belonging in postcolonial societies and people's practices of homemaking/ placemaking as aspects of state/nation building.

Cody O'Neil was former research fellow at the National Centre for Truth and Reconciliation. He is currently a Juris Doctor (JD)/Juris Indigenous Doctor (JID) candidate in the University of Victoria's new dual degree program in Canadian Common Law and Indigenous Legal Orders. Cody is a settler from the unceded Syilx Territory of the Okanagan Nation.

Paulette Regan is an independent scholar, researcher, public educator and co-facilitator of an intercultural history and reconciliation education workshop series. Formerly the research director for the Truth and Reconciliation Commission of Canada, she was the senior researcher and lead writer on the Reconciliation Volume of the TRC Final Report. Her book, *Unsettling the Settler Within: Indian Residential Schools, Truth Telling and Reconciliation in Canada* (UBC Press, 2010) was shortlisted for the 2012 Canada Prize. Her most recent publication is "Reconciliation and Resurgence: Reflections on the TRC Final Report," in *Resurgence*

and Reconciliation: Indigenous-Settler Relations and Earth Teachings.
Michael Asch, John Borrows and James Tully, eds., (University of Toronto Press, 2018).

Cathy Rocke, MSW, PhD, is an associate professor and the Associate Dean (Undergraduate Programs) at the Faculty of Social Work at the University of Manitoba. She completed her doctoral degree at the Arthur V. Mauro Centre for Peace and Justice at the University of Manitoba. Her current research is focused on addressing and evaluating how we reconcile the relationships between Indigenous and non-Indigenous peoples in Canada both on campus and in the community through inter-group dialogue. Prior to her academic career, Cathy's work experience includes developing post-secondary educational programs for Indigenous communities, diversity training for child welfare professionals, quality assurance for child welfare agencies, counseling victims of domestic violence, and child protection.

John Sinclair is a professor at the Natural Resources Institute at University of Manitoba. His research focuses on community involvement and learning in the process of resource and environmental decision-making. His applied research takes him to various locations in Canada, as well as East Africa and Asia. He is the current acting director of the Natural Resources Institute and has for a number of years served a chair of the University of Manitoba's Sustainability Committee.

Andrea Walsh is an associate professor in the Department of Anthropology at the University of Victoria. She is a visual anthropologist and curator who specializes in twentieth-century and contemporary Indigenous art and visual culture in Canada, as well as theoretical and methodological approaches to visual research. Her work critically reflects on and addresses discourses and actions of reconciliation and redress regarding relationships between Indigenous peoples and Canada. She works in partnership with elders and residential school survivors and their families to repatriate children's artworks created in residential and day schools and educate the public about this history through art exhibits. In 2019 she curated "There is Truth Here: Creativity and Resilience in Children's Art from Indian Residential and Day Schools," an exhibit at the Museum of Vancouver.

Melanie Zurba's research focuses on community-engaged research, environmental governance, collaboration, and social change. Melanie's PhD is in Natural Resources and Environmental Management from the Natural Resources Institute at University of Manitoba. Melanie's broader research has been geographically focused in Canada and Australia, but also spans the globe through her work on global policy frameworks that aim to support Indigenous rights, land tenure, and leadership in environmental decision-making. Melanie has been an active member of the International Union for the Conservation of Nature (IUCN), Commission on Environmental, Economic and Social Policy (CEESP), and the Theme on Governance, Equity, and Rights (TGER) since 2011.